From Presidio
to the Pecos River

From Presidio to the Pecos River

Surveying the United States–Mexico
Boundary along the Rio Grande
1852 and 1853

ORVILLE B. SHELBURNE, Jr.

Foreword by
DAVID H. MILLER

UNIVERSITY OF OKLAHOMA PRESS
Norman

LIBRARY OF CONGRESS CATALOGING-IN-PUBLICATION DATA

Names: Shelburne Jr., Orville B., 1932– author.
Title: From Presidio to the Pecos River : surveying the United States–Mexico boundary along the Rio Grande, 1852 and 1853 / Orville B. Shelburne, Jr. ; foreword by David H. Miller.

Description: Norman : University of Oklahoma Press, [2020] | Includes bibliographical references and index. | Summary: "Examines the U.S.-Mexico Boundary Survey's scientific exploration of the Rio Grande from Presidio to the mouth of the Pecos River by two American parties, one led by civilian surveyor M. T. W. Chandler in 1852, and the second led by Lieutenant Nathaniel Michler in 1853"—Provided by publisher.
Identifiers: LCCN 2020011871 | ISBN 978-0-8061-6710-7 (hardcover)
ISBN 978-0-8061-9309-0 (paper)
Subjects: LCSH: Chandler, Marine Tyler Wickham, 1819–1868. | Michler, N. (Nathan-iel), 1827–1881. | United States and Mexican Boundary Survey. | United States—Boundaries—Mexico. | Mexico—Boundaries—United States. Mexican-American Border Region—History. | Rio Grande (Colo.-Mexico and Tex.)—History.

Classification: LCC F786 .S53 2020 | DDC 972/.1—dc23
LC record available at https://lccn.loc.gov/2020011871

The paper in this book meets the guidelines for permanence and durability
of the Committee on Production Guidelines for Book Longevity
of the Council on Library Resources, Inc. ∞

Copyright © 2020 by the University of Oklahoma Press, Norman, Publishing Division of the University. Paperback published 2023. Manufactured in the U.S.A.

All rights reserved.
No part of this publication may be reproduced,
stored in a retrieval system, or transmitted, in any form or
by any means, electronic, mechanical, photocopying, recording, or
otherwise—except as permitted under Section 107 or 108 of the United States
Copyright Act—without the prior written permission of the University of Oklahoma Press.
To request permission to reproduce selections from this book, write to
Permissions, University of Oklahoma Press, 2800 Venture Drive,
Norman, OK 73069, or email rights.oupress@ou.edu.

"We have had rather a rough time and traveled a most singular country—I shall make a sketch of the country for you and will probably see more of interest than in following down this horribly desolate river."

—*Charles Parry to Major William H. Emory, November 4, 1852*

Contents

List of Illustrations	xi
Foreword by David H. Miller	xiii
Preface	xxi
Acknowledgments	xxiii
Introduction	1

Part I. The 1852 Chandler Surveying Party — 15

Men and Equipment of the 1852 Boundary Survey Party	17
Tracing the Route of the Chandler Party	32
Chandler's Surveying Methods	36
Surveying Begins	39
US and Mexican Versions of Boundary Map 22 near Presidio del Norte	50
Description of Boundary Map 22 Downstream from Presidio del Norte	51
Waiting for Supplies	57
The Boats Enter the Upper Canyons to Begin Surveying Boundary Map 21	58

Comparison of US and Mexican Boundary Maps
  of the Upper Canyons 66
The Camp at Comanche Crossing 67
Santa Elena Canyon 73
The Detour around Santa Elena Canyon 77
Connecting the Surveys above and below Santa Elena Canyon . . . 82
Chisos Crossing 88
Mariscal Canyon 98
Boquillas Canyon 105
Crossing the Rio Grande to Temple Canyon 114
Chandler's Boundary Map from Stillwell Bend
  to Reagan Canyon 120
Abandoning the Chandler Survey 123
The Trek to Santa Rosa 129
The Road to Fort Duncan 148
Results of the Chandler Survey 152

Part II. The 1853 Michler Survey — 157

Michler's Preparations: Equipment and Men 159
The Search for the "Initial Point" on the Rio Grande 161
San Francisco Canyon: The History of an Important Landmark . . . 170
The Boat Survey from Lipan Crossing to the Pecos River . . . 181
The Boundary Maps Based on the Boat Survey 183
Rapids below Lipan Crossing 186
Indian Trails Downstream from Lipan Crossing 188
Michler's Latitude Measurements 190
Results of the Michler Survey 193

Part III. Wrapping It All Up — 195

Later Surveys to Complete the Mapping of the Boundary 195
The Final Report and Maps of the US Boundary Commission . . . 197

Summary 202
Conclusions 208

Epilogue: The Men of the Boundary Survey 209
John Russell Bartlett (1805–1886) 209
William Hemsley Emory (1811–1887) 210
Marine Tyler Wickham Chandler (1819–1868) 211
Charles Christopher Parry (1823–1890) 212
Duff Cyrus Green (1828–1865) 214
Nathaniel Michler (1827–1881) 214
Edward Ingraham (1830–1862) 215
Christoph Conrad Stremme (1807–1877) 216

Appendices
A. Colonel Langberg's 1851 Expedition 217
B. 1855 Mexican Triangulation Stations near Presidio del Norte . . 221
C. The First Documented Boat Passage through
    Santa Elena Canyon 225
D. Chronology 229
E. Glossary 233
Notes 237
Bibliography 263
Index 275

Illustrations

Figures

1. US-Mexico Boundary in the Treaty of Guadalupe Hidalgo . . 2
2. Boundary Surveys across the Big Bend Region 12
3. Chandler's Boundary Maps 18–19
4. Men of the Boundary Survey 21
5. Rubber Boat Crossing the Colorado River 29
6. Mid-1800s Trails in the Big Bend Area 34–35
7. Nineteenth-Century Surveying Equipment 37
8. Sketch of Traverse and Triangulation Methods 38
9. Fort Leaton 42
10. River Trace Comparison: Presidio del Norte to Start of the Canyons 44
11. Three Dike Hill 48
12. Closed Canyon 49
13. Detail at Presidio del Norte 53
14. River Trace Comparison: The Upper Canyons 60
15. Hoodoos Rapids 61
16. Castle Rock 65
17. River Trace Comparison: Lajitas and Santa Elena Canyon . . 70
18. Trails at Santa Elena Canyon 72

19.	Rock Slide Rapids	74
20.	Ruins of San Carlos Presidio	79
21.	River Trace Comparison: Exit of Santa Elena Canyon to Mariscal Canyon	84
22.	View of the Chisos Mountains	87
23.	Punta de la Sierra from Chisos Crossing	90
24.	River Trace Comparison: Mariscal Canyon to Hot Springs Canyon	101
25.	Sierra del Carmen Mountain Front	103
26.	River Trace Comparison: Boquillas Canyon	106
27.	Pico Etéreo	109
28.	River Trace Comparison: Stillwell Bend to Reagan Canyon	112–13
29.	Views of Temple Canyon	116
30.	Hot Springs Pool	125
31.	Parry and Green Maps to Santa Rosa	130
32.	Trail to Camp #34	132
33.	Map of Santa Rosa Area	146
34.	Parry's Route from Santa Rosa to Fort Duncan	149
35.	Michler's Boundary Maps	158
36.	Johnston's Reconnaissance Map	162
37.	Lipan Crossing	167
38.	View of the Rio Grande	171
39.	John Gano's 1882 Map	173
40.	River Trace Comparison: San Francisco Canyon to Lipan Crossing	174
41.	River Trace Comparison: The Lower Canyons	177
42.	River Trace Comparison: Lipan Crossing to Langtry	187
43.	River Trace Comparison: Langtry to beyond the Pecos River	191
44.	1855 Mexican Triangulation Stations near Presidio del Norte	222

TABLES

1.	Geologic Formations of the Big Bend	47
2.	Landmark Locations on the 1857 Boundary Maps	54–55
3.	Classifications of Rapids	59

Foreword

David H. Miller

IN EARLY FEBRUARY 1848, when Nicholas Trist sat down with the Mexican representatives Luis G. Cuevas, José Bernardo Couto, and Miguel Atristáin in the town of Guadalupe Hidalgo near Mexico City to sign the treaty ending the Mexican War (also known as the Mexican-American War), he was under considerable pressure to make a quick deal. Trist, chief clerk to Secretary of State James Buchanan, had been sent to Mexico to negotiate a treaty to end the war. President James K. Polk, impatient and increasingly dissatisfied with Trist's lack of progress, recalled him to Washington, DC; but Trist, on the verge of a settlement, ignored the recall and quickly negotiated the Treaty of Guadalupe Hidalgo, which ceded almost half of Mexico to the United States. Although Polk wanted even more Mexican territory, including Baja California, he eventually agreed to Trist's treaty as written. Despite Trist's success in negotiating a treaty that included most of Polk's demands, Polk fired Trist as soon as he arrived back in Washington.

Neither Trist nor his Mexican counterparts had any detailed knowledge of the geography along the border of what became known as the Mexican Cession. In working out an agreement about the border, the negotiators relied on a colorful map published in New York by John Disturnell in 1847, a copy of which Polk had given Trist to take with him to Mexico City. Disturnell's cartography was based on Alexander von Humboldt's *Atlas*, published in Paris in 1811 to accompany his *Political Essay on the Kingdom of New Spain*. An imposing work for its time, Humboldt's *Atlas* was based on numerous manuscript maps and charts from Spanish archives, and his 1804 *General Chart of the Kingdom of New Spain* became the fountainhead of commercial maps of Mexico and the US Southwest for the next half century.

Unfortunately, Humboldt's maps contained significant topographical errors. One that caused Trist difficulties in negotiating the boundary between Alta and Baja California was a map section showing the Gila and Colorado Rivers emptying directly into an estuary at the head of the Gulf of California. The head of the gulf was represented as extending a full degree of latitude (about seventy miles) farther north than it does in reality, and, of course, the Gila empties into the Colorado and not directly into the gulf.

Another error concerned the location of El Paso del Norte (now Ciudad Juárez). Following the boundaries of New Mexico as represented on the late-eighteenth-century maps of Bernardo Miera y Pacheco and others, Humboldt had drawn a narrow New Mexico that extended only a few miles on either side of the Rio Grande, and from a point south of El Paso del Norte to the Upper Rio Grande north of Taos. On Humboldt's map, and on subsequent plagiarized maps, El Paso del Norte is situated in southern New Mexico.

It appears that the Mexican government never defined or surveyed the boundaries of New Mexico. However, this did not stop commercial cartographers from moving New Mexico's boundaries in a long succession of maps. Although El Paso del Norte was generally placed in New Mexico, on Disturnell's map it was placed a few miles north of the 32nd parallel (32°), instead of at its true location at 31°45′. Disturnell also placed the Rio Grande two degrees east of its actual location, an error of almost 120 miles. Since Disturnell showed New Mexico's southern boundary extending west three degrees (175 miles) from an inaccurately located Rio Grande, this created a dilemma as to whether the southern boundary of New Mexico should extend 175 miles west of the Rio Grande as Disturnell intended, or whether it should begin at the longitude depicted on the map, which would place two-thirds of the boundary *east* of the river's actual location, and thus only one-third (58 miles) extending to the west. This became an especially serious question when copies of Disturnell's plagiarized map were signed, sealed, and attached as part of the treaty, indicating that the boundary would be laid out on the ground as represented on the map.

The error concerning El Paso del Norte's location led to a compromise favoring Mexico (the Bartlett-García Conde Compromise of 1850), then to a rejection of that compromise by the United States, and finally a solution to the impasse when the United States purchased more land from Mexico, which was settled in the Gadsden Treaty (Treaty of Mesilla in Mexico). The Gadsden Purchase, ratified by Congress in 1854, established the present boundary between the two countries, and, among other things, meant the United States acquired sufficient land south of the Gila on which to construct a railroad across New Mexico and Arizona to California.

The Treaty of Guadalupe Hidalgo called for the creation of a joint United States–Mexico Boundary Commission to survey and map the new border as specified by the treaty. The treaty also stipulated that when the boundary maps were drawn and approved by both the US and Mexican Boundary Commissions, these fifty-four maps would become part of the treaty.

The two most important Mexican commissioners were General Pedro García Conde and José Salazar Ylarregui. García Conde (1806–51) had an intimate knowledge of the border area, having been born in Arizpe, Sonora. He was well educated, worked his way up through the military ranks to be a general, and possessed outstanding skills as a surveyor and mapmaker. In the early 1830s, he had conducted a survey of Chihuahua, which resulted in the first accurate map of that Mexican border state. Unfortunately for Mexico, he died of typhoid fever in December 1851. José Salazar Ylarregui then filled the position of Mexican commissioner. Salazar Ylarregui was also well acquainted with the border area and remained commissioner until the conclusion of the border surveys.

There were five American boundary commissioners during this same period, suggesting political and financial instability on the American side. The two most important American commissioners were John Russell Bartlett and William H. Emory.

John Russell Bartlett is best known for his *Personal Narrative of Explorations and Incidents in Texas, New Mexico, California, Sonora, and Chihuahua, connected with the United States and Mexican Boundary Commission* (1854), an account of his experiences on the boundary survey. Bartlett had never been to the Southwest, knew nothing about surveying, and was inept at managing his employees. In the middle of his tenure, he took a one-year hiatus, traveling across Mexico to Mazatlán, then north all the way to San Francisco, presumably collecting material for his forthcoming book.

William H. Emory was an officer in the prestigious US Army Corps of Topographical Engineers. An outstanding cartographer, he understood the importance of including information on a variety of scientific subjects in his published reports. He was also well acquainted with the borderlands from prior military work in the Southwest.

Article V of the treaty specified that the Mexican and American boundary commissioners would meet in San Diego within one year of the ratification of the treaty, "and proceed to run and mark the said boundary in its whole course to the mouth of the Rio Bravo del Norte."

The American commission arrived in San Diego by ship on June 1, 1849, and the Mexican commission, a few weeks later, on July 3. The task before them was daunting. The first step was to establish the initial point on the Pacific, which they accomplished on October 10, 1849.

The next step was to determine the location of the confluence of the Gila and Colorado Rivers, so that an azimuth line could be laid out across California from the initial point on the Pacific to the mouth of the Gila River. On September 8, 1849, Lieutenant Amiel Weeks Whipple and Charles C. Parry headed east from San Diego to the Colorado River near modern-day Yuma to map the confluence. Mexican surveyors joined them there to double-check Whipple's coordinates.

Meanwhile, on February 15, 1850, having completed their work in San Diego, the American and Mexican commissioners agreed to adjourn and to meet again in El Paso del Norte in early November, 1850, when they planned to survey the southern boundary of New Mexico west to the headwaters of the Gila, and then conduct a survey of the Gila River west to its confluence with the Colorado. They also intended to prepare plans for a joint survey of the Rio Grande downstream from a point above El Paso del Norte to the Gulf of Mexico.

John Russell Bartlett was appointed as the fourth US boundary commissioner in June 1850. After months of preparation, he left Washington, DC, for El Paso with a grand vision for the boundary survey. The geodetic survey of the international boundary was only an incidental part of his grand scheme, not his primary objective. He intended to make a detailed examination of the Southwest, including a study of the region's geography, flora and fauna, indigenous peoples, prehistoric ruins, and, of course, valuable gold and silver mines, with the goal of writing and publishing a detailed narrative of his travels.

Bartlett also intended to plot the location of a shipping canal along the Gila by floating down the Gila in specially designed iron boats that could also be used in surveying down the Rio Grande from El Paso del Norte to the Gulf of Mexico. Of course, he would need these boats for a side trip he planned to make up the Colorado River to explore the mysteries of the Grand Canyon. Before leaving Washington, DC, he had requested that the US Navy construct a flotilla of these iron boats. The thirty-foot, two-thousand-pound behemoths were each constructed in five sections designed to be riveted together in the field after traveling overland across southwestern deserts mounted on "truck wheels." The words "U.S. Boundary Survey" were neatly lettered on their hulls. Needless to say, these boats never left the Brooklyn Naval Yard.

Bartlett's bloated boundary survey party was in complete disarray when he arrived in El Paso del Norte on November 13, 1850, in a custom-built carriage. His commission was a spectacle of mismanagement and waste. His party included over 140 employees, many of whom were inexperienced political appointees, along with a few frontier ruffians as teamsters, and accompanied by a huge wagon train carrying an estimated 250 tons of supplies and baggage.

By contrast, the Mexican commission under Pedro García Conde was a lean and focused operation of talented surveyors when he arrived in El Paso del Norte a few days after Bartlett. García Conde might have immediately begun negotiations with Bartlett for the survey of the Rio Grande, but he chose instead to focus on a discussion of errors in the Disturnell treaty map.

A flood earlier in 1850 had caused the Rio Grande to make a significant change in course in the valley immediately downstream from El Paso del Norte, placing the villages of Isleta, Socorro, and San Elizario on the American side of the river. By postponing the survey for at least another year, García Conde hoped that in the interim the river might shift back to its former course, once again returning these three villages to the Mexican side of the border.

In discussions with Bartlett concerning the errors in the Disturnell map related to the actual locations of El Paso del Norte and the Rio Grande, García Conde convinced Bartlett that the boundary of New Mexico needed to be moved more than thirty miles north to correct these errors. After some discussion, Bartlett agreed to move the boundary north to the vicinity of the town of Doña Ana at $32°22'$ north. Their agreement—the Bartlett–García Conde Compromise—was signed in November 1850. It turned out to be the most controversial aspect of the boundary survey, was never approved by Congress, and ultimately helped lead to the 1853 Gadsden Purchase.

Article VI of the treaty stated that either Mexico or the United States could construct a road, canal, or railroad on either the left (Mexican) or the right (US) bank of the Gila River within one marine league (a little over three miles) of either bank, creating a railroad corridor about six and a half miles wide. It was very important to southern senators and congressmen that the Mexican Cession include sufficient land suitable for the construction of a southern transcontinental railroad to California. However, surveys along the Gila soon made it evident that a transcontinental railroad could not be constructed through the Gila's deep, narrow canyons.

Both the Rio Grande and the Gila River formed a significant portion of the international boundary, and they had to be carefully surveyed and mapped. It was a daunting task, extending almost two thousand miles from the Pacific Ocean to the Gulf of Mexico through rugged desert terrain. It is not surprising that the survey of the Rio Grande from El Paso del Norte to the Gulf of Mexico was the last major border survey conducted under terms of the Treaty of Guadalupe Hidalgo. It was the longest, the most difficult, and, in many respects, the most significant section to be surveyed.

The American and Mexican commissioners did not reach a final agreement for the survey of the Rio Grande until 1852. That summer, Emory and Salazar Ylarregui worked out an agreement dividing the survey of the Rio Grande into six segments, some to be surveyed jointly, and others to be surveyed by either the United States or Mexico. Although Mexico had originally been scheduled to explore and map the river through the Big Bend from Presidio del Norte to the mouth of the Pecos, the Big Bend, with its deep, precipitous canyons, was ultimately surveyed and mapped by American teams led by Marine Tyler Wickham Chandler in 1852 and Lieutenant Nathaniel Michler in 1853. These surveys form the major topic of Orville Shelburne's book.

Despite the significance of the Rio Grande survey, in writing about the United States–Mexico Boundary Survey, most historians have given the Rio Grande surveys short shrift. This is due in large part to the relative dearth of original sources relating to the surveys, and Major Emory is to blame for that lack. To avoid any future controversy over the results of the Rio Grande surveys, Emory decided to destroy all of the manuscript journals and documents in his possession once he finished writing his own reports.

Fortunately, Shelburne's discovery of Charles C. Parry's daily journal, including maps and sketches made during the Chandler Survey, has enabled him to produce the first detailed study of the boundary survey through the Big Bend. Parry's journal is truly an amazing find and a major contribution to Big Bend studies.

Parry had been born in England in 1823 and emigrated with his family to the United States in 1832. After graduating from Union College in Schenectady, New York, he studied medicine and botany at Columbia University. He moved to Davenport, Iowa, in 1846, where he practiced medicine. In 1848, he joined the boundary survey as a physician and botanist. His first assignment was to participate in Lieutenant Whipple's survey of the Gila and Colorado Rivers in 1849. He spent some time in California studying the state's botany before joining Chandler's 1852 survey of the Rio Grande through the Big Bend Country. Later, in the 1860s, he conducted extensive botanical surveys in the Colorado Rockies, and in 1867 he was employed as a naturalist on the Kansas Pacific Railroad survey across the Southwest.

Orville B. Shelburne's *From Presidio to the Pecos River* is the first detailed study of the boundary survey down the Rio Grande and through the Big Bend. His focus on Parry's detailed journal, maps, and landscape sketches made on the Chandler Survey adds a new dimension to the boundary survey. His careful analysis of the original boundary survey maps housed in the National Archives, supplemented by precise modern maps and re-photography is truly outstanding. *From Presidio to the Pecos River* is a major contribution to Big Bend studies.

Preface

IN THESE PAGES, we travel along with two US government surveying parties in 1852 and 1853 as they work their way along the Rio Grande, charged with the task of mapping the new United States–Mexico boundary across the wild country of the greater Big Bend area. What is still today a remote and infrequently visited area offered the men of the survey parties an adventure, if you will, sharpened by the perils of loss of food, clothing, and shelter while hurtling through unmapped rapids, accompanied by the ever-present threat of attack by roving bands of Comanche and Apache.

The first of the boundary survey parties that worked the Big Bend area was led by the civilian surveyor M. T. W. Chandler with a party that started down the river from Presidio del Norte (Presidio, Texas) in the fall of 1852. The second survey, in the summer of 1853, was led by Lieutenant Nathaniel Michler, an Army Topographical Engineer, whose party was charged with picking up where Chandler had left off and continuing down to the mouth of the Pecos River, 337 miles below Presidio.

Heretofore, information available on the routes and activities of both surveys has been sparse, based only on Chandler's and Michler's brief reports included in the Final Boundary Commission Report, a letter by the army officer in charge of the soldiers escorting the Chandler party reporting the completion of his assignment, and the private correspondence of Major William H. Emory, who led the overall boundary survey effort. The brevity and self-serving nature of these reports led to uncertainty about exactly where the surveyors went and what they did.

Initially, I had in mind a short article based on an analysis of digital copies of the eight original boundary maps that had been prepared in Washington, DC, in 1856–57 based on the fieldwork of the Chandler and Michler Surveys. These detailed maps along the Rio Grande are at a scale of 1:60,000, and they reside, unpublished, in the National Archives. My thinking was that the detail and variations in the accuracy of the maps when compared with modern topographic maps and satellite images would shed new light on the routes the surveyors traveled, methods they used, locations they worked, and, perhaps, locations they sketched in without actually surveying them.

While researching the biographies of the men who worked on these surveys, an unpublished journal kept by a member of the Chandler party came to light, which allowed a more extensive account of their adventure. That journal is the field notebook of Charles C. Parry, who was the medical doctor, botanist, and geologist for the Chandler party. Parry's 167-page daily record provides much new detail on the work of the surveying party. He included mileage covered each day; compass bearings to landmarks; salient events; geography, botany, and geology of areas they passed through; sketches of landscape and outcrops; and maps of the route traversed. Based on survey accounts published earlier, it had been thought that Chandler reached downriver to a point somewhere near Boquillas Canyon in today's Big Bend National Park, about 150 miles below Presidio del Norte; but Parry's journal clearly shows that the party in fact reached the Hot Springs Rapids in the Lower Canyons of the Rio Grande, 217 miles below Presidio del Norte.

The punishing challenges of surveying the Rio Grande across the Big Bend Country in the nineteenth century resulted in a patchwork of information that can now be better understood by merging historical and modern sources. My narrative at times includes details that help explain the historical context of these survey expeditions. And, I have included some textual features (such as longer image captions and information sidebars) that draw on modern knowledge to help illuminate methods used or actions taken that are connected to historical issues not as familiar today. I also try to connect important topographical features with what can be seen by today's intrepid adventurers and those who live on the edges of this still-wild area. I hope my accounting honors the men whose grit and determination gave us the first good maps of this mysterious region and offers the modern reader some insight into the interplay of history, politics, and exploration during an important era in the evolving history of the American Southwest.

Acknowledgments

I AM INDEBTED TO Becky S. Jordan, Reference Specialist of Special Collections, at the Parks Library at Iowa State University, who provided access to and copies of the field notebooks and correspondence of Charles Christopher Parry. Parry's detailed notebooks were the key to understanding the route and events of the Chandler surveying party during the fall of 1852.

Alex Chiba, the Curator of Map Archives at the Texas General Land Office (GLO) in Austin, was very helpful in locating, in their files, a draft report on the life of GLO employee Professor Christoph Conrad Stremme. The report confirmed that Stremme was the landscape artist for the Michler survey party of 1853. Cynthia Franco at the DeGolyer Library at Southern Methodist University in Dallas provided access to and copies of Robert T. Hill's geological notebooks of his 1899 exploration of the Rio Grande across the Big Bend. Amanda Masterson at the University of Texas Bureau of Economic Geology guided me through their files on the Big Bend area and provided digital copies of unpublished maps. Nancy R. Miller of the University of Pennsylvania Archives was kind enough to search out and provide alumni records on Marine Tyler Wickham Chandler. Dennis Boylan of the First Troop Philadelphia City Cavalry provided an unpublished photograph of trooper Marine T. W. Chandler.

Louis Aulbach, author of Rio Grande river-running guidebooks across the Big Bend, provided helpful advice and the use of his private photographs taken along the river. Beau Rolfe, a professional photographer, secured access to a remote site on the cliffs above the junction of San Francisco Canyon and the Rio Grande where he photographed the same view of the river shown in a woodcut in the Emory Report.

Ron Tyler, a Big Bend historian and retired director of the Amon Carter Museum in Fort Worth, gave encouragement and valuable advice on potential source material during early preparations for this work.

Kent McMillan of Austin, a professional land surveyor and friend, provided advice on nineteenth-century surveying methods and instruments. In addition, his translation and analysis of 1855 vintage Spanish-language triangulation records of the Mexican surveyors who mapped thirty miles of the Rio Grande downstream from Presidio del Norte to the Upper Canyons provided accurate locations for their grid of twenty-eight triangulation stations, which, in turn, showed how far down the river they had surveyed before abandoning further work for lack of supplies.

Dr. José Montelongo, of the Benson Latin American Collection Library at the University of Texas in Austin, provided an excellent digital copy of the unpublished 1857 Mexican Boundary Map 21, which he acquired, at my request, from the Mapoteca Manuel y Berra Museum in Mexico City. This map, covering the Upper Canyons of the Rio Grande, including Santa Elena Canyon, allowed a detailed comparison of the US and Mexican maps.

Carol Zuber-Mallison of ZM Graphics in Fort Worth transformed my sketch maps into the attractive professional maps seen in this book.

Morgan Morrison of Holland Photo Imaging in Austin prepared modern photographs and photocopies of the many historical images that appear in the book.

I am especially indebted to Susan Walters Schmid of Teton Editorial Services in Gardnerville, Nevada, for her extensive contributions throughout the years of preparation of the manuscript.

Professor David Miller, who taught history at Cameron University in Lawton, Oklahoma, and is an expert on Western overland trails, read the manuscript, offered constructive and supportive comments, and kindly agreed to write a foreword for the book.

Most of all, I want to thank Rita, my wife and life partner of sixty-four years, who consistently encouraged me to move forward, while providing critical review of my text during the years I worked on this project.

Introduction

On February 2, 1848, the Mexican-American War (1846–48) officially ended with the signing of what is commonly referred to as the Treaty of Guadalupe Hidalgo. It was negotiated and signed by Nicholas Trist of the US Department of State and officers of a special commission representing the Mexican government, and though ratification by the US Senate took additional time, President James K. Polk announced the treaty's final approval on July 4, 1848.

Article V of the treaty described the new boundary between the two republics in only a general way, but it outlined how the precise location was to be determined and documented. It was to start in the Gulf of Mexico, extend up the deepest channel of the Rio Grande to the southern border of the territory of Nuevo México, turn west along that border to the territory's southwest corner, go north to the Gila River, follow the Gila to its junction with the Colorado River, and, finally, extend from there in a straight line southwest to the Pacific Ocean to a point one marine league (three nautical miles) south of the port of San Diego (figure 1).[1]

The treaty specified that a joint American-Mexican boundary survey would be undertaken and that each country would appoint a boundary commissioner and a chief surveyor, all of whom would meet in San Diego within a year to begin work. That agreement to organize commissions and meet within a year proved to be far too optimistic. On the American side, not only had it taken five months to make small changes in the treaty and receive final approval by Congress, it

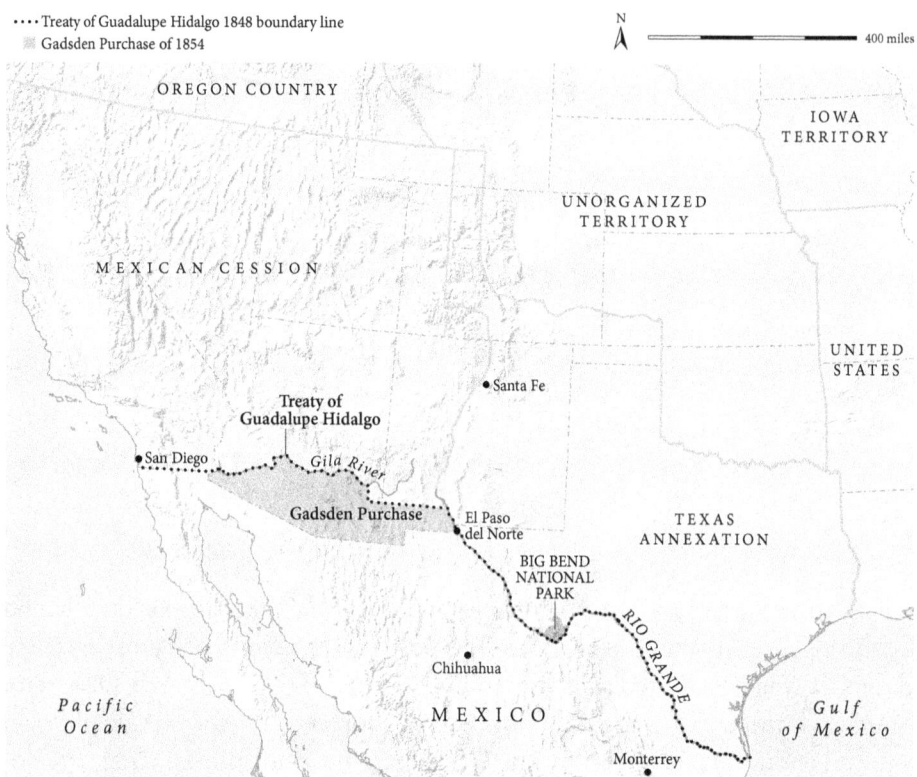

FIGURE 1. **US-Mexico Boundary in the Treaty of Guadalupe Hidalgo.** This simplified drawing superimposes the Bartlett–García Conde Compromise treaty line on an outline map of the United States today. Shown below the treaty line is the area of the 1854 Gadsden Purchase of additional land from Mexico, which today lies along the southern boundary of New Mexico and Arizona. Treaty line taken from Philip St. George Cooke's 1848 *Map of the United States (after the Treaty of Guadalupe Hidalgo)*, The Portal to Texas History, University of North Texas Libraries, https://texashistory.unt.edu/ark:/67531/metapth41375/m1/1/, accessed November 7, 2016. Map by Carol Zuber-Mallison.

took another year to organize and staff the commission and for its members to travel by steamer from the East Coast to Panama, where, in precanal days, they traveled on primitive roads overland to the Pacific coast to board another steamer to San Diego.

For its part in marking the boundary line, the Mexican government assigned competent, experienced surveyors to its commission. Their instruments were of somewhat lesser quality and fewer in number than those of the Americans, but the maps they produced were generally as good as those produced by the

Americans and sometimes better. The level of financial support from both governments ebbed and flowed during the years of the boundary surveys and was at times quite inadequate. The two countries' field parties worked independently to construct maps of the boundary line but jointly agreed on the locations of major turning points. The two parties generally worked well together and supported each other's efforts and results.

※ ※

The US Boundary Commission officers were finally named in January 1849. Just six weeks before his term as president ended, James K. Polk, a Democrat, named John B. Weller—a former congressman, a recently defeated candidate for governor of Ohio, and also a loyal Democrat—to the new position of boundary commissioner. For chief surveyor, Polk named another civilian, Andrew B. Gray, who had worked on the Texas–United States Boundary Survey of 1840. Major William H. Emory of the Army Corps of Topographical Engineers was named chief astronomer and commander of the army escort. The soldiers of the escort were to provide logistical support and protection from hostiles. Emory's main surveying assistants, also members of the Army Corps of Topographical Engineers, were Lieutenants Amiel Weeks Whipple and Edmund L. F. Hardcastle.[2]

For Major Emory, this was the beginning of eight years of work on the boundary survey, a task for which he was extremely well suited. He had graduated from West Point in 1831, where he had been well schooled in science, engineering, and celestial navigation. In 1838, when the US Army formed the new Corps of Topographical Engineers, Emory was recruited as one of the thirty-six original members of that elite group. He worked on the Canadian boundary survey in 1844–46. In June 1846, during the Mexican-American War, then Lieutenant Emory was named the Topographical Engineer reporting to General Stephen W. Kearny, whose Army of the West marched two thousand miles across the Southwest from Missouri to California. In 1848, when Emory's account of and maps based on his work with that expedition were published in Washington, DC, he became widely recognized as an expert on the Southwest region. His report bore the unassuming title "Notes of a Military Reconnaissance from Fort Leavenworth, in Missouri, to San Diego, in California," but it turned out to be a major step forward in understanding the nature and geography of the Far West. It proved especially valuable for adventurers traveling west to join the California gold rush.[3]

Emory would later use the format and basic elements of that very successful report when he prepared his monumental, two-volume final report of the United States–Mexico Boundary Survey, which was published in 1857 and 1859.

※ ※

The United States–Mexico Boundary Survey began work in the field in the late summer of 1849 near San Diego. Financial support from Washington soon began to falter, and by November, funds had dried up. The problem was that the new Whig president, Zachary Taylor, was not happy with President Polk's late-term appointment of John Weller, the Democrat from Ohio, to the post of boundary commissioner. Taylor wanted his own man in the job, so he offered the post to John C. Frémont.[4]

Frémont had also been one of the thirty-six original members of the Army Corps of Topographical Engineers, and he had led three high-profile expeditions to the Far West between 1842 and 1846. His published reports of those expeditions were widely read and had earned him the sobriquet "The Pathfinder." With strong support from his father-in-law, the influential Senator Thomas Hart Benton of Missouri, Frémont had become a leading figure in early California politics during and after the Mexican-American War. He had resigned from the army in March 1848, and was living in California, having become quite rich during that state's gold rush. Frémont, who was attempting to become a US senator for the new state of California, did not immediately accept or reject Taylor's offer of the boundary commissioner post.[5]

Widespread knowledge of the offer to Frémont led to a period of uncertainty about who was in charge of the American boundary survey party; Commissioner Weller found himself unable to cash drafts to cover survey operations in California. Major Emory, who was actually managing operations from his office in San Diego, used local army resources at nearby Fort Riley and limped along for a time. Finally, in January 1850, Weller and the Mexican commissioner agreed to discontinue operations and not attempt to extend the boundary survey east of the mouth of the Gila River. They agreed to meet in El Paso del Norte (now Ciudad Juárez, Mexico) and resume the survey from there on November 1. In spite of the official shutdown of the California survey, Emory remained in San Diego to wrap up work on the portion of the boundary line from the Pacific coast to the mouth of the Gila River, and he did not leave for Washington, DC, until October 1850.[6]

Introduction

In the meantime, in May, when it had become clear that Frémont would not accept the post, President Taylor had named a new boundary commissioner—John Russell Bartlett of Rhode Island. The forty-five-year-old Bartlett owned a bookstore in New York City, was an amateur ethnologist, and had strong Whig Party connections. Needing money to support his family, Bartlett had traveled to Washington with hopes of using his political connections to obtain the post of ambassador to Denmark. Instead, and in spite of his lack of surveying experience, it appears he received the boundary commissioner appointment at an annual salary of $3,000 as a consolation.[7]

Bartlett put together a large organization of Whig Party faithful with little regard for their qualifications for survey work; the group included friends and relatives interested in western travel. However, one of his political hires was in fact well qualified and would play a leading role in the survey. This man, Marine Tyler Wickham Chandler, was an experienced civilian surveyor and son of a Whig congressman from Philadelphia.[8]

New commissioner Bartlett's chief surveyor was Andrew B. Gray, inherited from the old Weller commission. Major Emory, chief astronomer for the old commission, was not initially picked for the new one for several reasons. First, Emory was still in San Diego, winding up the survey work completed prior to January 1850. Second, frustrated with the chaos in California, Emory had attempted to resign from his post, taking the position that the "mix" of leadership on the commission included civilians who had no understanding of or commitment to conducting a proper scientific survey, making it impossible for his Army Topographical Engineers to do their job. He made it clear that he preferred not to be assigned to such an organization in the future.[9]

Initially, Colonel John McClellan, also an Army Topographical Engineer, was named to Emory's old post of chief astronomer and head of the scientific corps. McClellan, however, did not last long in the job. Drunkenness and disruptive behavior during the four-month trip from Washington, DC, to El Paso del Norte, where operations were to begin, led to his recall before he had taken part in any surveying. Colonel James D. Graham replaced McClellan, although he would hold the post for less than a year.[10]

※ ※

Commissioner Bartlett, along with key members of his staff, left the East Coast on August 11, 1850. Bartlett planned to meet the Mexican commissioner, Pedro

García Conde, on November 1 at El Paso del Norte as his predecessor, Commissioner Weller, had agreed to do. Bartlett traveled by steamer from New York City to the port of Indianola, on Texas's southeast coast. There he hired teamsters and camp helpers for his wagon train and was joined by his assigned army escort; the large combined party began moving slowly west toward San Antonio.[11]

On the way, one of the new teamsters shot and killed a Mexican man who had challenged the teamster for trespassing. This was the first of a string of deaths involving the teamsters. Their wild and independent nature, when mixed with McClellan's open hostility to Bartlett's authority and Bartlett's inexperience in managing a large and diverse group of men, led to constant turmoil. In fact, by the time the entourage finally settled down three months later in El Paso del Norte, the known body count had reached nine: a citizen and a teamster were shot; a cashiered army captain committed suicide; two civilian party members, one the son of a US senator, were knifed to death; and four teamsters were arrested, tried, and hanged.[12]

After spending two weeks in San Antonio making final arrangements for the trip to El Paso del Norte, Bartlett decided to split up the huge party. Arguing that he needed to travel faster in order to reach El Paso del Norte in time to meet the Mexican commissioner, he handpicked thirty civilians, including servants and a tailor, for his "advanced party." They were to travel by horse and mule with six light wagons plus Bartlett's luxury coach, which he called a "New York Rockaway." The coach—a virtual "war wagon"—was equipped with multiple guns able to fire thirty-seven shots without reloading. It was also furnished with curtains, windows, and a folding bed.[13]

Bartlett's party was to take the "Upper Road" from San Antonio to El Paso del Norte, via Fredericksburg, Horsehead Crossing of the Pecos, and Guadalupe Pass. It was a slightly shorter and more interesting route than the better-known "Lower Road," which the main party, with heavy freight wagons, a mule train, and soldiers of the army escort, would travel. That route went west from San Antonio to Devils River; then north and west to Comanche Springs; continued west past the sites of what would later be Fort Davis, the town of Van Horn, and Fort Quitman; and then on to El Paso del Norte.[14]

Bartlett left San Antonio on the 625-mile trip on October 10, only twenty-one days before he was supposed to be at his destination; he could not possibly make it in time. On November 7, he was halted by early-season snow on Delaware Creek east of Guadalupe Pass while still 165 miles from his destination. Most of the mules were exhausted, but if the group stopped to refresh the animals, it would run out of provisions for the humans. Bartlett sent four men ahead to the army post at El Paso del Norte to bring back fresh mules and provisions. But because the four mules pulling his Rockaway coach were in relatively good shape, Bartlett decided the next day to press ahead with eight men, leaving the other six wagons to limp on. He arrived in El Paso del Norte on November 13, 1850, late but well ahead of the Mexican commissioner Pedro García Conde, who had stopped 225 miles away to enjoy the greater comforts of Chihuahua City while awaiting news of Bartlett's arrival. García Conde did not arrive in El Paso until December 1, appearing to have used the classic power play of arriving late and forcing your counterpart to wait.[15]

The meeting of the two commissioners had several purposes: to coordinate the independent efforts of the Mexican and American surveying teams, to agree on the location of key starting points of the line, and to seek early agreement on potential problems that might arise from differences in methods. The description of the trace of the boundary incorporated into the Treaty of Guadalupe Hidalgo was brief but adequate for most of its 2,000 miles. More than three-quarters of the boundary followed the channel of major rivers—about 1,300 miles along the Rio Grande and later about 350 miles along the Gila River in what is today Arizona. Between these rivers, straight-line segments defined the boundary. The first such segment was the far west end of the boundary in California. It began at the Pacific coast, three nautical miles south of the port of San Diego, and extended northeast for about 150 miles to the junction of the Gila and Colorado Rivers (see figure 1). Both the American and Mexican commissioners quickly agreed to the location of the end points of this segment, each to be marked with a stone monument.[16]

The second straight-line segment was two connected lines that totaled about 230 miles. One line ran east–west across the southern boundary of Nuevo México, and the other ran north–south along its western border. Locating these two lines turned out to be a significant problem. Their precise latitude and longitude had been unknown at the time the treaty was written. Aware of this uncertainty, the treaty's framers attempted to clarify their intention by noting in the text that the southern boundary of Nuevo México "runs north of the town called Paso" (El Paso del Norte) and by attaching the best map available to them—the *Mapa de los Estados Unidos de Méjico*, published in New York in 1847 by J. Disturnell. The map showed the town of Paso and the southern and western boundaries of Nuevo México; and, according to the map, the east–west-running southern boundary lay only 8 miles north of the town of Paso, while the north–south-running western boundary lay about 190 miles (more than 3 degrees of longitude) west of the town. The map also showed a latitude and longitude grid. However, Disturnell's positioning of Paso, the Rio Grande, and the boundaries of Nuevo México on the grid had been only educated guesses, and they turned out to be off by many miles.[17]

Shortly after the commission surveyors arrived at El Paso del Norte in November 1850, they used celestial navigation to determine the correct latitude and longitude for the town of Paso and found that the Disturnell map showed it to be 1 degree and 50 minutes (108 miles) too far east, and 30 minutes (34 miles) too far north. The dilemma then facing the boundary commissioners was whether to honor the distance in miles from the reference town of Paso to determine the southern and western border of Nuevo México, or to honor the latitude-longitude grid lines of the Disturnell map to determine those borders. Using distance measurements from the reference town heavily favored the United States, while using the Disturnell grid lines favored Mexico. For the Americans, the latter was doubly unfavorable, moving the boundary 34 miles north and 108 miles east of a location based on distance from the reference town.[18]

Commissioners Bartlett and García Conde worked out a compromise in which Bartlett yielded to the Mexican position honoring Disturnell's latitude, which set the southern boundary of Nuevo México 42 miles (8 plus 34) north of Paso. In return, García Conde agreed to a western boundary of Nuevo México (longitude) honoring Disturnell's approximate distance of 190 miles west of Paso. This was good for the United States in terms of total square miles, but bad in that it gave Mexico an east-west strip of land (34 by 190 miles), lying just north and west of El Paso del Norte—land thought to be the prime location for a transcontinental railroad and favored especially by the American southern states. Bartlett, being from Rhode Island, may not have placed a high value on this strip of land, since the northern, antislave states favored a transcontinental railroad route that lay much farther north near the center of the United States.[19]

Acting on Bartlett's direct orders, Lieutenant Amiel W. Whipple, sitting in for the chief surveyor Andrew B. Gray, who had been delayed by illness, signed the Bartlett–García Conde Compromise under protest, but it was never approved by Congress.[20] The Nuevo México boundary-line controversy would drag on for years, until it was finally resolved in December 1853 by the Gadsden Purchase, in which the United States purchased the disputed area, along with additional adjoining lands, from Mexico, securing about 30,000 square miles thought favorable for the railroad.[21]

In May 1851, Bartlett, thinking the Nuevo México boundary controversy was settled by his compromise with García Conde, moved his offices to the Santa Rita copper mines, 115 miles northwest of El Paso del Norte.[22] Leaving the mines with the stated objective of "investigating supply logistics" for his survey parties, Bartlett then traveled over 300 miles south to Ures, Sonora.[23]

In July, when chief surveyor Gray finally arrived at the commission office at Santa Rita, he strongly objected to the compromise boundary that Bartlett, now traveling in Mexico, had approved. Gray, supported by the Topographical Engineer Whipple and the recently arrived Colonel James D. Graham, formally challenged the Bartlett–García Conde Compromise. Uncertainty as to who was in charge of approving the compromise and Bartlett's continued absence delayed work on the survey west of El Paso del Norte through most of 1851.[24]

※ ※

The chain of command for the Boundary Commission was fuzzy, but it appears to have operated in this period with Commissioner Bartlett reporting to Whig Party career politician and Secretary of the Interior Alexander H. H. Stuart. Chief surveyor Gray reported to Bartlett and to Secretary Stuart. The commission's chief astronomer, Graham, a career soldier and a member of the Army Corps of Topographical Engineers, reported to Bartlett, Stuart, and the head of the Topographical Engineers, Colonel J. J. Abert, in Washington, DC.[25]

In fall 1851, Secretary Stuart had become increasingly unhappy with the lack of progress on the survey and specifically with the performance of his chief astronomer, Colonel Graham. After being named to the post, Graham had taken six months to gather his instruments and travel to El Paso del Norte. He did not feel well and remained there another month before moving west to the office at the Santa Rita mines where his surveyors were stationed. Once there, he refused to sign the Bartlett–García Conde Compromise, causing a further delay. Stuart had had enough. He ordered Major Emory, then in Washington, DC, to replace Colonel Graham as chief astronomer and proceed to El Paso del Norte to take charge of survey operations.[26]

※ ※

Although Emory had said earlier that he did not want to serve on a commission that was a mix of civilian and military leaders, after nine months back in

Washington, he was ready for a new field assignment. He took the job and quickly put together a team that included two naturalists recommended by his friend John Torrey, a botany professor at Princeton College. The two naturalists, Charles C. Parry and Arthur Schott, played important roles in the 1852 and 1853 boundary surveys that we will be examining in detail later.[27]

In mid-November, while Emory was en route to El Paso del Norte, his role was expanded by Secretary Stuart to include the post of chief surveyor, thus Emory was also replacing A. B. Gray, who had been relieved of his post because he refused to sign the Bartlett–García Conde Compromise. Holding both positions put Emory in charge of all field operations and meant he officially answered to Commissioner Bartlett and to Secretary Stuart. As part of his new post as chief surveyor, Emory was directed by Stuart to sign the Bartlett–García Conde Compromise. This presented Emory with a dilemma. Signing would put him at odds with his family and friends from southern states who supported a southern route for the transcontinental railroad, but refusing to sign would place his post as chief surveyor in jeopardy.[28]

We know from a December 1851 letter Emory sent in reply to an enquiry from Texas congressman Volney Howard that he believed neither the Bartlett–García Conde Compromise nor the alternate boundary line farther south that Gray had proposed would provide an adequate route for the railroad. What was needed was a new east-to-west boundary line that would pass well south of the mountains near Tucson.[29] Later, Emory's position became the prevailing view and the one considered in the 1853 Gadsden Purchase. In the end, Emory never signed the compromise because he could not do so until his post as chief surveyor was approved by Congress and that did not happen until a year after his appointment, by which time the Bartlett–García Conde Compromise had lost all congressional support.[30]

While the various boundary commission staff changes were taking place in 1851, Commissioner Bartlett remained out of touch, not only with Washington, DC, but also with his own men at both the Santa Rita mines and El Paso del Norte. He had been traveling about Mexico and California, purportedly arranging for provisions for his surveyors, but he was actually sightseeing across more than two thousand miles. He had first gone south to Santa Cruz, Arizpe, and Ures in Sonora, where he became ill with typhoid fever. After his recovery, he continued south to Mazatlán and Acapulco on the Pacific coast, and then went by ship to San Diego, where he arrived in February 1852. In San Diego, he met the boundary surveyor Lieutenant Amiel Whipple. Whipple had been working his way down the Gila River until he aborted his survey after running out of money and supplies about sixty miles before reaching the mouth of the river.[31]

Bartlett then took a ship up the coast to San Francisco "to procure supplies," taking time to tour the Napa Valley, and did not return to San Diego until April 1852. In May, Bartlett finally started overland for El Paso del Norte to reconnect with his surveyors. He continued to make side trips along the way, to the Pima Villages (near Phoenix) and the ancient ruins of Casa Grande in Chihuahua (125 miles southwest of El Paso del Norte). In August 1852, he finally arrived at El Paso del Norte, where Major Emory and his surveyors had their work well under way along the Rio Grande more than 200 miles farther downstream.[32]

※ ※

In late November 1851, when Major Emory had first arrived at El Paso del Norte to take control of survey operations, he found financial and organizational chaos. No one knew where Commissioner Bartlett was, and survey operations were at a standstill. He encountered about a hundred idle men, most not suited for survey work, and there was no money or credit for operations. Local merchants would not cash Emory's drafts, and survey employees had not been paid in months.[33]

Emory attempted first to find the commissioner, but when he could not, he quickly moved ahead on his own. He secured supplies through the help of his friend James Magoffin, an El Paso del Norte merchant, whom Emory had met in 1846 during the Mexican-American War when Emory had been with Kearny's Army of the West.[34]

Emory dismissed most of the idle men in El Paso del Norte, keeping the best-qualified ones to form three new surveying parties, and he set up his office at the village of Frontera, on the American side 8 miles north of El Paso del Norte. The first party, headed by the Topographical Engineer Lieutenant W. F. Smith, was directed to set up a celestial observatory for longitude calculations at San Elizario, Texas, 16 miles downriver from El Paso del Norte. For the second party, Emory sent Lieutenant Nathaniel Michler with the assistant surveyor Arthur Schott back down the San Antonio Road to set up an office on the Lower Rio Grande at Fort Duncan in Eagle Pass, Texas, about 800 river miles below El Paso del Norte. There Michler set up an observatory, and Schott began surveying along the river (figure 2). Emory sent out a third party, led by the civilian Maurice von Hippel. Traveling by boat and supported by an onshore mule train, this party was to survey the 240-mile section of river from El Paso del Norte down to

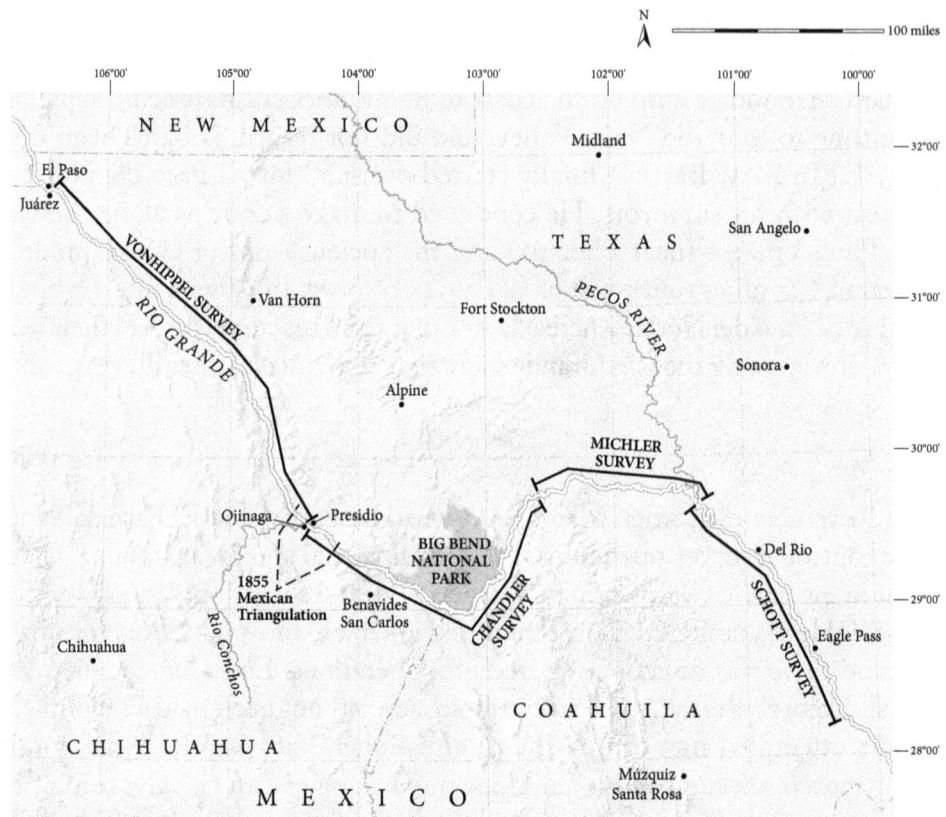

FIGURE 2. **Boundary Surveys across the Big Bend Region.** This map shows the span of five surveys along the Rio Grande from Presidio del Norte to the Pecos River: von Hippel (1852), Fernández (Mexican Triangulation; 1855), Chandler (1852), Michler (1853), and Schott (1852). Map by Carol Zuber-Mallison.

Presidio del Norte (the location today of the sister towns Ojinaga, Mexico, and Presidio, Texas).[35]

By summer 1852, Emory had things well enough in hand in El Paso del Norte to travel downriver to check on the progress of the parties he had sent out earlier. He arrived at Presidio del Norte on July 8, 1852.[36] Two months earlier, in May, von Hippel had finished the river survey from El Paso del Norte down to his camp located a day's ride above Presidio del Norte. He was awaiting new orders and financial support from Emory. Von Hippel needed money to pay off and dismiss packers who had stolen from him, and he wanted to pay his men, who had received no wages in eleven months.[37] In spite of the lack of funds, Emory directed von Hippel to continue the survey down the river below Presidio del Norte. Von Hippel balked, and in a letter to Emory on July 21, he asked for increased supplies, financial support, and fifty armed men for protection from roving bands of Indians. He had earlier sent out his assistant surveyor, Thomas Thompson, to scout the river below, and based on Thompson's report, von Hippel knew the survey below Presidio del Norte would be very difficult. Thompson had reported that steep canyons and rapids lay in their path, and as he was gone only five days, it is likely he knew this after going no farther than Colorado Canyon, about twenty-five trail miles below Presidio del Norte.[38]

On July 22, when it was clear Emory would not or could not meet his demands, von Hippel and his main assistant, E. A. Phillips, resigned.[39] Emory then asked his young clerk, Clint Gardner, to take temporary control of the von Hippel party, make an inventory of its men and supplies, and recommend what needed to be done to get the party prepared to continue the survey down the river and across the Big Bend. Over the next two weeks, Gardner supervised the surveying of the short section of river from von Hippel's camp down to Major Emory's new camp at his observatory on the American side of the Rio Grande across from Presidio del Norte.[40]

Before leaving Presidio del Norte, Emory assigned the civilian surveyor M. T. W. Chandler to lead a party to map the boundary along the Rio Grande from Presidio del Norte down to the mouth of the Pecos River. Chandler was unable to fully complete this extremely difficult section in 1852, so, early in 1853, Emory ordered Lieutenant Nathaniel Michler to survey the section from the point where Chandler had stopped, down to the mouth of the Pecos River (see figure 2). It is mainly the story of the men of the M. T. W. Chandler and Lieutenant Nathaniel Michler parties who surveyed the Rio Grande boundary across the Big Bend of Texas in 1852 and 1853 that will occupy our attention in the pages that follow.

PART I

The 1852 Chandler Surveying Party

IN THE LATE SUMMER AND FALL of 1852, the survey party led by Marine Tyler Wickham (M. T. W.) Chandler mapped 209 miles of the channel of the Rio Grande to define the new border between the United States and Mexico (see figure 2). The group started at Presidio del Norte and worked downstream across the Big Bend region and into the heart of the massive Lower Canyons. Some of the surveying was done in open valleys, but most of the time the surveyors worked in steep-walled canyons accessible only by boat. The party had to run churning rapids, where it lost two of its four boats and most of its provisions, camping gear, and clothing. It endured a tense encounter with a large band of Comanche at a major river crossing. The mule train escort had to make long, dry detours around the major canyons where the surveyors were working.

After three months, the men were dead tired, and their clothes and shoes were in tatters. Faced with an unbroken chain of precipitous canyons and unable to maintain contact with the mule train carrying their shelter and nearly exhausted supply of food, Chandler was forced to abandon the survey 125 river miles short of his goal: the mouth of the Pecos River. Leaving the river, the party spent the next three weeks walking 300 miles across the dry interior of Mexico to the US Army post at Fort Duncan on the lower Rio Grande.

The work done by Chandler and his surveyors formed the basis for five boundary maps in the larger set of detailed maps that documented the entire new boundary from the Gulf of Mexico to California and were signed in 1857 in Washington, DC, by leaders of the US and Mexican Boundary Commissions (figure 3).

⚜ ⚜

In the summer of 1852, when Major Emory moved his office and staff from the American settlement of Frontera, near El Paso del Norte, to Presidio del Norte, 240 miles farther down the Rio Grande, he had two objectives: (1) make arrangements for a party to extend the boundary survey down the river through and beyond the Big Bend, and (2) set up an observatory station to determine the latitude and longitude of Presidio del Norte to be used as a control point for the surveys.

Emory wanted the experienced civilian surveyor M. T. W. Chandler to lead the challenging and important survey down the Rio Grande, but Chandler was still en route from the East Coast after a leave of absence. While awaiting Chandler's return, Emory assigned his young clerk Clint Gardner to take temporary charge of the party and get it fully staffed and organized for the upcoming survey.

On August 8, one day after Chandler arrived in Presidio del Norte, Emory directed him to lead the survey party across the Big Bend and down to the mouth of the Pecos River, or to the point where he met the survey party led by Arthur Schott that was moving upstream from Fort Duncan at Eagle Pass, Texas. In Emory's letter to Chandler, he said: "I fully rely upon you for the successful accomplishment of this section of the work."[1]

Clint Gardner had hoped his temporary role would become permanent, and he was disappointed to return to his old job as Emory's clerical assistant. But later, in a letter to his mother, he rationalized: "Is it not better, for here I enjoy all the comfort—for the same pay—[while there] the dangers—of [many] different kinds are great."[2]

The likelihood that Chandler would successfully complete the task Emory had assigned him was quite remote. He was setting off into an unknown and wild section of the Rio Grande with massive canyons and rapids through which there had been no documented passage by man. It remains a wild and remote land even in the twenty-first century. Of the 336 river miles Emory asked Chandler to survey, 266 miles lie within the "Rio Grande Wild and Scenic River" designated by Congress in 1978 or in the adjoining canyons in Big Bend National Park and Big Bend Ranch State Park. Public access points to the river are sparse in the parks and in the Black Gap Wildlife Management Area (BGWMA) that adjoins the national park to the east. Outside of federal and state lands, access is tightly controlled by large ranches.

Men and Equipment of the 1852 Boundary Survey Party

Leaders

Marine Tyler Wickham Chandler, a mature and experienced surveyor, was a good choice to lead the party. He is usually listed as M. T. W. Chandler and was likely called Chandler by his coworkers. Born in Philadelphia in 1819, he was the son of Joseph Ripley Chandler—a loyal Whig Party member and a US congressman from Pennsylvania—and Mary R. Ward. Chandler received AB and MA civil engineering degrees from the University of Pennsylvania in 1837 and 1840. He worked as a surveyor for the city of Philadelphia and was elected to the post of city surveyor in January 1850. Immediately before joining the boundary commission, Chandler had been listed in the August 1850 federal census as living with his father and stepmother in Philadelphia.[3]

In late summer 1850, Boundary Commissioner John Bartlett hired Chandler, likely after he received a request to do so from Chandler's father, the Whig congressman. Although Chandler was an experienced surveyor, Bartlett put him "in charge of [the] Magnetic and Meteorological Department."[4] This probably means that the Army Corps of Topographical Engineers had responsibility for hiring all surveyors, so Bartlett had to find a nonsurveyor slot for Chandler.

While traveling from San Antonio to El Paso del Norte, Chandler recorded the barometric elevation along his route, and these measurements show that he traveled along the Lower Wagon Road with the army escort rather than by the Upper Wagon Road used by Bartlett's smaller advance party.[5] Because Chandler was the type of gentleman one would have expected Bartlett to choose for his small party, Chandler may have arrived late in San Antonio, after the advance party had already set out for El Paso del Norte on October 10, 1850.

Chandler arrived at El Paso del Norte in December 1850, and in July 1851, he was working in the US Boundary Commission office at Frontera. Also called White's Ranch, Frontera was a small Anglo settlement on the American side of

Figure 3. **Chandler's Boundary Maps** (*following spread*). This index map shows the locations of the five 1857 boundary maps that resulted from the 1852 Chandler Survey across the greater Big Bend area of Texas. Map by Carol Zuber-Mallison.

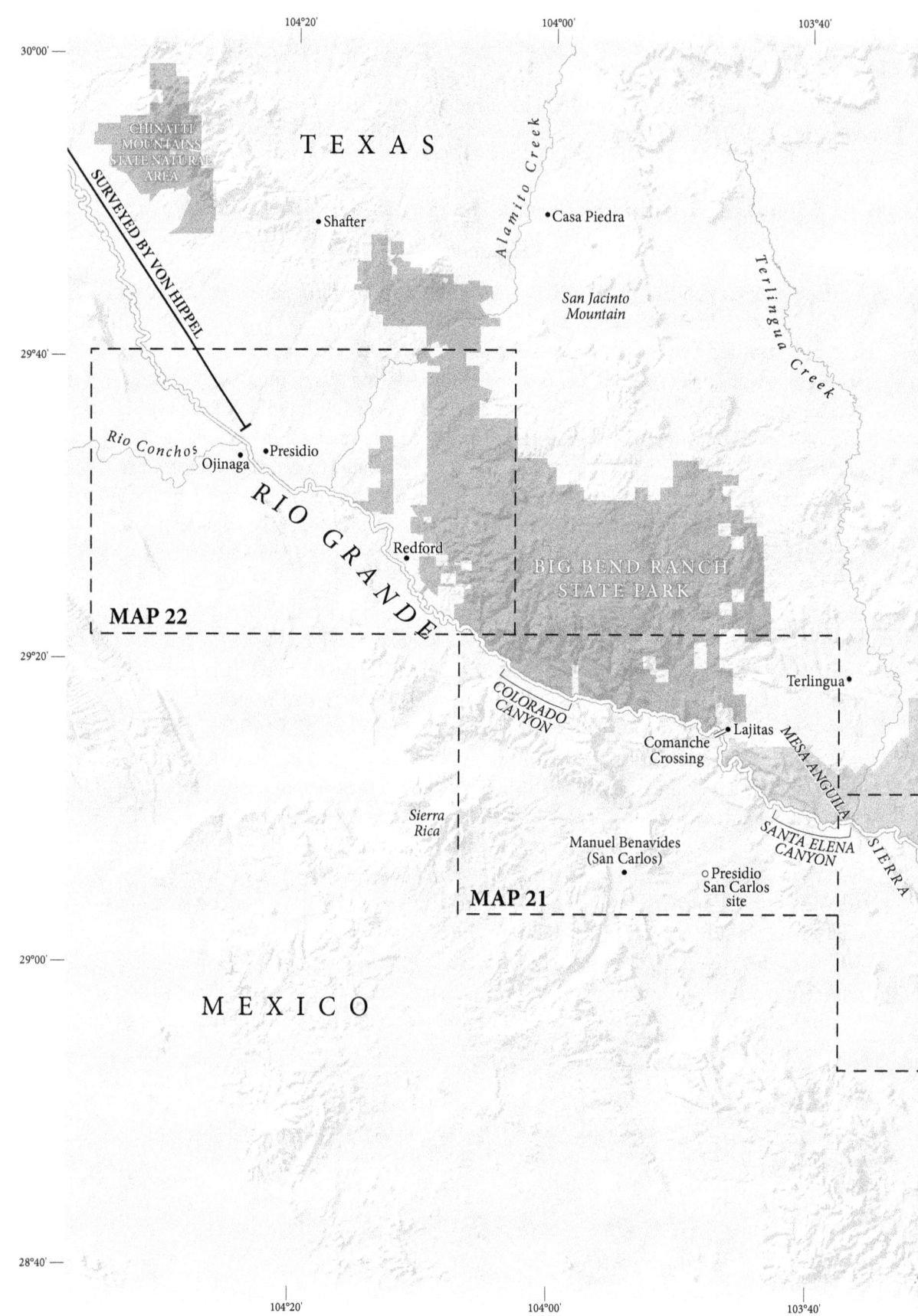

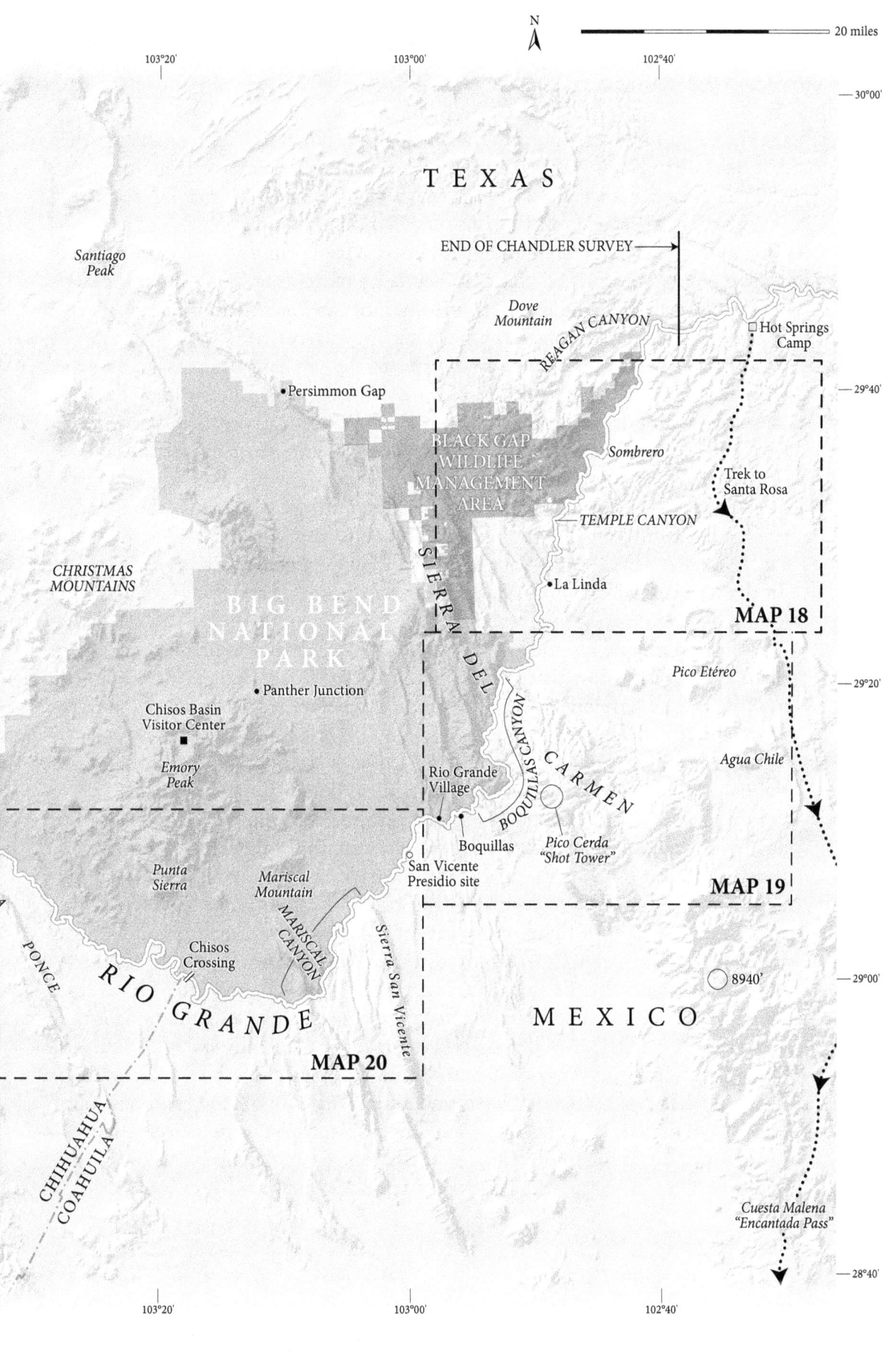

the river, eight miles north of El Paso del Norte.[6] Chandler met Emory for the first time when Emory arrived in the area in late November 1851. In January 1852, Chandler began a leave of absence, during which he traveled through New Orleans, where he met the family of Emory's clerk, Clint Gardner.[7]

Chandler made a favorable impression on Major Emory during their short acquaintance. In a draft of a letter to Secretary of the Interior A. H. H. Stuart, Emory described Chandler as "a gentleman of intelligence and integrity" and said he planned to put him in charge of a survey party.[8]

Chandler's main surveying assistants were the civilians Thomas Thompson from Connecticut and E. A. Phillips from Massachusetts. Little is known about these two men other than that they were experienced surveyors. Colonel John McClellan, the first chief astronomer (chief surveyor), hired these surveyors at the beginning of the Bartlett Commission. They arrived at El Paso del Norte in December 1850 but did very little surveying during 1851, because the controversy surrounding the Bartlett–García Conde Compromise had brought most surveying to a halt. In mid-November 1851, they were named assistant surveyors for the Maurice von Hippel party, which was to begin a survey at Frontera and move down the Rio Grande.[9]

When von Hippel resigned in July 1852 because Emory was unable to provide the financing, supplies, and protection he wanted, E. A. Phillips also resigned in support, but he rejoined the Chandler party before it started down the river below Presidio del Norte.

Charles C. Parry, who was already on Emory's staff, was named to serve as the naturalist, botanist, geologist, and medical doctor for the Chandler party (figure 4). It is Parry's unpublished field notebook that allows us to track the day-by-day progress and activities of the four months of the Chandler Survey.[10] Parry had been born in England in 1823 and at age nine emigrated with his family to the United States, where they settled on a farm in upstate New York. In 1846, at age twenty-three, Parry earned his medical degree from Columbia College in New York City and moved to Davenport, Iowa, to set up his medical practice.[11] Botany, not medicine, was Parry's passion, and after only a few months in Davenport, he left his medical practice to serve as a botanist for the geologist David Dale Owen, who was engaged in a federally sponsored survey of new lands in Iowa, Wisconsin, and Minnesota. While in school at Columbia, Parry had become acquainted with the noted Princeton botany professor John Torrey, and in 1848, Parry began to send Torrey plant specimens collected during his fieldwork.[12] He maintained a close relationship with Torrey, sending him

FIGURE 4. **Men of the Boundary Survey.** Left to right and top to bottom are Major William H. Emory, Commissioner John Russell Bartlett, civilian surveyor Marine T. W. Chandler, naturalist Charles C. Parry, Lt. Duff C. Green, and Lt. Nathaniel Michler. Emory: 1859 Emory Report, xi; Bartlett: New York Public Library Digital Collections online, image 122363; Chandler: courtesy The First Troop Philadelphia Calvary; Parry: *Proceedings of the Davenport Academy of Natural Science* 6 (1897); Green: George W. Cullum's *Register of the Officers and Graduates of the US Military Academy at West Point, NY*, Class of 1849, Graduate 1435; Michler: US Corps of Topographical Engineers website.

specimens and correspondence for decades. Emory also counted Torrey among his scientific friends, as Torrey had taught courses at West Point during the time Emory attended the school.[13] Emory had sent plants to Torrey beginning with his journey from Kansas to California with General Stephen Kearny's Army of the West in 1846. It is quite likely that Emory's hiring of Parry for the boundary survey in 1849 was based on a recommendation from Torrey.

Parry's work for the boundary survey began in June 1849 near San Diego. He was responsible for geological and botanical investigations in support of Lieutenant Amiel W. Whipple, who was charged with surveying to the junction of the Gila and Colorado Rivers—about 150 miles east of San Diego—then, jointly with the Mexican surveyor, selecting the spot to erect a permanent boundary marker. This marker would be the eastern terminus of the first straight-line segment of the boundary defined in the Treaty of Guadalupe Hidalgo. Parry completed his work for Whipple in December and returned to San Diego, where he worked on his plant collections and made excursions into the hills along the coast. It was during this time that Parry discovered a new species of pine, which he named "Torrey Pine" for his mentor.[14] Parry, carrying his collections, left San Diego by steamer for the East Coast in March 1851. In September, Emory asked Parry to take a new assignment with the US Boundary Commission and travel with him to El Paso del Norte, where Emory would direct the survey down the Rio Grande.

Parry's landscape and geologic sketches are key to documenting the Chandler party's route down the Rio Grande. Six of his drawings were converted to woodcut illustrations in the final Emory Report.[15] In addition, Parry's field notebook contains many geologic sketches of rock exposures, six of which were reproduced as line drawings in the geology summary he wrote for the Emory Report describing the nature of the country along the Rio Grande from El Paso del Norte to Fort Duncan, Texas.[16] Parry's field sketches do not show the level of artistic talent seen in the woodcuts in the final Emory Report, but this may mean either that he took greater care when making the larger figures destined for woodcuts or that someone embellished his sketches. At one point in his journal, after describing a view of the Chisos Mountains, Parry noted: "See figure 13." Since none of the numerous sketches in his notebook carry a figure number and none of his journal sketches appear as woodcuts, it seems likely that Parry made separate, larger landscape drawings for use in the final published report and that he numbered those drawings. No larger landscape sketches are among the Parry papers at Iowa State.[17] However, such drawings were probably destroyed in

Washington, DC, after being used to prepare the woodcuts for the final report. After completion of the final report in 1856, Emory directed that all work copies of maps, field notes, and other materials be destroyed in an attempt to minimize future second-guessing about the basis for the official boundary line as shown on the final boundary maps.[18] Fortunately for us, Parry did not destroy his personal field notebook.

Parry's Drawings in the Emory Report

It has been suggested that the assistant surveyor, Arthur Schott, made the geological drawings and sketches for the Chandler party.[1] However, the recent discovery of Charles C. Parry's daily journal makes it clear that Parry made the drawings along that section of the Rio Grande surveyed by Chandler.[2] Throughout 1852, during the Chandler survey, Schott remained on the lower Rio Grande, assisting Lieutenant Michler. In December 1851, Emory had sent Michler and Schott to Fort Duncan (Eagle Pass, Texas), where Michler set up an observatory to determine longitude and latitude while Schott surveyed the river below down to Laredo. Schott was back at Fort Duncan in late June when he began a survey upriver to the mouth of the Pecos. Schott is shown as the author of Rio Grande Boundary Maps 9 through 15, which cover the river from Laredo to the mouth of the Pecos River. On October 1, 1852, when the Chandler party was camped at Santa Elena Canyon, 150 miles to the west, Schott was in camp at San Felipe Spring (Del Rio, Texas), reporting problems with Indians in a letter to Major Emory.[3] Parry, who remained with the Chandler party from August through December 1852, mentioned Schott only once—on page 166 of his 167-page journal, in December when both Parry and Schott were at Fort Duncan.

NOTES

1. Ronnie C. Tyler, *The Big Bend: A History of the Last Texas Frontier* (Washington, DC: National Park Service, 1975), 82.
2. Charles C. Parry, "Field Notebook and Journal, Botany and Geology, U.S. Boundary Commission 1852, Texas and Mexico: The Papers of Charles Christopher Parry (1823–1890)." Special Collections, MS-290, Parks Library, Iowa State University, Ames, Iowa, 1–167.

3. Schott to Emory, Camp on Arroyo San Felipe (now Del Rio, Texas), October 1, 1852, William H. Emory Papers, Beinecke Rare Book and Manuscript Division, Yale University, WA MSS S-1187, New Haven, CT.

Second Lieutenant Duff Cyrus Green, assisted by First Sergeant Edward Quinn, was in charge of the army escort assigned to the Chandler Survey party. They provided protection from Indians and handled the mule train that transported the provisions. Duff Green was an 1849 graduate of West Point (see figure 4). In 1850, he was sent to El Paso del Norte, where he reported to Colonel Louis S. Craig, who was in charge of all military escorts assigned to the US Boundary Commission. Craig assigned Green to lead the escort unit serving Major Emory. When Emory and Green were camped across from Presidio del Norte in July 1852, Green agreed to a request from Emory to commit all his men to the Chandler party, which would soon start down the river.[19]

In early August, Green returned to El Paso del Norte and then went another forty miles upriver to Fort Fillmore to secure additional provisions and soldiers for the Chandler escort. When passing near El Paso del Norte on his return trip, Green encountered Commissioner Bartlett, fresh from a sightseeing trip to the historic Casa Grande ruins in Mexico. Bartlett informed Green that his commanding officer, Colonel Craig, had recently been killed by army deserters in California and that Green was now the senior officer of the boundary commission escort command. Bartlett ordered Green to abandon his planned escort of the Chandler party and instead accompany the Bartlett entourage along the San Antonio Road to protect them from Indian attack. To Lieutenant Green, it must have seemed inappropriate to dedicate his escort to a party traveling along the busy San Antonio Road, where unescorted mail coaches passed each week, while leaving an unarmed party of surveyors working along the Rio Grande frontier unprotected. Although concerned that turning down Commissioner Bartlett might damage his career, Green refused, choosing to honor his prior commitment to Emory to escort the Chandler Survey.[20]

Beyond these six men—Chandler, Thompson, Phillips, Parry, Green, and Quinn—we know only one other man by name: Charles Abbott. He was the boatman who, along with one or two companions, floated through the Lower Canyons of the Rio Grande from Hot Springs Rapids, where the main Chandler party abandoned the river, down to Fort Duncan at Eagle Pass, Texas. Parry mentioned Abbott by name in his letter to Emory from their camp at the rapids on November 4, 1852.[21]

Men, Equipment, and Supplies

No inventory of personnel has ever been located, but based on the scattered comments of participants and the size of other similar parties, I estimate the total number of men in the Chandler party, including the army escort, to be between sixty-five and seventy. I assume fifty for the mule train and army escort, as Parry noted there were fifty men at Presidio del Norte, and there would have been fifteen to twenty in the survey party proper.[22] Lieutenant Green commanded an escort of ten men when he arrived with Major Emory at Presidio del Norte in July 1852. Green then returned to Fort Fillmore in August in response to Emory's request for "a larger escort for the surveying party."[23] At Fort Fillmore, north of El Paso del Norte, Green acquired twelve additional soldiers, including Sergeant Edward Quinn, who had been with the main boundary commission escort led by Colonel Craig. These additional men raise the total number of soldiers reporting to Green to twenty-two.

Green said he started with a pack train of eighty mules.[24] According to W. D. Smithers, a well-known early Big Bend photographer and experienced packer, the usual army mule train in this era included sixty-four mules: fifty for cargo and fourteen for the packers to ride.[25] The additional sixteen mules suggest that Green started with a larger-than-usual train, and he must have had several additional mules for him and his sergeant to ride. This assumes the other soldiers walked. Green needed a couple of herders, because he took along some beef cattle for larder, perhaps a dozen beeves, one for each week they were on the trail, plus two that he gave to Indians along the way. He gave one beef to the Comanche at a river crossing on September 23, 1852, and much later he gave another to the Seminole near Santa Rosa, Mexico, when the party was only six days out of Fort Duncan, Texas. Thus, Green's total of fifty men could have been twenty-two soldiers, fourteen packers, and fourteen camp helpers, including herders and cooks. Fourteen camp helpers compares favorably with the nineteen cooks, servants, and laborers that Commissioner Bartlett had for a Rio Grande survey party near El Paso in 1851.[26]

For Chandler's survey team proper, I estimate fifteen to twenty men. In July 1852, Emory's clerk, Clint Gardner, made an inventory of the idle and disintegrating von Hippel party camped near Presidio del Norte. This indicated that only eleven men were still available versus a full strength of seventeen, which included American chainmen (to carry the chain used for measurement) and carriers of the surveying instruments. It is not clear if Gardner's seventeen included boatmen or camp helpers.[27]

Chandler's surveyors planned to travel by boat, so the number of men was limited by the capacity of the boats. Chandler gives no information in his report on the number or type of his boats, but scattered comments from Parry's journal allow an inventory. The party started with four boats: two made of India rubber and two made of wood, one larger than the other. With each boat carrying four or five men, they had space for sixteen to twenty men. In preliminary surveys made just below Presidio, Parry mentioned that the survey party had thirty men, but at that time they were working in the flatlands above the first canyon, while the boat party used the two rubber boats supported by a small onshore pack train to carry provisions.[28]

It is likely that the rubber boats were transported from the East Coast and the wooden ones were built in El Paso del Norte. Apparently, the same four boats had been used by von Hippel in his early 1852 river survey, because Parry later noted that the wooden boat Chandler abandoned at the entrance to Santa Elena Canyon "had accomplished the entire trip from El Paso [del Norte]." Von Hippel had known boats would be useful because in June 1850, two Topographical Engineers stationed in San Antonio had used wooden boats and pack mules to make a reconnaissance survey of the river from El Paso del Norte to Presidio del Norte.[29]

Chandler's heavy, flat-bottomed wooden boats did not last long in the big rapids in the canyons below Presidio del Norte. Parry reported that on September 14, the second day of the survey, at the entrance to Colorado Canyon at the second rapids just below the mouth of Rancherias Creek, "two of our boats swamped and much of the cargo [was] lost, including nearly our entire stock of provisions." These two boats had been "too heavily loaded" and must have been unmanageable in rough water.[30]

Late the next day, the wooden boats were found upside down in shallow water six miles downriver. One was beyond repair, but the other was still sound, and they were able to use it to continue downriver. Later, Parry noted that even the good boat was abandoned and cast adrift at the entrance to Santa Elena Canyon when the surveyors decided not to attempt a dangerous rapids created by a rock slide.[31] Without wagons, there was no way to carry the heavy wooden boat on the long detour around the canyon, whereas the smaller rubber boats could be deflated and carried by pack mules.

Although the two rubber boats were roughed up in the many rapids they navigated, both survived the entire journey from Presidio del Norte to Hot Springs Rapids, where the survey was abandoned—a distance of over two hundred miles on the river plus fifty-six miles deflated on the back of a mule during the detour around Santa Elena Canyon. At Hot Springs, Parry said: "Our rubber boats are not to be trusted[,] being full of holes, very leaky and rotten."[32]

In spite of the condition of the boats, in November, boatman Charles Abbott and unnamed comrades took the single best one and floated 227 additional miles down the Rio Grande through the heart of the Lower Canyons, past the Pecos River, and on to Fort Duncan, Texas. They averaged 23 miles a day for their entire trip of only ten days. This extraordinary and historic accomplishment was the first documented passage of a boat through the Lower Canyons of the Rio Grande.[33]

Rubber Boats

The Army Corps of Topographical Engineers pioneered the use of inflatable boats for exploration. Charles Goodyear's invention of the vulcanization process in 1838 made possible this type of boat. In the same year, John C. Frémont, who was a mathematics teacher on a navy sloop, was appointed a second lieutenant in the Army Corps of Topographical Engineers. While serving in the Corps, Frémont became famous for his early explorations in the Rocky Mountains, and newspapers gave him the nickname "The Pathfinder." Frémont used India rubber boats during his pioneering reconnaissance in the Rockies. He designed a boat and had it built at a cost of $190 (about $5,000 in today's economy) by Horace Day of New Brunswick, New Jersey. Frémont used the boat on the Platte River in 1842 (in present-day Wyoming). In the following year, Day built a second boat for Frémont. It was eighteen feet long, with four side compartments containing rubber cylinders eighteen inches in diameter and additional compartments front and rear. Inflation was accomplished with a bellows. Frémont used the second boat for exploring along the shore of the Great Salt Lake in September 1843.

In February 1854, when Topographical Engineer Lieutenant Amiel Whipple led an expedition to evaluate a possible railroad route along the 35th parallel, he used an inflatable boat, constructed on the spot using three inflatable pontoons and a small wagon frame, to cross the Colorado River near the Mojave Villages (now west of Kingman, Arizona; see figure 5). His naturalist/artist, Balduin Möllhausen, called it a "canvas boat," describing the contraption as "three large canvas bags lined with gutta percha—perfectly air-tight—pumped full of air by bellows and attached to the frame of a small wagon." The bags may have in fact been rubber and not the similar latex material gutta percha, because Möllhausen also referred to the rubber boat Frémont used on the Great Salt Lake as a "canvas boat." Möllhausen said that Topographical Engineer Lieutenant Joseph Ives brought the boat [the pontoons] with him from Texas. Using men shown in Möllhausen's sketch for approximate scale, Ives's boat appears to be about five feet wide and eleven feet long and designed for crossing rivers rather than floating down them.[1]

We do not know when Chandler's rubber boats were brought to the Rio Grande or who brought them. Parry first mentioned their use in the boundary survey in August 1852 at Presidio del Norte.[2] All of the members of the elite Corps of Topographical Engineers would have been aware of the use of this type of boat by Frémont. I assume that one of the three boundary commission chief astronomers, all Topographical Engineers charged with surveying the Rio Grande, brought the rubber boats to El Paso del Norte. These men were Colonel John McClellan in fall 1850, Colonel James D. Graham in fall 1851, or Major William H. Emory in December 1851.

Since I noted above that Lieutenant Ives acquired rubber pontoons in San Antonio in 1854, it is possible that Chandler's rubber boats were actually built or warehoused in San Antonio. Topographical Engineer Captain George Hughes reported that in 1846, on his way from San Antonio to the interior of Mexico during the Mexican War, he crossed the Rio Grande to Presidio del Rio Grande (now Guerrero, Coahuila) on a "flying-bridge" (pontoon bridge) put in place by a Captain Fraser, an engineer, who had built the pontoons in San Antonio. Unfortunately, these pontoons may have been wooden boats, since Hughes had access to wagons for transport and he does not say they were rubber.[3]

Part I: The 1852 Chandler Surveying Party

Notes

1. Ferol Egan, *Frémont: Explorer for a Restless Nation* (Garden City, NJ: Doubleday, 1977), 56, 112, 123, 149, 154; Balduin Möllhausen, *Diary of a Journey from the Mississippi to the Coasts of the Pacific with a United States Government Expedition*. 2 vols. Translated by Mrs. Percy Sinnett (London: Longman, 1858), 2:265.
2. "Our party composed of some thirty men with sufficiency of pack mules and two India Rubber boats." Charles C. Parry, "Field Notebook and Journal, Botany and Geology, U.S. Boundary Commission 1852, Texas and Mexico: The Papers of Charles Christopher Parry (1823–1890)" (Special Collections, MS-290, Parks Library, Iowa State University, Ames, Iowa), 1.
3. George W. Hughes, *Report of the Secretary of War, communicating, in compliance with a resolution of the Senate, a map showing the operations of the Army of the United States in Texas and the adjacent Mexican States on the Rio Grande; accompanied by astronomical observations, and descriptive and military memoirs of the country*, 31st Cong., 1st sess., 1849, SED 32, 18.

FIGURE 5. **Rubber Boat Crossing the Colorado River.** On February 27, 1854, an expedition led by Lt. Amiel W. Whipple used a rubber boat to transport equipment across the river near the Mojave Indian villages, near the southern tip of present-day Nevada. According to Balduin Möllhausen, who painted the scene, Lt. Joseph Ives constructed the boat on the spot using three inflatable pontoons brought from Texas and tied together with the body of a small cart placed upon them. He reported that the contraption "had the appearance of a Venetian gondola but proved to be of great capacity." "Pulling Boat in the Rio Colorado Near a Mojave Village," 1853, from Möllhausen, *Diary of a Journey from the Mississippi to the Coasts of the Pacific*, 265. Used by permission from Oklahoma Historical Society.

The Iron Boats Fiasco

While rubber and wooden boats were ultimately used by the US boundary survey crews along the Gila and Rio Grande Rivers, the first plan had been to use iron boats. This idea may have originated in a 1849 Christmas party conversation in Washington, DC, between Colonel John J. Abert, chief of the Army Corps of Topographical Engineers, and US Navy Lieutenant Edward F. Beale. A short time later, in early January 1850, Brevet Colonel John McClellan, who was on Abert's staff, wrote two letters about the iron boats idea to Secretary of the Interior Thomas Ewing. McClellan said Abert had suggested that six iron, or preferably copper, boats be built for the survey and that Beale had offered to oversee the construction of the boats at the navy facility in Brooklyn, New York. Curiously enough, Beale would, in 1857–59, become well known for experiments testing camels for use by exploration parties in the Far West.[1]

It appears that Abert's plan was to transport the boats to San Diego, California, where the boundary survey would begin. This suggests that the boats were to move first by ship to Panama, then by wagon across Panama, followed by another ship to San Diego, then overland by wagon east across California to the boundary line at the junction of the Gila and Colorado Rivers. From there, the boats would carry surveyors up the Gila to mark the river boundary line along the river extending east to its headwaters in New Mexico Territory. Then the boats would be moved overland by wagon east to the Rio Grande near El Paso del Norte, where they would be used to carry surveyors down the Rio Grande across Texas to the Gulf of Mexico.

This plan was almost immediately out of date. Because of the long delay in moving messages from San Diego to Washington, Abert was unaware that the US and Mexican boundary commissioners in San Diego had agreed on February 2, 1850, to delay the survey up the Gila River and instead move the site of further survey operations to El Paso del Norte on the Rio Grande and meet there on the first Monday of November.[2]

In June 1850, John R. Bartlett was named the new boundary commissioner, replacing John Weller, who had been dismissed in December 1849, and Bartlett inherited the iron boats project. He named two officers familiar with the iron boats to his staff. They were the astronomer and chief surveyor Colonel John McClellan, who had worked on the initial proposal of the boats for Colonel Abert, and US Navy Lieutenant Isaac G. Strain, who was to take charge of "navy matters" for the US Boundary Commission.[3]

In late August 1850, when Bartlett finally reached the Texas coast on his westward trip to the planned meeting of Mexican and American commissioners at El Paso del Norte, he noted that the navy had constructed four iron boats for the boundary commission. He failed to mention that the boats were still in New York. The fact that they had been left on the East Coast and not transported to El Paso del Norte suggests that the idea of using the boats for the survey had lost support.[4]

Further evidence that the iron boats were falling out of favor came in September 1850 when Bartlett recommended to the Secretary of the Interior that the iron boats be loaned to Lieutenant Strain for his proposed exploration of the lower Colorado River extending from the US-Mexico boundary line near the mouth of the Gila River down to the Gulf of California. Thus it appears that Bartlett became convinced the boats were not suitable for the boundary survey.[5]

In October 1850, Bartlett's chief surveyor, Colonel McClellan, was recalled after months of disorderly and drunken behavior. He was replaced by the Topographical Engineer Colonel James Graham, then in Washington, DC,[6] who quickly recognized the iron boats were not suitable for the survey. In two letters to Secretary of the Interior Stuart in April 1851, Graham reported that in January he had sent engineers to examine the four iron boats when they were at the Brooklyn Navy Yard. "They are made of galvanized iron, 30 feet long, 5½ feet wide, 1 foot 9 inches deep, and equipped with 8 oars, each 15 feet long, and [the empty boats] weigh over a half ton each. They are built in 5 detachable sections [to facilitate transporting overland]. They are altogether unsuitable for any service connected with the Boundary Survey. . . . They are too large, too heavy and require too many men to man them." Graham advised that "for the Gila and Rio Grande, canoes or light gum-elastic [rubber] boats will be best." He recommended an agent be sought in New York to dispose of the boats.[7] The fate of the boats has been lost to history, as no further reference to them has been found.

Notes

1. Graham to Stuart, April 9 and 12, 1850, US Congress, *Report of the Secretary of the Interior made in compliance with a resolution of the Senate calling for information in relation to the commission appointed to run and mark the boundary between the United States and Mexico*, 32d Cong., 1st sess., 1852, SED 119, 68–69; Gerald Thompson, *Edward F. Beale and the American West* (Albuquerque: University of New Mexico Press, 1983).
2. William H. Emory, *Report on the United States and Mexican Boundary Survey*, 34th Cong., 1st sess., 1857, Vol. 1, HED 135, 8.
3. Ewing to Bartlett, June 19, 1850, in Bartlett Papers; John R. Bartlett, *Personal Narrative of Explorations and Incidents in Texas, New Mexico, California, Sonora, and Chihuahua, connected with the United States and Mexican Boundary Commission, during the Years 1850, '51, '52, and '53*. 2 vols. (New York: D. Appleton, 1854), 1:4–6.
4. Bartlett, *Personal Narrative*, 1:4.
5. Bartlett to Stuart, US Congress, *Report of the Secretary of the Interior . . .* , 32d Cong., 1st sess., 1852, SED 119, 137. Strain's proposal was not approved. It would have been conducted inside Mexican territory and was clearly unrelated to the boundary survey.
6. Stuart to McClellan, October 10, 1850; Stuart to Graham, October 23, 1850, ibid., 32d Cong., 1st sess., 1852, SED 119, 93–96.
7. Graham to Stuart, April 10 and 20, 1851, James D. Graham, *Report of the Secretary of War, in Compliance with a Resolution of the Senate, the Report of Lieutenant Colonel Graham on the Subject of the boundary line between the United States and Mexico*, 32d Cong., 1st sess., 1852, SED 121, 108–9.

Tracing the Route of the Chandler Party

Parry's daily journal is the primary source for mapping Chandler's route. Parry traveled with the surveyors in the boats from Presidio del Norte to Comanche Crossing at Lajitas, Texas. Thereafter, he traveled with the army escort of Lieutenant Green. Daily journals from three earlier expeditions that crossed the Big Bend help us better understand the area, because they describe parts of what would later be Chandler's route. These three trips were the 1848 Hays-Highsmith Texas Ranger expedition from San Antonio, Texas, to San Carlos and Presidio del Norte, Mexico; the 1849 Forty-Niner gold rush wagon train that moved west from Fort Duncan, Texas, to Santa Rosa and San Carlos, Mexico; and the 1851 tour of frontier outposts by the Mexican colonel Emilio Langberg (figure 6).[34]

In August 1852, when Major Emory directed Chandler to continue the survey down the Rio Grande and across the Big Bend to the mouth of the Pecos,

Emory gave Chandler a map he had received in December 1851 from Colonel Langberg, a Danish soldier-of-fortune who served in the Mexican Army for many years. Langberg's map was based on an expedition he led in the fall of 1851 to assess border defenses and determine distances between outposts in northeastern Mexico. His original map is reported to be in the National Archives of Mexico, but it is very faded and covered in reflective plastic, thus making a legible photocopy impractical.[35] However, Langberg's daily journal describing the route and distances between camps has recently been translated and published, and this allows us to trace his route using modern maps.[36]

The first leg of Langberg's three-month expedition is relevant to the route of the Chandler party. This leg covered 340 miles in thirty-eight days. It began at the village of San Carlos (now Manuel Benavides), Chihuahua, which is southwest of Comanche Crossing on the Rio Grande at Lajitas, Texas; traveled southeast to cross the Rio Grande south of the Chisos Mountains; recrossed the river to the ruins of the abandoned Presidio San Vicente in Coahuila; went overland southeast to Santa Rosa (now Múzquiz), Coahuila; and, finally, turned northeast to the Rio Grande at the Mexican town of Piedras Negras, opposite Eagle Pass and Fort Duncan, Texas. (A complete discussion of the relevant portion of Langberg's trip and his map can be found in appendix A.)

Chandler did find Langberg's map quite useful. It helped guide him on the long detour around Santa Elena Canyon, allowed him to locate the Chisos crossing of the Rio Grande that Langberg had used, and helped him find the detour trail when his mule train needed to go around Mariscal and San Vicente Canyons. At the end of that detour, across from the old Presidio San Vicente, Chandler left Langberg's trail to continue down the Rio Grande, whereas Langberg had crossed the river to continue through interior Mexico to Santa Rosa and the Rio Grande near Fort Duncan, Texas.

About two weeks after Chandler left Langberg's trail at Presidio San Vicente, he again used Langberg's map when he abandoned his survey and left the Rio

FIGURE 6. **Mid-1800s Trails in the Big Bend Area** (*following spread*). Shown here are the Hays 1848 expedition, George Evans's 1849 Forty-Niner wagon train, Colonel Langberg's 1851 expedition in Mexico, Chandler's 1852 boundary survey, and Michler's 1853 boundary survey. Trace of trails based on author's reading of journals. Hays: Journal of Sam Maverick in Maverick, *Samuel A. Maverick, Texan*; Evans: Evans, *Mexican Gold Trail*; Langberg: Turpin and Eling, *Dust, Smoke, and Tracks*; Chandler: Parry Journal; Michler: 1853 Boundary Index Map 2, National Archives. Map by Carol Zuber-Mallison.

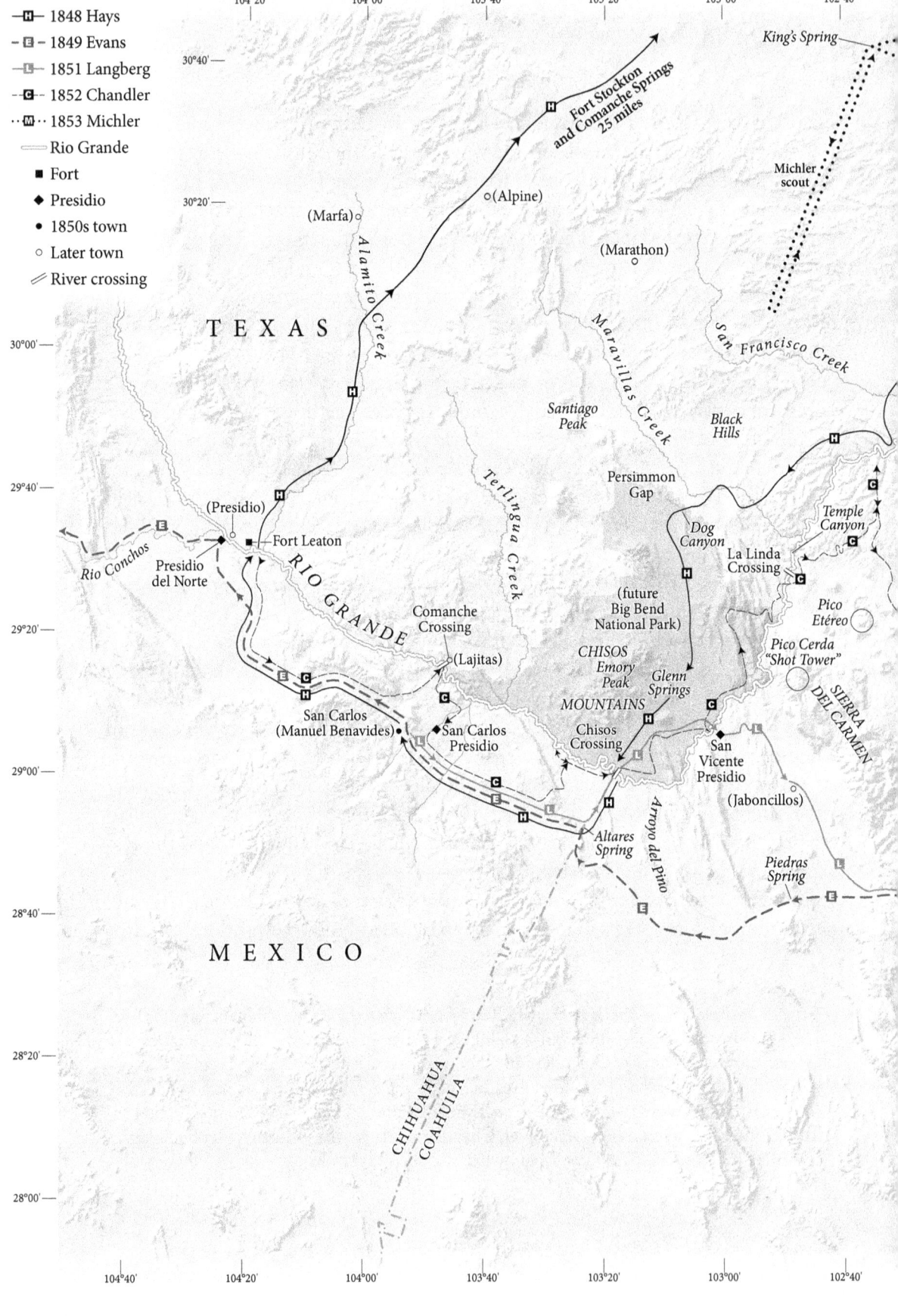

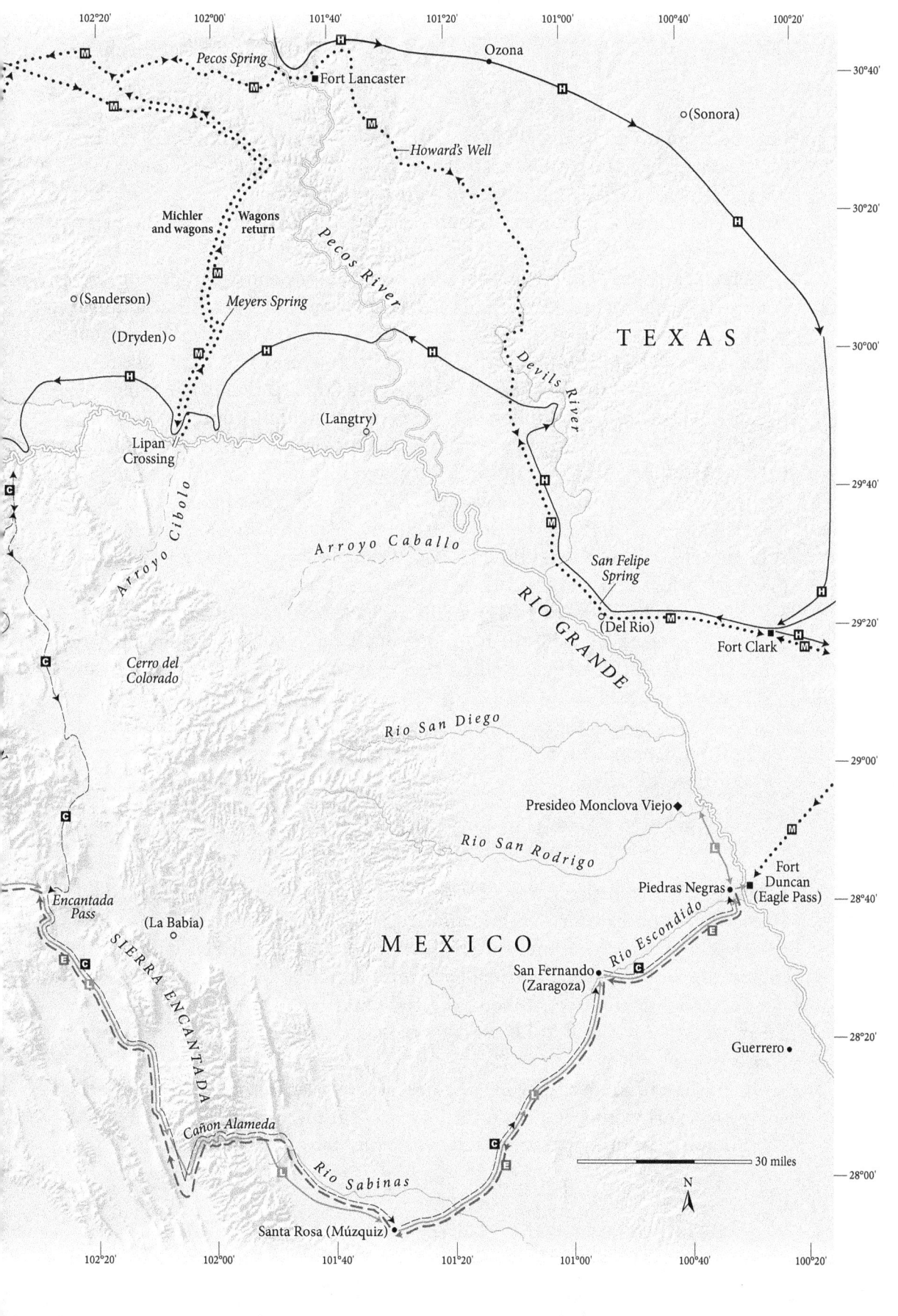

Grande to go overland across Mexico. He sought to rejoin Langberg's trail to guide him to the Mexican town of Santa Rosa (now Múzquiz), Coahuila. Leaving the Rio Grande, Chandler moved south, directly away from the river, then west, in an attempt to intersect Langberg's trail at the south end of the Sierra del Carmen range. Chandler found the trail in a mountain pass of the Sierra Encantada. He turned southeast to follow the trail to the entrance to Cañón de la Alameda, then went east through the canyon and south to Santa Rosa, and then northeast on established trails to Fort Duncan on the Rio Grande. With minor variations, which I will outline later, Chandler would move along the same route Langberg had used for over 280 miles. The only large section of the Langberg trail that Chandler did not follow was the 60 miles Langberg had traveled from Presidio San Vicente to the Sierra Encantada pass—a spot where wagon debris from a Forty-Niner wagon train could be found.

Curiously, the Chandler party was not free in their praise of Langberg, rarely mentioning his map. Parry noted that they were "leaving Langberg's trail" when they moved downriver from Presidio San Vicente. Chandler wrote in his letter to Emory when he abandoned the survey at the Hot Springs Rapids that his plan was to find and follow Langberg's route to Santa Rosa. Later Parry would mention they were "seeking the road to Santa Rosa," which was the Langberg route. Parry mentioned that finding debris from a Forty-Niner wagon train confirmed they had found Langberg's trail. The only way he could have known this was if he had seen the debris marked on Langberg's map. Thus, there in that Sierra Encantada pass, the trails of the Forty-Niners, Langberg, and Chandler converged (see figure 6).[37]

Chandler's Surveying Methods

Chandler anchored the start of his survey at the "known location" of Major Emory's field observatory. In July and August 1852, on the American side of the river opposite the Mexican village of Presidio del Norte, Emory determined the latitude and longitude by careful astronomical observations. The next astronomically determined longitude and latitude position would be 458 miles downriver at Fort Duncan, Texas, far beyond the limits of the Chandler Survey.[38]

Once Chandler moved beyond the observatory, the location of all his field survey stations would be determined by his "running of the line" down the Rio Grande. The principal surveying method used by Chandler was the simple traverse. This involved placing survey stations along his path of travel on the bank of the river and using a previously surveyed station to record the direction and distance to the next station. The result on a map is a zigzag pattern of straight lines of varying lengths joined end to end where the location of each new station down the traverse is determined by measuring the compass bearing from the old to the new station using a small theodolite (a combined telescope and compass) or a surveyor's compass (a compass with a peep sight). Each instrument was mounted on a stable tripod. The length of each line was

FIGURE 7. **Nineteenth-Century Surveying Equipment.** A surveyor's theodolite, surveyor's compass, and chain. Photograph by the author, made possible courtesy of Texas Society of Professional Surveyors, Austin, Texas.

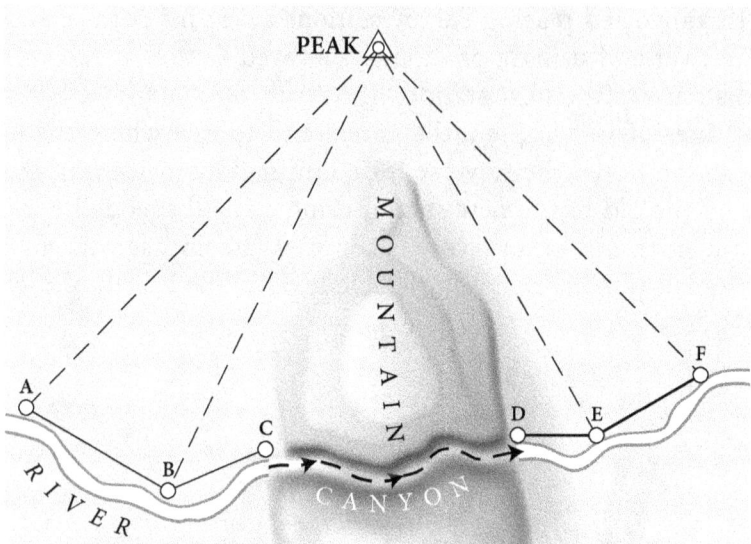

FIGURE 8. **Sketch of Traverse and Triangulation Methods.** This sketch map shows simple traverse lines connected by triangulation. The surveyor at traverse station A records the compass bearings to station B and to the peak to the northeast, then moves his instrument to station B and records the bearings to the peak and to station C at the canyon entrance. With the length of lines AB and BC measured on the ground by his assistant using a chain, he knows the positions of A, B, and C. Now, drawing lines on his map using the bearings from A and B to the peak, the lines will intersect at the correct map location of the peak. The surveyor then moves to the exit of the canyon to begin a new traverse at station D. He cannot see the peak from D, so he records the bearing to E, moves to E to record the bearing to the peak and to station F. His assistant will measure by chain the length of lines DE and EF. The surveyor can now draw on his map the bearing lines from the peak toward E and F, using the opposite direction of his bearing to the peak. There is only one location on the map (for triangle E-F-Peak) that will fit the triangle made up of the diverging bearing lines coming from the peak and line EF. The map position of this triangle determines the location of traverse stations D, E, and F relative to the peak and to the traverse stations A, B, and C above the canyon. Sketch by author, professional rendering by Carol Zuber-Mallison.

measured on the ground by an assistant using a surveyor's chain. (See figures 7 and 8 for a photograph of a vintage surveyor's theodolite, compass, and chain, and a sketch map of a traverse line.)

When Chandler reached the massive canyons of the Rio Grande, extending his survey through the canyons by traverse was no longer possible. His line of stations along the accessible banks would end at the entrance to a steep-walled canyon. He needed a different surveying method—triangulation—to connect his traverse line at the entrance of the canyon to a new traverse line starting at the exit of the canyon. This involved traveling downstream, without surveying, to set up a station at the canyon exit and then using triangulation to determine the location of the exit relative to the entrance. To accomplish triangulation, the surveyors needed to record the compass bearings from their traverse stations to a prominent peak that could be seen from traverse stations both above and below the canyon. See figure 8 for an explanation of the triangulation method.

For mapping the course of the river inside the inaccessible canyons, Chandler relied either on a rough sketch based on a visual reconnaissance of the canyon from the rim, as he did for Santa Elena Canyon, or he constructed a rough traverse line through the canyon by taking notes while making a rapid descent by boat, recording direction of the boat with a handheld compass and estimating distance by noting the time to float from one turn of the river to another. Distance estimates can be improved by measuring the time it takes for the floating boat to cross a measured distance along the bank. Chandler successfully used the "boat traverse" method in the Upper Canyons of the Rio Grande in the first week of his boat survey. Later, when the party reached the more challenging Santa Elena, Mariscal, San Vicente, and Boquillas Canyons, he resorted to sketch maps, and the accuracy of his mapped river trace inside those canyons is poor.

Since there is no written record of the methods used by Chandler, my interpretation is based on inductive reasoning and the types of instruments available to him. The body of information that guided me included the high accuracy of surveying where access to the river bank was good, the recommendation to use the simple traverse method by Colonel James D. Graham (Major Emory's predecessor), remarks by Chandler consistent with both traverse and triangulation surveying, and remarks by Parry about the successful triangulation of the location of Santa Elena Canyon.[39]

Surveying Begins

The Chandler party ultimately surveyed 209 miles of the Rio Grande below Presidio del Norte (see figure 2). Their last river camp was at Hot Springs Rapids, 8 miles downstream from the final survey point. From there they rode mules and walked 314 miles to Fort Duncan at Eagle Pass, Texas. In total, the party was out 101 days and made fifty camps. On this extraordinarily difficult, long, and hazardous journey they lost not a single man.

Charles Christopher Parry's unpublished journal, in which he recorded the route as well as botany and geology notes, allows me to reconstruct a day-to-day accounting of the trip. It is the only known daily record of the Chandler Survey and is supplemented here with details gleaned from published reports made by Lieutenant Duff Green, who led the army escort; M. T. W. Chandler's short report included in the final Emory Report; and Parry's geological summary (also part of the final Emory Report), as well as unpublished correspondence available in the Emory Papers at Yale University.[40]

Parry was not necessarily camped each night in the same place as Green or Chandler. For the first eleven camps—during the 51 river miles from Presidio del Norte to Comanche Crossing at Lajitas, Texas—Parry traveled with the surveyors along the river, either walking or in their boats, and he camped with them. After Comanche Crossing, Parry traveled and camped with Green's army escort and mule train, while the surveyors traveled by boat or walked. After reaching the entrance to Santa Elena Canyon, 11 river miles below Comanche Crossing, the entire party traveled and camped together during their five-day, 56-mile detour around the canyon. After Santa Elena Canyon, when the surveyors had only the two rubber boats with limited capacity for provisions, the surveyors and escort camped together almost every night, as they also usually did during the twenty-day journey across the interior of Mexico after the survey was abandoned at their Hot Springs Rapids camp in the Lower Canyons of the Rio Grande, 217 miles downstream from their start at Presidio del Norte.

The Chandler Survey actually had two beginnings. On August 16, 1852, they began a two-week effort to survey the course of the Rio Grande as it meandered across the floodplains lying between Presidio del Norte and the entrance to the first big canyons a few miles downstream from today's village of Redford, Texas. These first twenty-nine miles of river below Presidio del Norte formed a natural unit; the flat, accessible floodplains provided favorable conditions for surveying parties traversing along the bank while using a tripod-mounted theodolite or compass to record direction and a lightweight 100-foot "surveyor's chain" made of wire links to measure distance (see figure 7). For this "easy" section, surveyors could operate out of their Presidio del Norte base camp or temporary camps along the river. Below this section, steep canyons restricted access to the bank, requiring boats and a different survey method. Proceeding with the accessible section near Presidio del Norte allowed the surveyors to get an early start on their work while they awaited the return of Lieutenant Green, who had traveled to the El Paso del Norte area to secure the additional supplies and soldiers Emory had requested.

Parry, in his triple role as surgeon, botanist, and geologist for the Chandler party, traveled with the surveyors in this early phase of operations. Leaving from Emory's camp at the observatory, opposite the church at Presidio del Norte, Parry started down the river in an India rubber boat with the surveyors. Moving with him, onshore and in boats, was a thirty-man crew that included surveyors, a support group of camp helpers, and a mule train carrying provisions. On the first day, they floated three miles at a "rapid rate" due to the high stage of the river and set up a temporary camp (#1) about two miles west of the adobe-walled trading post called Fort Leaton (see figure 9).[41]

Fort Leaton

In 1848, Ben Leaton, an American veteran of the Mexican-American War, had taken over the ruins of a small abandoned Spanish fort across the river from Presidio del Norte, on what became the American side of the river after the Treaty of Guadalupe Hidalgo. Leaton acquired the land fraudulently and then repaired and expanded the enclosure for the protection of his home, trading post, and farm. Early American travelers to Presidio del Norte, such as men of the Hays-Highsmith Expedition in 1848, US Army Topographical Engineer Lieutenant Wm. H. C. Whiting in 1849, and various Forty-Niners heading to California, remarked on how much they enjoyed the hospitality and protection of Ben Leaton and his fort. But Leaton died while on a business trip to San Antonio in the summer of 1851. By the time the boundary surveyors arrived in the summer of 1852, other men dominated the trading business in the area, and the fort was becoming a relic. Julius Froebel, a German journalist and world traveler, who camped near the fort in May 1852, described it as "a large building surrounded by a mud wall." Later, Ben Leaton's widow and their son moved back into the fort. In July 1860, Lieutenant William H. Echols's camel caravan visited Presidio del Norte, and Echols remarked on the fine meal and watermelons he shared with Mr. Leaton (the son) at the fort.[1] Today the restored Fort Leaton is a Texas State Historic Site on Highway 170, three miles east of Presidio, Texas. It is managed by the

Texas Parks and Wildlife Department and open for visitors seven days a week.

NOTE

1. "Fort Leaton," *HOT*, accessed May 5, 2017; William H. Echols, *Diary of a Reconnoissance [sic] of the Country Between the El Paso Road and the Rio Grande River*," 36th Cong., 2nd sess., 1861, SED 1, 37; Julius Froebel, *Seven Years' Travel in Central America, Northern Mexico, and the Far West of the United States* (London: Richard Bentley, 1859), 409.

On August 17, while the surveyors were working near Presidio del Norte, far back up the river near El Paso del Norte, Lieutenant Green was on his return trip. He had met Boundary Commissioner Bartlett and turned down the request to abort his planned escort of the Chandler Survey and accompany the commissioner down the San Antonio Road for a meeting with Emory on the lower Rio Grande.[42]

FIGURE 9. **Fort Leaton.** The restored Fort Leaton, now a Texas State Historical Park on the River Road (FM 170), sits three miles east of Presidio, Texas. Photograph courtesy of Alastair Lyon.

On August 18, the surveyors moved their camp seven miles, "down to the ranch of Leon below Fort Leaton." This camp (#2) was probably on the American side near the mouth of Alamito Creek. The next day, Parry accompanied assistant surveyor Thomas Thompson's party, which was traversing along the bank of the river on the Mexican side. A few days later, Parry used Fort Leaton as a landmark by recording the compass bearing to the fort from his position on top of a distant mountain; this helped him determine the location of the mountain. Although it is not mentioned by the American surveyors, they must have regularly recorded the compass bearing to the fort from various stations along their survey lines, as the fort is prominently shown as a landmark on their map.

On August 20, the party mapped five miles of the river trace using traverse lines along the tablelands on the Mexican side and then crossed to the American side to make camp. This camp (#3) was near the present-day Mulato diversion dam, which diverts water from the river to an irrigation canal running ten miles along the Mexican side of the river.

On August 21, Parry reported finding volcanic rocks exposed in the hills adjoining the river. The course of the channel, which had been flowing east, now made a sharp turn directly south. This turn is three miles northwest of today's village of Redford, Texas. After traversing five miles of river, the surveyors camped (#4) near the site of the later village. On Sunday the twenty-second, Parry's friends John Milton Bigelow, Emory's staff physician, and George Clinton Gardner, Emory's clerk, came to visit from their camp seventeen trail miles upriver.

On August 23, after moving another six miles downstream to a spot near the beginning of some narrow canyons lying below the floodplains, the surveyors set up a more permanent camp (#5) that they would occupy until September 13. About halfway between camps #4 and #5 the surveyors must have passed the ranch of Colonel Langberg, on the Mexican side. The ranch, two miles north of today's Mexican village of El Mulato, is marked on both the Mexican and American versions of Boundary Map 22 (figure 10). Neither Parry in his journal nor Chandler in his report mentioned the ranch, but its appearance as one of the few landmarks on the final boundary map suggests it was often in view of the surveyors and used as a triangulation station.

Camp #5 was on the American side across from what Parry called "Muleta [sic] Ranch," on the Mexican side. This was the Mexican village El Mulato, which occupied a prominent narrow ridge adjoining the river channel. The village was

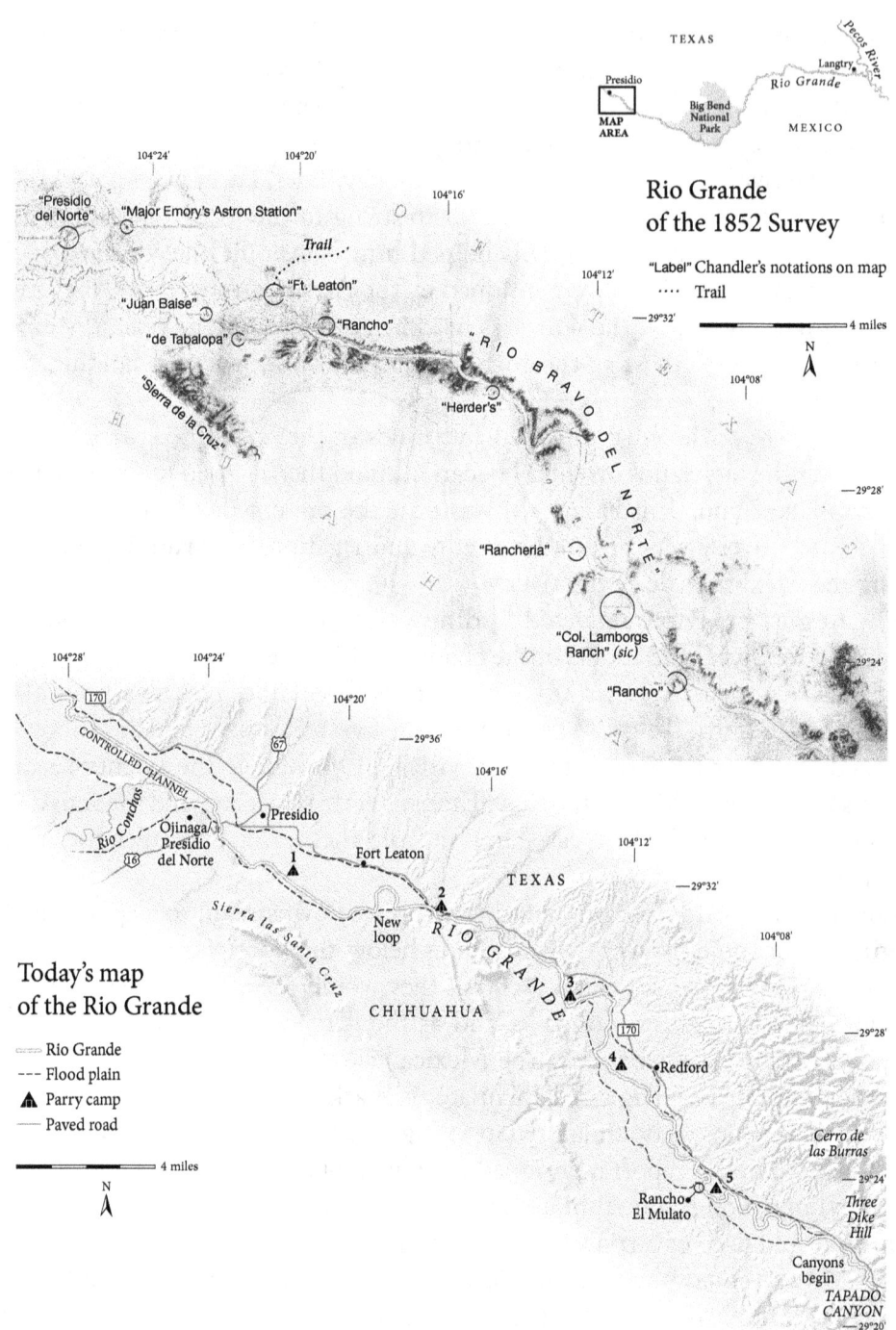

FIGURE 10. **River Trace Comparison: Presidio del Norte to Start of the Canyons.** The river trace of Chandler's Boundary Map 22 and a modern map of the Rio Grande, from Presidio, Texas, to the first canyon seven miles below today's village of Redford, Texas. Map by Carol Zuber-Mallison.

Part I: The 1852 Chandler Surveying Party

established in the eighteenth century and remains today as one of the oldest continuously inhabited villages in the Big Bend Region.[43]

The survey party initially spent several days finishing up surveying on the nearby flatlands and then used this camp as a base to prepare equipment for the difficult canyons that lay ahead. This camp would be the jumping-off point for the main survey that began on September 13. The first minor canyons began three miles below their camp; the first rapids were encountered at five miles, where Arroyo el Puerto enters from the Mexican side; and the major Colorado Canyon was eight miles southeast of their camp.

During his stay at camp #5, Parry made several explorations to nearby mountains and canyons. On August 24, he walked three miles east to a "Mountain Peak." The peak that fits Parry's geologic description and his direction and distance from camp is today named Cerro de las Burras (jenny mountain) and lies southeast of Redford (see figure 10). This peak is the culmination of a broad volcanic range, and Parry's sketch in his journal shows 200 feet of Cretaceous sediments dipping west at 15 degrees, overlaid by 400 feet of igneous rocks, topping out at 1,200 feet above the gently sloping tablelands below. Later, in 1857, when the Emory Report was published, Parry revised his interpretation of the Cretaceous age of the sediments in the lower part of the mountain to correctly show them as younger "volcanic breccia" (today's Tertiary age, Fresno Formation; table 1).[44]

Solving a Geographical Mystery

To document his mountain location, Parry recorded compass bearings from the peak toward local landmarks: 65 degrees west of north to Fort Leaton, 70 degrees west of north to the church at Presidio del Norte, and 80 degrees west of north to Santa Cruz Mountain just south of Presidio del Norte. Parry's bearings are magnetic bearings, taken directly from the needle of his handheld compass without correcting for declination. Magnetic declination (the difference between true geographic north and magnetic north) was 11 degrees to the east in 1852, as shown by the declination map in the Emory Report.[1] This means that Parry's compass needle would point 11 degrees east of true north. To determine the location of Parry's mountain peak, one can draw a line on a map starting at each of his three landmarks and then extend each line in the opposite direction of Parry's declination-corrected bearing. Parry recorded only a rough bearing, a multiple of

5 degrees; however, the three lines converge in a cluster around Cerro de las Burras, a 4,345-foot-high mountain 5.6 miles southeast of today's village of Redford, Texas, indicating that this was where Parry was standing when he recorded the bearings.

NOTE

1. William H. Emory, *Report on the United States and Mexican Boundary Survey*, 34th Cong., 1st sess., 1857, Vol. 1, HED 135, 258. A map of declination shows, by contours of equal declination value, the angle between true north and magnetic north. A point showing an 11-degree-east declination means a compass at that point would point 11 degrees to the right of true north.

On August 26, Parry began a two-day exploration of the river canyons below his camp #5. Three miles below camp he came to a point he called "start of the canyons," where the previously wide alluvial valley was suddenly narrowed by volcanic hills on both sides of the river channel. This location appears to be the scene pictured in a woodcut illustration labeled "Entrance to Cañón of Bofecillos" in M. T. W. Chandler's narrative in the Emory Report. The woodcut must have been made from a field sketch by Parry.[45] Today, there is no canyon named Bofecillos, but that name is applied to the range of volcanic mountains lying east of the village of Redford and north of the Rio Grande.

Parry described a singular geologic exposure on a hill north of the river and near the start of the canyons. Today, this hill is often photographed by geologists and is known as Three Dike Hill. It is admired because of the detailed geology visible on the near-vertical face unobstructed by any vegetation. The varying age relationships of three black igneous dikes cutting sharply across light-colored, older horizontal formations are strikingly displayed. The sketch in Parry's notebook, which was reproduced later in the Emory Report, accurately depicts the features of the outcrop (figure 11).[46]

Continuing to explore along the river, Parry reached the entrance to Colorado Canyon marked by the Rancherias Rapids, 33 river miles below today's international bridge at Presidio, Texas. The trail Parry followed down the river ended abruptly at the entrance to the canyon. The sheer walls of the canyon fall directly into the narrow river channel and block the trail. Searching for an alternate route, Parry found what he called "the cut-off," a well-worn Indian trail that took advantage of an open valley running parallel to the river and less than a

Table 1. Geologic Formations of the Big Bend

Age	Type	Formation (in feet)	Lithology	Landmarks
Recent	Terraces (Sedimentary)	(300)	gravel	Rio Grande
Tertiary	Volcanic	Black Gap, Rawls, Fresno, South Rim (1300)	lava, ash, tuff, sand	Black Gap WMA, Colorado Canyon, Emory Peak
		Chisos (2000)	lava, tuff, clay	Castle Rock, Lajitas Mesa, Punta Sierra
		Canoe (1200)	sand, tuff, lava	
	Sedimentary	Hannold Hill (600)	sand, conglomerate	
		Black Peak (900)	clay, sand, conglomerate	
		Javelina (600)	clay, wood	
		Aguija (1000)	dark clay, coal	Chisos Crossing
		Penn (400)	grey marl	
Cretaceous		Boquillas (800)	thin limestone	Comanche Crossing, San Vicente Canyon
		Santa Elena (800)	thick limestone	Santa Elena, Mariscal, and Boquillas Canyons
		Del Carmen (500)	thick limestone	
		Glen Rose (700)	shale, sand, limestone	Las Vegas de los Ladrones

Simplified after Ross Maxwell, *The Big Bend of the Rio Grande* (1968), table 1, p. 27.

SECTIONAL VIEW, SHOWING A SERIES OF VOLCANIC PRODUCTS,
TRAVERSED BY INJECTED IGNEOUS VEINS; CAÑON OF RIO BRAVO,
THIRTY-FIVE MILES BELOW PRESIDIO DEL NORTE.

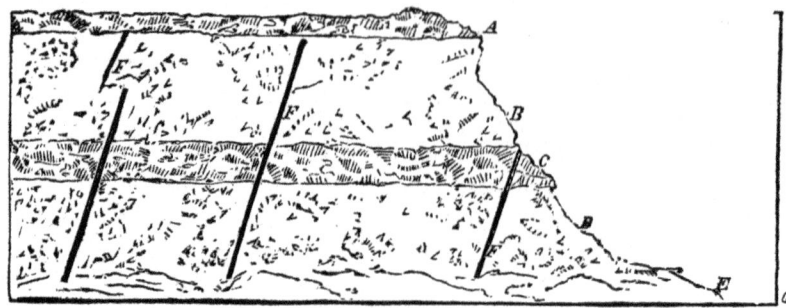

A. Dark-colored vesicular trap.
B. Volcanic breccia of a lightish brown color in horizontal strata.
C. Lava or trap-rock of close texture, dark-colored.
D. Breccia as above, having a light greenish color.
E. Igneous veins.

FIGURE 11. **Three Dike Hill.** Comparison of Parry's diagram and a modern photo. Today, Three Dike Hill is best seen from the River Road (FM 170) by looking east and just north of the road, at a north-side turnout 2.3 miles west of the bridge over Tapado Creek. (See the location on Boundary Map 22, figure 10.) Emory Report, 2:52; photograph by the author.

Part I: The 1852 Chandler Surveying Party 49

FIGURE 12. **Closed Canyon.** Today Parry's "Little Canyon" is called Closed Canyon. This type of very narrow but deep canyon is called a slot canyon. There is a roadside sign for the parking area and a trailhead on the south side of the River Road (FM 170) two miles east of the river access side road at the entrance of Colorado Canyon. (See location in figure 14.) Photograph by the author.

mile north of the steep canyon. This trail on the American side "came back to the river 5 miles below" (actually 6 miles).[47]

Along the cutoff trail, Parry found "a singular feature" that he described as "a miniature picture of the larger [Colorado] canyon." This is a scenic, half-mile-long slot canyon—a narrow but deep tributary canyon cutting through a mountain to reach the Rio Grande. The feature is known today as Closed Canyon, or Cañón Obscuro (obscure/dark canyon) in Spanish (figure 12). Parry noted it was only twenty feet wide at the entrance. It cuts, at a right angle to the river, through "the heart of the mountain" directly to the Rio Grande. The walls reach seven hundred feet high and are "almost shut out from the light of day." It has vertical pour-offs (waterfalls) along the canyon floor. When it reaches the Rio Grande, it throws a rock debris apron out into the river, forming a rapids.[48]

Parry continued down the cutoff trail to reach the Rio Grande near Panther Rapid, where he spent the night, fifteen miles below surveyor camp #5. The next morning, he "clambered with considerable labor to a high peak which commands a considerable view—some 1,200 feet above the river." This undoubtedly means Parry climbed to the top of Santana Mesa about two miles east of his camp (see figure 14). From that vantage, he was high above Dark Canyon of the Rio Grande and what is today known as Big Hill on the River Road (Texas Highway 170). From there it would have been obvious to Parry that Lieutenant Green's mule train could not possibly travel along the river and that a detour would have to be found around these canyons. Parry backtracked his trail to the entrance of Colorado Canyon and made camp.

On August 28, Parry returned upstream to the survey party outpost at camp #5. There are no other entries in his journal until September 12, when Parry and the entire Chandler party were making final preparations to depart Presidio del Norte and move down through the wild canyons of the Rio Grande.

US and Mexican Versions of Boundary Map 22 near Presidio del Norte

The US version of the final 1857 Boundary Map 22 was coauthored by Maurice von Hippel and M. T. W. Chandler. In May 1852, as part of his larger survey begun at El Paso del Norte, von Hippel surveyed the river channel, which extended across an eleven-mile section of Map 22 lying upstream of Presidio del Norte. The major portion of Map 22, which lay downstream of Presidio del Norte, was surveyed by Chandler in August 1852 using the line-traverse method (see figure 10).

The Mexican version of Boundary Map 22 was based on their survey done in 1855, three years after the Chandler Survey. In January, Mexican boundary commissioner José Salazar Ylarregui was in El Paso del Norte working with US commissioner Emory on preparations for the upcoming boundary survey along the Gadsden Purchase line, which ran west of El Paso along the boundary between Mexico and the present-day states of New Mexico and Arizona.[49] Salazar Ylarregui sent the Mexican surveyors Manuel Fernández, Francisco Herrera, and Miguel Iglesias down to Presidio del Norte to begin a survey from there down the Rio Grande. Salazar Ylarregui had made a reconnaissance survey of the river near Presidio del Norte in 1853, but the Mexicans made no detailed survey of the short section of river just above Presidio del Norte that is displayed on Map 22. Later, to complete their version of Map 22, they copied the US map of this upper section of river. Why Salazar Ylarregui would make the considerable effort to pursue the late survey below Presidio del Norte is not known. It may have been in response to concern that no Mexican survey had been done even though there were a large number of Mexican citizens living in Presidio del Norte and in settlements along the floodplains extending many miles down to the start of the Upper Canyons of the Rio Grande. These settlements included the ranch of Colonel Langberg of the Mexican Army and the nearby historic eighteenth-century village of El Mulato, twenty-two miles below Presidio del Norte.

The 1855 Mexican survey team used the accurate but time-consuming triangulation method to map that part of Map 22 lying downstream from Presidio del Norte. Their extensive triangulation grid of twenty-eight stations, including nine on the American side of the river, was used to construct the Mexican map. See appendix B for a table showing today's longitude and latitude positions of their triangulation stations. Most of their work was done out of a base camp in Presidio del Norte, but later, as they worked farther down the river, they moved their camp fifty miles southeast to the Mexican interior village of San Carlos, now Manuel Benavides, Chihuahua. Here, operations became more difficult because the river was twelve miles away and enclosed by deep canyons. They reported that the area was "infested with numerous bands of Comanche and Apache who were watching our surveyors—we met with the Indians and some became guides for our men." While at San Carlos, they extended their triangulation grid as far down the river (east) as 103°55'14", a point they named Mesa San Juan on the US side of the river about ten miles northwest of Comanche Crossing at Lajitas, Texas.

Always challenged by meager financial support from the Mexican government, the Mexican surveyors ran out of resources and suspended their survey in March 1855. In July, they returned to El Paso del Norte, and in the fall they assisted in the joint US-Mexican survey of the Gadsden Treaty boundary lines across the New Mexico and Arizona Territories.[50]

Description of Boundary Map 22 Downstream from Presidio del Norte

The course of the Rio Grande downstream of Presidio del Norte falls naturally into three topographic sections: two valleys where wide floodplains are home to frequent changes in the course of the river channel and a third section of low hills separating the two valleys. In the hill section, the river is confined to a narrow channel that has remained in a fixed position for hundreds of years.

In the first valley section below Presidio del Norte, the river flows through a floodplain seven miles long and up to two miles wide. Much of this low-lying area of deep soils was cultivated at the time of the survey and remains so today, especially on the Mexican side. Today, the course of the river has been stabilized by a human-made channel, which was negotiated by treaty. Because the river was uncontrolled in 1852, its channel meandered back and forth across the floodplain, often changing its location with just a single flood. We can reasonably assume Chandler's mapped trace of the river was reliable, since it is shown to lie within the limits of the floodplain and agrees well with the companion Boundary Map 22 made by the Mexican surveyors three years later. While today's channelized river trace is shorter than the one shown near Presidio del Norte on the US and Mexican maps, today's trace down the seven miles of floodplain below Presidio del Norte is actually one mile longer because a large, new meander loop has formed in the years since the 1850s, replacing an earlier straight section of river lying southeast of Fort Leaton.

Both the US and Mexican maps display excellent topographical detail and river trace in the vicinity of Presidio del Norte, but the Mexican map is superior in showing topography at much greater distances from the river (figure 13). The location of Emory's astrological observatory, which anchored the latitude and longitude starting point of the Chandler Survey down the river, now lies within the ephemeral floodplain of Cibolo Creek on the western outskirts of Presidio, Texas. Records of nineteenth-century land surveys indicate that Emory erected a monument to mark the location of his observatory. Texas General Land Office records of a survey of a small tract of land nearby in 1856 and the later resurvey notes of that tract in 1907 refer to a landmark called "Emory Astrological Point." A 1932 vintage army topographic map also shows an "Emory Monument," which appears to be the same spot.[51] A recent search for the Emory marker in the floodplain of Cibolo Creek came up empty-handed, so I must conclude the marker has been carried away or buried by flash floods in recent years.

It is important to be aware that Emory's original longitude determination at his Presidio observatory was 1.5 miles too far west, thus the observatory and all other nearby points on both the US and Mexican maps that were anchored to the observatory are shown west of their true position (table 2). Surveying along the river below the observatory, Chandler consistently overestimated the distance down the east-flowing river and, as a result, he more than fully offset his "too far west" start location by the time he had covered the 30 river miles that took him

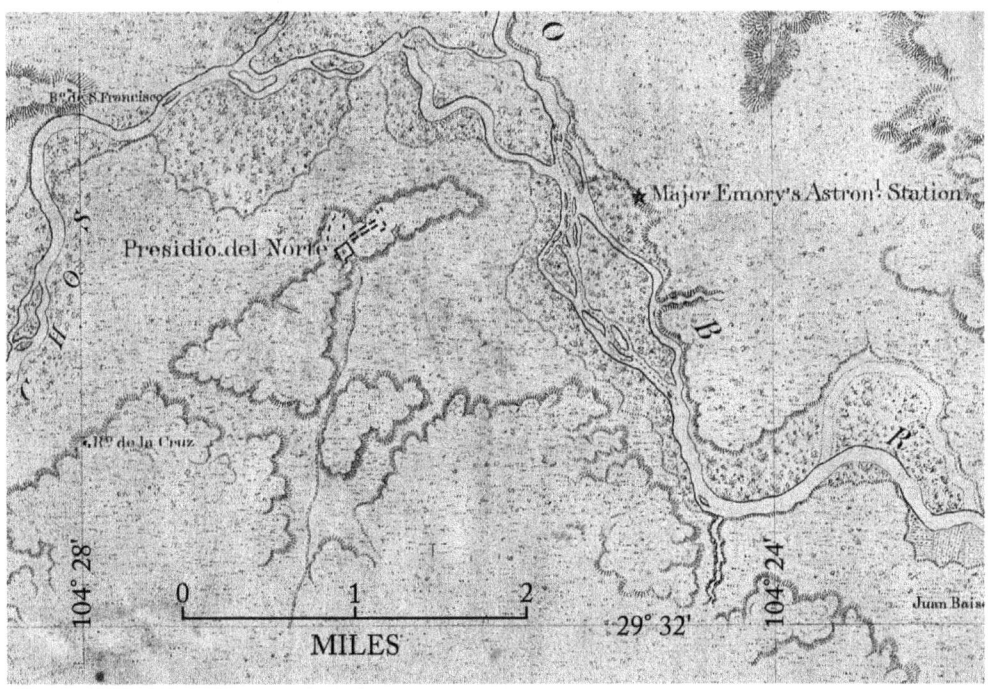

FIGURE 13. **Detail at Presidio del Norte.** This figure provides a closer view of Chandler's Boundary Map 22. Boundary Map 22, National Archives.

to the south margin of Boundary Map 22. In contrast, the 1855 Mexican survey maintained accurate distance and direction measurements relative to the starting point at Emory's observatory.

On Chandler's Map 22, the adobe walls of the Mexican fort of Presidio del Norte and its associated village buildings are shown on an elevated gravel terrace that is 1.75 miles west of Emory's observatory on the American side. Based on the map's scale, the fort's enclosure was a 450 × 300-foot rectangle that seems consistent in size with the description offered by Lieutenant William H. C. Whiting, who had dinner with the commander of the presidio during his 1849 reconnaissance: "The fortress is a rude adobe structure, oblong, without flanking defensives [no bastions], containing the church and barracks capable of holding five or six hundred men."[52] The site of the old presidio is now within the heart of today's town of Ojinaga, Chihuahua, on the natural high point of the gravel terrace, at or very near today's Nuestro Padre Jesús Church and the adjoining

TABLE 2. LANDMARK LOCATIONS ON THE 1857 BOUNDARY MAPS

Landmark Name	Boundary Map	Miles Too Far West	Miles Too Far East	Miles Too Far South	Miles Too Far North	True Longitude (Deg. Min.)	Surveyor
Presidio Observatory	22	1.5				104° 23.3'	Emory
Fort Leaton	22	1.2		0.1		104° 19.6'	Chandler
North Turn of River	22				0.3	104° 13.8'	Chandler
Mulato Village	22		0.3	0.2		104° 10.2'	Chandler
Start of Canyons	22		0.5	0.4		104° 6.6'	Chandler
Hoodoos Rapids	21		0.6	0.8		104° 5.5'	Chandler
Closed Canyon	21		1	0.8		104° 2.3'	Chandler
Unnamed Rapids	21		1.1	1.3		103° 53.9'	Chandler
Comanche Crossing	21		1.4	1.4		103° 46.8'	Chandler
San Carlos Creek	21		1.6	1.8		103° 43'	Chandler
Exit Santa Elena Canyon	21		1.6	2		103° 37'	Chandler
Island North of Camp	20	3			0.2	103° 29'	Chandler
Camp 17 Rancho	20	3		0.1		103° 28'	Chandler
Boquillas Crossing	20	3.2		0.8		103° 13.6'	Chandler
Entrance Mariscal	20	3.1		1.3		103° 10.4'	Chandler
San Vicente Presidio	19	2.6		0.4		103° 1.5'	Chandler
Boquillas Canyon	19	2.2		0.1		102° 54.9'	Chandler
Strawhouse Camp	19	2.4		1.6		102° 52.2'	Chandler

Landmark						Surveyor
Stillwell Bend	18	1.2			102° 48.8'	Chandler
La Linda Bend	18	1			102° 49.2'	Chandler
Sombrero Butte	18	0.8			102° 42.7'	Chandler
River Turns to East	17	0.7			102° 40.2'	Chandler
San Francisco Canyon	17	9.8			102° 19.2'	Michler
Lipan Crossing	17	10.4			102° 6.9'	Michler
Boat Wreck	16	8.6			102° 4.1'	Michler
Camp 3	16	6.4		0.2	101° 57.9'	Michler
Lozier Canyon	16	3.5		0.3	101° 48.4'	Michler
Camp 5	16	1.4		0.1	101° 39.7'	Michler
Camp 6	15		0.6	0.1	101° 27'	Michler
Mouth of Pecos, Camp 7	15		2.7	0.1	101° 22.3'	Michler
Amistad Reservoir	15		2.3		101° 16'	Schott
Devils River	14		1.9		101° 3.6'	Schott
Sycamore Creek	13		1.4	0.2	100° 47.5'	Schott
Fort Duncan	12	0.04			100° 30.4'	Emory

Landmarks along the Rio Grande from Presidio del Norte to Fort Duncan, showing the error in miles east or west and north or south of the landmark location shown on the boundary maps versus the true location of the landmark.

city plaza. As Whiting observed, the church was inside the presidio enclosure in 1849. The 1855 triangulation records of the Mexican surveyors include two stations at the church in the Presidio enclosure, which allows a determination of the correct latitude and longitude of the church site in 1855, and this confirms the church is located on the same spot today.

Other examples of excellent topographic detail by Chandler in the Ojinaga, Chihuahua–Presidio, Texas, area include the San Francisco ridge, which projects east into the wide floodplain formed by the confluence of the Rio Grande and the Concho River and was two miles northwest of the walls of the old presidio; the ridge just northeast of Emory's observatory, which today carries communications towers for the town of Presidio, Texas; the large Santa Cruz Mountain, three miles southeast of the old presidio; and the cultivated fields labeled as ranchos belonging to the Juan Baise and Tabalopa families on the Mexican side across from Fort Leaton.

After making its way through the floodplains of Presidio del Norte, the river enters a second section marked by nine miles of narrow channel among low hills that hold the channel to an unchanging path. A comparison of Chandler's map with modern maps and the Mexican map shows his trace was good, with one exception. The first leg of this section ran east–southeast for two miles and is shown accurately on the Mexican Map 22, but Chandler's map extends this leg to three miles, which, as a result, shifts all his subsequent landmarks one mile east. This was probably an error in the field record made by Chandler's surveyors.

In the third topographic section of Map 22, the river again flows for nine miles through the wide floodplains of today's Redford Valley, ending about eight road miles below present-day Redford, Texas, where the river enters the first of the Upper Canyons of the Rio Grande near the south margin of Map 22. Chandler's channel trace in the Redford Valley fits within the floodplain, as it must, but appears to be too straight. Both the Mexican Map 22 and modern maps show a more meandering river channel.

On balance, Chandler's river trace throughout Map 22 compares favorably with modern maps and the more accurate Mexican version (see figure 10); however, Chandler's distances are uniformly a bit long, so when he reached the east end of the area covered by the map—after thirty miles of river flowing in a southeast direction below Presidio del Norte—his locations had drifted two miles east and a half mile south (see table 2).

Waiting for Supplies

During the downtime in late August to early September while Chandler's party waited for Lieutenant Green to return from El Paso del Norte, several other important events took place. On August 30, Major Emory finally departed Presidio del Norte with a small party of his staff and no army escort to protect him from Indian attack. Emory traveled down to Fort Duncan on the lower Rio Grande to check on his survey party led by Lieutenant Nathaniel Michler. From Presidio del Norte, Emory said he traveled "the road which I opened." Emory implied this was a new route, and his clerk, Clint Gardner, traveling with him, called it "a new and unexplored route."[53] The only thing new about this ancient wagon route was Emory's presence on it and some minor roadwork his party did as it sped along at twenty miles a day.

Emory's "new" route had actually been used for centuries by many others: indigenous people and later Mexicans traveling from the Rio Grande to salt lakes, about 175 trail miles to the northeast in the Pecos River valley near Horsehead Crossing; the Spanish expedition of Captain Juan Domínguez de Mendoza, who, in 1684, traveled northeast from the Presidio del Norte area up to the Colorado River near Ballinger, Texas; and businessman Henry Connelley's wagons loaded with silver bullion going from Chihuahua City, Mexico, to Fort Towson (later part of Oklahoma) in 1839, and back in 1840.[54]

From Presidio del Norte, Emory traveled north to join the main San Antonio wagon road near Fort Stockton, east on that road for 300 miles to Fort Inge (Uvalde, Texas), and southwest to Fort Duncan on the Rio Grande, where he arrived on September 23 after an uneventful journey of 420 miles.[55]

In the meantime, back at Presidio del Norte, shortly after Emory had departed, Lieutenant Green and his wagons returned from El Paso del Norte with the additional provisions and soldiers Emory had requested for the Chandler party's army escort. On September 6, Green left his wagons on the American side, swam his mules to the Mexican side, and carried his provisions across in boats. He set up camp five miles south of Presidio del Norte and began to organize his eighty-mule pack train for the overland detour through Mexico. The plan was for the mule train to take the wagon road southeast about fifty miles to the Mexican town of San Carlos (Manuel Benavides, Chihuahua), then turn northeast for eighteen miles to Comanche Crossing of the Rio Grande (Lajitas, Texas) for the planned rendezvous with Chandler's boats.

On September 8, at the army escort camp below Presidio del Norte, Parry signed a contract with Lieutenant Green to serve as assistant surgeon for the US Army for a wage of $100 per month. During the next two and a half months, Parry only sparingly mentioned his role as a doctor and then only when he visited Mexican villages. His journal contains no mention of medicine, sickness, or injury of party members, except for one day in November at the Hot Springs Rapids when he notes prescribing a warm bath for his "rheumatic and syphilitic patients."[56]

In preparation for the start of the main portion of his survey through the canyons south of Presidio del Norte, Chandler had planned to cross to the Mexican side to make final arrangements with Green on September 7, but a sharp rise in the river delayed his crossing. On September 12, when the river had receded, Chandler finally crossed to the Mexican side to take care of business. At the end of that day, he took his boat downriver to join his surveyors at camp #5—the staging area his men had occupied for a month and from which they would launch the survey into the canyons the next morning.[57]

The Boats Enter the Upper Canyons to Begin Surveying Boundary Map 21

On the morning of September 13, 1852, Chandler and his men left behind the Presidio del Norte area where they had worked for two months. They left camp #5 in the two large wooden boats and the two India rubber boats and floated five miles through the lower Redford Valley, an area they had mapped in August. There the channel narrowed as they entered the first small canyon, and they referred to this point as the "start of the canyons." Parry noted it was twenty-five road miles below Presidio del Norte.[58]

The lack of access to the riverbank in the canyons and their speed of passage through them (documented in Parry's journal) indicates the party began rapid traverse surveying from the moving boats. This involved keeping a record of the compass heading of the boat as it moved from one point to another point within view of the first, while recording the float time between points. As their results testify, this method, though not nearly as accurate as traversing on land using theodolite or surveyor's compass and chain, can, with care, deliver a reasonably good map of the trace of the river.[59]

On the same day, back near Presidio del Norte, Green's pack train left the river and began its overland detour around the Upper Canyons of the Rio Grande.

TABLE 3. CLASSIFICATION OF RAPIDS

Class I: Easy	Fast-moving water with riffles and small waves. The few obstructions are easy to avoid. Not much training is needed and there is little risk to swimmers.
Class II: Novice	Water with wide, clear channels and medium waves. Obstructions can include rocks but are easily avoided. Training facilitates easy wave avoidance. Swimmers are seldom injured, and scouting is not needed.
Class III: Intermediate	Water contains highly irregular waves and strong eddies. Obstructions can include rocks and narrow but obvious passages. Swimmers may require assistance. Scouting is advisable.
Class IV: Advanced	Water with long, intense rapids that are powerful but predictable. Possible obstructions include rocks, highly constricted passages, and projecting ledges. Swimmers face moderate to high risk and will likely need assistance. Scouting is mandatory.

Green and Chandler had worked out a plan: Green would travel southeast on existing roads to the Mexican village of San Carlos, then take a well-known trail north to the Rio Grande at Comanche Crossing (Lajitas, Texas, today) to rendezvous with Chandler's boats. On the first day, Green had traveled only three miles when the mule train disintegrated into utter chaos, with the mules scattering away from the trail and losing their packs in the brush. Green reported: "My first day with pack mules, a description of which would be almost tautology [redundant], as all mules are alike. But I reached camp with only five mules out of our eighty and only two of the five had loads on them." He and his men spent the next day rounding up the mules, reorganizing the packs, and making purchases to replace some lost provisions. The group started down the road again on September 15.[60]

Parry, who had made no entries in his journal since August 29, resumed his journal on September 13. He left camp #5 early, walking about seven miles downriver to get ahead of the boats, and then waited for them at the first of the rapids in the Upper Canyons of the Rio Grande. See table 3 for the classification of rapids used hereafter.

The first rapids mentioned by the Chandler party is known today as Hoodoos Rapids, rated Class II–III. It lies two miles down the river from the start of the Upper Canyons at a point just below the mouth of Tapado Creek (buried treasure) on the American side and Arroyo Ventanas (windows) on the Mexican side (figures 14 and 15). The rapids is named for some "ghost like" rounded white columns of weathered igneous rock that overlook it from cliffs on the American side. Flanking the rapids on the west is a low island, and beyond it is a second

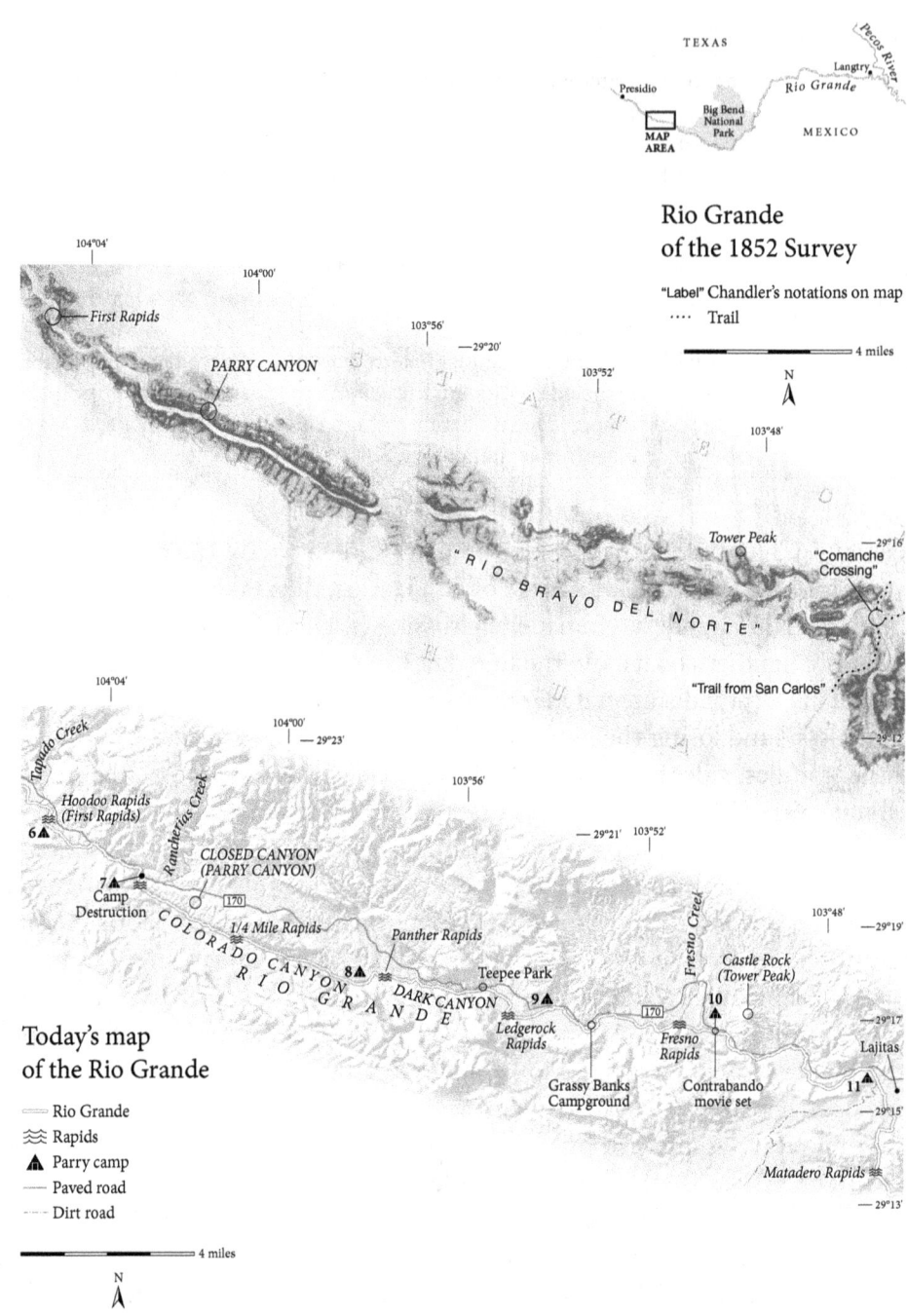

FIGURE 14. **River Trace Comparison: The Upper Canyons.** This dual-image figure looks at the river trace of Chandler's Boundary Map 21 as compared with a modern map for the area from the start of the Upper Canyons to Comanche Crossing at Lajitas, Texas. Boundary Map 21, National Archives. Map by Carol Zuber-Mallison.

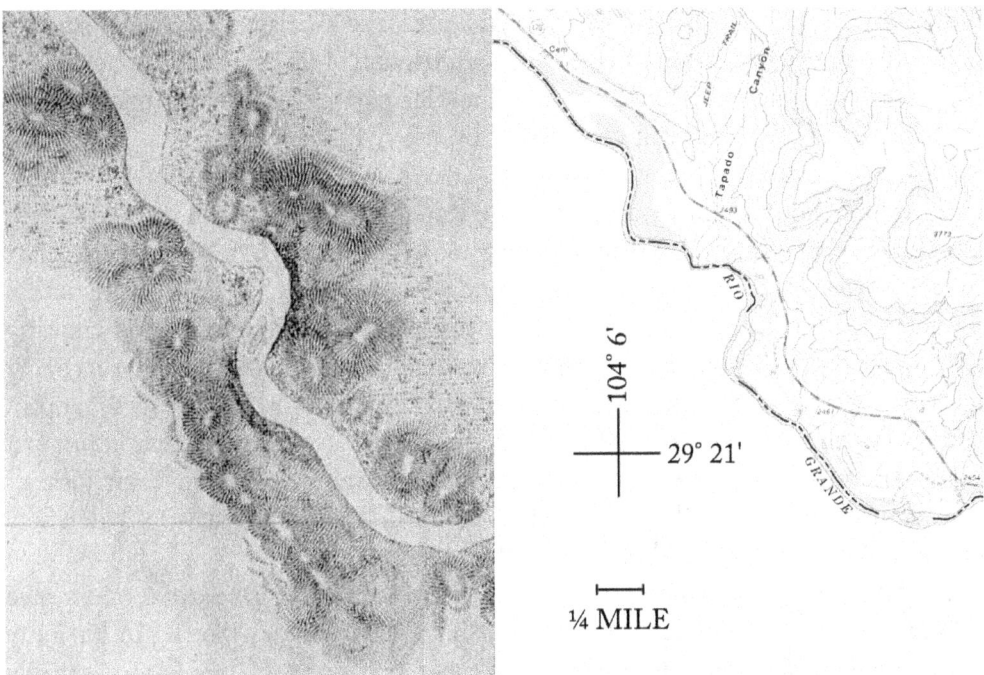

FIGURE 15. **Hoodoos Rapids.** This comparison of the Hoodoos Rapids shown on Chandler's Boundary Map 21 with today's USGS topographic map illustrates the detail provided by Chandler. Boundary Map 21, National Archives.

channel of the river. Chandler's map shows the rapids, the island, and the two channels, all of which can still be seen today from the cliff above. Parry, who was high above it on the ridge on the American side, watched as the first rubber boat came down the river. The boat was "delayed in making a portage and born[e] down over the rapids and filled with water." Fortunately, being a rubber boat, it did not capsize and dump its men or cargo. Parry ran upriver to warn the other three boats, and they successfully lined or portaged the rapids.[61] The group set up camp (#6) just below the rapids on the Mexican side, having covered seven miles their first day in the canyons.

The next morning, although his journal is silent, Parry must have again left camp early and walked three miles down the trail to the next rapids. Rancherias Rapids (also a Class II–III) lies just below the mouth of Rancherias Creek and just above the point where the Rio Grande enters the major Colorado Canyon (see figure 14). Chandler's Map 21 shows the rapids as a stippled area in the river channel. When the geologist Robert T. (R. T.) Hill and companions floated the

Colorado Canyon some forty-seven years later, the locals called it "Murderer's Canyon" because a dead man had been found washed up on the bank below the canyon. Given the experience of the Chandler party, it is easy to imagine that the "murder" may have been committed by the river itself.[62]

Both of Chandler's large wooden boats, heavily laden with provisions, bedding, and camping equipment, swamped in the Rancherias Rapids and were lost. This left only the two small rubber boats for the survey party. After the wreck, they retrieved from the water only "180 pounds of flour and a sack of beans and a few pieces of bedding." Everything else was lost, including eating and cooking utensils, tents, bedding, and provisions. No mention was made of their surveying instruments, but surely they lost some of them. After this "excitement," and in spite of having covered only three miles that day, they made an early camp just below the rapids at the entrance to Colorado Canyon to "count their losses." This camp (#7) Parry called "Camp Destruction," one of only two of their fifty numbered camps that he "honored" with a name.

Leaving Camp Destruction early on September 15, Parry boarded one of the rubber boats—"our bag boat." He obviously enjoyed the day, noting in his journal: "a very good day with plenty of work and rare sights." They floated rapidly down the river enclosed by Colorado Canyon's high walls and with the river running in a relatively straight southeast course. The loss of his provisions gave Chandler new motivation to move quickly down the river to the planned rendezvous with the mule train. He now had no choice but to do the surveying by taking notes as the party floated down the river; even if he came upon an open area of good access to the bank, the need to hurry precluded more accurate but time-consuming surveying.

Soon after entering Colorado Canyon, Parry reported passing his "little canyon" (see Closed Canyon in figure 14) and a bit farther down came to "a fearful rapid—waves tossing foaming water." This was likely Quarter Mile Rapids (Class II–III). The party hauled the boats ashore above the rapids to consider a plan. Apparently having no option to portage among the steep canyon walls, they decided they must run it, first taking off all their clothes to make swimming easier. They "shoved off into the boiling flood—thanks to our vessels [air chambers] which buoyed us up when an occasional wave splashed over us." Once past the rapids, "our feeling of exultation broke out in a shout."[63]

Later, apparently at the downstream end of Colorado Canyon, where the river channel widens and becomes less swift, Parry's rubber boat came upon one of the party's wrecked wooden boats, bottom up. They checked it out, but a large hole in the side made it beyond repair. A little farther along, they found the second wooden boat, and upon setting it right, found it to be entirely sound. To their surprise, they also found nearby a full, undamaged barrel of pork. A short time later, after covering nine miles for the day, they set up camp (#8) just above another rapids—Panther Rapids (Class II–III). This camp was likely at or near Parry's earlier reconnaissance camp of August 26.[64]

With the loss of the carrying capacity of the large wooden boats when they swamped at Rancherias Rapids, it seems likely that Chandler would have had to release some of his camp helpers or boatmen before entering Colorado Canyon in the smaller rubber boats. However, finding the one wooden boat intact would have given him back some of that carrying capacity, and one wonders if Chandler did in fact let men go or if he had the foresight to anticipate finding a boat and simply asked some of the men to make the three-hour walk overland using Parry's cutoff trail to the camp below Colorado Canyon. There is nothing in Parry's journal or the final report to indicate one way or the other, and there are no exact tallies of the total number of men before or after the boats were lost.

At this point, the Chandler party had surveyed the first ten miles of the Upper Canyons, and the results down to the exit of Colorado Canyon are shown on Boundary Map 21. The mapping of the river channel is good in direction, distance, and documentation of the turns of the river (see figure 14). Six rapids are shown in Colorado Canyon by stippled areas on the map. They seem rather too numerous and evenly spaced; modern river guides usually list only three rapids in this section: Closed Canyon, Thread the Needle, and Quarter Mile.[65] Only Closed Canyon Rapids at the mouth of that side canyon appears to be marked exactly in the right place on Chandler's map. His other rapids locations appear arbitrary, uniformly spaced along the entire length of Colorado Canyon as if his perception was that there were rapids all along the canyon route. It is possible that such a perception was correct when we take into account the high-water stage of the river in September 1852 and the fact that the location of earlier rapids will not always exactly match those of today. However, the usual location of rapids is near the mouth of a tributary arroyo or canyon where a flash flood of the arroyo dumps rock debris into the river channel, partially blocking it. These rapids are maintained by occasional floods, which change the details but allow the rapids to persist near the same location for hundreds of years.

Chandler's rendering of topography adjoining the river in Colorado Canyon is poor and shows no side arroyos entering the canyon other than Closed Canyon. He did pass several small side arroyos on his rapid descent but did not record them. Short of provisions, he was no doubt in a rush to get to the rendezvous with the mule train.

On September 16, the survey party passed the Panther Rapids just below their camp and soon entered the narrow canyon below the cliffs, with Santana Mesa towering above them. Today the scenic "Big Hill of the River Road" (Texas Farm to Market Road 170) occupies a narrow notch cut in the cliffs far above the river but only halfway to the top of Santana Mesa; the canyon is known as Dark Canyon (see figure 14). Beyond it the party moved past the site of today's Tepee Roadside Park and through the minor Madera and Flat Rock Rapids, which Chandler did not map. They camped above another rapids at the mouth of an unnamed arroyo on the American side. Although not present today, the rapids certainly was there in 1852. After traveling downriver a little over four miles that day, their camp (#9) was just downstream from some eroded white volcanic ash pillars on the north side of the River Road. These pillars, called "hoodoos," are known today as El Padre al Altar.[66]

On September 17, Parry wrote that they passed "several rapids": the first where they had camped; the second perhaps at today's rapids at Arroyo El Sauz, which Chandler did not map; and finally, the rapids at Fresno Creek, which Chandler did map. After floating four miles, the party reached camp #10 just downstream from the mouth of Contrabando Creek at the foot of a vivid red sandstone bluff on the American side. In the early 1980s, a movie set of several adobe houses and a little church was built near the foot of the red bluff. Several movies were made here, including *Lone Star*, *Uphill All the Way*, *Dead Man's Walk*, *Streets of Laredo*, and the music video *Hey Maria*. In 2015, the buildings were taken down by Big Bend Ranch State Park due to flood damage and public safety concerns, but there is a roadside sign and a parking area to visit the site.[67]

Parry made a rough landscape sketch in his notebook of a prominent rock spire one-half mile east of his camp. He named it "Tower Peak" and correctly noted it was a brown igneous porphyry underlain by a "black trap" (basalt). Today this rock spire is known as "Castle Rock" (figure 16).[68]

On September 18, after floating five miles down the river, the party arrived at Comanche Crossing. Parry reported that "three miles after a considerable canyon" the view widened to a more open basin as they approached the crossing. As planned, Chandler's surveyors camped (#11) on the Mexican side and waited for the arrival of Green and the mule train. Today at the old crossing, the Lajitas Resort sits on the Texas side and a small village on the Mexican side. For decades, there was an informal crossing here between the twin villages of

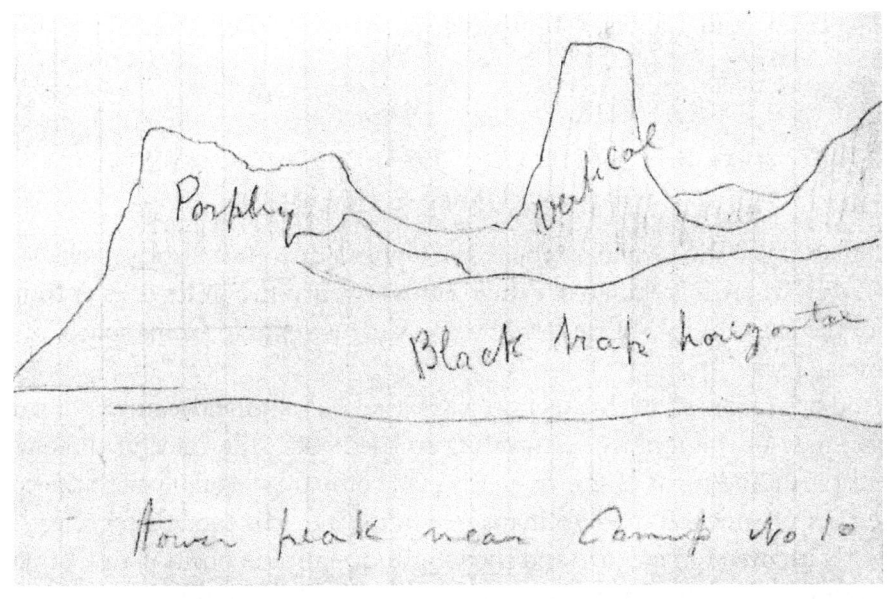

FIGURE 16. **Castle Rock.** A comparison of Parry's sketch and a modern photo of the scenic rock spire Parry sketched and named "Tower Peak." Today the Texas Parks guidebook to the River Road calls it Castle Rock. It lies half a mile northeast of the old *Contrabando* movie set, which in turn is on the River Road (FM 170) five miles west of Lajitas, Texas. Parry camped at the foot of the red sandstone outcrop seen in the photo. Alloway, *El Camino Del Rio–The River Road*, 17; PJ, 36. Photograph by the author.

Lajitas, Texas, and Lajitas, Chihuahua, but it was closed after September 11, 2001.

Comparison of US and Mexican Boundary Maps of the Upper Canyons

The course of the Rio Grande through the Upper Canyons is displayed on Boundary Map 21, where it is shown to extend across twenty-five miles of river from the start of the canyons east of Redford, Texas, downstream to Comanche Crossing at Lajitas, Texas.

Chandler's mapping of this section was based on handheld-compass headings and estimated distances while traveling in the boats. The trace of the channel with its twists and turns as shown on his map compares favorably with the course of the river channel on modern maps (see figure 14). His total distance estimate is slightly inflated (9 percent), and the longitude-latitude position of Comanche Crossing noted on his map is only two miles farther southeast than the true position (see table 2).

Although work by Mexican surveyors in 1855 led to an excellent Mexican version of Boundary Map 22 downstream of Presidio del Norte, they had just begun work farther southeast into the area covered by the adjoining Map 21. They had established only four widely spaced triangulation stations before they ran short of financial support and had to abandon their survey. It appears they did no surveying along the trace of the river boundary through the Upper Canyons. A side-by-side comparison of the river trace of the Mexican and US versions of Boundary Map 21 reveal that essentially all the river trace on the Mexican map is a copy of the American map. An exception is the first five miles of river trace at the north margin of the map where the Mexican map shows a curious river trace unlike the US map or modern maps.[69] We believe the five miles of odd river trace is a result of the requirement that a single boundary line must connect all maps in the final sets of both the Mexican and US versions of the Boundary Maps. The problem the Mexican mapmakers faced was connecting their accurate Boundary Map 22 of the area to the north with the less accurate but adjoining US Boundary Map 21 to the south. They had no Mexican-surveyed version of Map 21, so their only option was to copy the US map to complete their full set of maps. Yet, they could not simply trace the entire US Map 21 all the way north to its junction with Map 22 because the river trace at the south margin of Mexican Map 22 was two miles west of the river trace on US Map 22. The boundary had to be a single uninterrupted line, and the lines had to connect, map to map. To solve the problem, the Mexican mapmakers simply sketched in a "natural-looking river trace" across a five-mile transition zone at the north end of their Map 21, thus joining the river trace on their Map 22 with the trace on their version of Map 21.

The Camp at Comanche Crossing

Lieutenant Green's mule train joined Chandler at the crossing rendezvous on September 20. Green observed that Chandler was "eating his last piece of pork—and—had lost almost everything by destruction of the boats."[70] Green sent part of the mule train back up the trail to Presidio del Norte to replace "some things absolutely necessary," and that round trip took a week.

On September 23, the survey camp at Comanche Crossing was "startled by the cry: Indians," and Parry described the encounter:

> There was great hunting of guns and [rifle firing] caps and hurried enquiries of, lend me one of your pistols, etc. A band of Comanche came down to the crossing on the American side, opposite the survey camp. Our company of soldiers was formed into rank and marched down to the bank of the river. The Indians were impressed and ranged at a distance on the summit of a hill. Several Indians, under a white flag, came down to the crossing to await a confab. Lieutenant Green sent over a Mexican with a friendly message asking them to cross. Their chief with two others swam across. They said they were at peace with Americans and with the nearby Mexican village of San Carlos [Manuel Benavides], smoked a pipe with Lieutenant Green and concluded a treaty.[71]

This band of about fifty, under a chief whose name Green reported to be Mona but Chandler reported as Mano (hand), included a few women and two Mexican captives. They said their home was in Upper Texas, which suggests they were the Kotsotekas (Buffalo Eaters) Comanche of the Canadian River valley in the panhandle of Texas. Mano was probably the brother of the notorious Comanche chief Bajo el Sol. Mano and Mona were two of the many names used to refer to this chief; others include Mague, Mauwe, Mahua, and Mowway.[72]

Chief Mano and Lieutenant Green exchanged gifts—a horse for Green and a beef for Mano. The chief said they were on a foraging excursion to Durango, Mexico, but Parry observed that their equipment and arms indicated they were on a "robbing excursion." This would have been a round trip of about two thousand miles for the Indians. The band's peaceful demeanor at the crossing was likely due to Green's large, well-armed, and alert escort of soldiers. It might have been a different story if the large Comanche band had arrived at the crossing during the two days that Chandler's small group of poorly armed surveyors was camped alone at the crossing. Camping with a small party directly on a Comanche "highway into Mexico" was not a good idea, but in Chandler's defense, the rendezvous point at the crossing was the only one the surveyors knew about where there was a trail suitable for the mule train to reach the banks of the Rio Grande. It had been chosen before they left Presidio del Norte, when Chandler thought the escort, traveling by mule on established trails, would arrive first, but after the provisions and camping gear were lost on the river, the surveyors had moved down to the rendezvous point more quickly than planned.

In the period from 1840 to 1870, Comanche Crossing lay on the westernmost of three main Indian trails used to travel back and forth from the Texas-Oklahoma panhandle area to Mexico. The other two crossings lay farther down the Rio Grande: Chisos Crossing was about fifty miles down the river near the Chisos Mountains, and Las Moras Crossing was more than three hundred miles farther downstream. This easternmost crossing was on an early trail that passed by the large Las Moras (blackberry) Spring, which was twenty miles north of the river and later became the site of the US Army post of Fort Clark and today's town of Brackettville, Texas.[73]

The Comanche Trail at the Lajitas crossing continued west past San Carlos, to the Río Conchos far upstream from Presidio del Norte, then turned south along the headwaters of the Conchos and continued south toward Durango, Mexico.

In his journal, Parry offers a colorful description of the Comanche making their crossing at a spot where he also notes that the speed of the current was 4.3 miles per hour:

> Their cargo was securely bound in bundles [buffalo skins] then rafted across with the aid of horses. The river was hardly fordable and with a swift current was the occasion for some feats of agility and altogether presented an imposing scene. Most of them are lusty swimmers, one particularly attracted our attention by his robust prance and herculean profession [assertion]. I never saw such a frame on a human as I submitted to a friendly hug. I felt in the grasp of a giant. They seem to be pretty well prepared for their tramp, plainly calculated for a robbing excursion. Their arms were the bow and lance, a few rusty flintlocks, shield etc.[74]

On the day after their crossing, the Comanche continued west on the trail to San Carlos. Mano's earlier statement that he was "at peace" with San Carlos was a bit of an understatement. According to Emory, the Comanche had an ongoing trading arrangement with the town, whereby, on their return from raids into the Mexican interior, they traded stolen mules for supplies, including guns.[75]

While still camped at Comanche Crossing, Green had received "an express" from the army via El Paso del Norte and Presidio del Norte, warning him that Mano's band had recently killed four Americans on the San Antonio–El Paso Road. The army message appears to have mistakenly tied Mano's band to an earlier incident in which four Americans had been killed in November 1851 on the San Antonio road in Quitman Canyon, which was 85 miles east of El Paso del Norte and 155 miles northwest of San Carlos. That wagon train raid was much too far west to be along Mano's route from the panhandle of Texas and is a much better fit with a raid described in Santa Fe newspapers as having been carried out by a band of Indians that was probably Apache from southeastern New Mexico, who were also traveling to Durango, Mexico.[76]

While camped at Comanche Crossing, Chandler surveyed the eleven miles down the Rio Grande to the entrance to Santa Elena Canyon. It appears the surveyors spent considerable time over nine days using their instruments to carry traverse lines near the river. Not only was access good enough to allow them to travel along the riverbank, but they had ample time to do the work while they waited for Green's mule train to return from Presidio del Norte with replacement supplies. The surveyors produced an accurate map with considerable detail of the channel. While six rapids are shown, only one, Matadero, three miles below Lajitas, is recognized today (figure 17).

Chandler's map shows the trace of the Comanche Trail crossing the river channel at Lajitas as well as the approach trails on the American side and the trail leaving the river going west toward the Mexican village of San Carlos (Manuel Benavides). The trace of the Indian trail on the American side is shown going east about two miles then turning south, and is labeled "to Comanche Springs," whereas the Comanche Trail leaving the river actually continued east about four miles to Comanche Springs, then northeast another eight miles before turning north up Terlingua Creek. The surveyors, only interested in tracking the course of the river, probably took the word of their Mexican guide for the trail's route away from the crossing, and he described the trail used by the locals to go down to the mouth of Terlingua Creek at the exit of Santa Elena Canyon, not the Comanche Trail, which went east and north up Terlingua Creek. The Mexican version of Boundary Map 21 in this area was copied from the American map, but the Mexican version corrected Chandler's trail location and title to show the Comanche Trail continuing east from the crossing in spite of the fact that the Mexicans conducted no survey of the river in this area. This likely means that the Indian guides the Mexicans used while their 1855 survey base camp was in

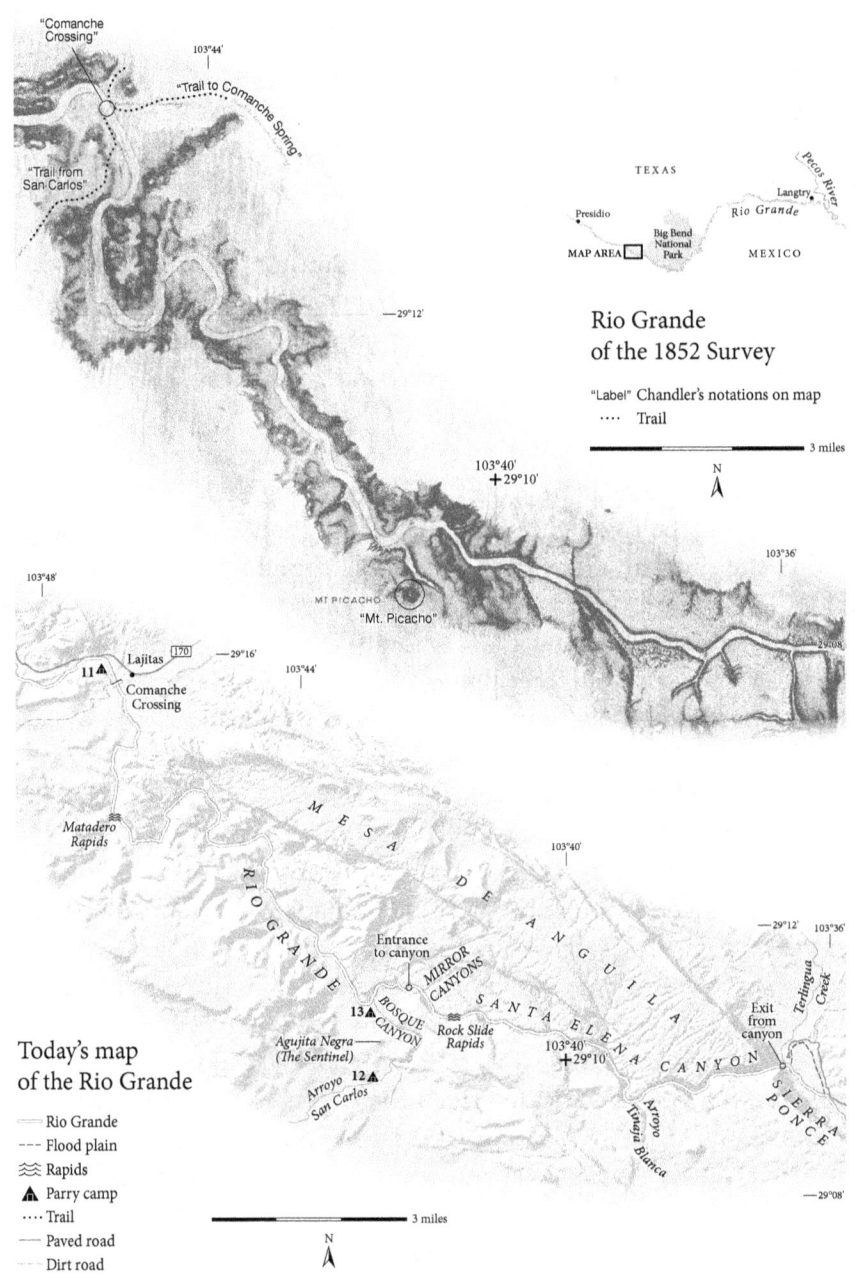

FIGURE 17. **River Trace Comparison: Lajitas and Santa Elena Canyon.** This comparison shows the river trace on Chandler's Boundary Map 21 and that on a modern map for the section from Comanche Crossing at Lajitas, Texas, to the exit of Santa Elena Canyon. Boundary Map 21, National Archives. Map by Carol Zuber-Mallison.

the village of San Carlos told them the trail continued east to join the valley of Terlingua Creek.[77]

In their work near Lajitas, Chandler's surveyors probably took advantage of a small mesa on the American side just one-quarter mile north of the crossing, where they had a view of the high point of the scenic Chisos Mountains twenty-eight miles to the east. Chandler later named that point Emory Peak. Recording the bearing to Emory Peak from the Comanche Crossing area would have been useful later in tying together, by triangulation, their survey work above Santa Elena Canyon and their detached survey of the river below the canyon.

On September 28, after spending ten nights at Comanche Crossing, the party broke camp early. Chandler's surveyors went down the river in the three boats, while Green's mule train escort made an overland detour because steep banks along the river were too difficult for the mules.

Beginning on this day and for the remaining months of the Chandler Survey, Parry traveled with Green and the army escort rather than with the surveyors. Space in the boats was limited, and Chandler likely wanted to use all the seats for men who would contribute directly to the surveying. A few days later, when the last wooden boat was abandoned at the entrance to Santa Elena Canyon, boat space was even further reduced. Parry was most likely happy to remain with the escort where he had more freedom to follow his interests in botany and geology and add to his collection of plants and rocks. He was, by nature, a botanist driven to discover new species of plants and document them with collections. Major Emory also had a strong interest in botany and had encouraged Parry to focus on plant exploration.[78]

Leaving Comanche Crossing, the escort went southwest up the trail toward San Carlos, then left that trail to turn southeast over the moderate highlands of the Sierra Los Encinos (live oaks), down to Arroyo San Carlos, and then down the arroyo three miles to water and camp #12. The mule train had traveled sixteen miles from the crossing. This camp was near the confluence of Arroyo San Carlos and Río San Antonio, just above the point where the combined streams enter the narrow Cañón del Bosque for a two-mile run to the Rio Grande (figure 18).

On the morning of the twenty-ninth, the escort moved down Arroyo San Carlos less than a mile, then left that drainage and turned northwest, going overland to pass just to the left of "a singular isolated pyramid peak with a tower shaped summit." Chandler's Map 21 labels this peak Mt. Picacho (peak), but neither Parry nor Chandler mentioned the name in their reports. Today,

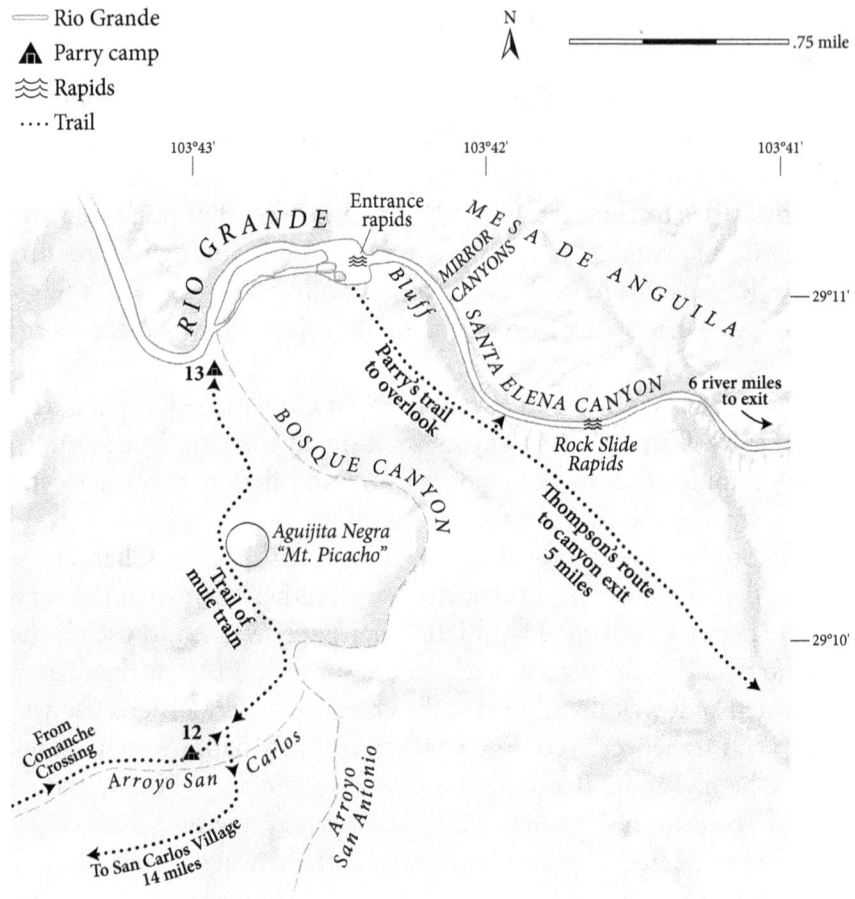

FIGURE 18. **Trails at Santa Elena Canyon.** Trails used by the Chandler party near the entrance to Santa Elena Canyon. Trails were drawn from descriptions in the Parry Journal. Map by Carol Zuber-Mallison.

Mexican maps show this butte as Cerro Agujita Negra (little black needle). When the American geologist R. T. Hill floated down the Rio Grande in 1899, he described this landmark as "a wonderful symmetrical butte a thousand feet high, the summit of which is [appears to be] a head presenting the profile of an old man, which we named the Sentinel."[79] Today, Rio Grande river runners in canoes and rafts still call this The Sentinel. They look for it as they float down the river to know they are approaching the entrance to the massive Santa Elena Canyon, which it guards.

Once past The Sentinel, the mule train escort continued north for a mile, then reached camp (#13) on the Rio Grande at the mouth of Cañón del Bosque (Río San Antonio on modern Mexican maps), where Chandler's surveyors had arrived earlier. The entrance to the massive Santa Elena Canyon lay only a half mile farther down the river.

Chandler's Boundary Map 21 shows excellent topographic detail in the immediate vicinity of his camp at the entrance to the canyon. Clearly shown is the last mile of Cañón del Bosque as it approaches the Rio Grande. Just below their camp, he indicates the Entrance Rapids and the high bluff, which sharply narrows the width of the channel at the beginning of Santa Elena Canyon. The correct and prominent placement on the map of the isolated Sentinel butte, less than a mile directly south of camp, indicates the surveyors used this landmark for a triangulation station.

Santa Elena Canyon

The Chandler party spent two days scouting the entrance to Santa Elena Canyon and the nearby "falls" to judge whether they could pass through with boats. The famous Rock Slide Rapids was not really a waterfall but a fall of giant blocks of limestone from the cliffs above. The limestone blocks partially block the channel to form rapids consisting of a series of narrow chutes in the river channel. The total length of the canyon is 7.2 miles, which Parry accurately estimated in his journal when he noted that the canyon extended 7 or 8 miles to its exit. In his December 1852 report to Major Emory, Chandler estimated the canyon to be 10 miles in length, but later his Boundary Map 21, completed in 1856, correctly showed it to be 7 miles. Thus, Chandler's early, overlong estimate was made prior to transcription of his raw field surveying records.

Chandler sent a team led by his assistant surveyor, Thomas Thompson, to reconnoiter the canyon and advise him on whether they should go through it or detour around. Thompson hiked up the mesa overlooking the rapids on the Mexican side to a viewpoint that was less than two trail miles southeast of and five hundred feet higher than their camp (see figures 18 and 19). He likely used a route similar to the one present-day canoeists use to get an early view of the rapids.[80]

Parry noted in his journal that a reconnaissance by the surveyors reached far beyond the rapids to a point on the crest of the mesa directly overlooking the mouth of Santa Elena Canyon: "Mr. Thompson reported reaching the peak above

FALLS OF RIO BRAVO, NEAR SAN CARLOS.

FIGURE 19. **Rock Slide Rapids.** These three images are all of the Rock Slide Rapids of Santa Elena Canyon. On the top left is a modern photograph, courtesy of Louis F. Aulbach, author of guidebooks for float trips through the Rio Grande canyons. On the top right is a landscape drawing by Thomas Moran, based on a photo taken by the geologist Robert T. Hill during his 1899 exploration and published in his January 1901 *Century Magazine* article. Below is a woodcut from the Emory Report that was based on a landscape sketch by Parry and included in the geologic discussion Parry wrote for the report (ER, 2:55).

Part I: The 1852 Chandler Surveying Party   75

the debouchment overlooking a beautiful panorama view of the river valley below spread out into a wide plain [the Rio Grande floodplain below the canyon]. The surveying party by a hard day[']s work brought the survey up to this point by triangulation."[81] Thompson was successful in determining the location of the exit of Santa Elena Canyon. He took compass bearings from the high point above the exit to landmarks whose location he had previously documented. The landmarks surely included The Sentinel butte near their camp—shown as a prominent peak named Mt. Picacho on Chandler's Map 21. For his triangulation, he must have recorded other bearings to landmarks, perhaps near Comanche Crossing to the west and Emory Peak to the east. That the surveyors reached the exit is confirmed by the fact that the bearing and distance from Picacho to the canyon exit taken directly from Chandler's Map 21 is almost the same as the true bearing and distance shown on modern maps.[82]

As the Thompson party had done, Parry climbed up the mesa on the Mexican side of the river to look down on and sketch the Rock Slide Rapids. Modern photographs of the rapids from the mesa show the same view depicted in Parry's sketch, which was converted to a woodcut landscape illustration in the final Emory Report. The woodcut is titled "Falls of the Rio Bravo."[83] For a comparison of Parry's sketch of the Rock Slide with a vintage landscape drawing by Thomas Moran and a modern photograph, see figure 19. Parry described the view in his personal journal by saying that "in all respects [it] was the most singular and grand I have ever beheld—seem[s] impossible that a river should have its course so near [to you,] but you stand on a projecting point and: THERE IT IS." Parry did not see, and doubted the existence of, falls, but he correctly reported a rapids caused by rockfall from the cliffs above. Parry thought boats could be portaged past the rapids but admitted that once boatmen committed to the canyon, there was no turning back and no way for them to climb out.[84]

As to the height of the canyon walls at the Rock Slide, Parry wrote that he counted "slowly" to twenty before a rock thrown from the top hit the river. Later in the Emory Report, he increased this to a count of thirty.[85] Parry must have been a fast counter or else he heard a late echo or secondary splash from the rock first hitting the wall and then the river. Directly above the Rock Slide, the canyon rises only seven hundred feet above the river, and one should hear a rock thrown from the top hit the water in less than eight seconds. Farther downstream at the canyon exit, which Parry did not reach, the canyon rises fifteen hundred feet above the river.

To map the course of the river through the seven-mile span between the entrance and the exit of Santa Elena Canyon, the surveyors had to resort to a rough sketch map based on occasional distant views of the canyon edge during their one-day hike to the triangulation point overlooking the canyon exit. The first two miles of the canyon, where Thompson traveled near the edge of the canyon above the Rock Slide Rapids, are well represented on Map 21. A short distance inside the canyon entrance, a fault line cutting at a right angle across the river forms two small canyons intersecting the river and lying directly opposite each other. Boatmen moving down the river today call these "the mirror image canyons." Chandler's map shows only the north canyon. Because the scouting party was high on the mesa south of the river, looking north to the main river canyon allowed them to see the notch formed by the north canyon on the exposed north wall of Santa Elena Canyon, but their view of the closer south canyon wall was blocked by the mesa surface directly in front of them, so they did not see the "mirror" effect.

The Rock Slide Rapids, which is 1.1 miles inside the canyon, is not apparent on Chandler's map. This is odd because Thompson reported that he had seen the rapids. Perhaps the little rapids the map shows at 2.1 miles was meant to be the Rock Slide. For the section from 2.1 miles below the canyon entrance down to the exit at 7.2 miles, the mapped trace of the canyon does not fit well with the actual course of the river. This section of the map must have been based only on Thompson's field sketch. Map 21 shows almost no topographic detail on the American side, probably because the surface of the west-sloping mesa appeared to be uniform in the distant view they had from the Mexican side of the mesa. More detailed topography is shown on the Mexican side because that was the ground over which Thompson had scrambled on his hike to the canyon exit. On the Mexican side, Chandler's map shows a canyon cutting down to the river 2 miles upstream from the exit; this is about the right distance to be the Mexican-side Arroyo Tinaja Blanca, the largest side canyon to join the main Santa Elena Canyon (see figure 17).

The magnificent east exit of Santa Elena Canyon, with its towering limestone escarpment cut by the narrow exit canyon, is displayed in such a subtle way on Map 21 that it can be missed at first glance. Shown bunched together in a quarter-mile zone against the east line of the map are a very narrow line of rubble running north across the river (the escarpment actually runs northwest); a tiny drainage inlet (the mouth of the large Terlingua Creek) on the north bank of the river just below the rubble; and a tiny island in mid channel, which appears to signal the beginning of the floodplain below the canyon exit (see figure 17).

Although subtle, Chandler's map shows the exit of Santa Elena Canyon at the proper "relative location" to Comanche Crossing and the canyon entrance. In terms of the true longitude and latitude of the canyon exit, his distance determinations were consistently a bit too long during the seventy miles of his general southeast travel since leaving Presidio del Norte; thus, he located the canyon exit too far east and too far south (see table 2).

After consulting with his scouts, Chandler decided he must detour around Santa Elena Canyon rather than risk the loss of his men in the "falls." In his report to Chandler after his reconnaissance of the canyon, assistant surveyor Thompson said he had used a telescope from the mesa and estimated the vertical fall of the rapids to be at least ten feet. His mention of a telescope suggests he may have carried a compact theodolite instrument to use for triangulation. Thompson also noted: "One of the men with me is a boatman and he expressed the opinion that it would be impossible to pass the falls in safety."[86]

The first documented passage of a boat through the canyon would not happen until 1882. For the story of that voyage by Presidio County surveyors and Texas Rangers, plus the later passages of a party led by the geologist R. T. Hill in 1889 and an International Boundary Commission party in 1901, see appendix C.

The Detour around Santa Elena Canyon

The Chandler party, heeding Thompson's warning of the "falls" at the Rock Slide, decided to take a long detour around Santa Elena Canyon on the Mexican side. Later, in a report to Emory justifying his decision to detour, Chandler said the "falls were 12 feet high, and separate from rapids on either side."[87]

In preparing for the detour, the surveyors could deflate the two rubber boats for the mules to carry, but there was no wagon to haul the last bulky wooden boat. They cast it into the river, later finding only fragments below Santa Elena Canyon.[88]

Although a shorter detour was available by returning to Comanche Crossing and then going down the American side of the Rio Grande to the exit of Santa Elena Canyon, Chandler chose to detour along the better-known route on the Mexican side. The Mexican route had several advantages. The Langberg map that Chandler carried showed a clear trail from the Mexican village of San Carlos to the Rio Grande below the canyon. Chandler's already established camp at the mouth of the canyon was only fourteen miles from San Carlos, and stopping there along the way would provide access to fresh provisions and the opportunity to hire additional Mexican laborers and guides.

In a letter to his commanding officer in Washington, DC, Lieutenant Green estimated his detour around Santa Elena at ninety miles, but the detailed mileage from Parry's journal shows the escort and mule train made a detour of only fifty-six miles, having stopped to camp on the river still fourteen miles short of the exit of Santa Elena Canyon.[89]

The detour around the canyon was the first time the entire Chandler party—surveyors and mule train—traveled together. They broke camp on the river and started west toward the village of San Carlos, backtracking the earlier route of the escort to their camp of September 29, then crossing Arroyo San Carlos to the right (south) bank, and continuing west along the arroyo to the ruins of the abandoned Presidio San Carlos. The presidio had been built in 1774 and abandoned about ten years later.[90] Today the exterior walls of the old presidio are still clearly visible on satellite images of the area. A photograph by the archaeologist Rex Gerald showed that parts of the chapel walls were still standing in 1968 (figure 20).

Parry's description of the presidio offers a quick step back in time to the rural economy of October 1852:

> The old Presidio occupying a level mesa on the right bank. The adobe walls occupying a square some 100 yards [actually 140] enclosing a large level court now grown up with *Larrea* [creosote bush]. The houses all open on the inside court and in its time must have contained a large population. The general contour of the walls still remain[s], the roofs having fallen in, the wooden part of the structure being less durable than the adobe. At this point in the river [creek] bottom, cultivatable land commences, continuing from here up to the town some 7 to 9 miles [and] composed of rich black soil, easily irrigated and now a continuous corn field. The remains of the Mission enterprise still exist in long walls of masonry for conveying water to the lower bottoms of the creek bed, [which] now runs over a pebbly bed [and] occasionally making a considerable fall over a conglomerate rock. The corn here is of remarkable rank growth, some stalks measuring 16 feet. The ears of corn being so high that it would require a man on horseback to reach them handily. This is the exclusive growth being planted in April or May and now just in fine roasting order. Good wheat is also raised here and with red pepper and tomatoes are mainly the whole growth. The wheat and corn are articles of export to supply the inhabitants of Presidio del Norte. Peaches flourish well and [are] tolerably abundant, but now [October] out of season.[91]

After traveling twelve miles from the Rio Grande, the survey party camped (#14) on San Carlos Creek just west of the old presidio. Parry rode up to the

Presidio de San Carlos. View of chapel from west corner of presidio.

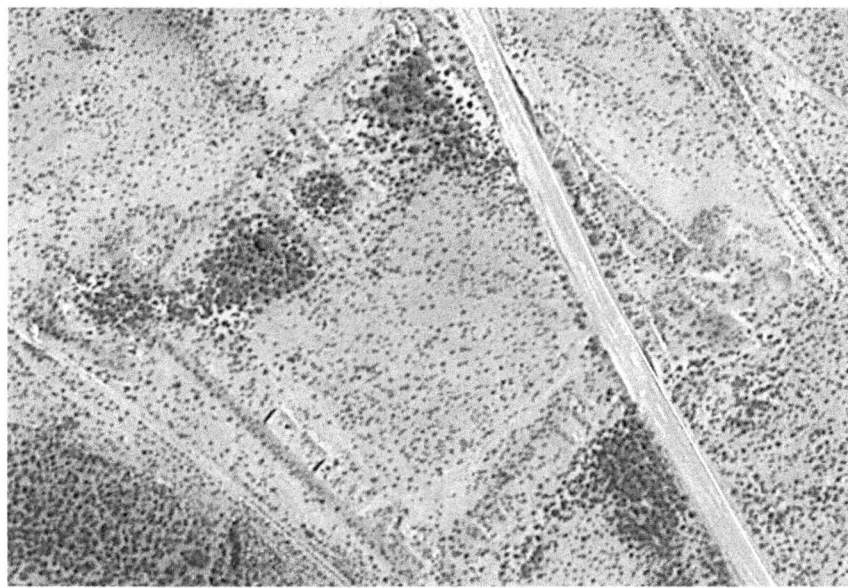

FIGURE 20. **Ruins of San Carlos Presidio, a 1770s vintage Spanish fort.** Above is a photo showing the 1968 condition of the chapel walls built into an exterior wall of the fort. (Photograph courtesy of Rex Gerald and the Santa Fe Museum of New Mexico Press.) Below is a recent oblique satellite view looking east. The walls of the enclosure are 140 yards on a side, with angular bastions extending out another 30 yards from the north and south corners. A dirt road crosses the ruins and an abandoned dirt airstrip is at the upper right. The presidio is seven miles east of the old town of San Carlos, Chihuahua, now named Manuel Benavides. The location is 29°06′22″ N and 103°47′58″ W. Google Earth Pro online, accessed December 17, 2014; Rex E. Gerald, *Spanish Presidios of the Late Eighteenth Century in Northern New Spain* (Santa Fe: Museum of New Mexico Press, 1968).

village: "The town as usual occupying a mesa on the right bank [west], surrounded by mountains nearly on all sides. I saw over the town the usual collection of adobe huts, cleaner than common, and appearance of thrift. Prescribed for a variety of ailments, partook of some of the country produce in the way of refreshment, and started back to camp near the old Presidio."[92]

On October 4, the Chandler party left their camp near the presidio ruins. They went west along the south bank of Arroyo San Carlos to join the good main trail and followed it southeast to the next camp (#15) at an arroyo among cottonwood trees. The twelve miles traveled and the camp's description indicate it was on Arroyo San Antonio near earlier camps made by Langberg in October 1851 and a Forty-Niner wagon train in May 1849 (see figure 6).[93]

On the fifth, they started out in a southeasterly direction on the trail Langberg had used. Later they left his trail on their right, turning east to strike the Rio Grande higher upstream and closer to the exit of Santa Elena Canyon. They continued east and then northeast, making an ascent up the gentle, west-dipping beds of limestone of the Sierra Ponce. They soon reached a point high enough to see the Chisos Mountains about twenty miles to the northeast. As they moved higher, they reached the divide and could see the Rio Grande below them about seven miles to the northeast. Parry described the descent from the divide as "rough and difficult, the last piece being a depression [notch] in the wall of limestone [the east face of the Sierra Ponce escarpment] stretching hence in an unbroken wall to the exit of the [Santa Elena] canyon."[94]

To cross the divide, Parry likely used a rough trail that passed about four miles north of today's Mexican village of Providencia. Here, near the southern end of the Sierra Ponce, the pass is about eight hundred feet above the plain leading down to the river. Parry's "wall of limestone" marks the eastern boundary of the Sierra Ponce, where gently dipping massive limestone beds are cut off by the large Terlingua Fault, resulting in a line of cliffs facing east. Langberg, in his journal, more accurately called this fault-bounded mountain range "Cuesta de Ponze" rather than Sierra Ponce. A cuesta is a linear hill or mountain very gently sloping on one side and very steep, or a cliff, on the other. The limestone cliffs of the Ponce gradually increase in height along their twenty-mile course to the northwest, until the massive cliffs rise fifteen hundred feet above the river at the exit of Santa Elena Canyon. The same cliffs continue northwest in a straight line on the American side beyond Santa Elena Canyon, where they form the abrupt east face of Mesa de Anguila.[95]

After a long day's journey of twenty-two miles, the party camped (#16) at a rock-bound pool of water. Parry's description reads: "a deep rocky basin, called ___ or wells. The surface of the rock is here marked with cavernous excavations." The missing word, now faded from his journal, is probably *tinaja* (earthen bowl)—the Mexican term used in the Big Bend area for small but deep pools of water in rock-floored ravines. A tinaja about twenty-five feet across can still be seen today via Google Earth at Parry's likely camp site at the bottom of a steep ravine. This tinaja location fits Parry's journal entry for the next day, which noted it was six miles to the Rio Grande. The "excavations" in the limestone that Parry mentioned must be mortar holes made by Indians grinding seeds and other foodstuffs. When using a heavy stick as a pestle in a depression in the limestone, over the years, a round hole up to an arm's length deep is made in the rock. These holes are very common on rock ledges near springs and tinajas throughout the Big Bend. It seems odd that Parry would not have known this, yet it is consistent with his apparent complete lack of interest in Indian relics; he never once mentions pictographs or other artifacts in his journal. It also suggests he spent no time chatting with the Mexican guides and packers. Since Parry reported an "Indian alarm" taking place during the night, some of the men of the party recognized the mortar holes as a sign of Indians in the area. This large tinaja may be the one Colonel Langberg referred to in 1851 when, five or six miles west of this tinaja, he said: "to our left [east] at some distance lie Aguaje del Leon [Waterhole of the Lion] and Cuesta de Ponze."[96]

Leaving camp early on October 6, the party traveled northeast on river terraces sloping gently toward the Rio Grande. Parry said they reached the river after six miles, "just above Vado Ponce" (Ponce Crossing). Chandler's report said they reached the river "some 20 miles below the canyon."[97] Parry's six miles and his landscape description suggest they first hit the river on the west side of Cerro Chino (Chinese), a 150-foot-high volcanic hill that is across the river and about five miles west of the site of the old Johnson Ranch in Big Bend National Park. This hill is, in fact, about twenty trail miles down the river from Santa Elena Canyon.

Langberg, in his 1851 journal, noted the Ponze (Ponce) crossing was two leagues (5.3 miles) above Chisos Crossing. The exact location of the crossing is not known, but I suggest it was about a mile west of the old Johnson Ranch site, either just below today's river gauging station on the American side, or a little farther down at the mouth of the Mexican arroyo La Saladita. That location is about right for Langberg's two leagues (by air) from Chisos Crossing and fits with Parry's statement about the "first junction with the river" being "just above Vado Ponce."

After the Chandler party reached the river, they moved another four miles upstream to camp (#17) on the Mexican side, near today's abandoned Rancho de Enmedio, which is a mile above the mouth of Smoky Creek in Big Bend National Park. Parry mentioned volcanic rock exposures on the trail up to their camp, which confirms they traveled along the river above today's site of the old Johnson ranch house because volcanic outcrops along the Mexican side do not begin until one mile above the site of the ranch house. From there, volcanic rocks occur near the river, off and on, for more than twenty miles up to a point just below the river exit from Santa Elena Canyon.

Connecting the Surveys above and below Santa Elena Canyon

The long detour around Santa Elena Canyon, during which the party did no surveying of their route, left Chandler with the problem of how to tie his traverse survey of the river above the canyon with his new survey below the canyon. There are no surveying notes to document what they actually did because of Emory's decree that all field notes be destroyed after the final boundary maps were prepared in 1856.[98] However, Parry's journal describes the surveyors' activities. He reported that they left camp #17 on October 7, crossed the Rio Grande to the American side, and walked four miles upstream so they could "view" the exit of Santa Elena Canyon: "the point above being connected by triangulation."[99] This confirms that the surveyors had earlier connected the location of the exit of the canyon into the triangulation net they had extended downstream from Comanche Crossing. Their plan must have been to reach a point in the valley downstream from the canyon exit where they had an unobstructed view back to the triangulation station on the top of the mesa so they could direct their instruments to that point from below, and with an additional bearing to another landmark—perhaps Emory Peak—in their view to the east, triangulate the location of the new station on the river below Santa Elena Canyon.

I assume Chandler tied the stations above and below the canyon with accuracy, consistent with the excellent surveying he demonstrated above Santa Elena Canyon and along the river for the thirty miles below the canyon. Yet, the extreme western portion of Chandler's Boundary Map 20, which should document the success of his triangulation tie between Map 21 on the west and Map 20 adjoining on the east, shows an absurd river track. It shows the river below the canyon exit flowing in a smooth arc to the southeast, extending only four miles to a triangular-shaped sandbar on the American side of the channel, whereas the actual distance from the canyon along the meandering river to that sandbar, still seen on modern maps, is eleven miles. Seven miles of river are missing from Chandler's Map 20! The sandbar was three river miles upstream from survey camp #17 and just south of the hill the surveyors likely used to take a compass bearing to the canyon exit (figure 21).

At first glance, this anomaly seemed to be a single extraordinary mistake in triangulation, yet it was much too far out of character with their accurate work in the area. Even the most junior survey helper, using the sun for a compass and guessing at the distance to the canyon exit from their triangulation station below the canyon, could have made a more accurate map. There must be another explanation for what appears to be an error.

An arbitrary location "adjustment" by the makers of the final set of boundary maps appears to be the source of this anomaly. Why an adjustment would be applied at this particular location along the western edge of Boundary Map 20 is not known. Perhaps it was because the American mapmakers could make an adjustment to Map 20 without having to reconcile their action with a map produced by the Mexican surveyors. The Mexican Commission did not survey the Rio Grande boundary across more than five hundred miles of the river extending from near Laredo, Texas, on the lower river, up through the Upper Canyons of the Rio Grande, thirty miles downstream from Presidio, Texas. Thus there were no Mexican maps to compare with American maps across a sequence of thirteen adjoining boundary maps.[100]

The need to make adjustments during the preparation of the final set of boundary maps was inevitable. US surveying parties generated twenty-nine separate and detailed boundary maps along the Rio Grande covering more than one thousand miles of river from the Gulf of Mexico to the New Mexico Territory. Many different surveying parties did the fieldwork over a period of three years, and it was up to five years before the final map set was prepared in Washington, DC. Yet all the maps in the final set had to fit together perfectly to show a single uninterrupted boundary line. As will be discussed later, in part II on the Michler Survey, the Map 20 adjustment is minor compared to what was needed to resolve a large disconnect in Map 17 at the junction of the Chandler and Michler Surveys in the Lower Canyons of the Rio Grande.

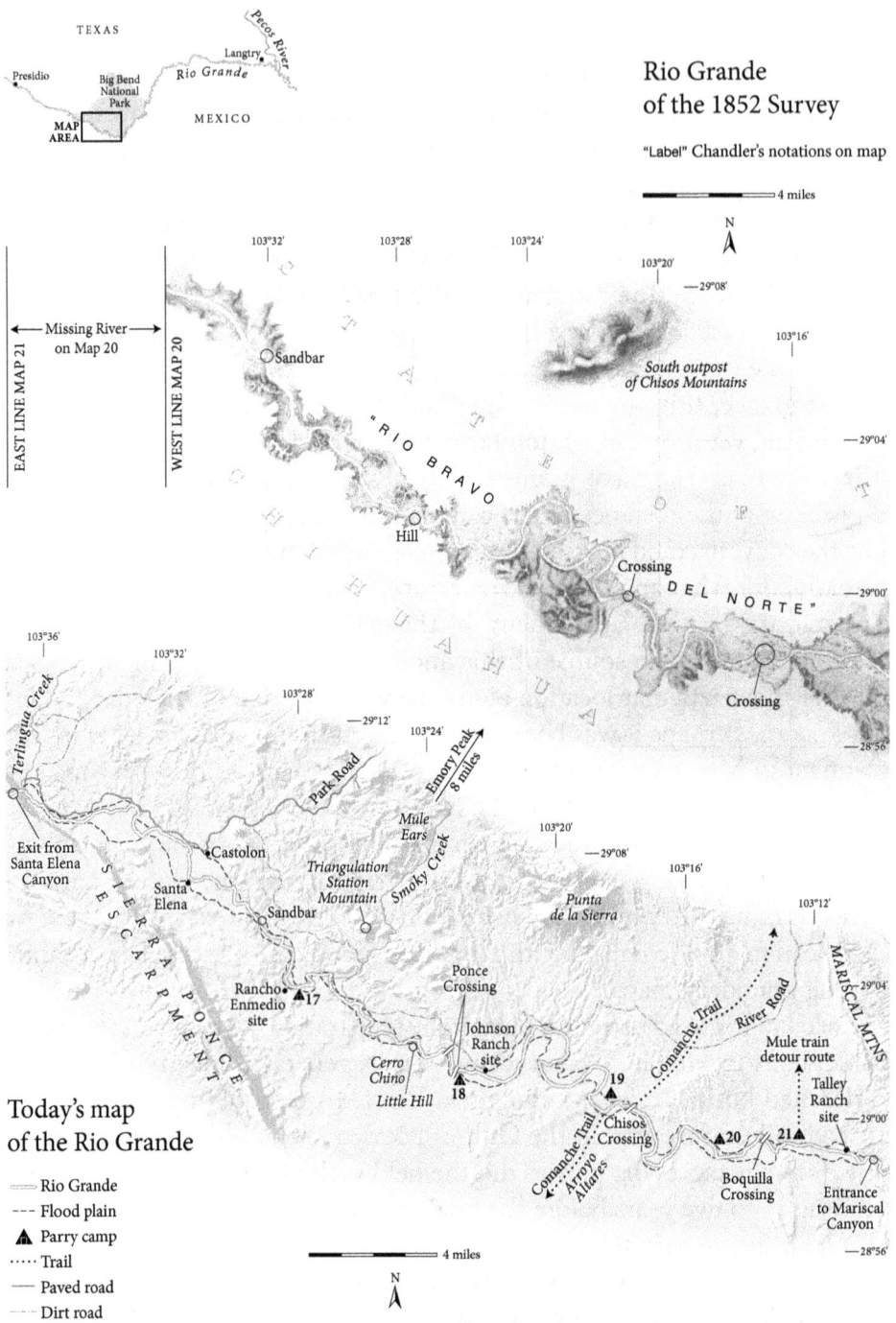

FIGURE 21. **River Trace Comparison: Exit of Santa Elena Canyon to Mariscal Canyon.** The river trace on the western half of Boundary Map 20 and on a modern topographic map for the area from the exit of Santa Elena Canyon to the entrance to Mariscal Canyon. An arbitrary shift of Chandler's Map 20 by mapmakers who moved it several miles to the northwest during final map preparations has resulted in the telescoping of Map 20 at its western edge and the absence of miles of the actual river trace on the Chandler map. Boundary Map 20, National Archives. Map by Carol Zuber-Mallison.

The map adjustment can be quantified by an analysis of the differences in the positions of landmarks displayed on Map 20 versus their true positions as shown on modern maps. This analysis indicates the adjustment made was to shift the entirety of Map 20 to the west 4.6 miles and to the north 2.2 miles. To remove the resulting overlap with the adjoining Map 21, the mapmaker then "erased" the column of overlap at the western edge of Map 20 and connected the now "dangling" trace of the river channel to the Santa Elena exit channel by drawing a smooth arc. There was no impact on Map 21, lying to the west, but landmarks on the repositioned Map 20, lying to the east, were more than 5 miles too close to landmarks of Map 21, and 11 miles of meandering river were compressed to 1 mile of fantasy.

Longitude and Latitude Position on Boundary Maps versus True Position

When Chandler began his survey at Presidio del Norte, he anchored his starting location to the "known" longitude and latitude of Major Emory's observatory across the river from Presidio del Norte. We know today that Emory's latitude location, based on his celestial observations, was near dead-on, but his longitude determination turned out to be 1.5 miles too far west (see table 2). By the time Chandler's surveyors worked their way downriver to the exit of Santa Elena Canyon 70 miles below the observatory, they had overestimated the distance traveled by almost 4 miles and showed the canyon exit location to be 1.6 miles too far east and 2 miles too far south. We can see from the table that with the arbitrary shift of the entire Map 20 to the northwest, made in 1857 during drafting of the final maps in Washington, DC, the mapmakers overcorrected, and the new adjusted locations show that the landmarks lying just below the canyon exit on Map 20 became 3 miles too far west and about a quarter mile too far north. Knowing the starting location error for the western edge of Boundary Map 20 was now 3 miles too far west is helpful. As one moves along the survey downriver from Santa Elena Canyon the relative accuracy of the point-to-point locations of landmarks on Chandler's Map 20 can be checked by noting whether the mapped longitude of his landmarks holds close to 3 miles too far west and the latitude remains near dead-on.

On the day the surveyors walked upriver to take a bearing to the canyon exit, Parry walked to a hill near camp and sketched his view of Emory Peak to the northeast. Chandler included this sketch in his narrative in the Emory Report, titling it "Mount Emory–Los Chisos mountains–Rio Bravo del Norte."[101] Elements of this sketch—the river coursing away from Parry (flowing northeast) in the foreground then turning right (southeast); the prominence of Emory Peak; the abrupt rise of the Punta de la Sierra (point of the mountains) ridge above the gently sloping terraces in the right middle ground—all fit a view from the hills on the Mexican side of the river near survey camp #17. This view of Emory Peak, sixteen miles away, looks almost directly over the scenic and distinctive Mule Ear Peaks, seven miles away, but they were not in Parry's view, being hidden behind the flank of (today's) Triangulation Station Mountain, rising above three thousand feet only three miles from where Parry was standing (figure 22).

In his journal, Parry described his view of the Chisos Mountains: "Northeast of our camp is the Chisos range forming a high broken ridge—rising up to basaltic peaks—see figure 13."[102] This reference by Parry to "figure 13" indicates that he was making a sketch of the range on paper separate from his notebook. None of the many rough sketches in the pages of his notebook are numbered. Neither Parry's original "figures" nor any landscape drawing later converted to a woodcut for the Emory Report were found in the Parry Papers at Iowa State. Most likely they, too, were destroyed after being used for woodcut illustrations in the final report, along with other "figures" that did not reach the woodcut stage. I suggest that Parry's "figure 13" was the original sketch for the woodcut landscape of the Chisos Mountains shown in the Emory Report (see figure 22).

After two nights at camp #17, the mule train broke camp and, "forced from the river by exposures of igneous rock" (Cerro Chino), traveled southeast on the Mexican side. They camped on the river, eight miles below their earlier camp and near Ponce Crossing on "a fine bed of grama grass." A likely spot for this camp (#18) is a river flat just below the mouth of Arroyo La Saladita on the Mexican side, three-quarters of a mile upstream from the old Johnson Ranch site.

Once past the arbitrarily compressed map section at the western margin of Map 20, Chandler produced an excellent map down to the entrance to Mariscal Canyon (see figure 21). This section of river, shown in the western half of Map 20, displays an accurate trace of the river channel. Where islands are shown, the side with the deeper channel is indicated, and topographic detail along the banks is excellent. The map even shows an isolated small hill of volcanic rock (fifteen by forty yards) that can be seen on the Mexican bank in satellite images taken today; it lies 2.3 miles west of the Johnson Ranch site in Big Bend National

Mount Emory—Los Chisos mountains—Rio Bravo del Norte.

FIGURE 22. **View of the Chisos Mountains.** Above is a landscape drawing by Parry of the Chisos Mountains, looking northeast from his camp #17 on the Mexican bank of the Rio Grande. Below is a recent photo taken from a point along Parry's same line of sight but closer to Emory Peak. The peak is the central high point on the horizon in both images. In the photo, the Mule Ear Peaks in the foreground form a U-shaped gunsight framing Emory Peak in the distance. The Mule Ear Peaks are not in Parry's drawing because his view of the "Ears" was blocked by his lower elevation on the river and the intervening Triangulation Station Mountain lying to his front. Emory Report, 83. Photograph by the author.

Park. The accuracy and detail level of the map indicates that the surveyors took advantage of the open country with good river access to build a careful traverse survey along the banks of the river and recorded bearings from their traverse stations to local landmarks such as the small hill so as to accurately position them on the boundary map.

Chisos Crossing

On October 9, Chandler and the surveyors moved down the Rio Grande by boat, while Parry and the escort moved their camp seven miles downriver. The mule train traveled across open river terraces about a half mile from the river itself. This more direct route avoided the dense brush and frequent changes in direction of the river channel as it meandered across the wide floodplain. They camped (#19) at a river crossing near the remains of a large Indian camp. Parry and Green called this crossing Vado de Fleche (ford of the arrows). Green reported that the ford was "two days march" below the mouth of Santa Elena Canyon.[103] This was just a rough guess by Green based on what the surveyors told him. He did not see the canyon exit, since his closest camp had been fourteen trail miles downstream, halfway between the canyon exit and Vado de Fleche.

Green and Parry's Vado de Fleche—twenty-two air miles but thirty-five river miles from Santa Elena Canyon—was the same crossing used a year earlier by the Mexican colonel Langberg on his way from the village of San Carlos to the ruins of Presidio San Vicente, but Langberg called this *vado* (ford) "los Chisos" (the Chisos). Historically there have been at least nine variations of the name used for this crossing of the Rio Grande along the Comanche Trail into Mexico. In chronological order they are: Paso de los Chisos, 1805; los Chisos, 1851; Vado de Fleche, 1852; El Vado Chisos, 1961; Paso de Chisos, 1966; Paso del Chisos, 1968; Chisos Ford, 1979; Vado de Chisos, 2008; and Chisos Crossing, which I will use.[104]

Chisos Crossing in the Historical Record

Both Parry and Langberg noted that the crossing was on a heavily traveled Comanche trail into Mexico. Langberg described it in 1851 as "being wider than any highway—so well worn that it seems [as] though engineers purposely built it."[105] Why the Chandler party, which was following Langberg's map, did not use Langberg's name for the crossing is a puzzle. Perhaps Vado de Fleche, used by Lieutenant Green, was the name provided by the Mexican guide he hired in San Carlos. Parry's journal entries on distance, the route description from the last camp before the crossing, and his description of a loose and rocky bed in the river fit the crossing Langberg used at the mouth of the Mexican Arroyo Altares. The gravel thrown into the river by the arroyo during flash floods form the shallow waters of the crossing. Langberg had reached this crossing after having stopped the day before to water his animals at the marsh farther up Arroyo Altares, about twelve miles southwest of the Rio Grande. In his approach to the Rio Grande, Langberg had traveled east from San Carlos, hit the Comanche trail above the marsh, turned left down the trail to the marsh, and continued along the trail on terraces above the arroyo down to the river. Support for calling the mouth of Arroyo Altares the location of Langberg's crossing comes from his note that his scouts found two other river crossings near the Chisos Crossing: Ponze, about two leagues (5.3 miles) upstream, and Boquilla, an equal distance downstream. Langberg's Boquilla crossing was the unnamed Indian crossing noted by Parry when he was six trail miles down the river from Chisos Crossing.

Langberg's Vado Ponze and Parry's Ponce Crossing were the same place; its exact location is not clear, but Parry's camp #18, which was just below his Ponce Crossing, was five air miles from Chisos Crossing. Thus, it appears likely that the Ponce Crossing was approximately three-quarters of a mile west of today's site of the old Johnson Ranch. Today, the name Ponze survives in Cuesta de Ponze and Sierra Ponce—two different names used for the same massive limestone escarpment on the Mexican side that parallels the river and runs for twenty miles southeast from the exit of Santa Elena Canyon.

While Colonel Langberg was camped at Chisos Crossing on October 7 and 8, 1851, one of his men made a sketch of the view to the north, which was preserved as one of the watercolors attached to Langberg's official report of his expedition and labeled "Vista de la Cierra de las Chisos" (figure 23).[106] The distinctive mountain profile is recognizable as the southern outpost of the Chisos Mountains, known today as Punta de la Sierra (point of the mountain). This sketch supports the locating of Chisos Crossing directly south of the Punta de la Sierra. The Punta—six miles north of the crossing yet rising two thousand feet above it—is often photographed by travelers along the backcountry River Road that runs between the Castolon Store and Rio Grande Village in Big Bend National Park. The surveyor M. T. W. Chandler clearly shows the Punta de la Sierra on his Boundary Map 20, unnamed yet correct in form, direction, and distance from the river. This was likely a landmark he used for triangulation surveying.

Figure 23. **Punta de la Sierra from Chisos Crossing.** Two views of today's Punta de la Sierra—Point of the Mountain. The Punta is a southern outpost of the larger Chisos Mountain range. In these views, the main Chisos range is hidden behind the Punta. The distinctive profile of the Punta is well shown in the landscape drawing, which includes, at the far left, the distant Mule Ear Peaks. The drawing "Lámina de la sierra de los Chisos" (illustration of the Chisos Mountains), is a watercolor contained in Colonel Langberg's report of his 1851 expedition. Below is a modern photo looking north from the gravel terrace just above Chisos Crossing on the Rio Grande. The close similarity of the mountain profiles, including the Mule Ear Peaks, supports the conclusion that the crossing that Langberg called "Los Chisos" is the same as today's Chisos Crossing near the abandoned "Woodson Place" in Big Bend National Park. Image of the watercolor courtesy of Solveig Turpin from the original Enrique Barchesky watercolor at Yale Collection of Western Americana, Beinecke Rare Book and Manuscript Library, Yale University, New Haven, Connecticut. Photograph by the author.

Other historical accounts that refer to Chisos Crossing include Ralph Smith's 1961 article "The Comanche Bridge between Oklahoma and Mexico, 1843–1844," wherein Smith included a map showing the location of El Vado Chisos. While his small map does not allow a precise location fix, the distance of about ten miles west of the apex of the Big Bend of the Rio Grande fits my suggested location. Smith states this was the most used Comanche crossing in the period from 1840 to 1870. It was their usual route when traveling south to the Bolson de Mapimi, a huge region in western Coahuila and eastern Chihuahua characterized by intermountain basins with springs and internal surface drainage forming lakes and dry lakes. This region, which begins about fifty miles south of the crossing and extends south for another two hundred miles, was a favorite staging area for Comanche raiding parties into the Mexican states of Durango and San Luis Potosí (see figure 6). Raiding parties often arrived in the fall and spent the winter camped there.[107]

In October 1848, the Hays-Highsmith Expedition had crossed the Rio Grande at Chisos Crossing. That expedition had been organized and financed by San Antonio businessmen who wanted to find a better wagon road to El Paso del Norte.[108] The expedition's leader was retired Texas Ranger John Coffee (Jack) Hays, who put together a group of about thirty-five men, including the businessman Samuel Maverick and the frontiersman Richard (Dick) Howard, the namesake of Howard's Well, an important spring on the San Antonio Road.[109] Hays left San Antonio on August 27, 1848, and was joined en route by an escort of thirty-five Texas Rangers led by Captain Sam Highsmith.[110]

Samuel Maverick's daily journal of the expedition records their route (see figure 6). After a wandering start, they joined a wide and well-used Comanche trail and turned south near today's north entrance to Big Bend National Park at Persimmon Gap. Moving south, they stopped at several water holes, first Bone Springs, then forty-two miles southeast to a spring, probably Willow Springs, then southwest to Glenn Springs. They continued southwest down a dry arroyo to reach the Rio Grande at Chisos Crossing. Most arroyos coming to the river on the American side in this area of Big Bend National Park flow straight south, but an unnamed arroyo, just west of the ruins of the old "Woodson Place," runs southwest, hitting the river across from the mouth of the Arroyo Altares on the Mexican side. Maverick said their crossing was two hundred to three hundred *varas* (185–280 yards) above the arroyo he had followed in his approach to the Rio Grande.[111] Today, the shallow-water gravel flats that form the crossing start about three hundred yards upriver from an arroyo near the ruins of the old Woodson ranch house. This southwest-flowing arroyo lines up with the northeast-flowing Arroyo Altares across the river on the Mexican side. This lineation led the makers of a 1952 geologic map to show a possible fault, which they indicated by a line on their map that connected the two arroyos and ran for several miles, both ways, away from the river.[112] In any event, the paired southwest-northeast trend of the two arroyos formed a natural pathway for the Comanche trail to cross the Rio Grande. These arroyos fit the direction the Comanche needed to travel as they moved between the freshwater sources of the Arroyo Altares marsh in Mexico and Glenn Springs in the United States, both a one-day trip from the Rio Grande.

After crossing the Rio Grande, Maverick reported in his journal that the group traveled south-southwest on the Comanche Trail, then left it and turned west for thirty miles to reach the Mexican village of San Carlos. A distance of thirty miles to San Carlos shows that Maverick left the Comanche Trail near the marsh on Arroyo Altares and supports the idea that they had earlier crossed the river at Chisos Crossing, which was back down their trail at the mouth of Arroyo Altares. Jack Hays, in his report to Texas Ranger Colonel Peter Bell, said they crossed the Rio Grande thirty-five miles below San Carlos (Chisos Crossing is actually thirty-seven air miles).[113]

Some published trail maps show that the Hays party crossed the Rio Grande farther downstream, near the old Presidio San Vicente. But Maverick's journal said San Vicente was three leagues below their crossing (actually six leagues). A crossing at San Vicente would have required Hays to travel south-southeast (not south-southwest) as they moved away from the river to avoid the Sierra San Vicente, and then turn west to reach the village of San Carlos. This would have meant a total trail distance of about one hundred miles beyond the crossing, rather than the forty-eight trail miles to San Carlos reported by Maverick.[114]

Notations on detailed maps in Louis Aulbach's 2007 canoeist guide for the Rio Grande show a crossing he calls Paseo de Chisos (Pass of the Chisos) at the location of Chisos Crossing, just downstream from the mouth of Arroyo Altares and upstream from the old Woodson ranch house. Aulbach confirms this was a major crossing of the Comanche Trail. In a 1993 master's thesis on the history of the Johnson Ranch, Glen Willeford also confirms that Paso de los Chisos was near the Woodson ranch site.[115]

Natividad Lujan, who lived in the village of San Carlos during the second half of the 1800s and whose stories of Big Bend history were recorded by the historian O. W. Williams, said that Paso de Chisos (Chisos Crossing) was about forty miles (actually thirty-seven) from San Carlos and was located at the boundary

Part I: The 1852 Chandler Surveying Party

of the Mexican states of Chihuahua and Coahuila. Lujan said the Comanche would usually cross at Lajitas, Texas (Comanche Crossing), on the way south to Durango, Mexico, and then cross at Paso de Chisos on the return north. He said they wanted to be farther from the Mexican soldiers at Presidio del Norte on the return trip because at that time they were traveling slowly with a large number of stolen mules and horses.[116]

It has been reported that the boundary line between the Mexican states of Chihuahua and Coahuila intersects the Rio Grande at Chisos Crossing. Early maps are inconsistent in their placement of the state boundary line. A map made by a joint Mexican-American effort in 1993 (the Joint Operations Graphic [JOG] series) shows the Mexican states' boundary intersecting the river 1.7 air miles northwest of the mouth of Arroyo Altares at a point on the river that does not appear favorable for a crossing.[117] A later map made by the International Boundary and Water Commission (IBWC) in 2008 shows the Chihuahua-Coahuila boundary (correctly, I believe) at the mouth of Arroyo Altares, but retains an old Vado de Chisos label at the old boundary location upstream. I think the Vado de Chisos label on that map is an artifact taken from older maps, and that the correct Chisos Crossing is just below the mouth of Arroyo Altares on the Mexican side and just above the Woodson ranch house on the American side.[118]

Any question of the location of the Chisos Crossing should have been settled by Chandler's Boundary Map 20, but his map shows neither the crossing nor a clear Indian trail leading to or from it, even though the journals of Sam Maverick, Colonel Langberg, and Parry all reported a prominent trail at the crossing. Chandler's map does show a wide river channel marked with a stipple pattern at what should be the crossing site, indicating shallow water favorable for a crossing.

Chisos Crossing to Mariscal Canyon

The Chandler party spent the tenth of October bringing across most of the animals and pack train supplies. A number of the animals were taken above the ford to swim across so as to avoid injury in the shallow ford "full of loose rocks." The main camp tents remained on the Mexican side another night; the baggage was floated over in the rubber boats early the next morning.

At this point in his narrative report to Emory, and included in the final Emory Report, Chandler discussed two prominent peaks used for reference points during his survey in the Big Bend area. He said these two landmarks were distinct and almost always visible. The first was the highest point in the Chisos Mountains, for which he proposed the name Mount Emory. This is known today as Emory Peak—the highest point in the Big Bend area at 7,825 feet—and it is fifteen miles north of Chandler's camp.[119]

It is odd that Chandler chose this point in his narrative to discuss Mount Emory. He could not see Emory Peak from the camp at Chisos Crossing, as it was hidden behind the high South Rim escarpment of the Chisos Mountains. For about forty-five miles of river—from just below the Johnson Ranch site down to the area of Langford's Hot Springs (just upstream of the Rio Grande Village campground of Big Bend National Park)—Emory Peak is hidden behind the intervening South Rim escarpment. The rim, rising above 7,400 feet, rings the peak on the south and is only a little over a mile from it. For triangulation landmarks to the north across this section of river, Chandler must have used other distinctive outpost peaks of the Chisos Mountains, such as Triangulation Station Mountain, Punta de la Sierra, or Elephant Tusk Mountain.

The other prominent landmark peak, noted but not named or described by Chandler, would have been in his view to the east in the Sierra del Carmen mountain front, near the river but on the Mexican side, thirty-three miles east of Chisos Crossing. This is Pico Cerda (bristle peak), a singular tower that rises from the high limestone escarpment of the Sierra del Carmen range. Although it has been known by a variety of names, including Shot Tower, the peak is located in Mexico and the official name as shown on current Mexican maps is Pico Cerda, so I use that here.

What's in a Name? Pico Cerda or Shot Tower?

Pico Cerda is a favorite of photographers today and the official name of the Mexican peak that can be seen in almost all photos of the mountain front taken looking east from Big Bend National Park (see figure 25). It reaches an elevation of 7,024 feet and is shown on Mexican topographic maps as Pico Cerda but is sometimes called El Pico, Shot Tower, or Schott Tower by local residents. Parry called it simply "the peak of Mount Carmel." The geologist R. T. Hill called it "The Boquillas Finger" when he made his historic boat trip through the Big Bend canyons in 1899.[1] Charles Smith, in a 1970 report on the geology on the Mexican side of the river, called it "Pico Puerto Rico" for the now abandoned Puerto Rico mine lying two miles southwest of the peak.[2] The legendary Big Bend National Park geologist

Ross Maxwell thought this landmark was called Shot Tower because early Texas land surveyors used the tower as a reference point by taking a "shot" (bearing) to the tower with their surveying instrument.[3] Virginia Madison and Hallie Stillwell, in their book on Big Bend names, *How Come It's Called That?*, suggest it may be called Shot Tower because it looks similar to the towers used to make lead shot.[4] The industrialist, photographer, and river runner Henry B. du Pont, who floated the Rio Grande Canyons in 1940, 1941, 1946, and 1952, labeled this peak "Shot Tower" on a photograph he contributed to his friend J. O. Langford for his 1952 book, *Big Bend: A Homesteader's Story*.[5] Du Pont may have been the first to note that the limestone spire looked like a shot tower. E. I. du Pont de Nemours and Company (usually shortened to DuPont) was an important supplier of ammunition, and Henry du Pont, vice president of the company, would have been familiar with the process of making lead shot by dropping molten lead from a tall cooling tower. The geologists Peter Flawn and Ross Maxwell called it "Shot Tower" in their 1958 article on the Mexican Sierra del Carmen.[6] The name "Schott Tower" appears to have evolved from Shot Tower. Some have suggested the peak was named for the talented artist and boundary surveyor Arthur Schott, who some have thought was a member of the Chandler party and the author of a landscape drawing showing the tower. But Charles Parry made the landscape drawings of the tower, and throughout the time of the Chandler Survey, Schott was working far downriver, leading his own survey party up the Rio Grande between Fort Duncan and the mouth of the Pecos River.[7]

Notes

1. Robert T. Hill, "Running the Cañons of the Rio Grande," *Century Magazine*, January 1901, 383.
2. Charles I. Smith, *Lower Cretaceous Stratigraphy, Northern Coahuila, Mexico*, Report of Investigations No. 65 (Austin: Bureau of Economic Geology, University of Texas, 1970), 101.
3. Ross A. Maxwell and John W. Dietrich, *Geology of the Big Bend Area of Texas: Field Trip Guidebook* (Midland: West Texas Geological Society, 1972), 105.
4. Virginia A. Madison and Hallie Stillwell, *How Come It's Called That? Place Names in the Big Bend Country* (Marathon, TX: Iron Mountain Press, 1997), 44.
5. J. O. Langford, *Big Bend: A Homesteaders Story*, with Fred Gipson (Austin: University of Texas Press, 1952), 88.

6. Peter T. Flawn and Ross A. Maxwell, "Metamorphic Rocks in Sierra del Carmen, Coahuila, Mexico," *Bulletin: American Association of Petroleum Geologists* 42, no. 9 (September 1958): 2247.
7. Schott to Emory, San Felipe Spring (Del Rio, TX), October 1, 1852, William H. Emory Papers, Beinecke Rare Book and Manuscript Division, Yale University, WA MSS S-1187, New Haven, CT.

On the morning of October 11, the mule train left camp on the American side just upstream from Chisos Crossing. A short distance east of the camp it crossed the well-beaten main Comanche Trail leading to and from the crossing. After an easy day's travel of five miles along the elevated terraces above the river, the mule train came back down to the river to camp (#20) with the surveyors.

Writing in his journal that evening, Parry noted that during the day they had passed sections of river bottom with "plots suitable for cultivation" located in a twenty-mile section of Rio Grande bottomland characterized by large meander loops and wide floodplains that extend from the old Johnson Ranch site down to another early ranch—the "Talley Place"—at the entrance to Mariscal Canyon.[120] This section has more trees and grassland than the steep and barren banks farther up the river or the rocky canyon below. Lieutenant Green and others suggested this was a good area for an army outpost.

Lieutenant Green Recommends an Army Post on the Rio Grande

In December 1852, after the Chandler Survey was aborted and the surveyors and the army escort had walked across interior Mexico to Fort Duncan on the lower Rio Grande, Lieutenant Green sent a mission report to his commander in Washington, DC. In his report, Green recommended that a new military post be located near the river flats below Chisos Crossing, making his case in some detail.

Unfortunately, Green had failed to sign his report from Fort Duncan, and by the time it was returned to him for signature, the boundary survey had been temporarily discontinued and Green and his men had been posted to San Antonio. Before returning his now signed mission report to Washington in June 1853, Green added the note that Colonel Joseph E. Johnston of the

Army Corps of Topographical Engineers, also stationed in San Antonio, shared his opinion of the favorability of this site.

It is unlikely that Johnston had actually seen the location recommended by Green. Johnston's sketch maps of his Trans-Pecos expeditions in 1849 and 1850 show his nearest approaches to the Rio Grande in the Big Bend were Fort Leaton, seventy-five miles to the northwest, and Cherry Springs, seventy-five miles to the north. Nevertheless, Johnston may have had a favorable opinion of the Chisos site based on conversation with his friend Richard A. Howard, also a San Antonio resident, who had seen the Chisos Crossing area. Howard had been Johnston's guide for his 1850 reconnaissance as well as the guide for the 1849 Hays-Highsmith party that crossed the Rio Grande at Chisos Crossing on their way to the village of San Carlos, Mexico.

Later, in July 1860, Lieutenant William Echols, on a reconnaissance mission using camels, reached the Rio Grande at the exit of Santa Elena Canyon and recommended that an army post be located in a different section of the wide floodplain near the present Castolon Store in Big Bend National Park, about twenty miles upstream of Green's recommended site.[1] No army post was ever established in Green's recommended area, but a temporary army encampment named Camp Santa Helena was occupied in 1919–20 at Echols's site near Castolon.[2]

NOTES

1. William H. Echols, "Diary of a Reconnoissance [sic] of the Country Between the El Paso Road and the Rio Grande River," 36th Cong., 2d sess., 1861, SED 1, 48.
2. Clifford B. Casey, *Soldiers, Ranchers and Miners in the Big Bend* (Washington, DC: Office of Archeology and Historic Preservation, Division of History, National Park Service, 1969), 22–25.

On the morning of October 12, Parry and the escort left their camp (#20) and started across a dusty, mile-wide flat paralleling the river channel. After a short distance, they reached another Indian crossing: "The river spread out in a variety of channels over a pebbly bottom—the lower [river] bottom grown with cottonwood, willow and dense undergrowth of *Aster spinosus*" (also known as Mexican devil weed, a vine with white flowers).[121] Chandler's Boundary Map 20 shows a low island mid river with channels on both sides.[122] This must be the Boquilla Crossing that Langberg said was about two leagues (5.3 miles) downriver from

Chisos Crossing. Parry's trail distance of six miles from his crossing site confirms that the Chandler party and Langberg crossed the Rio Grande at Chisos Crossing.

After a short journey of three miles beyond Boquilla, the mule train stopped to make camp (#21). They had reached their point of departure for a long detour around Mariscal Canyon. On this night, both surveyors and escort would be in the same camp, which Parry noted was three miles above the entrance to Mariscal Canyon.

Mariscal Canyon

Parry called this two-part canyon complex San Vicente Canyon. Later, R. T. Hill called it Big San Vicente and Little San Vicente. Today, the larger, upstream canyon is referred to as Mariscal Canyon, and the downstream one, as San Vicente Canyon. Both were formed by the Rio Grande, which cut its way through anticlinal limestone mountains. A valley—the Solis Graben—separates the two canyons.

When the Chandler party first left Presidio del Norte, the operating plan had been to carry enough provisions and shelter in the four boats so that the surveyors could work on the river for a week without needing to meet with the mule train carrying the bulk of their supplies. That plan had, of course, come unraveled on the second day out of Presidio del Norte when they lost the two big wooden boats. Later, the surveyors deflated their rubber boats to carry them on pack mules so the entire party could travel together during the long detour around Santa Elena Canyon. To get around the barrier of Mariscal Canyon, the surveyors and the mule train would have to follow different routes. The surveyors entered the canyon in the rubber boats, and the mule train detoured away from the river and mountains to meet them at the canyon exit. At this first major canyon below Santa Elena, Chandler had to change the way he operated. The rubber boats could carry only enough food for one day and only the most minimal shelter needed for a night. With no place to resupply on the frontier, the surveyors had needed to stay in daily contact with the mule train. This method was problematic because the mule train could not follow the surveyors through even a moderate canyon. The mules had to make an overland detour and come back to the river below the canyon. If the detour took more than a day, the surveyors would be short of food and shelter. Such an operation was a risky game when the length of the canyons and the detour routes were unexplored. Once Chandler's boats entered

Part I: The 1852 Chandler Surveying Party

a steep canyon, they were committed to going all the way through because the surveyors could not paddle upstream or climb out.

The party knew from their copy of Colonel Langberg's map that from the entrance to the Mariscal–San Vicente canyons the detour trail around them to the old Presidio San Vicente below the canyon was about eight leagues (twenty-four miles). They most likely assumed the distance along the river to the canyon was a bit shorter, and hoped that, with luck, they could float through it in one long day. But once the Chandler party went beyond these two canyons, they would be entirely on their own. When they came to any new canyon, they would have no Langberg map, no Mexican guide, and no idea of the length of the canyon or the distance of the detour being taken by the mules. They would have to either stop and scout out a detour around the canyon and a suitable rendezvous point, or blindly enter it and hope Lieutenant Green would quickly find a route around the canyon. The need for the surveyors to rush all the way through a canyon in a single day or go hungry helps explain why the accuracy of their maps of the river channel inside large canyons is usually quite poor.

Both parties got an early start on October 13. Chandler's boats entered the canyon, and the mule train detoured north away from the river, guided by Langberg's map. The detour skirted the western side of Mariscal Mountain, then turned east around the northern tip of the mountain at the future site of the Mariscal quicksilver mine (mercury ore). Langberg called the curving shape of the route around the mountain the "turning of the mountain." The mule train then moved southeast and arrived back at the river to complete eighteen miles of detour and set up camp (#22) at the exit of San Vicente Canyon, about three miles upstream from the ruins of the old presidio. This camp was at or very near the present site of the ruins of the old "Rooney's Place" on the north bank of the river in Big Bend National Park.[123] Parry's description of the eastward-dipping rock exposures and the types of enclosed fossils he found near the camp show that he was on the Upper Cretaceous Boquillas formation, which is exposed at the Rooney site. (See the geologic time scale, table 1.) Here the mule train waited for the boats of the survey team to make their way through the canyons.[124]

The surveyors, however, did not arrive at the mule train camp at the end of the first day, as everyone had hoped. They were delayed by the overturning of one of the rubber boats, "scattering blankets and tents, mostly lost." They spent a rough night in the canyon with minimal food and shelter, but set out early on the second day and arrived at the rendezvous camp on the morning of October 14.[125]

The surveyors had floated eighteen miles through the double canyon, and it is assumed they kept rough notes of the course of the river using handheld compass headings and distance estimates; however, their map of the configuration of the river channel did not turn out well. A comment in Parry's journal implies Chandler himself may not have been on the river but instead hiked across the mountain above while his men passed below in the rubber boats. In any event, Boundary Map 20 shows a very simplified approximation of the river trace (figure 24). None of the Class II–III rapids that occur in the first three miles—Rock Slide, Tight Squeeze, Compton's—are shown on Chandler's map. A single line across the river near the correct location may represent the Class I Entrance Rapids. Well delineated by Chandler is the modern river runner's camping spot of "Cross Canyons," about three miles inside Mariscal Canyon where two small canyons enter from opposite sides. Good map detail for the first few miles of the canyon and lack of detail later may mean their boat wreck was early on the first day, and that after the delay of salvaging what they could from the wreck, they moved as fast as they could and paid little attention to mapping the river. The map does show the Solis Graben as a zone of low riverbanks separating the steep canyons of Mariscal and San Vicente.

The lack of accuracy in mapping the uninhabitable canyons may not have been an important concern to Chandler because he knew he could accurately reestablish his location on the river once he was beyond the canyon walls and had a clear distant view to triangulate his position using his landmarks in the Chisos Mountains to the north and Pico Cerda to the east. That he had good success doing this is demonstrated by the fact that his mapped location for the abandoned San Vicente Presidio just below the canyons is close to the true compass bearing and distance from the canyon entrance (within one degree of bearing and one mile of distance). In other words, Chandler's relative locations of his surveying lines above and below the canyon, while not exact, are very good, and fit his previously noted pattern of distance determinations that are usually 5–10 percent too long.

The first map to show an accurate trace of the river through Mariscal and San Vicente Canyons was not made until the early 1880s, when it was done by the Presidio County surveyor John Gano when he made the first land surveys in the area. Later, R. T. Hill, a professor at the University of Texas, made an excellent sketch map of the trace of the river in his notebook during his boat trip through the canyons in 1899.[126] Hill had been appointed to the new position of chair of the Geology Department at the University of Texas at Austin in 1888, but by 1890 he had resigned and returned to work for the United States Geological Survey.[127]

FIGURE 24. **River Trace Comparison: Mariscal Canyon to Hot Springs Canyon.** The river trace on the eastern half of Boundary Map 20 compared to a modern map. The accuracy of Map 20 is poor through Mariscal Canyon and the adjoining San Vicente Canyon, where the surveyors traveled by boat, but very good farther east where access to the river bank was favorable for traverse work by the surveyors. Boundary Map 20, National Archives. Map by Carol Zuber-Mallison.

We assume Hill's maps of the river were based on his careful notes of direction and distance while floating in his boat, but it is possible he had with him an early copy of the Gano map. His contacts at the university or the Texas General Land Office in Austin may have provided him a copy of that map.

At the Chandler Survey camp near Rooney's Place (#22), Parry walked about half a mile downstream to a low hogback ridge of Cretaceous rock at the river's edge to make a landscape sketch looking east from the American side to the distant Sierra del Carmen mountain front on the Mexican side. In this sketch titled "View of Presidio de San Vicente and Sierra Carmel [Sierra del Carmen]," the right turn of the river and the ruins of the Presidio San Vicente in the middle ground slightly to the right of Pico Cerda on the horizon fit the view from the hogback looking downriver toward the ruins of the old presidio (figure 25).[128]

On the fourteenth, the party remained an extra day in camp near Rooney's Place to refresh the surveyors. The following day, Parry's trail down the river passed the old presidio, but he did not cross the river to visit it. The Presidio San Vicente is the same vintage (1774–81) as the San Carlos Presidio he had visited earlier. The surveyors reported: "The walls are in pretty good preservation and the church is quite neat and in good repair—a note on the wall records that Colonel Langberg was there on October 9th, 1851 on his way to Santa Rosa." Today, it is difficult to recognize the outline of the old presidio because it sits among recently built ranch buildings on the outskirts of the Mexican village of San Vicente, Coahuila. With difficulty, some lineation of the original exterior walls can be viewed on Google Earth.[129]

When Parry passed the old presidio, he remarked: "At this point we leave Langberg's track which we have mainly followed before." This is one of the few references to the utility of the Langberg map. Chandler's Boundary Map 20 shows the location of Presidio San Vicente and two trails leading away from it. The trail labels must have been taken from Langberg's map, since the surveyors had no way to know where they led. The south trail is labeled "Trail to San Carlos," and the one to the northeast, "Trail to Santa Rosa." The south trail was an alternate and longer route to San Carlos that followed a route around the south end of Sierra San Vicente. Langberg and the Chandler mule train had both approached the old presidio via the shorter route from San Carlos that used Chisos Crossing and then went around the north end of Mariscal Mountain on the American side. Neither Chandler's map nor Parry's journal notes an Indian trail on the American side across from the old presidio even though several published early trail maps have shown a branch of the Comanche Trail coming to the river across from the

VIEW OF PRESIDIO DE SAN VICENTE AND SIERRA CARMEL.

FIGURE 25. **Sierra del Carmen Mountain Front.** Top: a sketch by Parry of his view looking east from his camp two miles west of the ruins of the 1770s vintage San Vicente Presidio. In the middle ground are the walls of the presidio. The Sierra del Carmen mountain front, including the sharp tower, Pico Cerda, are on the horizon, sixteen miles away. Below: a closer view of the Sierra del Carmen front and Pico Cerda from today's road to Boquillas Canyon. Emory Report, 2:59. Photograph by the author.

old presidio. This was likely an early branch of the Comanche Trail, blocked by construction of the presidio in 1774 and less traveled thereafter.

Langberg crossed the river to reach the presidio and mentioned the crossing was difficult, wider and deeper than the earlier Chisos Crossing.[130] On Chandler's map, the unlabeled crossing appears to be a half mile below the presidio where midchannel islands are shown. Today's San Vicente village crossing is 1.5 miles downstream from the presidio site and just downstream from the village of San Vicente, Coahuila.

Shortly after passing a point across the river from the old presidio, the escort stopped to camp (#23). They were just five miles from the previous night's camp and "a short distance above boquilla [the constriction] by which the river enters the Mount Carmel Cañon" (Boquillas Canyon). Actually, they were still more than ten river miles upstream from the canyon and near the site of the now abandoned early-1900s village of San Vicente, Texas. At this camp, Parry described his view of the massive Sierra del Carmen mountain front to the east as "picturesque—ridge broken by projecting points—separate pinnacles." Parry does not single out Pico Cerda, which would have been by far the most dominant pinnacle in his view.[131]

Parry left camp early on the morning of the sixteenth to explore down the river on the American side. He soon turned east with the river and came to the mouth of a wide arroyo (today named Tornillo Creek) coming down from the northwest to join the Rio Grande. Here he found fresh water at one spot in the otherwise dry gravel bed of the arroyo.

Moving farther down the north bank of the river, he observed, "A short distance below the arroyo, passing some projecting ledges I come to a most singular spring of clear water gushing out of the rock crevices directly on the river bank—looked inviting—but temperature I would guess is 170 deg.—its issue a brook tumbling into the turbid Rio Grande." This is an excellent description of the natural state of Langford's Hot Spring—a popular point of interest today when traveling the paved Big Bend National Park Road to the Rio Grande Village Campground. It is disappointing that Parry did not mention the signs that Indians often camped here, including mortar holes and the many pictographs still seen today on his "projecting ledges" near the spring.[132]

The mule train traveled along the hills above the river to detour around Hot Springs Canyon. After nine miles, they came back down to the river and camped (#24) on a wooded river flat that is today the site of the Rio Grande Village Campground. The men probably camped near the spring found at the east end

Part I: The 1852 Chandler Surveying Party   105

of the campground. They were three trail miles from the entrance to Boquillas Canyon, and the party spent four nights here waiting for the scouts to find a trail that would carry the mule train on a detour around the canyon. Parry and the surveyors noted several hot springs between their camp and the canyon entrance on both the American and Mexican sides of the river.

Boquillas Canyon

Parry used one of the "waiting days" at camp #24 to walk downriver and explore the entrance to Boquillas Canyon. Along the way, he noted the marshy springs on the Mexican side but did not go across to examine them. At the canyon entrance, he measured the walls to be 136 feet apart, wider than the earlier canyons, and he saw several sand beaches within the canyon, leading him to believe it would be less hazardous for the boats than earlier canyons had been.

While in the canyon, Parry had some excitement:

> I climbed the first high ridge some 500 feet above the river—I happened to cast my eye up to the opposite wall where there was a precipice some 800 feet above the river & was attracted by a strange object which I thought I could perceive to move. Not relishing the idea [of] being so close an object of observation of an Apache Indian, I backed out of view and then, looking up once more, the object had vanished. Having no arms & not caring to risk a fight, I streaked it back to camp & Indian or no Indian was glad to find shelter under the American flag.[133]

A woodcut showing the entrance to Boquillas Canyon is included in the final Emory Report in a section written by Parry and titled "General Description of the Country." This woodcut, "Entrance to the Cañon of Sierra Carmel [del Carmen]," was surely based on a sketch by Parry. It was included to illustrate the character of the major canyons of the Big Bend area. The woodcut takes some liberty in projection and scale, which makes the canyon appear more imposing than it really is. The view shows two Indians in the foreground, perhaps a tongue-in-cheek reference to "the Indian" Parry thought he saw in the cliffs above the entrance.[134]

Chandler's men produced a very good map of the eighteen-mile section of the Rio Grande between San Vicente and Boquillas Canyons. Access to the river was good, and they had ample time to do careful traverse surveying while waiting for the scouts to find a mule train detour around Boquillas Canyon. This section included the last ten miles of Boundary Map 20, ending in the small Hot Springs Canyon, followed on Boundary Map 19 by seven miles of river below Hot Springs Canyon and above the entrance to Boquillas Canyon (see figures 24 and 26).

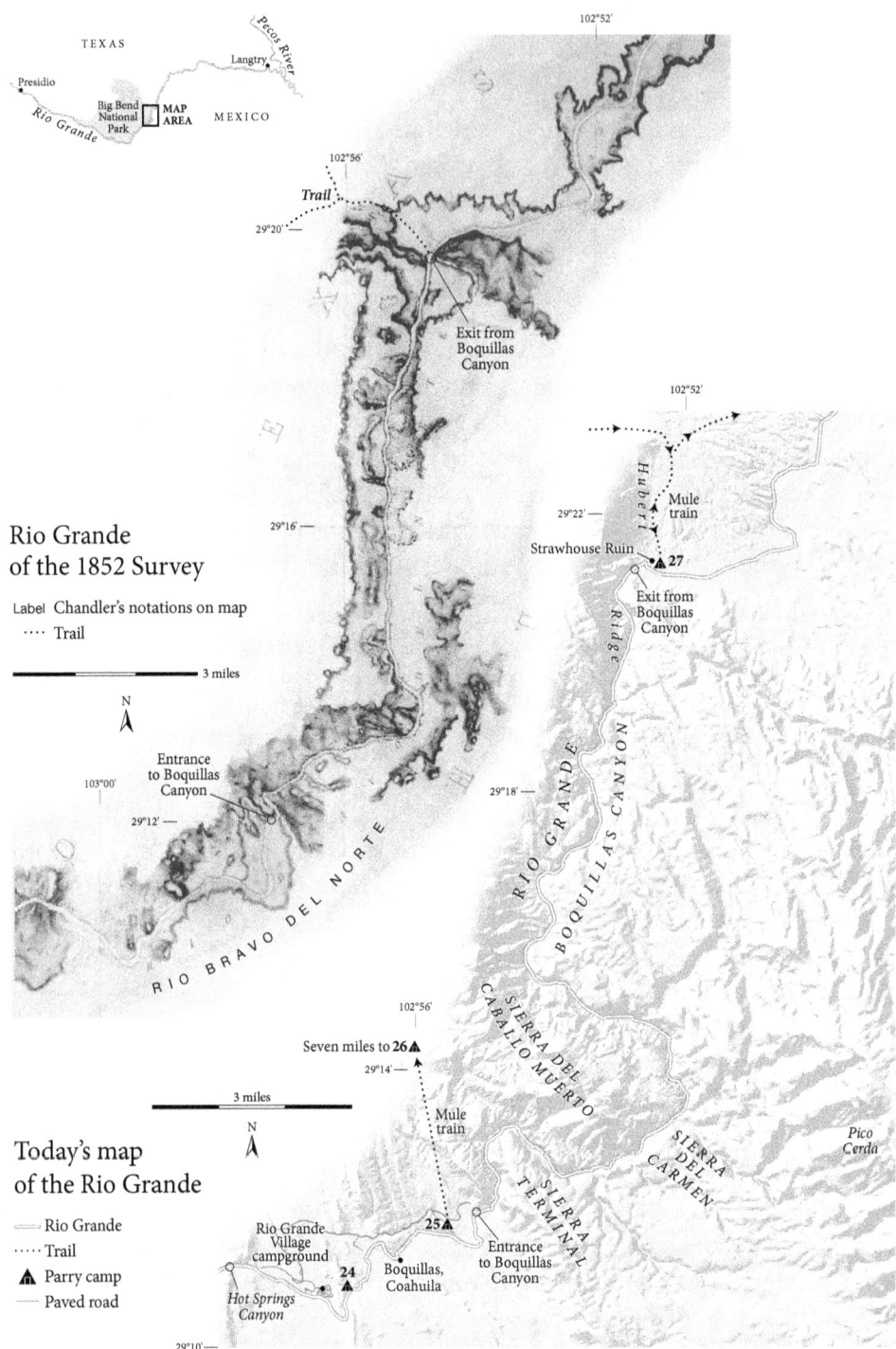

FIGURE 26. **River Trace Comparison: Boquillas Canyon.** The river trace of Chandler's Boundary Map 19 (dashed line) and a modern topographic map through Boquillas Canyon. The character and distance along the river shown on Chandler's map is a poor fit with that of the modern map. Boundary Map 19, National Archives. Map by Carol Zuber-Mallison.

The scouts returned on the night of October 19 to report that a rocky and waterless detour of thirty-six miles on the American side lay ahead for the mule train. At midday on the twentieth, they moved their camp (#25) two miles downriver to shorten the next day's long detour around the canyon. Early on the morning of the twenty-first, the surveyors started into the canyon in their boats, and the mule train started northwest, away from the river. The mules went up a dry arroyo (today's Ernst Valley), where their route followed today's Straw House Trail of Big Bend National Park. At "about 10 miles, where there were huge blocks" of limestone in the arroyo, they left the arroyo and ascended a steep hill to their left. The "huge blocks" would have been a problem for the mules. Satellite images today show the worst section of blocks in the arroyo along the Straw House Trail is eight to ten miles above the Rio Grande. After leaving the trail, the mule train appears to have drifted too far west, going miles out of their way. They made a high and dry camp (#26), at a distance of twenty miles, somewhere west of today's Straw House Trail but still short of the divide leading down to Telephone Canyon. Today, the divide leading to that canyon on the Straw House Trail is only eighteen miles from the Rio Grande.

A short distance after leaving camp the next morning, they reached a divide and made a rough descent to a "wide arroyo running east" (Telephone Canyon). They must have joined the canyon about four miles above today's junction with the Straw House Trail. A higher junction helps explain why Parry logged thirty-four miles for the detour from his Rio Grande camp near the entrance to Boquillas Canyon to his river camp at the exit of Boquillas Canyon, whereas the total distance on today's Straw House Trail is only twenty-five miles.

Once in Telephone Canyon, they moved east down the arroyo, then reached more open country at the mouth of the canyon and turned south down low gravel terraces adjoining a dry arroyo now named Heath Creek. They reached the river at the exit of Boquillas Canyon and camped (#27), having covered fourteen miles for the day and thirty-four miles from the camp on the Rio Grande. Their camp was just east of the later site of the "Straw House," a primitive shelter used by a Mexican *candelillero* (harvester of candelilla cactus to render wax). There is likely little left of the shelter ruin today. Ross Maxwell, in his 1968 guidebook on the geology of Big Bend National Park, included a 1936 photograph showing flattened debris marking the site of the shelter. He said this shelter had walls of candelilla, chino grass, and carrizo cane with a candelilla-thatched roof, and was located on the Texas side at the mouth of Boquillas Canyon. The Straw House location is marked on the 1966 Geologic Map included in Maxwell's guidebook.[135]

From his camp at the canyon exit, Parry noted that "a fine landmark—a singular high mountain called Pico Tena—is a few degrees north of east."[136] It is a puzzle why Parry consistently used this name for the landmark. No references, other than those of Parry, could be found that used this name for any mountain in this area. Perhaps a Mexican packer with the mule train said this was the name, or Parry's transcription of the sound of the word left something to be desired. Based on Parry's bearing to and description of the mountain peak, on that day and later in his journal, the peak is the well-known landmark Pico Etéreo (ethereal peak), a name in use at the time by the Mexicans. It is mentioned in Langberg's 1851 journal as Pico de Etéreo and shown as Pico de Eteria on an 1805 Spanish map of presidios along the Rio Grande.[137]

It is a jagged igneous peak fifteen miles east of Parry's camp and rising about 4,000 feet above the level of the Rio Grande to reach an elevation of about 5,600 feet. From Parry's camp, his compass would have shown a magnetic bearing of twelve degrees north of east to Pico Etéreo, whereas the true bearing corrected for declination was 1 degree north of east. See figure 27 for a modern view similar to Parry's.

Parry reported that "the main peak of Mount Carmel is about due south." This is today's Pico Cerda, aka Shot Tower, ten miles away at a direction of 19 degrees east of directly south. Parry also noted that the course of the river below his camp was a bit north of east, and this fits the general river course today, which is about ten degrees north of east. About two miles downstream from their camp, the river turned north and maintained a generally north-northeast direction for the next thirty-seven miles.[138]

Reflecting that they had been traveling northeast for a long time, Parry observed: "We cannot be far from the Pecos and the San Antonio Road." It is easy to understand how after all the hard marches they had made, they thought they were close to their destination—the Pecos River. However, it was still 93 air miles farther east across the heart of the Lower Rio Grande Canyons to the mouth of the Pecos River and 113 miles east to the nearest point on the San Antonio Road at the "first crossing" of Devils River.[139]

The surveyors finally arrived at the mule train camp at the exit of Boquillas Canyon on the morning of October 23. They had spent two and a half days and two nights on the river without food or shelter. What kind of trouble they encountered in what should have been an easy passage is unknown. All Parry said was that "they got entangled in the mountain ranges adjoining the river and were left there without food."[140]

FIGURE 27. **Pico Etéreo**. The jagged profile of this landmark peak on the Mexican side rises above 5,600 feet. This modern view is looking east from seventeen miles away on Texas Highway 2627. In 1852, Parry had a similar view of what he called "a fine landmark," from his camp #27 on the Rio Grande, fifteen miles from the peak. Photograph by the author.

"Entangled" makes it sound like they may have had men walking on the shore who became separated from the boats by steep canyon walls. We can only guess that in an attempt to take a bearing to distant landmarks to use for triangulation to determine their position, some surveyors had left the boats to climb a high peak and, in the process, missed a rendezvous with the boats moving downstream. There are only seventeen miles of river from the entrance to the exit of Boquillas Canyon and there are no large rapids to have upset the rubber boats. If the men remained in the boats, they should have been able to float the distance in one day. The poor job they did of mapping the course of the river in the canyon indicates they did little or no surveying and may have been distracted by other events. The surveyors arrived exhausted and hungry, and the entire party remained camped an extra night at the canyon exit to rest the men.[141]

Chandler's mapping of the Rio Grande through Boquillas Canyon on his Boundary Map 19 is poor (see the comparison with a modern map in figure 26).

The surveyors had good reason to hurry through the canyon, being concerned it might be as far to the exit as the thirty-four-mile detour route the mule train was taking. The river trace shown on Map 19 is too straight and too short, displaying only eleven of the actual seventeen miles of river. In the final Emory Report, Parry reported that the canyon extended only eight miles. His short estimate may have been meant to apply to the straight-line distance, which is nine miles on Chandler's map. But Parry also badly underestimated the distance from the river to Pico Etéreo as five miles, whereas the peak is never closer than twelve miles from the meandering river. Raw visual estimates of distance in remote mountains and deserts frequently fall short of actual distance. The clear mountain air offsets the expected buildup of haze when judging distance, and size alone is near useless with only massive mountains in view and no human-made infrastructure for scale.[142]

Chandler's Map 19 shows about three miles of the trail the mule train used to both approach and depart from their camp at the exit of Boquillas Canyon. While the location of their camp is not far off, the direction shown for the trail as it leaves the camp points 65 degrees too far to the west, versus the actual due north. Such a western direction for the trail would have taken the mules over the steep limestone bluffs of Hubert Ridge rather than across the gently sloping north-south drainage of Heath Creek they most certainly walked down. This had to have been either a mistake in the survey notes or a failure of Chandler's memory when he instructed the mapmaker four years later.

To determine the map location of the exit of Boquillas Canyon relative to its entrance, Chandler faced a new challenge. He had moved east of the high and continuous Sierra del Carmen range, which now blocked his view of all landmark peaks whose location he had documented earlier, except one—Pico Cerda. Now able to record only the one bearing to Pico Cerda from his survey station at the canyon exit, he needed to record a second survey station at a measured distance and direction from his exit station. Then, moving his instrument to the second station, perhaps a quarter mile down the river to the east, he could take a second bearing to Pico Cerda from that station to construct a triangle on his map. Knowing two angles and the length and position of one side of his triangle, he could determine the distance to Pico Cerda at the apex of the triangle, and thus the relative positions of the canyon exit station, the second station, and Pico Cerda. Chandler's calculation of the location of the canyon exit turned out fairly well. His final boundary map shows a distance and bearing from the canyon entrance to the exit of Boquillas Canyon to be 9.1 miles at N17°E, whereas true was 10.9 miles at N12°E.[143]

Once in the open country beyond the exit of Boquillas Canyon, the surveyors had good access along the river for an accurate traverse survey. The northernmost six miles of Boundary Map 19 provide a good picture of the river meanders, which extend to a point just upstream from the large meander of Stillwell Bend. In the first leg after exiting Boquillas Canyon, the map shows the river flowing 2.5 miles east, whereas it actually turns north in 2 miles; but, beyond that, the distance and direction of the river trace on the map are very good.

Overall, Map 19, which covers twenty-eight river miles from Hot Springs Canyon of Big Bend National Park, through Boquillas Canyon, and downstream to the Stillwell Bend, is the least accurate of Chandler's five boundary maps. One wonders if this may be due, in part, to a less attentive or less skilled draftsman working on Map 19. We know that in the Washington, DC, office a different draftsman produced Chandler's higher-quality adjoining Maps 18 and 20.[144]

On October 24, the surveyors continued downriver in their boats while the escort followed Indian trails on the American side, first going north back up the dry arroyo they had come down (Heath Creek). At three miles they turned east, crossed another arroyo (today's Brushy Draw), then traveled over a mesa (Sierra Larga) and down a wide arroyo to the river to camp (#28) just upstream of a rocky canyon. They had covered six miles on this day. The location of the camp, as described by Parry, fits a spot near the present site of the Adams Ranch House at the mouth of Stillwell Creek. It appears that the escort and surveyors met in camp each night as planned, since the absence of the surveyors would have been a problem worthy of mention by Parry.[145]

The next day, to avoid a new canyon, which contains the small Black Gap rapids, the mule train detoured around the canyon on the American side. They followed the Indian trail shown on Chandler's Boundary Map 18 as heading north out of their camp (figure 28). The trail rises about seven hundred feet across the flank of a west-dipping cuesta, then turns east, down a steep ravine cutting through the cuesta, and continues east to the river. They set up camp (#29) near today's Carl A. Gerstacker Bridge, where the paved Ranch Road #2627 dead-ends at the Rio Grande. The bridge, built by Dow Chemical in 1966 and named for Dow's chairman of the board, is now closed, but earlier it crossed to the Mexican mining

FIGURE 28. **River Trace Comparison: Stillwell Bend to Reagan Canyon** (*following spread*). The river trace of Boundary Map 18 compared to a modern map. This is the best of Chandler's five maps—an accurate trace of the river channel with rich details of onshore features along the banks. Boundary Map 18, National Archives. Map by Carol Zuber-Mallison.

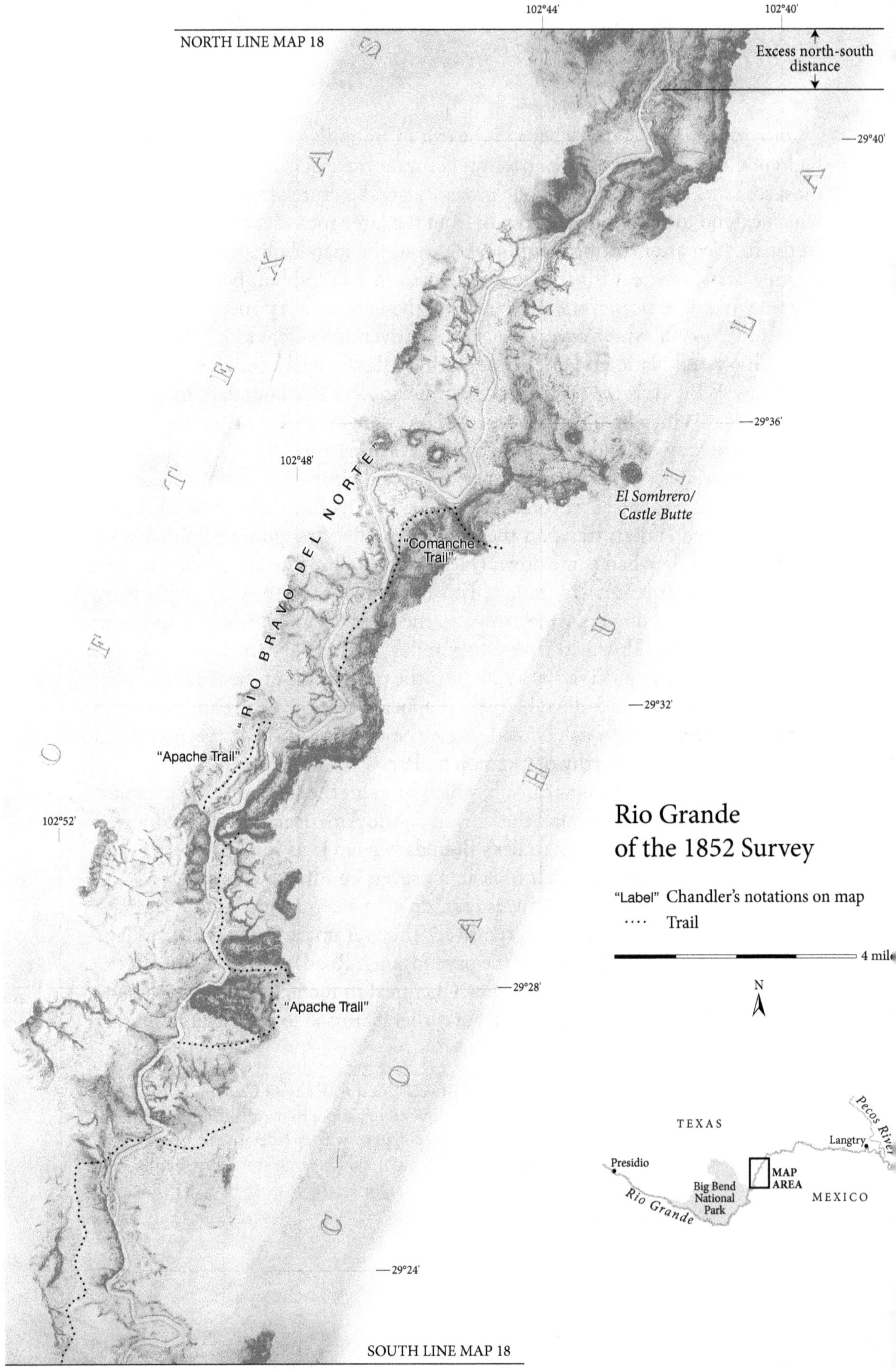

NORTH LINE MAP 18
102°44'
102°40'
Excess north-south distance
29°40'
29°36'
102°48'
"RIO BRAVO DEL NORTE"
El Sombrero/
Castle Butte
"Comanche Trail"
29°32'
"Apache Trail"
102°52'
Rio Grande
of the 1852 Survey
"Label" Chandler's notations on map
Trail
4 mil
N
29°28'
"Apache Trail"
29°24'
TEXAS
Pecos River
Langtry
Presidio
MAP AREA
Big Bend National Park
Rio Grande
MEXICO
SOUTH LINE MAP 18

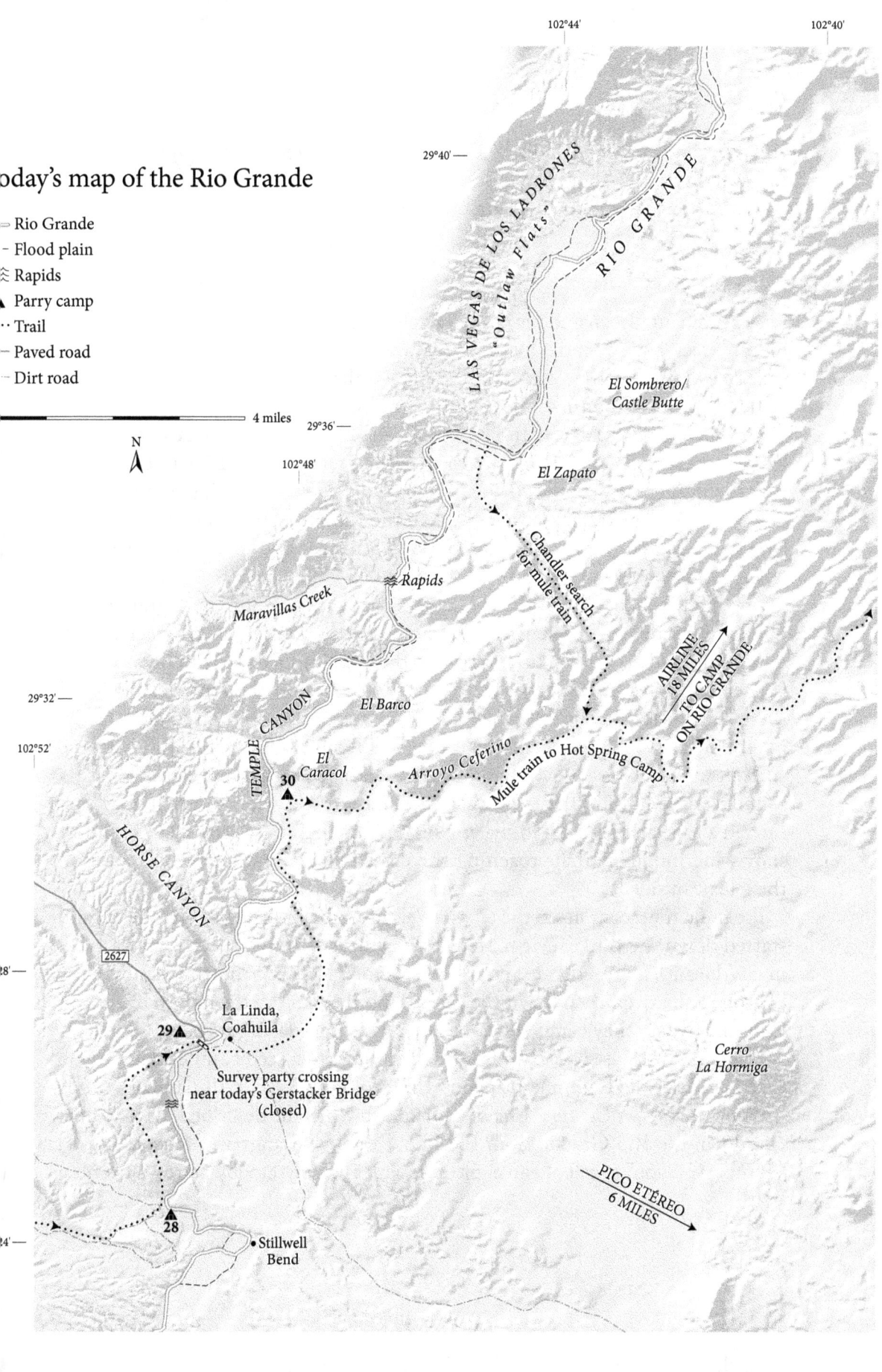

village of La Linda, Coahuila.[146] Parry gives no mileage for this day's travel, but the trail distance is about five miles. There is today a four-wheel-drive trail from Adams Ranch that follows the first part of their route.

Crossing the Rio Grande to Temple Canyon

For Lieutenant Green and his mule train to meet the surveyors on the river each night, Green had to send out scouts in advance of the main party to find a route the mules could handle away from the steep walls of the canyons along the river channel. Most of the time, the scouts were able to find an old Indian trail that served the purpose. A clear Indian trail headed north down the American side led the scouts to the river bank opposite the later village of La Linda. It was clear that the trail crossed to the Mexican side, and there was nothing going farther downriver on the American side. So, like the Indians, the scouts crossed to the Mexican side and there picked up the good trail that allowed them to continue down along the river.[147]

One might wonder about the challenge of moving an entire mule train across the Rio Grande, but it seems the crossing went smoothly. On October 26, the mule train and escort began crossing to the Mexican side, with Green noting matter-of-factly: "Advance guard reported no trail on the American side—I therefore crossed to the Mexican side." Chandler's description alludes to the potential for trouble but confirms there was none: "With great difficulty the whole train was passed over without loss." Parry's journal makes the crossing sound routine, noting the river was two hundred feet wide and that they first carried a rope across to aid in the crossing. Chandler's Boundary Map 18 simply shows the Indian trail approaching the crossing and continuing northeast on the Mexican side.[148]

The mule train completed the crossing early on the morning of October 27 and started down the trail. Their route went northeast to cross the arroyo La Hormiga (the ant), up to a divide and down to Cañón Zeferino, northwest down the canyon to the river, then down the river along the bank to the mouth of Arroyo Ceferino, where they camped (#30) after a day's journey of six miles.

This camp was just upstream from the entrance to a scenic, mile-long canyon that is today called Temple Canyon. The geologist R. T. Hill named Temple Canyon in his 1901 *Century Magazine* article in which he described his 1899 boat trip down the Rio Grande from Presidio, Texas, to Langtry, Texas. Hill used "Temple Canyon" to refer to an eight-mile series of canyons downstream from La

Linda Valley, including today's Heath Canyon, Horse Canyon, Temple Canyon, and Bourland Canyon.[149]

The most photographed part of Temple Canyon lies about six miles down the river from La Linda, where the view looking downstream toward the Mexican side shows a unique detached stone column (figure 29). Fishermen this author met at their nearby camp were impressed with this scenic canyon and called it "Finger Canyon."[150] The canyon cuts through the high hills of the Cerro el Caracol (snail) on the Mexican side. Parry made a landscape sketch of this view showing the detached column on the east wall above the river. Hill had surely seen Parry's drawing in the Emory Report, and during Hill's 1899 trip through the canyon, he took a photograph replicating Parry's view. He published that photograph in a 1934 *Dallas Morning News* review of his earlier historic river exploration. Apparently, the stone spire reminded him of a church steeple, hence Temple Canyon.[151]

The detached column illustrated by Parry and Hill can be seen in most present-day photographs of Temple Canyon taken by adventurers floating the wild and scenic canyons (see figure 29). Parry's Temple Canyon drawing carries the caption: "Cañon Below Sierra de Carmel [Sierra del Carmen]." This is the most downstream landscape drawing of the Chandler Survey, and Chandler included it in his section of the final Emory Report to document how far he had reached.[152] Temple Canyon was 185 miles below their starting point at Presidio del Norte but still 153 river miles from the survey's hoped-for final destination at the mouth of the Pecos River. The accuracy of the final Boundary Map 18 and the first few miles of Map 17 show that Chandler's men continued to survey an additional 24 miles of river downstream from Temple Canyon before they abandoned their work.

In his earlier magazine article (1901), R. T. Hill had shown a different view of a canyon labeled "In Temple Canyon." The view is a drawing by artist Thomas Moran, based on a photograph by Hill. That view appears to be looking upstream toward the west wall (American side) of the canyon. There are no spires, and the formations are shown to be dipping gently to the left. We know it is of the west wall because geologic maps of this canyon show formations dipping to the south (left if you are facing west).[153]

Parry's journal mentioned that downstream from Temple Canyon, some ridges near the river had a thin cap of black igneous rock, "the first I have seen since leaving the Chisos Mountains." The mountains he saw north of Temple Canyon are today in the Black Gap Wildlife Management Area (BGWMA) on the

Cañon below Sierra de Carmel.

FIGURE 29. **Views of Temple Canyon.** Looking north (downstream). Top: woodcut from the Emory Report showing the detached spire. Below: a modern photo showing the spire and the thin black cap of volcanic rock on the distant horizon mentioned by Parry. Emory Report, 84. Photograph courtesy of Rolf Laub.

American side, where outcrops of Cretaceous limestone near the river have a thin black cap of Tertiary-age volcanic rocks (see modern photograph in figure 29).[154]

It is unfortunate that Parry did not travel the scenic section of river below Temple Canyon, as he would no doubt have had interesting comments on three items in particular: the igneous rocks of today's BGWMA to the west; the often-photographed isolated towering butte of Cretaceous limestone on the Mexican side (Cerro el Sombrero), which rises 1,400 feet above the river and which R. T. Hill named "Castle Butte"; and the anomalous ten-mile section of lowlands along the river that today carry the name "Las Vegas de los Ladrones" (meadows of the bandits, or robbers' flats). In the late 1880s and early 1890s, these meadows were the hideout for a small outlaw band of Texans who stole horses, rustled cattle, and robbed a train before they were tracked down and killed or captured by Texas Rangers.[155]

On October 28, the mule train set out on what would be the final detour. Leaving the camp near Temple Canyon, the surveyors went downriver through the canyon in rubber boats, while the mule train went east directly away from the canyon (see their trail in figure 28). Lieutenant Green did not have time to scout a detour route in advance; his plan must have been to move away from the river a short distance, going east up the arroyo near camp, then turn north up some arroyo of opportunity and continue north up to its head, cross the divide, and then follow a new arroyo draining north or west to bring the mule train back down to the river. He hoped to accomplish this in one day and camp on the river with Chandler by nightfall. The mule train started east on an Indian trail going up the Arroyo Ceferino. They continued up that arroyo to its head, crossed a "gentle swell" (low divide) at about twelve miles, and descended to Arroyo La Presa Reventada (the breached dam), which Parry said was "flowing south toward Pico Tena [Pico Etéreo]." This was not good.[156]

They needed an arroyo draining north toward the Rio Grande, not south. So they turned north to go farther up the arroyo in an attempt to reach a new divide, on the other side of which they hoped to find an arroyo draining north or west back down to the river. Parry said only that they found this new route "impractical." It is likely that an advance scout went up to the divide at the head of the arroyo, looked north from the crest and saw at his feet a steep 300-foot drop to the southwest-flowing Arroyo La Tinaja del Toro (waterhole of the bull), with no way down for the mules. In addition, he would have seen three or four additional east–west-trending ridges, just as high as the one he was standing on, that would have to be crossed to reach the river, which was at least five miles to the northwest. "Impractical" was most certainly an understatement! The only option was to go back down and find another branch of their arroyo with better river access. They backtracked to the point where Arroyo La Presa Reventada turned east, followed it east and northeast to its head, crossed a divide at an elevation of about 4,200 feet, and made a rocky descent to another arroyo, but that arroyo was flowing east, not north. They were now in an upper branch of the large Arroyo San Rosendo. The continuing search for a favorable crossing of the divide had pushed them farther and farther east, away from the Rio Grande and away from their intended rendezvous with the soon-to-be-desperate surveyors.[157]

At dark, still moving east while looking for a way to turn north to the river, they found limited rainwater in rock depressions and camped (#31). A short distance below camp the Arroyo San Rosendo joined the large Arroyo La Herradura (horseshoe), whose drainage was north toward the river. Here, a 150-foot sharp limestone hill pointed northeast into the junction of the two arroyos to form a landmark Parry called "point of [the] mountain."[158]

Not far from camp, Lieutenant Green "found a fine new beaten trail heading in the opposite direction to the one I had been marching." This was an Indian trail, not a surveyor trail, and indicated Green was scouting ahead of the mule train camp and had passed the "point of mountain" where Arroyo San Rosendo joined La Herradura and turned north; thus, Green had found tracks going south, away from the river, when he was headed north down the arroyo toward the river. Since Parry was back in camp with the mule train, he did not see the new tracks going south up Arroyo San Rosendo until the following morning (October 29).[159]

Meanwhile, back on the Rio Grande, Chandler's men spent the first day (the twenty-eighth) surveying downriver from the Temple Canyon camp, while the mule train was vainly searching for a way back to the river. The surveyors expected to meet Green and the mule train somewhere downriver at the end of day. When Green did not show up on the first night, Chandler's men were in immediate trouble, and that night they endured the first of several nights without food and bedding.[160]

On the morning of the twenty-ninth, Lieutenant Green, concerned about the surveyors, who he knew had spent the night without food or shelter, broke camp at first light, hoping to quickly reach the river and find Chandler and his men. They followed the Arroyo San Rosendo north down to the Rio Grande. They reached the river at one o'clock in the afternoon and they made camp (#32), fourteen miles from their last camp. There at the mouth of the arroyo are large hot springs on the southeast bank and a Class III rapids on the river. Not finding the surveyors at the river, Green knew that Chandler's men were facing a second night without rations or bedding. Unfortunately, Green had hit the river much too far downstream to help Chandler. The mules could not move up the river from their Hot Springs camp, because they were surrounded on all sides by massive canyons. Green had no way of knowing how many miles of wild river separated him from Chandler's men, but his long detour had carried him to a point thirty-six river miles below their last river camp with the surveyors at Temple Canyon. This distance to their rendezvous camp must have been three times farther down the river than he and Chandler had hoped.[161]

Meanwhile, back at Chandler's camp on the river somewhere below Temple Canyon, the men awoke on the morning of the twenty-ninth after their first night without food or bedding. Now they were in full survival mode. The surveying was over except for a few notes on estimated direction and distance and maybe a sketch map, all to be done while rapidly descending in the rubber boats.

Up to this point, Chandler's operating plan required his surveyors, traveling in small boats, to be in daily contact with the supplies carried by the mule train. Since Chandler had no map and no guide who had ever seen the river course below Temple Canyon, he had no way of knowing that he was entering a much different section of the Rio Grande, one dominated by continuous and massive canyons that extended down the river for the next eighty miles. Under the new conditions, there would be no way his surveyors could maintain daily contact with the mule train traveling overland.

When Green and his mule train did not show up on the river by the morning of the twenty-ninth, Chandler decided to immediately go into the mountains to search for them. He likely told his men to wait until the next day, then either continue down the river in the boats or follow his trail into the mountains; both were high-risk options, but they were the only ones they had. In the end, the men did both. Parry reported that scattered groups of surveyors reached the Hot Springs camp at different times using various routes. In his search for the mule train, Chandler took with him his trusted assistant E. A. Phillips. The obvious choice for their search route was the Comanche Trail, which Chandler clearly shows on his Map 18 (see figure 28). The trail runs directly south, away from the river and up Arroyo La Piedra Parada (rocky meadow), which comes down to the river ten miles downstream from the surveyors' last camp with the mule train at Temple Canyon. The arroyo is located about two miles up the river from Cerro el Sombrero (also known as Castle Butte) and just across the river from today's BGWMA fishing shelters #15 and #16. This is the last Indian trail (the farthest downstream) recorded on Chandler's maps, suggesting he was camped nearby and had scouted the onshore area. The arroyo and trail held a consistent south-southeasterly direction away from the river and offered a low divide that was only fifteen hundred feet higher than the river. This trail led Chandler south to intersect Lieutenant Green's trail to the Hot Springs camp. It was a route exactly like this, but going in the opposite direction, that Green had searched for in vain to take him north to the river. Green had passed the subtle junction with this trail before noon on his first day out from their Temple Canyon camp. If he had recognized the dim side trail and followed it up the small unnamed arroyo for one mile, then turned north with the trail to go over the low divide and down to the Rio Grande, he would have arrived on the river near Chandler's camp well before dark on the first day of his detour. This trail was a less traveled route, and Green's only chance to have discovered it would have been to see a few tracks branching off to his left as he passed by on the more heavily traveled trail up the large Arroyo Ceferino in which he was moving east.[162]

I think Chandler and Phillips left their river camp and followed the Comanche Trail of Chandler's later boundary map for five miles up Arroyo La Piedra Parada to the divide, then south and west down a small arroyo where they found the tracks of Green's mule train in Arroyo Ceferino. Once on Green's trail, they easily followed the tracks east up the larger arroyo. By shortcutting Green's wandering backtracks, Chandler and Phillips could have reached the mule train camp at the Hot Springs in a total of thirty-two miles from their Rio Grande camp. This was quite an accomplishment for the two men to cover that distance with no food and only what little water they found in the rocks along the way. Yet, they did it! They reached the Hot Springs at eleven o'clock at night. If they started from their camp on the river at first light, they averaged a quick pace of two miles per hour. Lieutenant Green reported: "Greatly to my relief, at about eleven o'clock at night [on the twenty-ninth], Mr. Chandler and his assistant Mr. Phillips came into camp, having struck my trail and marched in one day what required two for the mules."[163] Of course, the thirty-nine miles the mule train had covered in the two days after leaving Temple Canyon had included some route finding and backtracking.

Chandler's Boundary Map from Stillwell Bend to Reagan Canyon

Chandler and his men produced their finest map of the boundary along the Rio Grande in the last few days before they were forced to abandon the survey. In spite of it being the final map, Boundary Map 18, made during the "last gasp" of the increasingly difficult work along the river, this is the best one of the five maps of the 1852 survey—a triumph of commitment and fortitude (see figure 28). The map's accuracy indicates that Chandler still had use of his instruments (the theodolite or tripod-mounted surveyor's compass) in spite of the many upsets of his boats. The map shows an accurate river trace and is rich in topographic detail, including the trace of numerous onshore Indian trails. Part, if not most, of the fine detail of this map is due to the careful work of the talented draftsman E. Freyhold, who drafted the final map in the Washington, DC, Boundary Commission office.

Map 18 covers a thirty-six-mile section of the river that extends from Stillwell Bend, shown at the south margin of the map, downstream to a point just below the mouth of Reagan Canyon, at the north margin. The prominent, eastward-projecting Stillwell Bend is correctly displayed in Chandler's trace of the river channel. Topography and trails near the river are shown in good detail, including the trail the mule train used to travel five miles down the American side to the next river bend across from the present-day village of La Linda, Coahuila. About halfway between the east-projecting river bends at Stillwell and La Linda, Chandler's map shows a midchannel island that is still there today and is associated with the Black Gap Rapids.

The location of the river crossing made by the mule train at La Linda is clearly indicated on Chandler's map by trails that approach the river from both sides. Earlier, the mule train had made crossings of the Rio Grande at Presidio del Norte and at Chisos Crossing, but neither of those crossings was shown on Chandler's earlier maps.

In the six-mile section of river below the crossing—from La Linda down to Temple Canyon—the map shows good detail of the mountains, ridges, terraces, and floodplains along the river. This includes the Cerro el Caracol mountain ridge on the Mexican side, where cliffs abut the river to form the scenic rock spires of Temple Canyon.

Excellent detail continues for eleven miles below the Temple Canyon camp (#30) down to Cerro el Sombrero (Castle Butte). This level of detail, which indicates they were working onshore, is a surprise because the surveyors had no support from the mule train while in this section and had only a day to get the work done. Bourland Canyon can be seen on the American side just below Temple Canyon, and a little farther downriver an island is shown at the mouth of Maravillas Creek, marking the rapids that occurs there today. Seven miles farther downstream, today's large, west-pointing meander loop is seen, as well as an Indian trail that shortcuts the loop and then goes south up Arroyo La Piedra

Parada. This trail is surely the one Chandler used later when he went in search of the lost mule train.

A mile downstream from the big loop, the scenic Cerro el Sombrero lies a little over a mile directly east of the river. This may be the point on the river that the surveyors reached on the night of the twenty-eighth, the first night they camped without food when the mule train was not there to meet them. The butte is prominently and accurately shown on Chandler's map, indicating that he recorded compass bearings to this landmark from his traverse lines. At this point in his survey, almost two hundred river miles from the observatory-documented latitude and longitude at his starting point of Presidio del Norte, Chandler's map accurately shows the position of Cerro el Sombrero as less than a mile south and west of its true position (see table 2).

Across the seven-mile section of river below Cerro el Sombrero down to the site of BGWMA fishing camp shelter #25 in Las Vegas de los Ladrones, the distance, direction, and shape of the river channel remain accurate, but onshore detail is lacking. This suggests that the river mapping of this section was done quickly by boat, using handheld compass and estimated distances.

The last, most downstream mile of Chandler's Boundary Map 18, and the adjoining five miles of Lieutenant Michler's Map 17 must have been based on a sketch map or notes made by Chandler's boat crew as they rushed downstream to rendezvous with the mule train at Hot Springs Rapids. On Michler's map, the shape of the meanders of the river and the distances are only approximate, and two prominent canyons that junction with the Rio Grande on the American side—Big Canyon and Reagan Canyon—are not shown.

However, Chandler's men made an essential contribution to Michler's Map 17. They were the only boundary surveyors to actually see this section of the Rio Grande in 1852 or 1853. They documented the shape and location of a very important major turn of the river where the course, which had been north for thirty miles, abruptly turned directly east. At the top of this turn on Boundary Map 17, a large tributary canyon is shown coming down to the Rio Grande from the north, but this tributary does not exist. It probably was added in final map preparations in Washington, DC, in 1856, to honor earlier maps in the files of the Topographical Engineers' office that mistakenly showed San Francisco Creek joining the Rio Grande at this turn of the river. Or, perhaps the boatman who made the sketch map of the turn misplaced Reagan Canyon, the nearest tributary, which enters the Rio Grande from the north less than a mile upstream from the big turn to the east.

Just downstream from the major turn, Chandler's sketch map correctly showed a straight, west-to-east, two-mile leg of the river. The east end of this leg is the most downstream point displayed on Map 17 that fits the true course of the Rio Grande. Beyond that point there is no agreement between the river trace shown on Michler's Boundary Map 17 and the true course of the river. This sudden end to documenting the actual river trace is thought to be where Chandler's men stopped keeping any record of the course of the river during their frantic descent in the rubber boats to the rendezvous camp at Hot Springs Rapids. In spite of the fact that the first five miles inside Michler's Map 17 were based entirely on the observations of Chandler's men, Chandler was not recognized as a coauthor of Michler's Boundary Map 17. (Part II covers the making of Boundary Map 17 in more detail.)

Abandoning the Chandler Survey

Finally, on October 30, all of the small groups of surveyors had reached the rendezvous camp at Hot Springs. The last group had been without food and shelter for three days. Some arrived by walking and others by rubber boat. Those who arrived by boat said they had come through large canyons, portaged many rapids, and covered a river distance from the Temple Canyon camp that was likely similar to that traveled overland by the escort. This was a good guess, as Hot Springs camp was thirty-six river miles below Temple Canyon versus the thirty-nine trail miles covered by the wandering mule train.[164]

The Chandler party spent a week at the Hot Springs camp. They rested from their recent ordeal, bathed in the hot springs, decided to discontinue the survey, wrote letters explaining their decision, planned their return route, and prepared their equipment for the long overland journey. Chandler's decision to halt the survey was "very reluctantly arrived at," according to Lieutenant Green, but it appears to have been agreed to by all. They really had no choice. Factors they listed in letters included low provisions, lack of bedding, worn out clothes and shoes, and the rotten and leaky rubber boats. There was simply no way for the escort and the surveyors to stay in daily contact while moving through the major canyons. What was needed to survey the canyons was enough boat capacity to carry surveyors, equipment, and provisions to operate for more than a week without the support of the mule train and escort. Only if they still had all four of the boats they had started with at Presidio del Norte would they have had a chance to operate in the Lower Canyons.[165]

To illustrate the futility of continuing the survey, Lieutenant Green reported that his advance scouting party from the Hot Springs camp had traveled a three-day detour without water to make a river distance of only six miles. Looking at present-day topographic maps, this was likely an upstream scouting party. The only spot on the river that appears to fit Green's description is a detour to the mouth of Arroyo La Yegua (the mare) on the Mexican side, about six river miles above the Hot Springs. To reach that spot by mule from Hot Springs would have required marching up arroyos to the south and west, crossing a divide, and then turning northeast down La Yegua to the river—a detour of at least thirty miles.[166]

While at the Hot Springs camp, Parry enjoyed warm baths at the spring and remarked that he hoped to transport a (water) sample for chemical analysis. He said: "Near the mouth of the arroyo and just on the river bank is a fine hot spring gushing out its clean tepid water into large rocky basins." This is an excellent description, even today, of the spring on the Mexican bank just below the rapids (figure 30). Parry, ever the reluctant doctor, noted: "I have availed myself of the proximity to get off my hand all the rheumatic and syphilitic patients with a standing prescription of a warm bath."[167]

While camped at the Hot Springs, Parry climbed a high mountain just above his camp to gain a distant view of the surrounding country. He saw a valley to the north, which he supposed was the Pecos River, but it was still forty-five miles to the northeast and could not have been what he saw. He must have mistaken the closer San Francisco Creek drainage, fifteen miles to the north, which, like the Pecos, flows southeast but joins the Rio Grande far above the mouth of the Pecos. From the high vantage point, Parry recorded the direction to major landmarks using his pocket compass. He reported that Pico Etéreo lay in a direction of five degrees east of directly south, and Pico Cerda lay ten degrees west of directly south. Knowing these bearings to the two landmarks, which appear on modern maps, we can with confidence determine Parry's location.[168] And knowing the Hot Springs camp location is important because it confirms that the Chandler party reached a point on the Rio Grande some seventy miles farther down the river than Boquillas Canyon, which has been reported as the point where Chandler abandoned his survey.[169]

There is no indication that Parry shared his landmark bearings to Pico Cerda and Pico Etéreo with Chandler, the party leader. There is not even a hint that the location of the Rio Grande at the Hot Springs camp was known when the final set of boundary maps was prepared in Washington, DC, in 1856. It is tempting to conclude from this that the relationship between Parry and Chandler at this

FIGURE 30. **Hot Springs Pool.** Today's rock-lined "Hot Tub" on the Mexican bank at Hot Springs Rapids on the Rio Grande. Chandler's men enjoyed frequent baths at this spring at their last camp on the river, October 30 to November 4, 1852. PJ, 100–5. Photograph courtesy of Greg Anderson.

point in the stressful expedition was cool at best; or, perhaps Parry did mention the bearings, but Chandler chose to ignore them rather than have to explain later to Major Emory why he used the doctor's rough compass bearings instead of having his surveyors go up the mountain to record proper bearings using their tripod-mounted compass.

Many years later, in 1899, the geologist R. T. Hill used a free afternoon at his camp at the same Hot Springs Rapids to climb to the top of a mountain south of camp. His sketch map and the bearings in his notebook indicate he climbed the same peak Parry had forty-seven years earlier. Hill measured and described the geologic layers during his ascent, and, with a barometer, determined the height to be 1,650 feet above the river, which agrees with modern topographic maps. Hill reported a "superb view" from the top and noted compass bearings of twenty degrees west of south to what he called "the Carmen Finger" (Pico Cerda), and eighty degrees west of north to "the middle one of three little black peaks." Hill's "little peaks" lay twenty-seven miles to the west, and today are called the Black Hills. These three small volcanic peaks are lined up east to west along a five-mile fault zone, fifteen miles northeast of the Persimmon Gap entrance to Big Bend National Park. They can be seen today to the northeast during the last ten miles as one follows the highway south from the town of Marathon to Persimmon Gap. Hill's magnetic bearings were reasonably accurate for a quick sighting using a hand compass.[170]

Doctor Parry reported in his journal that on "Election Day" (November 4, 1852), the Chandler party made final preparations for the journey across Mexico. Both Chandler and Parry wrote letters to Major Emory before their departure, as military men of that era were prone to do. Chandler explained his decision to abandon any further work on the survey and to travel across the interior of Mexico to reach the US Army post at Fort Duncan on the lower Rio Grande. He planned to use his copy of Langberg's 1851 map as his guide and proceed as directly as he could to intersect Langberg's trail to the Mexican village of Santa Rosa. From the Hot Spring camp, they would first go south about sixty miles to pass around the south end of the lofty Sierra del Carmen range. Then they would turn west to intersect Langberg's trail from San Vicente Presidio, where they would turn southeast and follow that trail to Santa Rosa. From there, they would go northeast on the well-established trail to Fort Duncan on the Rio Grande. Chandler said he hoped to reach Fort Duncan in eighteen days, whereas Parry estimated it would take two weeks; it took them twenty days.[171]

The boatman Charles Abbott, with two or three companions whose names are unknown, secured Chandler's approval to take the best one of the two remaining rubber boats and "risk their lives" by floating the Rio Grande to Fort Duncan rather than making the long walk in their homemade shoes. Abbott, if he made it, was to deliver Parry's and Chandler's letters to Major Emory, who was thought to be at Fort Duncan.[172]

Chandler's letter to Emory reported that he had carried the survey "to a canyon near this camp." We assume Chandler is making a general reference to the Rio Grande canyons he surveyed downstream from his camp (#30) at Temple Canyon. In that area, about nine miles directly west of the Hot Springs camp and near the El Sombrero butte, the river was still flowing north and had yet to reach the long-anticipated major turn to the east toward the Pecos River. The depiction of that turn on the final boundary maps would have to depend on the rough sketch map made by Chandler's surveyors as they floated quickly down the river to reach the final camp at Hot Springs Rapids.[173]

Chandler's letter reported that he must abandon the survey because his boats could only carry enough provisions for one day, and the continuous canyons would not allow him to stay in touch with the pack train. He said his men had recently gone without food for seventy-eight hours. He reported that he had "made arrangements to connect this point [Hot Springs Camp or his last mapped canyon?] by triangulation with the mouth of the Pecos River, should the boat crew come to the Pecos within two days."[174] It is unclear what "triangulation plan" Chandler had in mind. There is no evidence that he made any triangulation bearings at the Hot Springs camp. Perhaps he thought he was close enough to the Pecos to ask Abbott to keep a two-day record of the estimated distance and direction his boat traveled down to the Pecos and use that very rough traverse survey to determine the location of the Hot Springs camp relative to the "known" longitude and latitude of the mouth of the Pecos, but that is not really triangulation. In any event, Chandler's plan did not work because it took Abbott about a week of extreme effort past many dangerous rapids to reach the Pecos, 119 miles downriver from their Hot Springs camp. Abbott did make a rough sketch map of his trip and delivered it to Fort Duncan, but it appears the pride of the Army Topographical Engineers would not allow them to use a sketch made by a common laborer, as there is no evidence it was used in preparing the final boundary maps.[175]

Parry, in his letter to Emory, said he did not go in the boat with Abbott because he "did not like to trust my collection [of plants] to the risk of capsize."

He committed to make a sketch of the country along his overland route to Fort Duncan, saying: "I will probably see more of interest [along the overland route] than in following down this horribly desolate river." Parry, the obsessive plant collector, knew he would get no new plants bouncing down the river with Abbott. In the end, Parry met his commitment to Emory. His daily journal includes notes on plants and nine single-page sketch maps of the route, showing the terrain, compass bearings to landmarks, and mileage to Fort Duncan. We know Parry carried pen and ink to record in his journal, as he mentioned at one point having dropped and broken his inkbottle. Parry's maps of his route occupy a full page in his 4" × 6" notebook, and each map usually covers two or three days' travel. Some maps are dim, but only one, covering two days of travel over La Encantada Pass in Mexico, has faded entirely away. The maps and Parry's associated notebook narrative allow one to closely follow his route except for the twenty-six miles of trail over La Encantada Pass, where we must depend on his narrative and a rough sketch map made by Lieutenant Green.[176]

Parry, like Chandler, asked Abbott to make notes on the character of the banks along the river during his descent in the rubber boat to assist Major Emory in outfitting a new party to finish the survey.[177] Arthur Schott, who later worked on the final preparation of Michler's Boundary Map 17 covering the Lower Canyons, reluctantly admitted to Major Emory that conversations with Abbott and the rough sketch map Abbott made of his journey had been helpful: "I found Abbott, the man belonging to Mr. Chandler's party, more and better provided to answer my questions as I expected. He made a sketch in his own primitive manner, which of course, as it is based only on guessing without any aid of instruments, cannot be of much worth."[178]

The reality was that Abbott, the common laborer, and his comrades in the boat were the only members of the 1852 survey or the later 1853 Michler Survey to actually set eyes on the twenty-six miles of the Rio Grande from Hot Springs Rapids down to the mouth of San Francisco Canyon. Michler's Boundary Map 17 showing that section of river was later simply "sketched in" across the unknown by the Topographical Engineers in Washington. The boatmen's "uneducated" observations were the only and the best information available but seem to have had no impact on the map. Abbott's original "primitive" sketch of the course of the river, mentioned by Arthur Schott, has not survived, but it was surely better than Michler's generic tight meandering pattern of the river displayed on his Boundary Map 17.

The Trek to Santa Rosa

The Chandler party departed the Rio Grande on the fifth of November "not expecting to see it again until Eagle Pass." They started south, back up the wide Arroyo San Rosendo, which they had come down a week earlier. On their right they passed the spot Parry called "point of mountain," and their old trail near their old camp #31, but they continued straight south on "a plain Indian trail up a wide grassy valley." Parry's "point of mountain" was about twelve miles from the Rio Grande at the junction of the Arroyo San Rosendo, which turned west, and the tributary Arroyo La Herradura, which continued south. They traveled up La Herradura past thickets of scrub oak to the arroyo's head and climbed up to a divide. After twenty-two miles, they found limited rainwater in depressions in the rocks and made camp (#33; figure 31).[179]

The divide where they camped lies along the crest of the Sierra del Bravo, a gentle anticlinal area of hills along the southern margin of the larger highlands of the Serranía del Burro, which is an extension into Mexico of the Cretaceous rocks forming the high Edwards Plateau of Texas.[180] Parry took compass bearings from the divide: Pico Etéreo (his Pico Tena) ten degrees east of south and Pico Cerda (his Carmel Peak) twenty degrees west of south. These bearings, corrected for declination, indicate he was at a point on the divide twelve and a half miles north of Pico Etéreo and six miles north of the present site of Rancho Nuevo, Coahuila. It is interesting to note that now the angle between Parry's two bearings to his mountain landmarks from the divide were thirty degrees apart, whereas his earlier, more distant bearings from the Hot Springs camp on the Rio Grande to the same landmarks were only fifteen degrees apart. The widening of the apparent angle between the landmarks from fifteen to thirty degrees confirms that Parry had moved much closer to his landmark mountains.[181]

Finding enough water each day for the large party of men and animals during the long journey to Santa Rosa caused constant anxiety. The party was probably about fifty men at that point, as some of the laborers and mule packers had likely deserted along the way. When conditions on the survey became destitute, the Mexican laborers had the option of simply returning to their home villages. The number of mules would have fallen below the eighty Lieutenant Green had at the start. It seems reasonable that about fifty mules remained, and most of them would have been needed for carrying packs. Chandler had mentioned in his letter to Emory that the alternative for the boatmen who had floated down the river from the Hot Springs camp was to "walk" to Fort Duncan in homemade shoes,

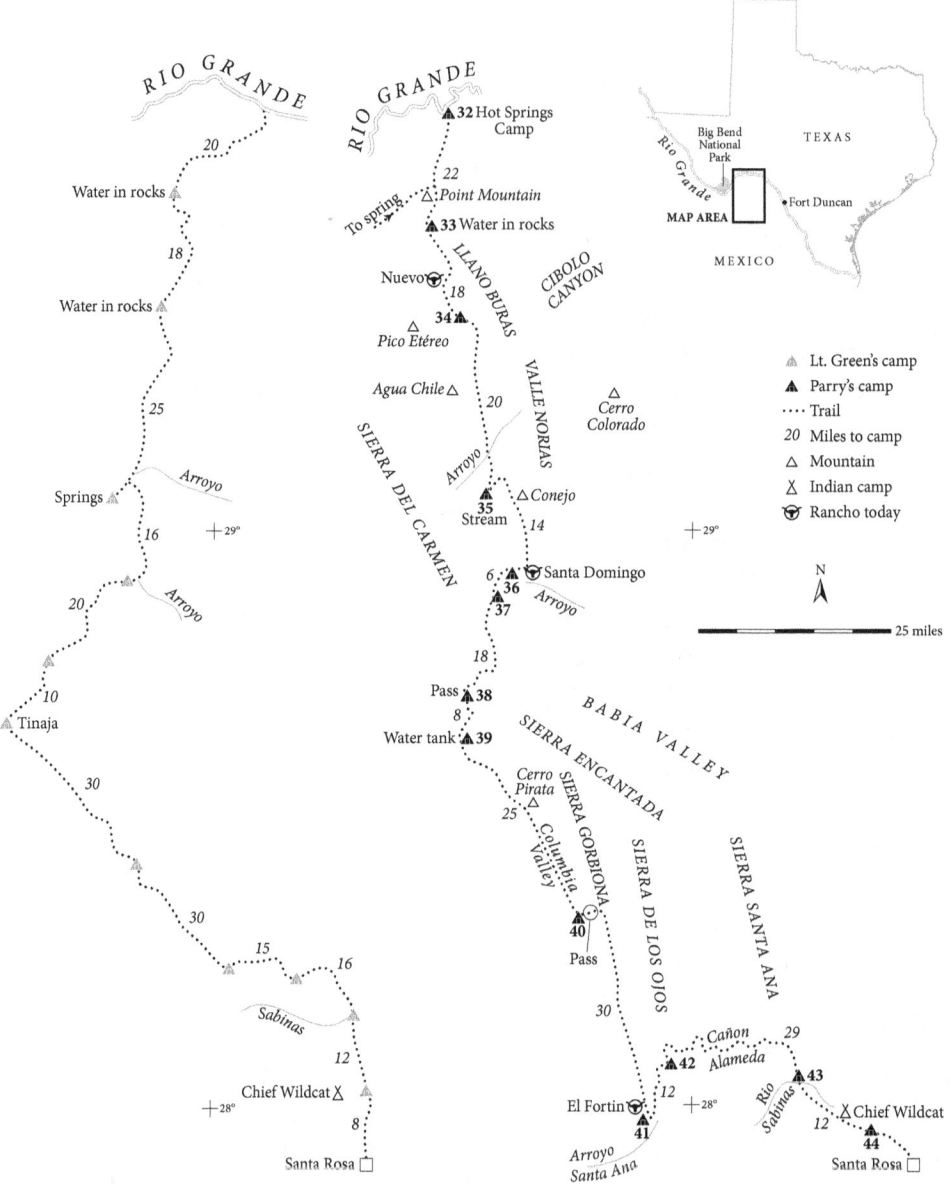

FIGURE 31. **Parry and Green Maps to Santa Rosa.** A comparison of route maps by Green and Parry across Mexico from Hot Springs Camp on the Rio Grande to the town of Santa Rosa (Musquiz/Múzquiz), Coahuila. The original sketch maps have no scale; therefore, for comparison, a scale is constructed for both by using the true distance in miles from Hot Springs Camp to Santa Rosa. Green's map trace was redrawn by the author from Tyler, "Exploring the Rio Grande," 10; Parry's map is a composite of his sketch maps.

but fifty men and fifty mules need a lot of water after marching all day. This meant that often the entire party could not camp at the same spot; they had to break up into smaller groups when water sources were small and scattered. This explains why the distance between some of the camps reported by Parry varies by one or two miles from the distance reported by Lieutenant Green. Also, the group followed the common practice of sending out a small advance or "explorers" party to scout ahead for the best route and sources of water. Green's report said he traveled sixty-three miles in the first two days after leaving the river, while Parry reported sixty-two miles for three days of travel. This must mean that Green was in the advance party, which skipped one of the camps used by the main party.[182]

After remarking the night before that they would be moving off the divide and down into a valley trending southeast, Parry says:

> We pass by a pleasantly smooth descent down the mountain slope and enter a grassy valley which widens as it proceeds over a wide basin plain of a uniform white color given by the coarse dead grass. . . . We pass along the western edge of this plain and leaving it on our left pass up an ascending slope connecting with the same basin lying between two rocky ridges and make toward a gash on the right side where we hope to find water. Encamp on the southern side of the gorge near the mountain base. Small rainwater in holes, enough for the men. Mountain ranges [are] Cretaceous [limestone] having an eastern dip. Topographic sketch on next page.[183]

Parry's map and detailed narrative of the journey allow us to tag along vicariously on the journey using a current satellite image of the area. See figure 32 for a side-by-side comparison of Parry's sketch map and a modern satellite image. At the foot of the smooth descent down the mountain slope they passed near the site of today's Rancho Nuevo. The light-colored grassy plain to his left (east) is Llano Los Buras. He passed between two rocky ridges, Cerro la Fortuna (fortune) on the left and Lomas el Hacha (hatchet hill) on the right. The gash on the right where he camped is the arroyo La Ventura (luck). Their camp (#34) was eighteen miles from the previous camp and six miles directly east of Pico Etéreo, which Parry would not have seen because ridges near camp blocked his view.[184]

Anxious to find a better supply of water, the party broke camp at sunrise on the seventh. It moved southeast over a gentle swell and then up a broad valley in the direction of "distant southern mountains." Parry was probably referring to peaks reaching above 9,000 feet, twenty-five miles southwest of him in the present-day Maderas del Carmen Protection Area (forest preserve) of the Sierra del Carmen. Nine miles from camp and off to the right of the trail was a "conspicuous jagged

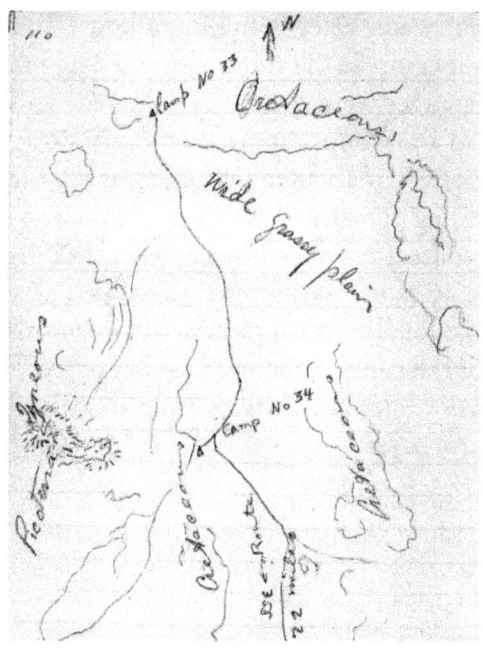 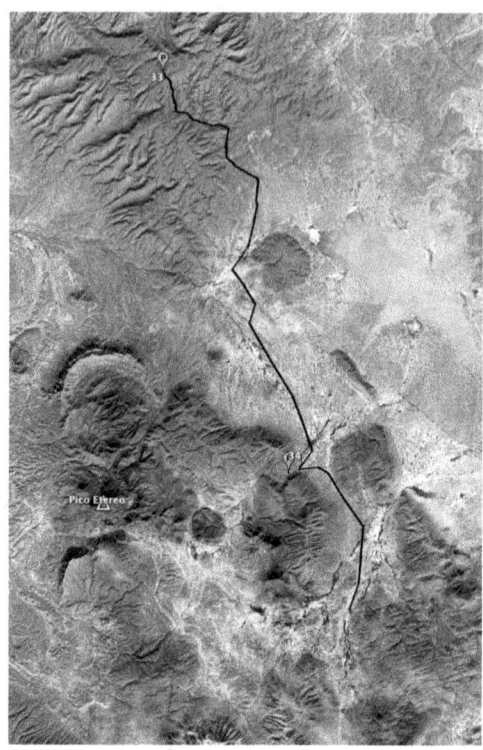

Figure 32. **Trail to Camp #34.** A comparison of Parry's topographic sketch map of his trail to camp #34 with today's satellite view. PJ, 145, courtesy of Special Collections, Parks Library, Iowa State University, Ames, Iowa; Google Earth Pro, accessed 12/15/2018.

mountain covered in pines and oaks with a core of granite and flanking beds of limestone and igneous rocks of brown color." This description fits the 5,502-foot collapsed volcanic cone–shaped mountain Cerro Aguachile (watery chili), which was three miles west of the trail and is today the site of a fluorite mine. Later in the day they found a "stake" left by their advance party to help guide them to the next camp. Continuing south, they crossed the wide Arroyo El Burro draining east. Having covered twenty-two miles that day, the party camped west of a rocky spur, at the base of an igneous hill by a stream of clear water. Their camp (#35) was just southwest of today's village of José María Morelos, Coahuila. The water at this camp was the first flowing water they had seen since leaving the Rio Grande three days and sixty-two miles earlier. Parry remarked: "The animals and us do justice to it." Green's sketch map shows "springs" for this camp where the party stayed for two days to rest and rehydrate.[185]

Parry used the extra time to explore west of camp, where he described surroundings that included igneous rocks, a gurgling brook among willows, live oaks, abundant Indian trails, and old Indian camps. The advance party scouted ahead and returned to report a plain Indian trail headed in their intended direction (south) with plenty of water but no sign yet of "the road to Santa Rosa"—the trail of Colonel Langberg.[186]

Leaving camp #35 on November 10, they went east around the rocky spur and south on the Indian trail. On their left they passed "a conspicuous peak rising out of the plain." This is today known as Cerro el Conejo (rabbit), which rises to an elevation of 4,741 feet. The plain extending east of the peak is the wide Valle las Norias (watermills) through which Arroyo El Cíbolo (buffalo) flows north, then northeast through the canyon of El Cíbolo to reach the east-flowing Rio Grande at a point seventy miles upstream from the mouth of the Pecos River. The Chandler party continued down the Indian trail following along the western margin of the plain, with igneous rock to their right (west) and Cretaceous limestone ten miles away across the plain to the east. They passed near the site of today's Hacienda Guadalupe, then through a narrow valley of limestone with live oak, walnut, and cherry trees (three miles north of present-day Rancho Santo Domingo). They continued south-southeast until near the end of the day, when they turned west up a valley. Their fourteen miles of travel brought them to camp (#36) on the south bank of a clear stream among live oaks. They were probably one or two miles west of Rancho Santo Domingo.[187]

Their turn to the west followed their general plan to first travel south to pass below the higher peaks of the Sierra del Carmen and then turn west to intersect Langberg's "Road to Santa Rosa." Had they instead continued southeast another twelve miles, they would have come to the La Babia Valley, a wide, flat, and well-watered valley that is today the home of large ranches and Mexican Highway 53. Following that valley's relatively straight course southeast fifty miles would have brought them out in open country only thirty-five miles north of their destination of Santa Rosa. A La Babia route would have avoided many miles of difficult mountain travel awaiting them along Langberg's Road. While it is easy today to point out this alternative, it must be said in Chandler's defense that he had no general map of the area to follow; he had only the mapped trace of Langberg's route to guide him and the knowledge that following that route would without a doubt take him to Santa Rosa.

The next day the group traveled only six miles to the south-southwest, leaving one valley to cross a divide into another valley and camped (#37) near its head.

They were in the foothills of the Sierra del Carmen where water is easy to find. The short journey from one creek to another, and no mention of a trail, suggests they were uncertain of their course. The specific location of their camp is not clear, but there is no reason to think it was not six trail miles south-southwest of the previous camp as Parry's sketch map shows. This camp is within the high mountain valley of Rancho el Álamo (cottonwood ranch).[188]

On November 12, they continued crossing the outer ridges of the Sierra del Carmen, "undulating ridges—first traveling south then more to the west through several ranges, now limestone." The sketch map in Parry's notebook that covers the route from camp #37 to camps #38 and #39 has faded away over the years, leaving a blank page. Without Parry's map and with few landmarks in his narrative, the route must be reconstructed using the notation of eighteen miles traveled, the mention of starting on igneous rocks and later encountering limestone, and the rough sketch map in Green's report. The rock outcrops suggest they were traveling southwest because limestone outcrops begin four miles southwest of the estimated site of camp #37. Since Parry does not mention a climb, they must have stayed below and east of the high igneous plateau of Mesa de los Fresnos (ash trees), which is a 5,600-foot-high grassy plain with scattered clumps of ash and oak. Near the end of the day they made "an assent of the mountain range which has an extensive view to the north and west."[189]

The party camped high on a limestone divide, high enough to have frost in mid-November, probably about 5,400 feet. Parry described it as "singular—and last view to the west-northwest of the Chisos Mountains." His rough bearing to the Chisos suggests that the camp (#38) was in the area where the southern end of the Sierra del Carmen range meets the northern end of the Sierra de la Encantada (enchanting) range, likely near today's mountain pass on Mexican Highway 53. The western culmination of the pass is called La Cuesta del Plomo (lead) and the eastern is called La Cuesta de Malena. The Chandler party must have been on the western side of the pass, since Parry said they were in limestone outcrops, whereas the Cuesta de Malena area at the east end of the pass is known for its scenic towers of igneous rock.[190]

The next day they began to descend the mountain "on a south slope, over rocky swells in a southeast course, looking down on an extended grassy plain" (Encantada Valley). After eight miles, they "encamped [#39] on the lower swells above this plain where deep ravines have water for animals, in tanks, difficult of access." Green on his sketch map labels this camp "Tinaja" (see figure 31).[191] Deep ravines and difficult access in this same area were also mentioned by George

Part I: The 1852 Chandler Surveying Party   135

Evans in 1849, Colonel Langberg in 1851, and Major Flores in 1881.[192] Turpin and Eling report that ranchers use these water sources today even though they remain difficult to access.[193]

During the descent from the pass, Parry observed: "We here fall into the remains of a wagon trail made by some Californians who succeeded in getting their wagons but a short distance from this point and were obliged to abandon them." The wagon debris confirmed the Chandler party had joined the "Road to Santa Rosa," as Langberg had noted wagon debris in this section of the mountain pass when he came through in October 1851.[194]

In the Tracks of Forty-Niner Wagons

A wagon train of "Forty-Niners" joining the gold rush to California had used the Sierra de La Encantada Pass in May 1849 (today's pass on Mexican Highway 53). Twenty-nine-year-old George Evans had been one of the adventurers, and he kept a detailed and interesting journal that was eventually published in 1945.[1] Evans began his journey in February 1849 by sleigh from his home in Iowa, then took a boat to New Orleans and Port Lavaca, Texas. He traveled by wagon to San Antonio, and from there rode a mule while in the company of others using wagons. From San Antonio they moved southwest to Fort Duncan (Eagle Pass, Texas), crossed the Rio Grande into Mexico, and continued southwest to Santa Rosa (Múzquiz, Coahuila). Then they turned northwest on primitive trails to the village of San Carlos (Manuel Benavides, Chihuahua), north to Presidio del Norte, west to Chihuahua City, and north to Tucson, Los Angeles, and San Francisco. Evans arrived at the "diggins" east of Stockton, California, in October 1849. He failed to find his fortune and died from an undisclosed illness a year later in Sacramento at the age of thirty-one.

The exact makeup of the Forty-Niner party changed along the way, but it was a mix of wagons and mule packers. While traveling their trail between Santa Rosa and San Carlos, the party was made up of 84 men and 250 mules and horses. Evans does not mention the number of wagons. From Santa Rosa, they went north, then west through the Cañón de la Alameda (Arroyo Santa Ana), then north up to the pass over the Sierra de La Encantada where the wagon debris occurs (see figure 6). Between Santa Rosa and the Encantada Pass, they traveled up many of the same Indian trails Langberg and

Chandler would later travel on their way to Santa Rosa. The three trails—the Forty-Niners', Langberg's, and Chandler's—all came together at the Sierra de La Encantada Pass where the wagon debris was located. The Forty-Niners approached from the south then turned west; Langberg approached from the north and continued south; Chandler approached from the east and then turned south. Once down from the pass, the Forty-Niners had moved west across the desert flat to the landmark spring at San José de las Piedras, and then northwest to water in a marsh in Arroyo de los Altares. From Altares west to San Carlos their route was the same trail Langberg followed in the opposite direction in 1851. From the Altares marsh, Langberg had turned north to the Chisos Crossing of the Rio Grande.

Contrary to Parry's note that the Forty-Niners had abandoned their wagons, Evans reported only one wagon was destroyed on the Encantada Pass (the debris noted by Parry), and one other was abandoned about forty miles farther west in the desert beyond Piedras Spring when the mule team gave out from lack of water. All the other wagons made it to San Carlos.[2] The minimal loss of wagons was extraordinary for such a difficult journey of three hundred miles along primitive Indian trails through the mountains and deserts from Santa Rosa to San Carlos. Beyond San Carlos the wagon train separated into subgroups that took varying routes to Chihuahua City and beyond. Leaving San Carlos, Evans went north to Presidio del Norte, west to Chihuahua City, northwest to Tucson, then west and north to the goldfields east of San Francisco, California.

Notes

1. George W. B. Evans, *"Mexican Gold Trail: Journal of a Forty-Niner,"* edited by Glenn S. Dumke (San Marino, CA: Huntington Library, 1945), 43–74.
2. Ibid., 71.

The Boatmen Reach Fort Duncan

Meanwhile, on the lower Rio Grande, 100 miles to the east, the boatman Charles Abbott and his companions arrived at Fort Duncan, Texas, on November 14 in the Chandler party's last rubber boat. They had floated, portaged, and paddled 235 miles of the Rio Grande from the Chandler camp at Hot Springs Rapids in only ten days. Nothing is said of the men's condition upon arrival, but they must have been at the ragged edge of their endurance. Abbott delivered the Chandler and Parry letters, which were forwarded to Major Emory, who only two days earlier had left Fort Duncan to go farther down the river to meet with Boundary Commissioner Bartlett at the army post of Ringgold Barracks near today's Rio Grande City, Texas.[195]

Abbott and his men made the first documented passage of any boat through the dangerous rapids in the Lower Canyons of the Rio Grande. While it is possible some early trappers worked their way through these canyons, no credible claim of an earlier passage has surfaced to date. The claim that in 1850, a party led by "Captain" Love poled a fifty-foot keelboat 967 miles upriver from Ringgold Barracks, near McAllen, Texas, is laughable, as that distance over impossible rapids would have carried him all the way to Presidio del Norte.[196] A later undocumented claim of a boat passage, which appears very unlikely, is the Civil War (1862–65) story of three Union soldiers who escaped from Confederate captors at El Paso, Texas, and paddled two dugouts all the way to the Gulf of Mexico.[197] If indeed three escapees made it to the Gulf, it is more likely they paddled to Presidio del Norte and then walked across interior Mexico to Texas.

After Abbott, the second documented passage of a boat through the Lower Canyons was that of the John T. Gano party of Presidio County surveyors and Texas Rangers in January 1882. The third, and best known, was that of the party of the geologist R. T. Hill in October 1899. All of these were described earlier.

In the years between the Gano and Hill passages, there is evidence that early fur trappers took boats through the Lower Canyons. An old trapper named James McMahon, who guided R. T. Hill in 1899, said he was on three boat trips through the Rock Slide Rapids of Santa Elena Canyon. Based on a story McMahon told Hill, at least one of those trips continued down the river through the Lower Canyons. On October 23, 1899, while camped at Hill's camp #18 near what today is called Lower Madison Falls, McMahon recounted how on an earlier boat trip he had been caught in a flash flood on the river near that spot.[198]

After 1882, boat parties exploring the Lower Canyons had the option of taking out their boats at the new railroad village of Langtry, Texas, about twenty-five river miles upriver from the mouth of the Pecos River. In 1899, the R. T. Hill party took their boats out and boarded the train at this spot. Langtry came into being as a work camp on the north bank of the river when the railroad construction crews arrived in 1882. First named Eagle Nest, it was renamed after the railroad engineer George Langtry. The village became famous for the saloon/courtroom of Justice of the Peace Roy Bean, who called himself "The Law West of the Pecos."

The Trek Continues

On November 14, still in the wagon tracks of the Forty-Niners, the Chandler party descended the rocky swells below their camp (#39) at the tinajas and entered a wide valley plain trending southeast. This is the Northern Encantada Valley, a grassland basin bordered by limestone ridges and sloping gently from an elevation of 4,700 feet down to 4,400 feet. Parry reported: "In twelve miles we pass on the left several round knolls of seeming igneous [rocks]." This is the Cerro del Pirata (pirate), an igneous intrusion that projects into the valley from the east and separates the Encantada Valley on the north from the Columbia Valley on the south. Parry continued: "Distant mountains to the south are quite elevated—strata dip west—the plain over which we pass forms a regular basin having only drainage to the central depression." The high mountains to the south are the Sierra Atravesada (cutoff) and Sierra de los Guajes (gourds), which are about twenty miles away; they reach an elevation of 7,743 feet and expose Cretaceous limestone dipping west. The internal drainage of the basin noted by Parry is a common feature of basins that are surrounded by mountains.

At the end of day, after twenty-five miles of travel, they made a dry camp (#40) at "the entrance to a puerto" (pass). This is the Puerto de la Gorriona (sparrow), which is a dry arroyo cutting through the Sierra de la Gorriona, a southern spur of the Sierra de La Encantada. Langberg referred to this pass as "the point of La Encantada" and described it as a "completely dry, rocky stream bed."[199]

Green was traveling in a separate group that did not camp with Parry's on this or the next two nights. Green's sketch map shows that he traveled thirty miles to the next camp, rather than the twenty-five recorded by Parry, indicating that Green did not stop at the mouth of the pass but pressed on in a vain search for water. Green's group remained ahead of Parry's until they camped together again after reaching the abundant waters of the Río Sabinas on the night of November 17.

On the morning of November 15, 1852, Parry's traveling group started east through the Gorriona Pass. After three miles, the pass opened to a wide, dry basin plain. This is the northern part of Valle el Fortín (little fort valley). Here they turned south down the valley and moved along the dry arroyo. Their route was "bounded by Cretaceous mountains of considerable elevation" (Sierra Atravesada and Sierra Orégano on the west and Sierra Hermosa de Santa Rosa on the east). At a distance of twelve miles, they passed on their left a rocky swell projecting into the now narrow valley.[200]

Farther south, as they followed the Forty-Niners' wagon tracks, they left the Valle el Fortín and crossed a low divide on their right. In doing so, they unknowingly departed from a more direct route down the valley to the entrance to the Cañón de la Alameda, the tree-lined canyon they had to use to cross the mountains and reach Santa Rosa. As they continued south along the wagon tracks, they came to another valley with a freshwater marsh where they camped (#41). Parry noted that "this is the first fresh water since camp number 39"—the Tinaja camp, two days and fifty-five miles back up the trail.[201]

The next morning, Parry reported: "The pioneer [scouting] party says the trail ahead is cut off by an immense marsh." They had camped on the north side of a marsh running along Arroyo Santa Ana, and the pioneer party report indicated they could not continue south, the direction they had been traveling, because the marsh occupied the entire bed of the arroyo to their front. Parry continues: "They find a new trail heading northeast, [which] seems the wrong direction but wagon tracks say to follow it." It was the right direction but seemed wrong because the Parry group, in traveling south for two days, had traveled too far south, and they needed to go back to the north to reach the entrance to Cañón de la Alameda and get through the mountains to Santa Rosa. It turned out that the roundabout Forty-Niner wagon route Parry had backtracked added several miles of extra travel, but it had the advantage of abundant fresh water at the marsh.[202]

The marsh area where Parry camped was along the Arroyo Santa Ana, about five miles upstream from the entrance to Cañón de la Alameda, through which Arroyo Santa Ana flows. In May 1849, Evans's California-bound Forty-Niners had camped at the marshes, where they watered their stock and filled all their containers for the long waterless trail north to the tinaja in the foothills of the Sierra de La Encantada. Langberg, in 1851, on his way to Santa Rosa, had taken the direct route down Valle el Fortín but stopped at the entrance to the canyon and sent a small party to scout the marsh lying southwest of the canyon. The marsh is today called Ciénaga del Zacate (hay meadow marsh). He mentioned it was a well-watered area, a crossroads of the Indians, and a strategic location where the Spaniards had earlier kept twenty-five men at an outpost of the old Presidio Santa Rosa. This outpost was the source of the name El Fortín (the little fort) for the valley and for today's nearby Rancho el Fortín.[203]

While Parry was on his way to the marsh, Lieutenant Green's advance party traveling ahead had taken the direct route down Valle el Fortín to the entrance to Cañón de la Alameda. Green's party found water and camped three miles inside the canyon.[204]

Leaving camp #41, Parry's group traveled northeast along the north bank of the marsh and soon entered Cañon de la Alameda. About five miles inside the canyon they found "a fine stream of clear water" and camped (#42) not far from the spot where Lieutenant Green had camped the night before. Most of the journey through the canyon was on a dry, rocky bed, but in a few favored places along the twenty-six-mile arroyo, water that had been moving unseen in the gravel beds below came to the surface. Those points of access to surface water support several ranches in this area today.[205]

On this same night, Green's advance group was camped about thirteen miles farther down the arroyo. Green's sketch map shows he traveled only sixteen miles the next day to reach the Río Sabinas, where Parry and Green would camp together again on the night of November 17. See figure 31 for maps of their differing travel routes as sketched by Parry and Green.

Comparing the Parry and Green Maps: Hot Springs to Santa Rosa

Both Parry and Green made sketch maps during the thirteen-day journey across Mexico from their camp at Hot Springs on the Rio Grande to the village of Santa Rosa (see figure 34). Their maps are very similar, which supports the accuracy of both and confirms that their starting point from the Rio Grande was the Hot Springs Rapids. Parry's map shows twelve camps en route and a total of 222 miles, while Green shows eleven camps and 220 miles. When water for a camp was limited and scattered, the men separated into small groups, camping at different spots. On those occasions, the maps of Parry and Green will indicate different camp locations and distances.[1]

Green explained that the directions for his trail as given on his sketch map might be a bit off because he did not have a compass. Green thought he was traveling west of south when he was actually going directly south. As a result, locations shown on his map had drifted about thirty-five miles too far west by the time he reached Santa Rosa. Parry used a compass, and the direction of travel shown on his map is accurate. Neither Green's sketch map nor any of Parry's maps display a scale, but in the comparison shown in figure 31, an apparent scale for both maps was equalized, based on the actual straight-line distance of 143 miles from their Hot Springs camp to the town of Santa Rosa.[2]

During the first sixty-three miles after leaving the Rio Grande, the men found only standing rainwater in shallow rock depressions. Both maps show two camps in this section, and Green labeled them "water in rocks." This means temporary pools of rainwater in depressions in solid rock. The third camp at sixty-three miles was at a spring with ample flowing water where the whole party camped for two days. Contrary to his map showing two camps, Green's narrative says he traveled the sixty-three miles to the spring in two days, thus making only one camp. One camp indicates Green was in a small advance party that skipped one of the "dry" camps en route to press ahead to find the spring. Upon leaving the spring, Green and Parry traveled apart along the next forty-six trail miles, passing over Encantada Pass and down to the ample water of the "Tinaja" camp shown on Green's map, where they camped together and Parry said the water was "in tanks" (deep depressions in solid rock along the bed of a creek, capable of storing ample water) but difficult to reach (Parry camp #39).[3]

Parry and Green traveled separately below the Tinaja camp, moving down the Encantada and Colombia mountain valleys and through the Cañón de la Alameda to the Río Sabinas, where they once again camped together only one day's march from Santa Rosa (camp #43).[4] Parry had traveled a few miles farther than Green because Parry followed the wagon tracks of the Forty-Niner wagons past the entrance to Cañón de la Alameda and had to turn back north to reach it.

NOTES

1. Parry Journal ("Field Notebook and Journal: Botany and Geology: U.S. Boundary Commission 1852"; hereafter cited as PJ), Charles Christopher Parry Papers, MS 290 (Parks Library, Iowa State University, Ames, Iowa), 107–45; Ronnie C. Tyler, "Exploring the Rio Grande: Lt. Duff C. Green's Report of 1852," *Arizona and the West* 10, no. 1 (1968): map B.
2. Distance measured on Google Earth satellite image, accessed October 4, 2013.
3. PJ, 125.
4. PJ, 138.

In his journal, Parry described his travel through the canyon on the morning of the seventeenth:

Down the arroyo mostly in its dry pebbly bed, making several sharp curves to accomplish its eastern course through the mountain range. Some two or three miles below camp running water makes its appearance forming a fine dashing stream. In a short distance the stream again sinks and finally the canyon opens on a wideish valley stretching north and south, our course now is east-northeast, soon we entered the second canyon, [the formations] dip west at 45 degrees, the canyon extends for about two miles and then opens into the wide Santa Rosa Valley—entering the valley our course is south-southeast toward the eastern point of Santa Rosa Mountain [now called Sierra de Múzquiz].[206]

Parry's route along the arroyo had followed, as all travelers must, the swinging meander loops of the narrow canyon that cuts through the mountain range. The "wideish valley" (1.5 miles wide) and the steeply dipping Cretaceous rocks are on the west flank of the Sierra de Santa Ana Anticline. The resistant limestone in the core of that anticline forms a two-mile-long second, but short, canyon with an exit opening into the extensive Santa Rosa Valley. For travelers moving west from Santa Rosa, this exit is their entrance to Cañón de la Alameda and is called Puerto de Santa Ana (Santa Ana Pass). Here at the exit, Parry turned southeast toward the old town of Santa Rosa. Today the town is named for favorite son Melchor Múzquiz, who became president of Mexico. Six miles beyond the canyon exit (at twenty-nine miles total for the day) Parry's group joined Green's advance party and camped (#43) on the north bank of a "large river flowing south" (southeast). This is the spring-fed Río Sabinas, "one day[']s march from Santa Rosa."[207]

Langberg's 1851 route through the Cañón de la Alameda was a variation of those of Parry, Green, and the Forty-Niners (see figure 6). At Parry's "wideish valley," about four miles west of the eastern exit of the canyon, Langberg turned south, leaving the arroyo to make a gentle climb of five hundred feet in five miles to go over a mountain pass he called Los Cojos (cripples) and then dropped down to the headwaters of the Río Sabinas. Today, at the southern foot of the pass, Los Cojos is the name given to a tributary of the headwaters of Río Sabinas. Langberg had camped about six miles upstream from the later campsite of the Chandler party. He described it as "one of the most picturesque places that can be seen—the current is swift and the river is quite deep—banks covered with beautiful Mexican bald cypress." From this camp, Langberg had moved directly overland to Santa Rosa, arriving "from a direction rarely taken by travelers" (from the west), and as a result causing alarm among townspeople on edge because of recent Indian raids.[208]

The Seminole near Santa Rosa

Once the Chandler party left their camp on the Río Sabinas heading for the nearby village of Santa Rosa, they encountered the Seminole Indian band of

Chief Wild Cat. This band had arrived near Santa Rosa less than a year earlier to settle on new lands granted them by the Mexican government. Wild Cat, or Coacoochee, as the Indians called him, was a respected chief. He had been born in Florida in 1810 and fought the Americans in the Seminole Wars there. He was captured in 1841 and sent, along with other Seminole and Black Seminole, to the reservation at Fort Gibson, Indian Territory. Today, the eastern Oklahoma town of Fort Gibson is on the same site. Wild Cat spent the years from 1845 to 1849 traveling about Texas and northern Mexico in an attempt to form a confederation of Indian tribes. That effort failed, but based on favorable overtures he received from the Mexican government, he formed an immigrant group and started for Mexico in 1850.[209]

Wild Cat's immigrants included the Mascogo, also known as the Black Seminole or Maroons. The Mascogo were descendants of black slaves who, decades earlier, had escaped to Florida from the Carolinas. They had their own separate camps, but they were associated with Seminole villages.

In July 1850, about three hundred of Wild Cat's followers—including Seminole and Mascogo and about one hundred Kickapoo Indians who had been enlisted by Wild Cat as he passed through Texas—entered Mexico at the river town of Piedras Negras (black rocks) across from Fort Duncan and Eagle Pass, Texas. The state of Coahuila welcomed them, believing they would be helpful in defending the state against devastating raids by Comanche and Lipan Apache. The immigrants separated into three main camps outlying Piedras Negras: the Seminole settled about twenty miles west, near San Fernando (Zaragoza, Coahuila); the Mascogo, fifteen miles north of Piedras Negras at El Moral (mulberry); and the Kickapoo, twenty-five miles south near Guerrero, Coahuila.[210]

In October 1850, the Mexican government approved an agreement granting Wild Cat's immigrants about 70,000 acres of land in an area northwest of Piedras Negras that lay between the San Rodrigo and San Antonio Rivers. The Seminole were not happy with the granted lands, claiming they were too dry, and in November 1851, they asked to be moved to other lands. The government proposed a well-watered alternate location at El Nacimiento (the source) at the headwaters of the Río Sabinas, eighty-five miles southwest of Piedras Negras and just north of the town of Santa Rosa (Múzquiz). The Seminole and Mascogo began arriving at the new site in late 1851 (after the Forty-Niner and Langberg expeditions but before Chandler arrived at Santa Rosa).[211]

In early 1852, Wild Cat traveled to Mexico City to gain formal approval of the new lands near Santa Rosa, which included about 18,000 acres of pasture and river bottom. With approval secured in July, he was back in Santa Rosa by the first of September. Thus, Wild Cat and his followers had been on their new lands only a short time when Chandler arrived on November 18. A Lipan raiding party had attacked the Seminole soon after they started their settlement, so they were understandably alarmed by the sudden appearance of Lieutenant Green's large party of armed and mounted men approaching from the north. At that time, the Seminole camps were in the open prairie below the headwater springs of the Río Sabinas. Apparently, they felt more secure in the grasslands, which provided distant views to guard against surprise by an approaching raiding party. Later the Seminole would move upstream to the more desirable, but more confining, foothills area of the headwaters. Today there is an active Kickapoo Indian village at the headwaters site and a Mascogo (Black Seminole) village four miles downstream.[212]

A smallpox epidemic hit Santa Rosa and the El Nacimiento settlements of the Seminole in the winter of 1856. Wild Cat died in January 1857, after which most of his band returned to the Indian Territory (Oklahoma). The relationship of the Seminole and Mascogo had grown increasingly strained over the years, but some Mascogo still live in the El Nacimiento area.[213]

In 1870, US Army Major Zenas Bliss formed a detachment of thirteen Black Seminole Scouts from a small group that had settled near Fort Duncan. The scouts were so successful in identifying and following the tracks of Comanche and other raiding Indian bands that threatened the border region that a year later the army increased their number to thirty-one.[214]

In 1872, some of the scouts were transferred forty miles north to Fort Clark (Brackettville, Texas), where in 1873 they gained a permanent commanding officer—Lieutenant John Bullis. During the next nine years, led by the energetic and capable Bullis, the scouts achieved their greatest success, playing a key role in army operations throughout the region, including participating in major battles between the army and renegade Comanche in Palo Duro Canyon in the Texas panhandle and tracking Comanche, Kickapoo, and Kiowa raiders moving across the Big Bend region to their temporary camps in Mexico. After 1880, Indian raiding lessened, and the need for scouts diminished. Lieutenant Bullis was reassigned and left Fort Clark in 1882. In 1912, the last sixteen Black Seminole Scouts were mustered out of service.[215] Today there is a Kickapoo village of about six hundred named El Nacimiento near Chandler's old camp on the Río Sabinas north of Múzquiz (old Santa Rosa). Most of the Kickapoo travel to work on farms in the United States and Mexico but return to winter at El Nacimiento.[216]

Part I: The 1852 Chandler Surveying Party   *145*

The Encounter with Chief Wild Cat

Parry reported that across the Río Sabinas from his camp was "a deserted adobe building," which he labeled "house" on his sketch map. It had undoubtedly been abandoned because it was a lone house along the main trail leading to Santa Rosa yet so far from town that it would receive no support if attacked by raiders. Langberg, a year earlier, had described the northern outskirts of Santa Rosa as "beautiful plains abundant in pasture grass and water but abandoned because of the continuous raids of the Indians."[217]

Chandler's men and the Seminole encountered each other on November 18. Parry's sketch map of the Santa Rosa area clearly shows the camps and the area of the encounter (figure 33). Lieutenant Green and an advance party of six men left their camp on the Río Sabinas early in the morning, traveling by mule. The plan was to go to Santa Rosa (Múzquiz), reported to be eighteen miles down the road, to explain to local officials the unexpected presence of Americans in Mexican territory and ask for permission to pass through the town. At three miles from his camp, Green came upon a Seminole camp and was stopped by "some negroes—from Wild Cat's Band" who thought the ragged Americans were a party of Indian raiders. This was a Mascogo camp about two miles above the present-day Mascogo community of Comunidad Negros Mascogos, where there is a neighborhood park sponsored by the Mascogo Tribe.[218]

Wild Cat's main Seminole camp at this time was about five miles farther down the Río Sabinas, on a tributary known today as Arroyo El Nogal (walnut). There was no Kickapoo camp in the area because they had not yet moved west from their camps closer to the Rio Grande. The black man who stopped Lieutenant Green agreed to guide him to Wild Cat's main camp, but when Green approached Wild Cat's camp, the man panicked and ran his mule back to the Mascogo camp. Green became concerned: "Thinking that some foul play was about to be attempted, I returned to my camp to bring up the whole party."[219]

Parry's sketch map in his journal shows the "Negro Village" (Mascogo) on the west side of Río Sabinas, about two miles below the survey party camp, and Wild Cat's camp about five miles farther down (see figure 33). When Green, now joined by the entire party, again passed the Mascogo camp, it was deserted. About a mile beyond the deserted camp, a Mascogo rode up and told Green that the chief wanted Green and his party to stop, but Green continued marching ahead. Soon another messenger arrived asking Green to come alone to meet with the chief. Green told the messenger to "inform Wild Cat I would stop for a short time and if

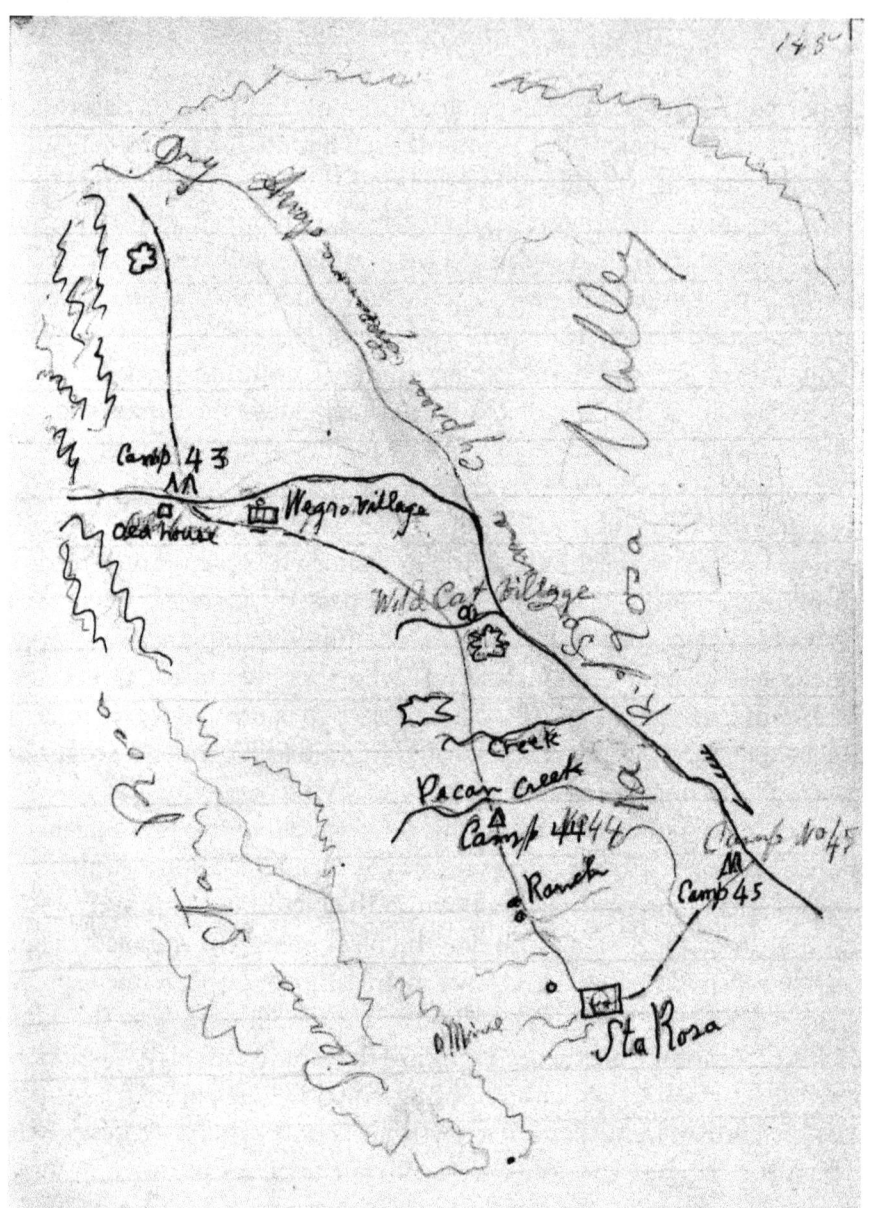

FIGURE 33. **Map of Santa Rosa Area.** A page from Parry's journal covering events of November 17–19, 1852. His "No. 43" is the survey party camp on the Río Sabinas. "Negro Village" is a Black Seminole camp. "Wild Cat Village" is the camp of Seminole Chief Wild Cat. "Mine" is the silver mine west of Santa Rosa owned by the American doctor Long of Santa Rosa. PJ, 145; courtesy of Special Collections, Parks Library, Iowa State University, Ames, Iowa.

he did not soon come out to meet me, I would march on." Soon Wild Cat arrived and demanded to know why Green was in the country, remarking that he had fifty men in the grass. In response, Green told him: "For each man of his, I had three." Wild Cat became more conciliatory and replied that "he was peaceful." The Americans continued down the road toward Santa Rosa. Parry remarked that they were "only interrupted in our march by a second-thought request from Wild Cat to give him a beef, which was complied with." It is interesting to note that Green was still driving beeves for his larder at this late stage, even though he had been traveling for more than two months and had covered more than four hundred miles of rough country since leaving Presidio del Norte.[220]

The entire survey party continued marching several miles beyond Wild Cat's village to camp (#44) on a tributary of the Río Sabinas that Parry called Pecan Creek. Both Green's and Parry's maps show this camp to be twelve miles below their first camp on the Río Sabinas. Green's map also indicates that their Pecan Creek camp was eight miles from Santa Rosa. These distances and the pattern of the creeks on the sketch maps indicate that Parry's Pecan Creek camp was on today's Arroyo La Lajita (flat rock), and Wild Cat's camp was on today's Arroyo El Nogal. Leaving Sergeant Edward Quinn to set up camp, Lieutenant Green pressed ahead to Santa Rosa and arrived "a little before dark." He met with "The Presidente" and gained permission to pass through town the next day. Green mentioned he met Dr. Long, an American medical doctor, who had lived in Santa Rosa for many years and was very helpful in Green's dealings with the Mexican authorities.[221]

Parry Visits the Town of Santa Rosa

On November 19, Parry left early from their camp on the outskirts of Santa Rosa to visit the old town,

> passing over a well watered and timbered country, . . . the prevalent shrub being Mimosa . . . at four miles passing a cattle ranch where I was bid Good Morning in English by a well dressed Negro—two miles further came to the town of Santa Rosa beautifully interweaved in trees of cypress and pecan. The town having a fine rural character divided into garden houses of stone and adobe. The whole surface is cut up with clean running brooks for the purpose of irrigation. The town has a very antique appearance particularly noticeable in the graveyard and church. The plaza with various Mexican stores is in the center of town. Met with an American doctor [Long], a long-time resident here, a prompt, energetic looking man and a thorough going American. He entertained us quite hospitably. He owns a mine some seven miles from town of which he gave me a specimen. The ore seems

to be a fine quality argentiferous galena [silver ore, mostly lead but containing silver]. The great trouble in working the mine was water, requiring constant pumping.[222] (See figure 33 for mine location.)

The doctor gave Parry a quick tour of the town, and then Parry departed to the northeast toward the "Rio Sabinal" (Río Sabinas). Parry stopped five miles from town at an hacienda and sugar factory among fields of sugarcane. Parry observed: "The factory is clean and well managed. We were entertained with syrup and pilones [sugar loaves]. The raw material [is] cast into small conical cakes of half a pound and sold at retail." Two miles farther Parry reached the Río Sabinas, a clear creek, twenty feet across. He camped (#45) among the cypress on the west bank of the creek after having traveled fifteen miles from his previous night's camp. One of the escort soldiers told Parry: "General Wool had made his camp at the same spot [on his way to Monterrey]." This referred to the Mexican-American War and General John E. Wool, who in the fall of 1846 had been on his way from San Antonio, Texas, to Chihuahua City. Later, Wool would abort the mission to Chihuahua and support General Zachary Taylor in the important battle of Buena Vista in February 1847.[223]

The Road to Fort Duncan

The Chandler party traveled on a well-established wagon road from Santa Rosa along the ninety-six miles to Fort Duncan at Eagle Pass, Texas (figure 34). Going east from their camp on the west bank of the Río Sabinas (#45), they crossed the stream "reaching about to the mules['] bellies" and then three miles over a divide to cross the Río Álamos (Cottonwood River), another clear stream. Parry noted, "The Mexicans say the two streams join about nine miles below." Beyond the Álamos, Parry went northeast for fifteen miles over a gently undulating plain to reach an arroyo where they camped at a rocky pond. Parry's sketch map shows this camp (#46) was on the Arroyo San José.[224]

The next day, November 21, they continued northeast and north over smooth country, then left the San José valley to cross a limestone swell to another grassy valley, then over a higher ridge to a deeper valley with trees in the distance. Moving farther down, they reached richer soil supporting occasional live oaks, and fifteen miles along they came to a flat, "springy" place with water in shallow puddles among chaparral where they camped (#47). Parry called the camp "Cavasera," but we do not know why; perhaps it was someone's name (Cava Sera).[225]

Part I: The 1852 Chandler Surveying Party

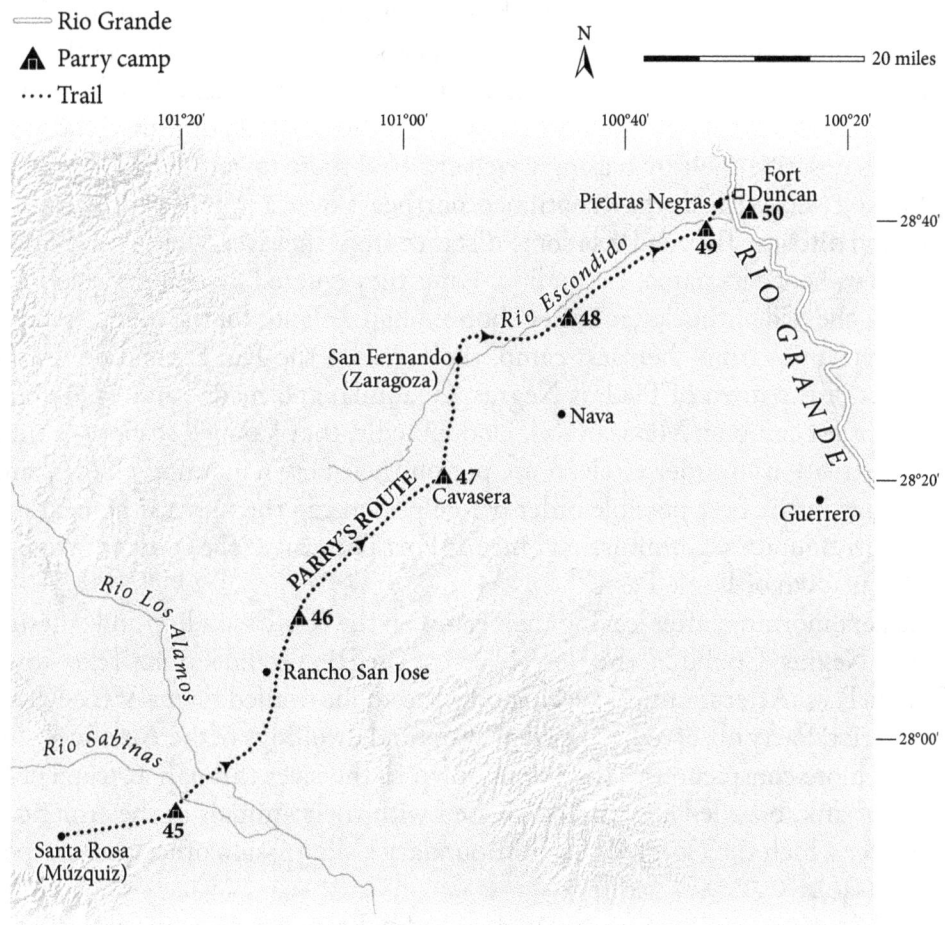

FIGURE 34. **Parry's Route from Santa Rosa to Fort Duncan.** Map showing Parry's route and camps along the final leg of his journey across interior Mexico to the boundary commission office at Fort Duncan. PJ, 150–59. Map by Carol Zuber-Mallison.

After leaving camp the next morning, the party passed through country with clumps of trees and clear lagoons. After ten miles, they crossed a shallow stream, the Río Escondido (hidden), and reached the town of San Fernando (now Zaragoza, Coahuila), about which Parry said: "The town occupies a flat some 30–40 feet above the river, finely shaded by large trees of cypress, pecan and oak. The houses [are] set off with gardens and orchards of fig and peach and give quite a rural character. The buildings are of the usual Mexican character, rather neater than ordinary. The plaza is spacious and the church rather dilapidated."[226]

They continued through town and headed northeast, passing sugarcane fields irrigated by the Río Escondido. They then crossed the river to the south bank and soon after made camp (#48) after a day's travel of eighteen miles. In noting that they made camp to the left of the road, Parry for the first time used the word "road" to describe their increasingly well-traveled route toward Fort Duncan.[227]

On the twenty-third, they continued northeast over a grassy plain with dry irrigation ditches. The road was some distance from the river, which was hidden from view, hence its name: Escondido. Later they entered more broken country and near the end of the day, a "mirey" bottomland difficult for the mules to cross. At fifteen miles from their last camp, they crossed the Río Escondido on the outskirts of the town of Piedras Negras, Coahuila, and made camp (#49). This was their last camp on Mexican soil. Undoubtedly, they stopped so close to their final destination in order to clean up, put on their best remaining clothes, and put things in the best possible order before presenting themselves the next day to the US Boundary Commission office at Fort Duncan at the southern edge of the Texas town of Eagle Pass.[228]

The next morning, after leaving their camp on the Río Escondido and entering Piedras Negras, Coahuila, they looked across the Rio Grande to the Texas town of Eagle Pass. After months of seeing only the adobe-walled towns of the Mexican interior, Parry observed: "The stone walls and dwellings of the American side are still more conspicuous." They went down to the river through a steep cut in the riverbank, boarded a ferry, and crossed with their animals to the American side, after which they located the US Boundary Commission office and camped nearby (#50).[229]

On November 24, Chandler reported to the US Boundary Commission office at Fort Duncan, where Lieutenant Michler was the senior Topographical Engineer. Major Emory had left Fort Duncan twelve days earlier, shortly before Charles Abbott's rubber boat arrived after its ten-day journey down the Rio Grande from the Hot Springs camp.[230] Emory was headed 250 miles farther downriver for a planned meeting at Ringgold Barracks (Rio Grande City, Texas) with Boundary Commissioner Bartlett, who was traveling east across interior Mexico. Lieutenant Green must have checked in with the army's commanding officer at Fort Duncan, Major Thompson Morris.[231]

Chandler and his men would have presented a pitiful sight—their clothes in rags, their shoes long ago worn out and replaced by homemade "raw cow-skin moccasins," their strength gone, and their bodies emaciated and sick from the months of poor diet. Yet there was news for Chandler to report in his letter to

Emory on the twenty-fifth: "I hasten to announce the safe arrival at this place with my party all safe."[232] Not losing a single man after what they had been through was a victory, but the bad news for the major was that the party had failed to complete the survey of the section of the river he had assigned to them—they had not reached the mouth of the Pecos River.

The entire Chandler party, including the army escort, remained at Fort Duncan from November 24 until the end of the year. Chandler sent a report to Emory on December 1, and Lieutenant Green sent a report to his commander in Washington on December 16. In addition to recovering from their ordeal, they were waiting on some resolution of the financial problems of the boundary survey. Commissioner Bartlett did not arrive at Ringgold Barracks to meet with Emory until December 20. On the twenty-second, Bartlett and Emory agreed that the lack of funds meant they must disband the US Boundary Commission. The two men sent a message announcing the abandonment to Fort Duncan and then departed for the East Coast.[233]

During the month of downtime at Fort Duncan, Parry recorded various observations in his notebook. The river, he noted, was at a low stage in December, exposing sandbars and islands. The water level at that time was eight to fifteen feet below the floodplain, which was covered during high-water times of the year. The previous summer, the Fort Duncan hospital weather station had recorded twenty-six inches of rain falling in one twenty-four-hour period, which had caused extensive flooding. About thirty feet above the river bottom was a wide terrace on which the buildings of both Eagle Pass and Piedras Negras were located. About one-half mile back from the river bottom were projecting sandstone bluffs, about eighty feet high, containing dark-brown iron nodules and some soft coal. These dark rocks, most common on the Mexican side, had given their name, Piedras Negras, to the town. In the hills nearby, Parry found silicified fossils of bivalves and ammonites, petrified wood, and coal seams—all in a higher formation that he thought was Tertiary or Late Cretaceous in age. He was right. A current geologic map shows the Late Cretaceous Olmos formation is exposed near the river.[234]

Parry grew tired of his long stay at Fort Duncan: "About the place little need be said. It owes its existence to the military post. The chief trade is smuggling into Mexico. There is not a foot of cultivated land, no gardens and no fruit. Maize [corn] is brought from the Mexican interior or the Presidio Rio Grande [at Guerrero, Coahuila] over 25 miles below on the river, the usual price: $3 per fanega" (about $2 per bushel).[235]

At Fort Duncan on December 30, M. T. W. Chandler received a letter from Major Emory at Ringgold Barracks, advising him of the suspension of the US Boundary Commission due to lack of funds. Chandler and Parry were directed to bring their field records and report in person to Major Emory in Washington, DC. Parry was to bring his plant and fossil collections. Parry and Chandler left Fort Duncan soon thereafter, headed for San Antonio on the first leg of their journey. It appears Lieutenants Michler and Green moved to army posts in San Antonio because that is where Michler was in April 1853 when he received orders from Emory to resume the Rio Grande survey, and where Green was in June when he finally signed the report he had mailed earlier from Fort Duncan without his signature. Most of the remaining civilian employees of the commission at Fort Duncan were released after receiving their back pay from funds derived from the sale of surplus equipment owned by the commission.[236]

Results of the Chandler Survey

Given the limited resources available to Chandler, Major Emory had charged him with an impossible task. It was made even more difficult because it was the first time Chandler had been put in charge of a large boundary surveying party in the field. He was asked to survey an unknown distance through an unknown section of the Rio Grande. At the outset, he would have known only that the straight-line distance from Presidio del Norte to his objective at the mouth of the Pecos River was approximately two hundred miles. About the river he knew only that below Presidio del Norte it flowed generally southeast for about one hundred miles, passing through big canyons with reportedly huge "falls," then made a big bend to flow northeast for another one hundred miles through more canyons, and then turned east for another one hundred miles before joining the Pecos River, which was itself still in a deep canyon. Chandler knew there was a risk of Indian attack, because the section of river they were to work was crossed by a number of well-beaten trails used by large armed bands of Comanche for their frequent raids from Texas into northern Mexico.

As it turned out, Chandler had been asked to survey 336 miles of the Rio Grande through deep canyons and rapids where no human had ever made a documented passage. He made a heroic effort. He began in mid-September and in a little over two months surveyed 209 river miles of the Rio Grande below Presidio del Norte. At the end, he made his last camp on the river at Hot Springs Rapids, 217 miles below Presidio del Norte, reaching a point considerably farther down

Part I: The 1852 Chandler Surveying Party

the river than he has heretofore been given credit for. He thought he was very close to his final objective—the mouth of the Pecos—but it was still 119 miles farther down the river. The surveying work of the Chandler party produced a fine set of five maps that are a part of the official set of fifty-four boundary maps that were jointly approved by the American and Mexican boundary commissioners in Washington, DC, in 1856 (his maps are numbered 18 through 22). He accurately traced the river's course except inside the precipitous canyons of Santa Elena, Mariscal–San Vicente, and Boquillas.

No one died, but in the ordeal of wrecked boats; lost supplies and instruments; and long, dry detours around canyons, he exhausted his resources and men, leaving them destitute, in rags and fragments of shoes, and weak from shortness of rations. He had no choice but to abandon his survey. To keep his surveyors moving down the river, they had to camp with the mule train each night because only the train had the capacity to carry the required food and shelter. Yet it was impossible for the surveyors to stay in daily contact with the mule train once the party entered the Lower Canyons of the Rio Grande, where continuous, massive walls of stone enclosed the river.

After he abandoned the survey, Chandler had only a rough idea where his final camp on the Rio Grande was located; but, in twenty days, he led his men as they walked and rode mules overland 320 miles back across interior Mexico to the army post at Fort Duncan, Texas, on the lower Rio Grande. For a good part of that distance they had no map to guide them, so they used Indian trails of opportunity headed in the general direction they wanted to go, all the while anxious about finding enough water for the men and animals. Chandler and his party arrived back on the Rio Grande at Fort Duncan on November 24, 1852. It would be late February 1853 before Chandler would meet Emory back in Washington, DC, to deliver his field records from the survey.

※ ※

Charles C. Parry's 167-page unpublished daily journal of the 1852 Chandler Survey party allows greater precision in tracing the route of the surveyors than has heretofore been available from the brief and guarded accounts of the party leader, M. T. W. Chandler, and his army escort commander, Lieutenant Duff Green. Parry was not only a medical doctor but also a talented and perceptive naturalist. His daily journal recorded distance and direction traveled and described in some detail the terrain, plants, trees, and geologic formations, while also collecting and preserving plant and rock specimens for later study. Parry's descriptions make it possible to recognize many of today's named landmarks along the survey party's route. Additionally, he provided a wealth and variety of useful information: the number and makeup of the men of the Chandler party, the number and types of boats they used; a historical "point-in-time" description of the types of weapons carried by Comanche raiders and their method of crossing the Rio Grande; the crops grown in remote Mexican villages; and the state of preservation of the abandoned buildings of the eighteenth-century Spanish presidios of San Carlos and San Vicente.

Parry was the first botanist to visit the Big Bend region and identify its plant species. He collected specimens of plants, fossils, and rocks, which he protected and carried back to Washington, DC, for further analysis by leading American scientists whom Major Emory had engaged to write the extensive and artistically illustrated natural history appendices included in the final Emory Report. The appendices included sections on geology and paleontology by James Hall, botany by John Torrey and George Engelmann, and zoology by Spencer Baird and Charles Girand.

Parry's geological notes provide the earliest general picture of the ages and types of rock formations along the Rio Grande as the river cuts across the greater Big Bend region. From Presidio, Texas, down to Comanche Crossing at today's village of Lajitas, Texas, Parry found only volcanic igneous rocks. At Lajitas, he noted Cretaceous-age sedimentary limestone beneath the volcanic beds, thus demonstrating that the volcanic rock was younger than the Cretaceous rocks. For about 40 miles below Lajitas he found a mix of volcanic and Cretaceous rocks. In the middle of this section was the giant Santa Elena Canyon, which Parry correctly observed was cut into massive limestone of Cretaceous age. In a distant view to the north from below the canyon, he correctly reported that the Chisos Mountains were composed of igneous rocks. He noted that the volcanic rocks exposed along the river near the exit of Santa Elena Canyon extended downstream only to a point 20 miles below the exit, and then Cretaceous-age bedrocks dominated the remaining 125 miles downstream to the farthest point the Chandler party reached on the Rio Grande at Hot Springs Rapids. He noted that Cretaceous-age limestone was at the core of the towering and scenic limestone canyons of Mariscal, San Vicente, Boquillas, Temple, and the remote Lower Canyons of the Rio Grande. Near the end of the Chandler Survey, when Parry was camped near Temple Canyon, he noted a thin black volcanic layer capping the crest of distant limestone mountains on the American side of the river. This was the earliest mention of the dark Tertiary-age basalt formations that dominate the landscape in what is today the Black Gap Wildlife Management Area of Texas.

After the Chandler party aborted their survey of the Rio Grande, Parry continued to keep a record of botany and geology along their 320-mile "escape" trek across interior Mexico, where they went first south and then east across the state of Coahuila to Fort Duncan on the American side of the Rio Grande. As before, most of the bedrock along his route was Cretaceous limestone. But he also noted the scattered occurrences of younger intrusive and extrusive igneous rocks, and the dominance of igneous rocks on the eastern flanks of the Sierra del Carmen range of Coahuila.

Parry's field notebook records only scientific observations on botany, geology, and landscape. He makes no comment on native wildlife, even though deer, mountain lions, coyotes, snakes, birds, and fish were surely abundant along the river. He has no comment on artifacts or pictographs, which he must have seen. To his credit, he never complained or was critical of the conduct of the leaders or members of the party, even though there must have been ample opportunity to vent his frustration as the party struggled through the unknown and hostile land under the stresses of extreme physical effort, poor food, limited shelter, scarce water (when away from the river), and the need for leaders to quickly make "best guess" decisions about which direction to travel and when and where to camp. Not in his journal, but in a letter to Major Emory at one stressful point late in the expedition he wrote: "these horrible canyons." In his journal, Parry did not once mention the name of the party leader, M. T. W. Chandler, usually mentioning only "the surveyors." On rare occasions Parry mentioned his friend, assistant surveyor Thomas Thompson, and the army escort commander, Lieutenant Duff Green.

The Chandler party remained at Fort Duncan through December 1852. Major Emory was 250 miles farther down the Rio Grande at Ringgold Barracks (Rio Grande City, Texas) awaiting the arrival of Commissioner Bartlett for their planned meeting to discuss the lack of funds needed to continue the surveys.

Commissioner Bartlett had agreed to meet with Emory when he was in El Paso del Norte in August 1852. Never one to hurry, Bartlett did not leave until October. Rather than follow the usual but lonely route through Texas to the lower Rio Grande—the Lower Wagon Road that Major Emory had used—Bartlett chose to travel a route more interesting to him—across interior Mexico through the historic Spanish cities of Chihuahua City, Torreón, and Monterrey. For protection from Indians, Bartlett accepted the offer of an escort from Colonel

Langberg of the Mexican Army. Langberg offered ten soldiers but delivered only five. On the first leg of his journey, in the mountains between El Paso del Norte and Chihuahua City, Apache raiders attacked Bartlett's party, killing one of his men. It is ironic that during what was supposed to be a safe route, this was the only fatal Indian attack against any employee group of the boundary commissions in the seven years they operated in the field. Bartlett continued his journey, visiting the cities and finally crossing the river at Camargo, Tamaulipas, to meet Major Emory at Ringgold Barracks in late December 1852. They agreed that the US Boundary Commission must disband due to lack of funds. After Christmas, they started back to the East Coast: Bartlett to his home in Providence, Rhode Island, and Emory to Washington, DC.[237]

In terms of managing the operations of the boundary survey, the tenure of Commissioner Bartlett was a disaster. He, with his large entourage of gentlemen friends, simply traveled here and there throughout the western United States and Mexico for two and a half years, pursuing whatever new experience interested him, often thousands of miles removed from the boundary, while being out of contact with survey operations for months at a time and not delegating his powers during his absence. The boundary survey operations under Bartlett were a "fiasco" as documented in the recent book of that same title, which details the personal correspondence of a witness to events—Major Emory's young clerical assistant, George Clinton Gardner.[238] However, to Bartlett's credit, it must be said that he wrote and published a detailed, interesting, and informative account of his western wanderings, illustrated with his sketches and including historic drawings and paintings by noted artists he had enlisted, such as Seth Eastman, Henry C. Pratt, and others in his party. His travelogue became a classic of nineteenth-century Americana.[239]

When the US Boundary Commission was disbanded at the end of 1852, Emory's men had surveyed almost two-thirds of the 1,300 miles of the US-Mexico boundary along the Rio Grande. This included 350 miles of the river between El Paso del Norte and Presidio del Norte done by Maurice von Hippel; 209 miles below Presidio del Norte completed by M. T. W. Chandler; and 243 miles below the mouth of the Pecos River carried out by Arthur Schott. At that point, the sections remaining were the 127 miles above the Pecos to the point where the Chandler Survey had stopped and the 365 miles of the lower Rio Grande from Fort McIntosh (Laredo, Texas) down to the Gulf of Mexico.

PART II

The 1853 Michler Survey

IN MAY 1853, five months after the Bartlett boundary commission disbanded, Congress authorized a new, third commission. Incoming US president Franklin Pierce named Robert B. Campbell, a loyal Democrat, to the post of boundary commissioner. Campbell had been a congressman from South Carolina and later the US Consul in Cuba, but he had since retired and moved to San Antonio, Texas. Major William H. Emory was again named chief astronomer and chief surveyor. He and Campbell were a successful team, with Campbell taking care of relations with Washington, DC, while Emory led all field operations.[1] Emory's priority was to complete the survey along the Rio Grande where two sections remained—one, thought to be about 100 miles in length, extended upstream from the mouth of the Pecos River, and the other entailed about 350 miles of the lower river below Laredo, Texas, down to the river's mouth at the Gulf of Mexico.

Even though the new boundary commission did not have final approval, Emory jumped the gun on April 4, 1853, when he sent orders from Washington to twenty-five-year-old Topographical Engineer Lieutenant Nathaniel Michler in San Antonio, directing him to complete the survey of the first of the two unfinished portions. This was the section that lay between the two surveys that had ended in October 1852.[2] It connected the farthest downstream point on the Rio Grande reached by M. T. W. Chandler's party and the mouth of the Pecos River—the farthest upstream point reached by Arthur Schott's party (figure 35).

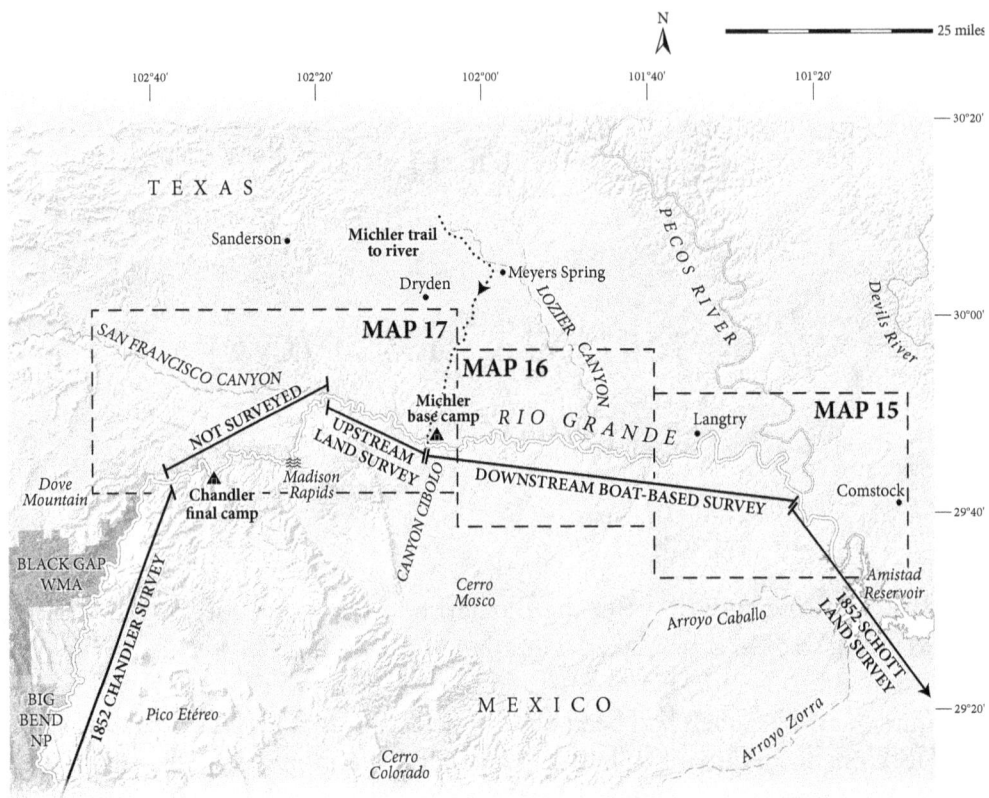

FIGURE 35. **Michler's Boundary Maps.** This index map shows the locations of Boundary Maps 15, 16, and 17 based on Michler's 1853 survey. Boundary Maps 15, 16, 17, National Archives. Map by Carol Zuber-Mallison.

Emory's orders to Michler referred to the unfinished section as "Fort Vicente [Presidio San Vicente] to the Pecos," even though he knew that Chandler had continued to survey some distance down the river beyond the ruin of the old fort. It seems Emory used the fort as the starting point for two reasons. First, at the time he wrote the orders, he did not know precisely how far downriver Chandler had gotten. Locating the exact final point would have to wait for analysis of the field surveying records by the Washington, DC, office, and Chandler had not yet arrived in Washington with the records. Second, no other named landmark—no village, flowing stream, or named canyon—was available for Emory to use as a reference point downstream from the fort's adobe ruin.[3]

MICHLER'S PREPARATIONS: EQUIPMENT AND MEN

Once Michler received his orders in San Antonio, it took him several weeks to recruit his survey team members and arrange for provisions and equipment. He had three wooden boats—a flatboat and two smaller skiffs—built and then disassembled to travel in wagons. The more versatile India rubber boats, like those used in the 1852 Chandler Survey, must not have been available on short notice in San Antonio, even though Major Emory had earlier recommended their use.[4]

Only a few members of the Michler Survey are known to us by name. The party leader, young Lieutenant Michler, had graduated seventh in his class from West Point in 1848. At that time, he was promoted to Brevet Second Lieutenant in the elite Army Corps of Topographical Engineers and ordered to report to the chief Topographical Engineer, Colonel Joseph E. Johnston, at the San Antonio office of the US Army's Department of Texas. Michler was assigned to the outpost office in Corpus Christi, where he accomplished some impressive early work in South Texas, including an 1850 river reconnaissance in which he and fellow Topographical Engineer Lieutenant Martin L. Smith led a reconnaissance party that poled a flatboat over four hundred miles up the Rio Grande, from Ringgold Barracks (Rio Grande City, Texas) to a point they estimated to be eighty river miles upstream from the mouth of the Pecos River.[5]

Michler had been assigned to the US Boundary Commission in fall 1851, at which time he reported to Major Emory and traveled west from San Antonio with him to arrive at El Paso in November. Shortly thereafter, Emory sent Michler to Fort Duncan at Eagle Pass, Texas, on the lower Rio Grande to set up an observatory and map the river boundary nearby. Michler was still at Fort Duncan when the Bartlett commission disbanded in December 1852. He returned to the US Army's Topographical Engineers office in San Antonio and was there in April 1853 when he received Emory's orders to undertake a new survey to cover the gap between the Chandler and Schott Surveys.[6]

I found no roster of the men who made up Michler's 1853 survey party. The only members Michler mentioned by name were the three he singled out for praise in his final report to Emory. They were his lead surveying assistants, the civilians E. A. Phillips and Edward Ingraham, and his geologist-naturalist, Conrad Stremme.[7]

E. A. Phillips had been hired in 1850 as an assistant surveyor and assigned to the US Boundary Commission office at El Paso del Norte. In early 1852, he was an assistant surveyor in the von Hippel party that mapped the Rio Grande from

El Paso to Presidio del Norte. In fall 1852, he was made an assistant on the new Chandler party. After that party disbanded in late 1852, Phillips went to San Antonio, where he was recruited for the new Michler Survey. In addition to his surveying experience, Phillips could be helpful to Michler in identifying the final point on the Rio Grande reached by Chandler—the point where Michler was supposed to begin his survey.[8]

Edward Ingraham was born in Philadelphia in December 1830. When he was about fifteen, his family moved to a large plantation on the Mississippi River south of Vicksburg. In June 1849, when the first boundary commission began work at San Diego, Ingraham was on Emory's staff, where the eighteen-year-old civilian was listed as a "junior computer."[9] One possible explanation for how a kid from Mississippi came to be a member of Emory's staff lies with Ingraham's maternal uncle, then Lieutenant and later Civil War Major General George G. Meade, who, like Emory, was a West Pointer, a Topographical Engineer, and a veteran of the Mexican-American War.[10] When Emory traveled to El Paso in fall 1851 for his new assignment to the second boundary commission, Ingraham was again on his staff. In spring 1852, Emory sent Ingraham, with an escort of thirteen soldiers, to the Pima Villages, three hundred miles west of El Paso del Norte, in a vain attempt to find the "missing" Boundary Commissioner Bartlett.[11] Emory must have been impressed with Ingraham, sending him on other troubleshooting missions, including to Fort Inge (Uvalde, Texas) in June to set up a new storage facility, to New Orleans in November 1852 to solve a banking problem, and to his staff in Washington, DC, in early 1853. When the third boundary commission was organized in the spring of 1853, Emory sent Ingraham to San Antonio to serve as an assistant surveyor for Michler.[12] It is likely that Michler was not entirely happy to have a twenty-two-year-old friend of the major assigned to his team, preferring instead to pick his own men.

Christoph Conrad Stremme (also known as Conrad C. Stremme) was Michler's geologist and naturalist. Stremme was a forty-six-year-old German immigrant who had studied at the University of Sciences in Berlin and later at the University of Giessen, where he received his PhD in 1841. He then taught architecture at the prestigious University of Dorpat (now University of Tartu) in Estonia. To escape political turmoil, he came to America, arriving at Galveston in 1852. How he so quickly came to Michler's attention is a mystery; perhaps Michler's assistant, Arthur Schott, also a German, met Stremme in San Antonio where there were many German immigrants or in the nearby German settlement of New Braunfels. It is notable that five scenes Stremme sketched along the Rio Grande were converted to woodcut illustrations and included by Michler in his portion of the final Emory Report.[13] No other members of Michler's party are known to posterity by name.

There is no indication of an army escort like the one commanded by Lieutenant Duff Green for the earlier Chandler party. Michler carried his supplies in wagons, rather than using a more versatile mule train as had Chandler.

It would have been advantageous to bring along one of the boatmen from the Charles Abbott party. Having floated down the river to Fort Duncan from Chandler's final camp, one of these men could have recognized points along the river and helped Michler identify the proper starting location, but there is no indication that Michler did this. As a trained Topographical Engineer equipped with surveying instruments, Michler may have thought it unlikely that a common laborer could help him determine his location. Michler's actions during the survey suggest that he was rather a stuffed shirt, and it is not hard to imagine him taking such an attitude.[14]

What extant information there is suggests that the Michler party was small—about thirty men. Of these, only a core group of about ten would have been in the boat survey party that proceeded down the Rio Grande from their base camp, while the larger wagon party backtracked their overland approach route. Space in the one flatboat and two small skiffs was limited. Michler mentioned having two oarsmen in each skiff and two Mexican boatmen whose swimming rescued the flatboat once when it crashed into a canyon wall.[15] The three boats together would have had six boatmen plus Michler, Stremme, Phillips, and Ingraham. A landscape drawing of the mouth of the Pecos made by Stremme confirms that he was in the boat party. Michler's wagon party, which he referred to as "the main party," was probably about twenty men, comprising teamsters, herders, and camp helpers. This had been the number of laborers suggested by Emory during early planning for what later became the Michler Survey.[16]

The Search for the "Initial Point" on the Rio Grande

Emory's April 4 orders to Michler instructed him to begin his survey where the Chandler Survey had ended, despite the fact that no one really knew where that was. Chandler himself had only a rough idea of his longitude and latitude in the closing days of his fieldwork on the river. As noted previously, obtaining a good location for the final point was dependent on analysis by US Boundary Commission office staff in Washington, DC, and Chandler had not arrived there in time

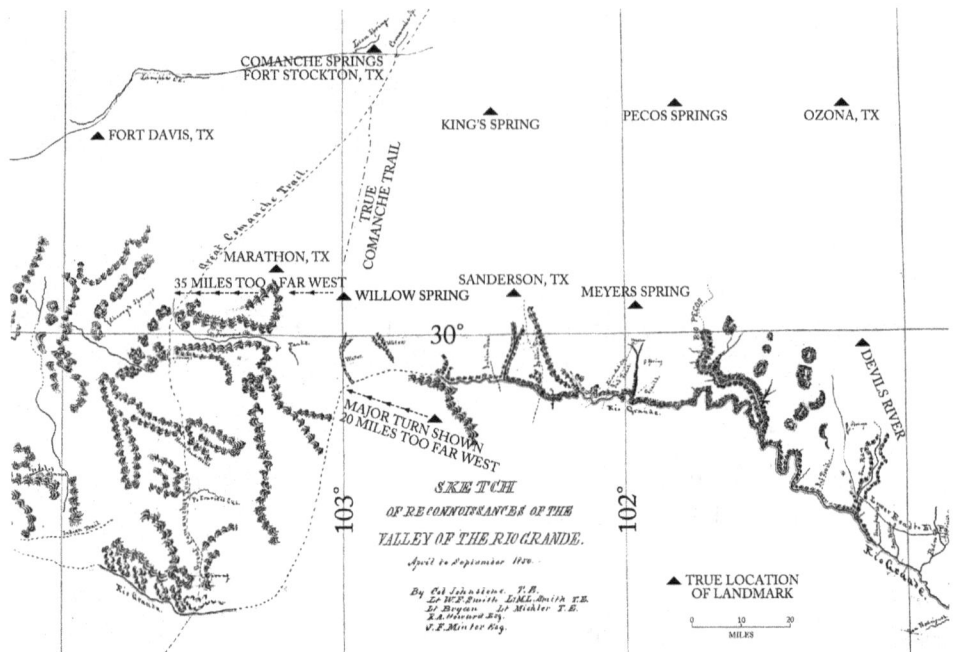

FIGURE 36. **Johnston's Reconnaissance Map.** Colonel Joseph E. Johnston et al.'s *Sketch of Reconnoissances [sic] of the Valley of the Rio Grande, April to September, 1850.* Johnston commanded a group of US Army Topographical Engineers stationed in Texas. This map was a compilation of expeditions by Johnston and his men, including Lieutenants W. F. and M. L. Smith, F. T. Bryan, N. H. Michler, and the civilian guides R. A. Howard and J. F. Minter. This was the best map available to Michler at the beginning of his 1853 survey, and it had a strong influence on his plans for carrying out his upcoming survey of the Rio Grande. National Archives, RG 77, Q-26.

for the work to be done before Emory's order went out to Michler.[17] Chandler could only say that he had surveyed a short distance beyond a major turn where the river changed course to flow east after flowing north for about fifty miles. Michler would have to determine the "initial point" for his survey on his own.[18]

In planning his route from San Antonio, Michler must have relied heavily on the 1850 map by Colonel Joseph E. Johnston (Michler's commanding officer when he first came to Texas in 1848) titled *Sketch of Reconnoissances [sic] of the Valley of the Rio Grande, April to September, 1850*.[19] Michler was listed as one of seven coauthors of the map and surely carried a copy with him as he moved along his route (figure 36).

I estimate that the Michler party departed San Antonio in mid-May, six weeks after Emory sent his April 4 orders from Washington. About three weeks would have been needed for the orders to move by telegraph to New Orleans, by ship to Indianola, and by horse to Michler in San Antonio. Then it would have taken another three weeks for him to bring together supplies and staff.[20]

Michler set out west from San Antonio on the well-traveled lower wagon road toward El Paso del Norte. About 150 miles west of San Antonio, where the road approached the massive canyon marking the junction of the Rio Grande and the Pecos River, it turned north and then northwest for another 150 miles to cross the Pecos River farther upstream where valleys were wider and more favorable for wagon travel.[21]

Pecos Springs was one of those places where the hills flanking the river were lower and it was easier to cross; it was there that Michler left the El Paso wagon road and headed overland to the west (see figure 6). He was familiar with the topography of the area because he had traveled west along the road in November 1851 and returned east on it the following month. Once he left the wagon road, it is likely an experienced scout guided the party along primitive trails. It appears their route west began in today's Sheffield Draw, which drains east to join the Pecos River just below Pecos Springs. After fifty miles traveling generally west, which Michler described as "circuitous," they reached a plentiful spring and camped. Michler called this King's Springs. Apparently Michler's guide knew the spring by name. The historian William Goetzmann has noted that Michler followed "King's Road" to King's Springs, which suggests that the spring and the road to it were known at the time, although I have found no map published before 1853 that shows either the road or the spring.[22]

Michler's route to King's Springs is displayed on Boundary Commission Index Map 2, which accompanied the final set of 1857 boundary maps.[23] Today the exact location of the spring is in doubt. Michler reported it as fifty trail miles "nearly due west" of Pecos Springs. This is a good example of how historians and others sometimes have to simply make their best guess for a location using whatever data is available. The spring is indicated on figure 6 in an arroyo at the midpoint of two potential locations based on the distance and compass bearing from Comanche Springs (Fort Stockton, Texas) and Pecos Springs taken from Boundary Commission Index Map 2. This estimated location is twenty-seven miles east-southeast of Comanche Springs and thirty-nine air miles west of Pecos Springs, a location that today is in a dry arroyo that drains into Independence Creek. Michler described the spring as "deep—gravel bottom—protected from the sun by shelving rocks—without bush or tree to mark its place."[24] A spring site without the trees that usually signal the presence of water in this otherwise barren landscape would be almost impossible to locate on today's satellite images or topographic maps. Only a few scattered springs are in this general area today, unlike in the 1880s when the first settlers reported "water in all the draws in the vicinity."[25]

In his 2002 book, *Springs of Texas*, Gunnar Brune locates Michler's King's Springs four miles west of my suggested location, but picking one from the few surviving springs of the present day to be the one where Michler camped is problematic. Brune also lists a "King Springs" that can be confused with Michler's spring but lies thirty-seven miles to the southeast. That spring, labeled "King Spring" on a 1917 topographic map, is only forty trail miles from the Rio Grande, too close to the river to fit Michler's report that he traveled ninety miles from his King's Springs to the Rio Grande.[26]

While the main party camped at King's Springs, Michler sent a small scouting party to the southwest toward "Los Chisos" (the Chisos Mountains in today's Big Bend National Park) to see if a route in that direction was feasible for the wagons. The scouts returned to camp after going "almost sixty miles southwest" and reported the route to be "impractical—steep cliffs—sharp igneous stones."[27]

That Michler, guided by Johnston's 1850 map, traveled fifty miles west after leaving the El Paso wagon road and then sent his scouts another sixty miles southwest indicates that he believed his initial point to be near a major eastward turn of the Rio Grande as mentioned by the Chandler surveyors—a turn that appeared to be shown on Johnston's map at about ninety air miles west of the mouth of the Pecos River (see figure 36).

Michler's scouting party must have traveled south of southwest, since they did not report encountering the heavily traveled and conspicuous Comanche Trail, which ran south from Comanche Springs (Fort Stockton, Texas), even though the trail passed only twenty miles west of King's Springs. They most likely ended their reconnaissance about forty air miles from King's Springs in the high limestone plateau country, still more than twenty miles from the Rio Grande.

Contrary to the scouting report, there are no igneous rocks near the party's route; they traveled exclusively over Cretaceous sedimentary limestone, though perhaps they confused some angular siliceous cobbles (generally rounded rock fragments between 2.5 and 10 inches in diameter) in surface gravels with igneous rock. They may have had a distant view of igneous rocks, either the prominent volcanic butte Santiago Peak, still forty miles to the southwest when they began their return to King's Springs, or, on a clear day, perhaps the Chisos Mountains, at seventy miles. Still, Michler would make this same mistake again when describing a spot on the Rio Grande, which leads one to wonder if the man simply did not know what an igneous rock was.

Michler Is Misled by the Longitude Estimates on Johnston's Map

Johnston's 1850 reconnaissance map of the Rio Grande Valley was the best map available to Michler for locating the initial starting point for his survey.[28] While the longitudinal (west/east) position of landmarks such as Pecos Springs along the well-traveled San Antonio–El Paso wagon road were known with a good degree of accuracy, in the unexplored country farther south along the Rio Grande, longitudinal positions shown by Johnston were only his rough estimates. As it turned out, Michler's target point of the major eastward turn of the Rio Grande was shown on Johnston's map twenty miles west of its true position. Thus, Michler thought his initial point was twenty miles farther west of Pecos Springs than it actually was. This explains why Michler sent his scouts southwest from King's Springs when his initial point—the Chandler Survey end point he needed to connect with—actually lay almost directly to the south.

Michler Changes His Route

Once Michler accepted the scouting report that a southwest route from his camp at King's Springs was impractical, he needed an alternate plan. Surely he looked again to Johnston's map for guidance. It showed four north-south Indian trails branching off from Johnston's reconnaissance trail to reach the Rio Grande at distances ranging from thirty to sixty miles west of the mouth of the Pecos River (see figure 36). Finding one of the trails would mean Michler could follow it to take his wagons down to the river and then work upriver to approach the point where he needed to begin his survey—the "initial point."

Michler needed to go south from King's Springs, but the grain of the drainage and the Indian trails led southeast down the headwater arroyos of Independence Creek. Thus, as a practical matter, to gain distance south he had to travel southeast, diagonally back toward the Pecos River. While doing so, Michler searched for a trail of opportunity heading more directly south to the Rio Grande. He traveled on a good Indian trail down the wide Independence Creek valley for forty miles (about four days) before he found a favorable branch of the Indian trail leaving the creek to head south and ascend the plateau above the creek. The trail was heavily used, but by horses not wagons, so they must have found the ascent difficult. Once on the plateau above the creek, the trail was easier for the wagons, but again it turned more to the southeast, seeking water, and led to a picturesque spring that Michler described as "noticeable for its beauty—falling over a precipice of forty feet—a favorite camping place of the Indians—many paintings of men and animals covering the rocks."[29] Brune in *Springs of Texas* confirms that Michler stopped at what today is Meyers Springs, ten miles northeast of what would later be the railroad village of Dryden, Texas.[30]

By the time Michler reached Meyers Springs, he had given back 30 of the 50 hard-won westward miles he had earlier achieved by traveling west from Pecos Springs to King's Springs. Leaving Meyers Springs, the party followed a wide Indian trail headed southwest, which soon took advantage of a change in the pattern of the drainage. The topographic grain of the arroyos, which earlier had been east toward the Pecos, now was south toward the Rio Grande. Michler approached the Rio Grande along a divide separating two arroyos heading down to the river where there was a major Indian crossing with shallow water and gentle banks on both the north and south sides (figure 37). Michler's wagons had now covered 90 miles of primitive trail since leaving King's Springs and 140 miles since leaving the El Paso Road at Pecos Springs. He described the crossing as "the only place we could reach the river in our wagons."[31] Michler named it "Lipan Crossing" because Lipan Indians were often seen at the crossing and "made themselves useful as guides."

Today this spot is called Shafter Crossing, named after Lt. Colonel William Shafter, who, in June 1876, led a punitive expedition of cavalry and Black Seminole scouts that crossed here on their way into Mexico in pursuit of an Indian band that had been raiding Texas ranches.[32]

The Michler party reached the Rio Grande in the first half of July, and in his report to Emory, Michler noted the "scorching July sun" along the trail to Lipan Crossing. He had only a rough idea how far upstream he was from the mouth of the Pecos. Michler did not recognize this crossing (had not seen it before), so would have concluded that he was more than eighty river miles above the Pecos, because two years earlier he and fellow Topographical Engineer Lieutenant Martin L. Smith had made a boat reconnaissance that went more than four hundred miles up the Rio Grande, reporting that they had poled their flatboat on the river to a point eighty miles above the mouth of the Pecos.[33] Later, as Michler continued to work on his 1853 survey and prepare his final maps, he held

Lipan Crossing—View down the river.

FIGURE 37. **Lipan Crossing.** View east and downstream from the American side comparing a drawing by Michler's naturalist Conrad Stremme with a modern photo. Today this is known as Shafter Crossing, named for Colonel William Shafter, who crossed here in the 1870s seeking to punish Indians for raiding Texas ranches. Emory Report, 75. Photograph by the author.

to his belief that Lipan Crossing was more than eighty miles above the Pecos. In his final report, a view of Lipan Crossing (reproduced in figure 37) carried the caption "eighty-five miles above the Pecos," thus, five miles above the point he and Smith had reached on the earlier reconnaissance.[34]

Johnston's 1850 map provides confirmation that Smith and Michler's flatboat reconnaissance did reach a point near Lipan Crossing. That map was the first to show an expressive and accurate pattern of the meanders of the Rio Grande upstream from the mouth of the Pecos River. The map's accuracy was made possible by the work of the two men, and they were listed as coauthors of Johnston's map. Equally telling is the sudden loss of accuracy in the shape of the meanders of the river on Johnston's map as he sketched the river farther west, first with a mildly wavy solid line and then with a dashed line. Beyond the accurate trace provided by Smith and Michler, the Johnston map continues to show the river trending west-northwest for about fifty miles before making a major turn south toward the Big Bend, and this turn was shown more than twenty miles too far west.

Surveying Begins Upstream

When Michler arrived at Lipan Crossing, he set up a permanent base camp and sent his surveying crew west across the low hills bordering the river on the American side. It is likely their instruments for this land-based portion of their survey were a compact theodolite for direction and a light surveyor's chain to measure distance—the same type of equipment used by the Chandler party to carry out their traverse surveys. They likely used triangulation to measure distance across steep canyons where they could not carry the surveying chain. The boats they had brought with them from San Antonio would not have been useful for carrying the party upstream, since Michler had already learned that even in the small skiff two good oarsmen could not move against the current.[35] In any case, the fast water of Agua Verde Rapids would have stopped the boats less than three miles above their camp.

Michler's description of the problems of access near the river indicates that his men were working entirely on land, moving from one headland to another overlooking the river. He reported that his men had great difficulty measuring their surveying lines near the river because their access was blocked by deep canyons: "We had frequently to make detours of twenty-five to thirty miles, in order to advance our work a few hundred feet."[36] It appears the surveyors returned to the base camp at Lipan Crossing each night. As the distance from the base camp to the work site increased each day, their working hours decreased. It probably took them about three weeks to survey the twenty miles upstream to a point where they were blocked from continuing the survey any farther up the river by a deep and precipitous side canyon that came down from the north to intersect the east-flowing Rio Grande.

This canyon barrier also marked a major turn of the Rio Grande. The survey up the river had moved generally west upstream from Lipan Crossing, but here the river turned to the south. Looking south from their vantage point high on the headland above the canyon junction, the surveyors saw a half-mile-long section of the river flowing toward them through a deep, narrow canyon with high and precipitous walls that continued to grow in height farther upstream. In their work from Lipan Crossing up to this point, the surveyors had seen a gradual increase in the height of the canyon walls enclosing the river, starting at two hundred feet near the crossing but reaching seven hundred feet where they met the barrier canyon.[37] Much higher canyon walls, on the order of fifteen hundred feet above the river, would have faced Michler had he gone farther up the river into the heart of the Lower Canyons.

Upstream Surveying Abandoned

At this juncture, Michler discontinued any effort to extend the survey farther upstream. He really had no choice. His method of work—having his men scramble along the headlands far above the banks of the river during day trips and return each night for the food and shelter of the base camp at Lipan Crossing—had reached its limit. It was successful when the distance was no more than ten to fifteen miles from camp and the headlands were about five hundred feet above the arroyos coming down to the river. It would not work farther up the river where distance from camp exceeded twenty miles and the height of headlands rapidly increased. Michler had no way to move a base camp upriver. There was no access along the river for his wagons, or even a mule train, and the boats were too small to carry enough provisions, even if they could find a way to pole or paddle against the current.

Michler, the highly trained West Point Topographical Engineer, would have known before he left San Antonio with wagons and boats that it was exceedingly unlikely he would be able to reach the point on the Rio Grande where Chandler had abandoned his survey in 1852. In his party, Michler had assistant surveyor E. A. Phillips, who had been a member of Chandler's party. Phillips and

Michler knew Chandler's final camp on the river had been enclosed by canyons whose precipitous limestone walls towered more than fifteen hundred feet above a fearful rapids in the narrow river channel; the only access to Chandler's camp had been a narrow, rocky arroyo on the Mexican side. The most Michler could have reasonably hoped for was to reach a point somewhere close enough to have a distant view of Chandler's final camp site.

In Michler's defense, it was reasonable for him to conclude that the twenty-mile upstream survey his men had finished above Lipan Crossing had reached a point on the river quite close to Chandler's final camp. After all, Chandler had estimated his last camp on the river was less than one hundred miles from the mouth of the Pecos River, and Michler thought the barrier canyon reached by his surveyors was more than one hundred miles from the Pecos (eighty-five to Lipan Crossing plus twenty to the barrier canyon).

To document the most upstream point reached by his crew, Michler included in his report to Emory a landscape sketch of the canyon along the river drawn by his naturalist Stremme (figure 38 shows a comparison of Stremme's sketch with a recent photograph). The view in that sketch is up the Rio Grande channel looking south from a point high on the plateau on the American side; in the Emory Report, this illustration is titled "Cañon—one hundred and five miles above mouth of the Pecos."[38] In it, one sees massive limestone formations dipping gently downstream toward the artist, and in the distance, to the south where the river makes another turn, a gentle anticline in the canyon walls. That anticline can be seen on a modern geologic map of the area.[39]

San Francisco Canyon: The History of an Important Landmark

Michler's surveyors did not recognize that the major canyon preventing them from extending their survey farther upstream was actually the termination of San Francisco Creek. This creek emptied an extensive drainage basin whose headwaters sixty miles farther west were an important source of fresh water for travelers and were shown by name on Johnston's 1850 reconnaissance map, but at that time, no one knew where San Francisco Creek joined the Rio Grande. Stremme's landscape sketch is focused on the Rio Grande and gives no hint that the barrier canyon on his immediate right had been plunging east for tens of miles as it approached the Rio Grande. Nor does the sketch reveal that less than one-half mile before joining the river, the San Francisco Canyon makes a sharp

Cañon—One hundred and five miles above mouth of the Pecos.

FIGURE 38. **View of the Rio Grande.** View upstream, southwest, from the cliffs above the mouth of San Francisco Canyon. Top: a woodcut illustration in the Emory Report, made from a sketch by Conrad Stremme in July 1853. Bottom: a recent photo from what is judged to be the same position and view as Stremme's. Emory Report, 77. Photograph courtesy of Beau Rolfe.

turn directly south before joining the Rio Grande. Stremme must have seen this right-angle turn in the canyon from his vantage point but did not recognize its importance and did not show the canyon in his drawing, nor is it mentioned in Michler's narrative report. The final Boundary Map 17, completed later in Washington, also does not show San Francisco Canyon approaching from the west. The map only shows the canyon splaying out to the north and northeast with no branch corresponding to San Francisco Creek extending to the west.

It would be a long time before anyone realized that this big dry canyon was the mouth of San Francisco Creek. For the next thirty years, mapmakers who bothered to suggest where the headwaters of San Francisco Creek connected to the Rio Grande usually showed the junction forty miles too far upstream near the mouth of Reagan Canyon, where the river makes another major turn to the east. Adding to the early uncertainty, an 1881 *Military Map of the Rio Grande Frontier* showed San Francisco Creek connecting with the Rio Grande at the mouth of Sanderson Canyon, six miles downstream from San Francisco Canyon.[40]

The junction of San Francisco Creek and the Rio Grande was correctly located on a map for the first time in March 1882 when Presidio County assistant surveyor John T. Gano submitted a new map to the office of the county's chief surveyor in Fort Davis (figure 39 and appendix C).[41]

Gano's map was also the first to accurately show the trace of the Rio Grande through the Lower Canyons. In total, his map showed the trace of fifty-six miles of the river as it crossed what is today Brewster County, from the mouth of Maravillas Creek in the Black Gap Wildlife Management Area downstream to the mouth of San Francisco Creek. His map was the product of a boat-based survey in which he was escorted by a contingent of Texas Rangers led by Captain Charles Nevill. Gano's handwritten note on the map says: "The surveys were actually made in the field by me during the month of January 1882." Nevill recounted their trip down the river in a letter to his father and in a report to his commander.[42] Nevill's correspondence and Gano's map document the second passage by a boat through the Lower Canyons of the Rio Grande, thirty years after the first passage by Chandler's boatman, Charles Abbott, in November 1852.[43]

Eastern Half of Boundary Map 17: Lipan Crossing to San Francisco Canyon

The results of the Michler Survey crew's traverse work along the hills on the American side upstream from Lipan Crossing is documented in the eastern

Part II: The 1853 Michler Survey

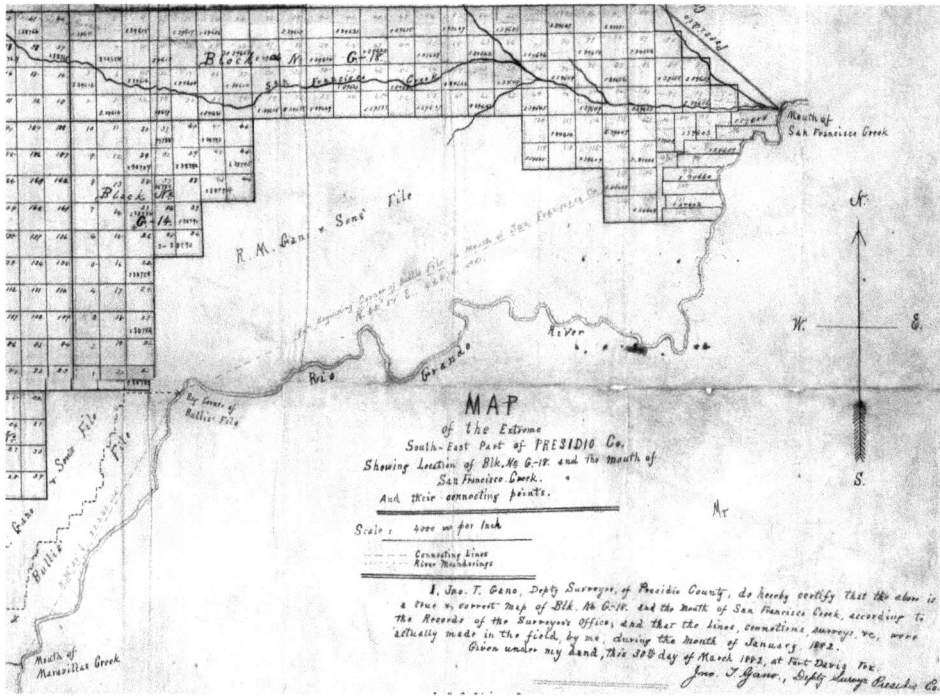

FIGURE 39. **John Gano's 1882 Map.** This unpublished map of a part of Presidio County is important in the history of mapping the Rio Grande because it was the earliest map to correctly display the course of the Rio Grande through the Lower Canyons and the first to show where San Francisco Creek joins the Rio Grande. The map documents the passage of the Gano party through the Lower Canyons, the second successful boat passage through the towering canyons. Courtesy of Texas General Land Office online, map 10985.

half of Boundary Map 17. The overland survey produced an accurate map. The meander pattern and distances between landmarks on the boundary map compare favorably with modern maps along the river (figure 40). The level of detail on the topography near the river falls off with increasing distance upstream from Lipan Crossing, most likely a function of less time available for surveying with the increased travel time to and from the base camp. In Michler's final report to Major Emory, he noted that in one case a thirty-mile detour by his men was required to advance the survey along the river a few hundred feet.[44] To detour, they had to move away from the river along the rim of a tributary canyon; find a suitable, less deep place to cross the canyon; and then come back down the other side of the canyon to the river. Looking at jeep trails on satellite images, the only

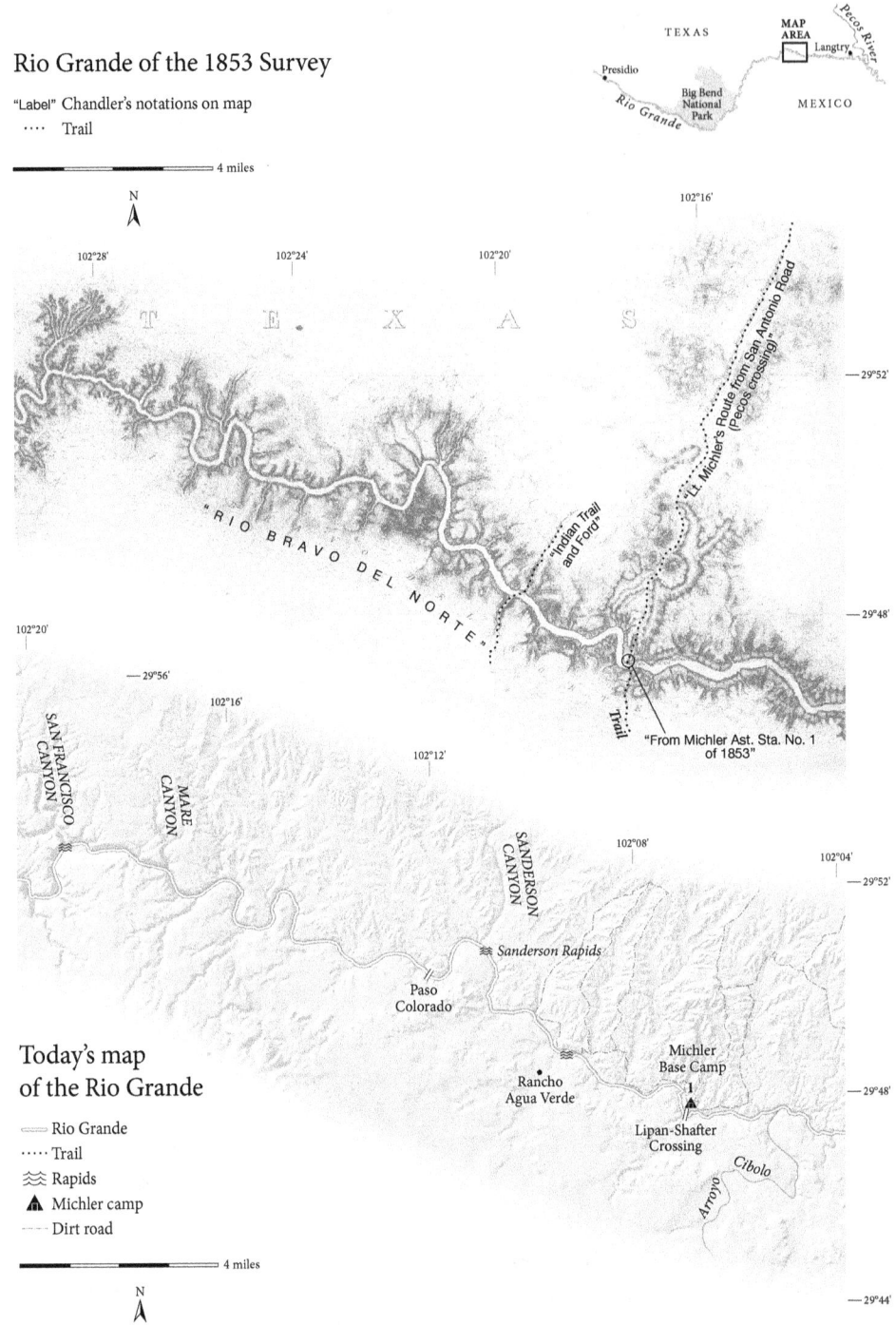

FIGURE 40. **River Trace Comparison: San Francisco Canyon to Lipan Crossing.** A comparison of the eastern half of Michler's Boundary Map 17 with a modern map for that portion of Map 17 downstream from the mouth of San Francisco Canyon. This part of Map 17 is accurate and was based on careful overland traverse lines using theodolite for direction and chain for distance along headlands near the river. Boundary Map 17, National Archives. Map by Carol Zuber-Mallison.

place where a thirty-mile detour appears necessary for men riding mules is the Sanderson Canyon, seven miles upstream of Lipan Crossing. The other canyons, although still deep, could have been detoured in only eight miles.

To map the river trace, the surveyors did not have to set foot on the immediate bank of the river. They needed only to have instrument men and flagmen occupy points along the bluffs overlooking the river. This they could do by traversing from one headland to another overlooking the river, and even though the headland might be five hundred vertical feet above the river and seven hundred horizontal feet from the river, they needed only to estimate the horizontal distance from their headland to a point in space directly above the river to correctly place the river on their map. The general character of the topography adjoining the river on Map 17 is correct in showing cliffs enclosing the river. Topographic detail is meager though somewhat better on the American side, where the surveyors worked, than it is on the Mexican side. Only the large tributary canyons of Sanderson and Mare, on the American side, seven and eighteen miles above Lipan Crossing respectively, appear correct in form and location. Smaller American side canyons such as Red House, Taylor, Jabalina (Javelin), and Britton cannot be recognized among the generic side canyons shown on the map.

Rapids on the river are indicated on Boundary Map 17 by a stippled pattern in the channel. The rapids are usually correctly shown on the map because the surveyors had a good view of the river from the headlands. The first rapids was at the Lipan Crossing base camp. Moving upstream, the next rapids and a river crossing were three miles above, at today's Agua Verde Rapids (Class II) at the mouth of Mexican-side Arroyo Agua Verde. Next, at seven miles, was Sanderson Rapids (Class II) at the mouth of Sanderson Canyon. Two miles farther upstream, at the mouth of an unnamed small arroyo on the Mexican side, the map shows rapids where today there is a ford named Paso Colorado.[45] The most upstream rapids shown on Map 17 is at the mouth of Arroyo Los Maromeros (acrobats), eleven miles above the surveyors' Lipan Crossing camp. There is no rapids or crossing at that site today. They did not record the small rapids that lies at the mouth of Arroyo Las Pompas, where Paso Las Pompas Crossing is today, fifteen miles above their base camp, or the large San Francisco Rapids (Class II+) at twenty miles above.[46] The surveyors could not see the San Francisco rapids from their position on the headland seven hundred feet above the rapids. Their view of the rapids was hidden behind the intervening steep north wall of the canyon directly beneath them (see figure 38).

Map 17 shows only two Indian trails crossing the Rio Grande. On the American side, the last eleven miles of the Indian trail Michler traveled on his approach to the Rio Grande at Lipan Crossing were shown. That trail was shown to extend another mile on the Mexican side. At Agua Verde Rapids, three miles above their camp, the map shows a trail coming down from the northeast, crossing near the rapids, and continuing south up Arroyo Agua Verde on the Mexican side. Johnston's 1850 map shows one other Indian trail coming down to the river about ten miles upstream of Lipan Crossing. Modern maps prepared by the US Customs Service show four additional crossings, but these are probably recent cattle ranch crossings of no historical significance.[47]

Western Half of Boundary Map 17: The Heart of the Lower Canyons

Michler's surveyors ended their upstream work at the mouth of San Francisco Canyon, abandoning any further attempt to reach the targeted "initial point." The result was an unsurveyed gap of the river's course farther upstream to the point reached by the Chandler party in 1852 (see figure 35). In a letter to Emory summarizing his survey, Michler falsely stated: "The initial point of our survey was found to be a little over forty miles above [upstream of Lipan Crossing]—It was next to an impossibility to approach the river for the first twenty miles of the survey [initial point to San Francisco Canyon]—this section being cut up by deep arroyos; steep hills covered with rocks of igneous origin intervene and jut to the waters edge. The river here is very tortuous."[48] Michler's letter to Emory continued the ruse of his completion of a full survey, stating: "On arriving at the mouth of the Pecos—the survey, 125 miles in extent, was completed."[49] Michler did not write his letter until March 1856, by which time both Chandler and Michler would have prepared preliminary copies of their adjoining Boundary Maps 18 and 17. With these maps in hand, they would for the first time be able to estimate the distance of the unsurveyed gap lying between the two maps (figure 41).

The plain truth was that Michler made no serious attempt in 1853 to reach his "initial point," and in his report to Emory, he only indirectly implied that the initial point lay 20 river miles upstream from the point actually reached by his surveyors. He did not visit the river at any point upstream from the mouth of San Francisco Canyon. He surveyed only 94 miles of the Rio Grande lying above the mouth of the Pecos River, not the 125 miles he claimed. Figure 41 shows a comparison of the river trace Michler sketched in on Map 17 versus the actual river trace. His sketched-in portion of the Rio Grande carries no detail

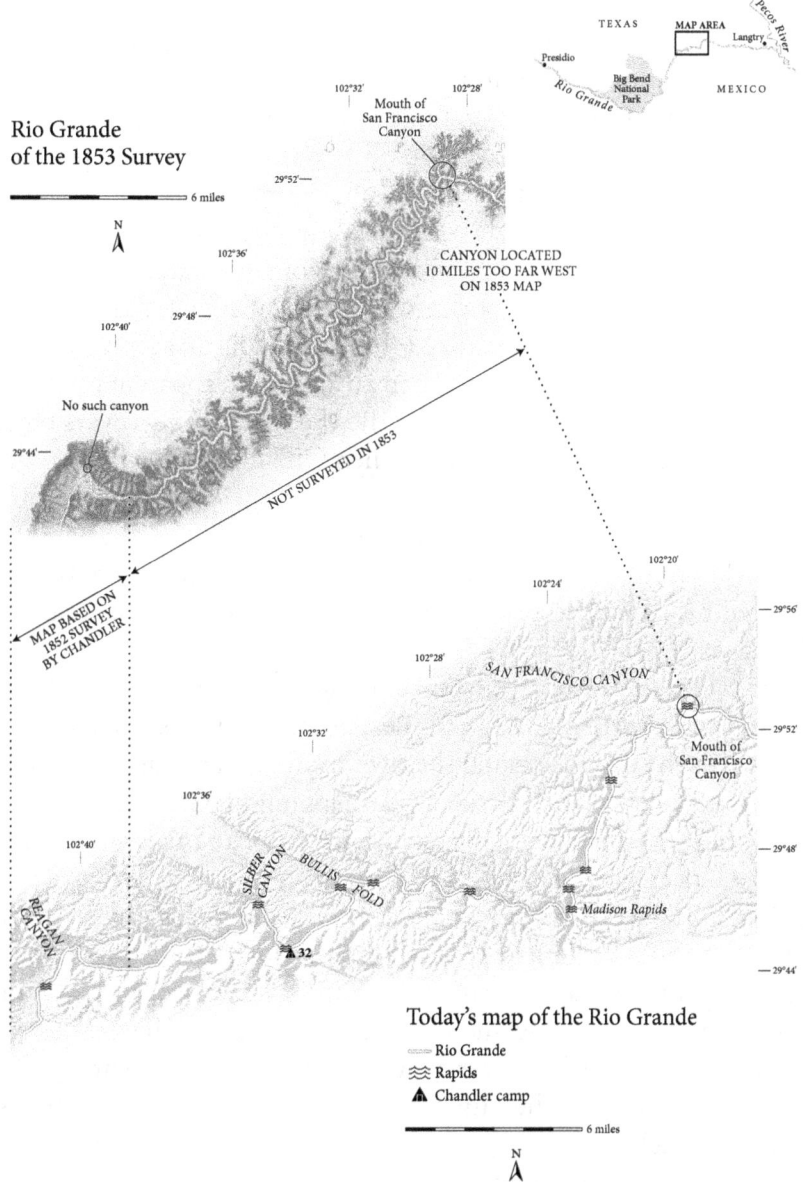

FIGURE 41. **River Trace Comparison: The Lower Canyons.** A comparison of the western half of Michler's Boundary Map 17 with a modern map for the forty-mile section of the river beginning at the Big Canyon area of the Black Gap Wildlife Management Area and extending downstream to the mouth of San Francisco Canyon. This includes the heart of the massive fifteen-hundred-foot-deep Lower Canyons of the Rio Grande. The two maps present strikingly different views of the course of the river. With the exception of about five miles of river trace at the extreme southwestern limit of Map 17, which was based on the work of Chandler's men while hurrying down to their final camp in rubber boats in 1852, the trace of the river on the western half of Map 17 is a complete fabrication by Michler. Neither he nor his men witnessed any part of it beyond the distant view they had of the first half mile of river lying upstream from the mouth of San Francisco Canyon. All Michler had to guide the river trace pictured on his map was a poor estimate of the approximate compass bearing and straight-line distance between the two end points. Boundary Map 17, National Archives. Map by Carol Zuber-Mallison.

to suggest that his party had visited this part of the river, such as rapids, Indian trails, or arroyos coming down to the river. The Lower Canyons are very deep and are eroded massive Cretaceous limestone. There are no igneous rocks near the river's edge as described by Michler. The nearest igneous exposures at the river are more than 150 miles upstream.[50] The river channel is not "tortuous" with tight meanders of small amplitude like those shown on Michler's sketch; rather, the trace is characterized by long straight sections separated by sharp turns, a typical drainage pattern where hard bedrock is broken by faults or joints.

Michler and Emory likely rationalized that not having an accurate map of a few miles of remote and inaccessible canyon in an area of no apparent economic value would not be an important omission. Nor did the Mexican surveyors prepare any map of this section of the river. In 1856, when Chandler and Michler worked to complete their final boundary maps and reports in the Washington, DC, office, Chandler altered his 1852 letter to Emory to be consistent with Michler's new estimated location for the joining of their surveys at 125 miles above the Pecos. He wrote that his party had reached a point "since shown to be about 125 miles above the Pecos."[51]

The actual surveying gap in distance along the river between the work of Chandler and that of Michler was 34 miles, not the 20 miles Michler estimated. The true gap was the distance along the river from San Francisco Canyon, where Michler had stopped, to the last credible mapping by Chandler just beyond a major eastward turn of the river. Michler's estimate of 20 miles within the Lower Canyons was short for two reasons. First, he thought the San Francisco Canyon was 105 river miles upstream from the mouth of the Pecos, but it was only 94 miles. Thus, he thought he had reached a point farther upstream and farther west than he really had, and he also thought he was closer to Chandler's last point, which he knew lay somewhere to the south. Second, he had not seen and did not know the trace of the river as it flowed across the unsurveyed gap. As a result, he underestimated the number of miles added by sharp changes in the river's direction, such as those at Silber Canyon, Hot Springs Rapids, Madison Rapids, and Bullis Fold (see figure 41).

Today, we can determine with confidence where Chandler ended his surveying by comparing the river trace shown in the southwest corner of Boundary Map 17 with the actual river trace on a modern map, noting the point where Chandler's heretofore accurate mapping of the course of the river (on Michler's map) abruptly broke down. This indicates that Chandler's men stopped surveying at a point 127 river miles above the Pecos. That position for Chandler's final point on the river, and thus Michler's targeted initial point on the river, is, by the happenstance of offsetting errors by Michler, almost the same distance that Michler reported in his letter to Major Emory: "125 miles above the Pecos."[52]

It must be pointed out that when Chandler's surveying operations broke down and the scattered elements of the party gathered on the river at Hot Springs Rapids, their camp was 8 miles downriver from the point where they recorded their last notes on the course of the river. Thus, Chandler's final camp was only 119 miles above the Pecos River. While camped at Hot Springs, Chandler did no surveying and had only a rough idea of where he was relative to the Pecos. In his letter to Emory from the Hot Springs camp, he made no comment about location other than that he had "carried the survey to a canyon near here." The location of Chandler's final camp on the Rio Grande was not indicated in any way on Michler's Boundary Map 17. Not only did Michler not know the exact location of Chandler's camp on the river, but showing Chandler's approximate camp location at a point more than 15 river miles inside of Michler's Map 17 would have been difficult to explain, since Michler claimed he alone had surveyed the entirety of Map 17.[53]

Today, the location of Chandler's final camp is known because Parry recorded in his journal a detailed description of the unusual site as well as compass bearings to distant landmarks. His bearings from the top of a mountain overlooking the camp accurately document their location (see Chandler's final camp location on the modern map comparison portion of figure 41).[54]

When the final boundary maps were being prepared in Washington, DC, Emory must have decided that, given the uncertainty of the trace of the river in this area, Chandler's "final point" on the river and thus Michler's "initial point" would be arbitrarily set at the latitude where Chandler's Map 18 joined Michler's Map 17 (29°41′30″).

As a result of this arbitrary latitude for joining the maps, which did not fit the boundary of the actual work done by Chandler in the field, the most upstream seven miles of the river trace on Michler's Boundary Map 17 were actually sketched in from the field notes of Chandler's men, who had floated down the river in boats. Chandler's river trace shown on Michler's map is correct in form and good in distance. Starting at the south end of Michler's map and moving north, Chandler's sketch correctly showed the river flowing north for two miles. Then he documented the important right-angle eastward turn of the river toward the Pecos. This turn had long been anticipated as the Chandler party had surveyed north for weeks, moving downstream from today's Big Bend National Park. On

Map 17, the topography shown adjoining the river channel in the vicinity of the major eastward turn is highly generalized, and it was probably based on brief notes or memory during the frantic rush of the boats down the river to find the mule train. Missing on Map 17 are Big Canyon and Reagan Canyon, which join the river on the American side just upstream from the major eastward turn, but included is a nonexistent canyon at the apex of the turn. This false canyon, coming down from the north, may have been added to honor the commonly held but erroneous belief of mapmakers during that time that the San Francisco Creek joined the Rio Grande at this major eastward turn. Chandler himself did not see the turn of the river sketched by his boat crew because he had left the river on foot to go into the mountains in search of the mule train that was carrying his food and camp gear.[55]

The Chandler party made an important contribution to Boundary Map 17 by documenting the location and form of a major turn of the river, but Michler did not list Chandler as coauthor of his map. Recognizing the Chandler party's contribution to a portion of the river assigned to Michler may have been viewed as "untidy" by Emory, drawing attention to the reality that Michler did not visit this part of the river depicted on his map.

It is not known how or by whom the trace of the river was filled in for the unsurveyed gap. From office work done in Washington, DC, after all field surveys were completed, the mapmakers would have determined the longitude and latitude of the end points of the unsurveyed gap, and thereby, the bearing and straight-line length of the gap. It appears they then simply connected the end points with a meandering line to mark the river trace.

An apparently unused source of information available to Michler on the course of the river across the unsurveyed gap was the rough sketch map made by Chandler's boatman Charles Abbott of his daring adventure down the river. Parry had asked Abbott to make notes along his route and deliver them to Major Emory if and when he reached Fort Duncan.[56] As we know, Abbott reached the fort in just ten days, beating the overland party by ten days. Michler does not mention Abbott or his map, but Michler and his assistant Arthur Schott were at Fort Duncan when Abbott arrived on November 14, 1852. In a letter to Emory, Schott reported: "I found Abbott[,] the man belonging to Mr. Chandler's party, more and better provided to answer my questions as I expected. He had made himself a sketch in his own primitive manner, which of course, as it is based only upon guessing without any aid of instruments[,] cannot be of much worth."[57]

Part II: The 1853 Michler Survey　　　　　　　　　　　　　　　　　　　　　181

In spite of Schott noting with surprise that Abbott could answer questions about the river trace and had prepared a rough map, it appears that Schott concluded Abbott's information was too unreliable to be of any help in the preparation of their final boundary map, even though Abbott and his companions had been the only members of the Chandler or Michler parties to actually see this section of the Rio Grande. Abbott's sketch map of the river has not survived, but it seems unlikely that the generic wiggle depicting the river trace on Boundary Map 17 came from Abbott's sketch.

The Boat Survey from Lipan Crossing to the Pecos River

Michler's approach route to the Rio Grande and the upstream survey to San Francisco Canyon were more difficult and time-consuming than he expected. Running short of time and perhaps provisions, he decided to use his boats to conduct a rapid survey down the river from Lipan Crossing. To justify not using the more accurate method of traverse surveying onshore with instruments and chain, Michler noted it was "impracticable to survey on land without taking an interminable length of time." We do not know if Michler's time constraint was self-imposed or had come from Emory. That he went to the considerable trouble of bringing boats in wagons from San Antonio suggests that Michler had planned to use this quicker option all along, preferring to reach the relative comforts of Fort Duncan as soon as he could after spending several months in his frontier tent.[58]

When the disassembled wooden boats carried by the wagons were put together at Lipan Crossing, the boards had dried and warped during the long, hot trip; the boats were leaky and fragile, but they floated.[59] With limited space in the boats, Michler sent the wagons and most of his men back overland, noting that "the train was sent back by the road to Eagle Pass."[60] The wagons backtracked the way they had come, over the rough Indian trail north to Meyers Springs and Independence Creek. Then, as they continued northwest up that creek toward King's Springs, they found a cutoff trail headed north that bypassed King's Springs but saved them thirty miles of travel (see figure 6). They went east to join the San Antonio Road, south to cross the Pecos, farther south to cross Devils River, then east past Fort Clark (Brackettville, Texas), to Fort Inge (Uvalde, Texas), and finally turned southwest to Fort Duncan (Eagle Pass, Texas). According to Michler, he and the wagon train arrived at Fort Duncan within hours of each other.[61]

With the two small skiffs and the larger flatboat, the Michler party started down the Rio Grande within a day of August 6, 1853. We know this because Michler recorded eleven nightly camps on the way to Fort Duncan, and he sent Emory a letter reporting his survey was complete on August 18, 1853.[62]

Michler described his method of surveying while floating down the river as "taking the direction [by handheld compass] of the [river] courses and timing the passage from bend to bend—when opportunity offered, the speed of each boat was ascertained by distances accurately measured on land—making allowances for change of current [speed] and other causes of error [wind]."[63]

Michler supplemented the direction and time records made while floating in the boats during the day with a celestial determination of latitude made with the sextant each night.[64] Unfortunately, an accurate north-south position (latitude) was not of much help in determining distance between landmarks along the river, since the course of the river was primarily easterly, and latitudinal positions remained relatively unchanged from camp to camp.

The longitude of the camps along the river, shown in tables in the final Emory Report, were estimated values determined later by east-west measurements taken directly from the completed boundary maps themselves. In effect, the longitudes reported by Michler were based on the compass and clock notes taken in the floating boat; as a result, they are only rough estimates. Michler's longitude positions were anchored at the mouth of the Pecos River by a tie with Arthur Schott's longitude calculation based on his more accurate overland traverse survey, which in turn was anchored to Emory's even more accurate celestial determination of longitude at the Fort Duncan observatory, more than a hundred miles from the Pecos.[65]

Immediately after Michler left the low, open banks on both sides of the river at Lipan Crossing, the boats entered limestone canyons, lower here—on the order of one hundred to three hundred feet deep—but the steep banks confined the men and boats to the channel. Early on the first day, at the first major rapids, only three miles from base camp, the awkward flatboat crashed into a wall, "tearing away her entire front."[66] They spent the remainder of the day repairing the boat. This wreck was at today's Zacate Rapids, where Arroyo El Zacate on the Mexican side empties into the Rio Grande, throwing a rock debris apron out into the river and pressing the narrow river channel against a sheer limestone wall on the American side. Because the "wreck" camp was so close to Lipan Crossing, it was the only camp on the trip to the Pecos with no sextant-based latitude recorded. Michler called this camp 2, with the start at Lipan Crossing as camp 1.

Part II: The 1853 Michler Survey

In the Emory Report, Michler provided a lively description of being carried rapidly down the canyons on the way to the Pecos: "Rapids are numerous—insurmountable to navigation—for 30 miles above the Pecos one continuous rapid."[67] His "constant rapids" are at odds with the more tranquil state of the river today and with his earlier experience of polling a flatboat up this same section of the river. Perhaps the difference was a high river stage in August 1853 but a lower one in fall 1850 when he and Lieutenant Smith had poled up the river. It is a puzzle why Michler makes no comment regarding that earlier poling expedition when traveling this section of the river. Surely he recognized unique sections of the river he had seen three years earlier. Chances are he had come to suspect that he and Lieutenant Smith had overestimated how far up the river they had poled, and he wished not to explain their earlier claim of reaching eighty miles above the Pecos.[68]

The boats reached the final point of their survey—camp 7—at the mouth of the Pecos River about August 12, six days after leaving Lipan Crossing. Not counting the first short day, the boats averaged 14 miles per day. This speed indicates they spent little time onshore except to camp at night. At the mouth of the Pecos, Michler tied his survey to the final point of the survey that Arthur Schott, moving upriver from Fort Duncan, had completed in October 1852. Now moving quickly downstream without surveying, Michler covered the last 116 miles in five days and arrived at Fort Duncan about August 17. He averaged 23 miles per day, about 2 miles per daylight hour, a speed similar to that of Charles Abbott in his desperate 235-mile trip through the Lower Canyons and down to Fort Duncan in November 1852.

In a letter dated August 18, 1853, at Fort Duncan, Michler reported to Emory, then at his observatory at the mouth of the Rio Grande, that he had completed his survey down to the mouth of the Pecos River.[69]

The Boundary Maps Based on the Boat Survey

The boat survey from Lipan Crossing down to the mouth of the Pecos was documented on three boundary maps authored by Michler: the easternmost four miles of Map 17, all of Map 16, and the west half of Map 15. The span of coverage for each of these maps is shown in figure 35, which also shows that the "footprint" of Map 17 is twice as wide as that of Map 16, in spite of the fact that the original boundary maps are the same width. The distortion in apparent width comes about because the east and west margins of each boundary map are shown on the index map at the true longitude where the margin of each boundary map cuts the river. In other words, the index map displays the true longitudinal span that Michler mapped, not what his map claims he mapped. Map 16 appears narrow on the index because Michler overestimated the east-west distance of Map 16 by 31 percent. In contrast, Map 17 appears wide on the index because Michler underestimated the east-west distance of that map by 19 percent.

Setting aside the problem of west-east distance distortion, the boundary maps based on the boat survey faithfully show the course and character of the Rio Grande. The distinctive shapes of the meanders compare favorably with modern maps because Michler's inflation of distance is uniform, and because the river flows in a channel cut into solid rock that has changed very little since 1853.

While the pattern of meanders on Michler's maps is excellent and looks to the eye to be the same as on a modern map, Michler's west-to-east distances along the river below Lipan Crossing were consistently much too long. On average, the distance from one landmark on the river to another landmark is 29 percent too long; almost all sections along the river are inflated to that extent, but just above and below the boat wreck, short sections are 50 to 100 percent too long. If you make a transparent overlay of a Michler map along the boat survey, then reduce it by 29 percent, the overlay is a very good match with a modern map of the river.

The "west-east stretch" can be demonstrated by comparing the true straight-line distance between two landmarks with the straight-line distance for those same landmarks as shown on a boundary map. For the entire length of the boat survey, Michler's maps show a straight-line distance of fifty-eight miles from Lipan Crossing to the mouth of the Pecos, whereas the actual distance is only forty-five miles (29 percent too long). In terms of the distance along the channel of the meandering river, Michler reported eighty-five miles to the Pecos from Lipan Crossing, whereas the true river distance is seventy-four miles. He is only 15 percent too long by that measure, because his river course through the meanders is too straight (too short), partially offsetting his otherwise overlong estimates of distance. The meandering of the river on Michler's maps adds thirteen miles to his straight-line distance, whereas an accurate river trace on today's maps shows the meanders add twenty-two miles.

Michler said he calculated his distance from point to point along the river by recording the time it took for his boat to reach each point and then applied his estimated speed of the floating boat.[70] His overestimates are systemic, that is, they occur throughout the trip down the river; they are not restricted to a random mistake here or there.

Part II: *The 1853 Michler Survey*

Why are the west-east distances inflated? The easy answer would be that Michler thought the boats were going faster than they really were. He had no way to determine the speed of the current except to record the time it took to float across a short distance measured by chain where he had access to the bank of the river. Areas of good bank access are those where the river is wider and the current is slower. Most of the time he was moving down a narrow canyon where the current is faster. Michler knew this, and had to estimate how much faster the boats traveled in the canyons; perhaps he increased the speed estimate too much.

The explanation for the overlong distance estimates may actually lie elsewhere. Michler knew that his estimate of boat speed was an approximation, and he would have looked to other information to judge whether or not the speed he was using was about right. I think Michler may have used higher boat speeds in his distance calculations in order to make his east-west distances on his new boundary maps fit better with the east-west distances along the Rio Grande shown on Johnston's 1850 reconnaissance map, which Michler used to guide his expedition (see figure 36).[71]

Johnston's map showed the Rio Grande extending west from the mouth of the Pecos for ninety air miles, then turning south toward the Big Bend Country. It is likely that Michler thought his surveyors had reached Johnston's major turn to the south at the barrier canyon (San Francisco) twenty miles upstream from Lipan Crossing. If that were so, Michler's expectation would have been that his boat survey would confirm that Lipan Crossing was about seventy air miles west of the Pecos. Yet I suspect that when preliminary plots of his boat survey records were made later in the Washington, DC, office, they indicated the Pecos to be about fifty air miles from Lipan Crossing. Michler would not have been pleased with such a large discrepancy relative to Johnston's map and would have used any flexibility he had to increase the distance and reduce the discrepancy. Since Michler had no flexibility to change the accurate traverse survey upstream from Lipan Crossing, his only option was to shift his boat-derived locations to the west by increasing the estimated boat speeds as much as seemed reasonable. Another benefit for Michler of shifting his locations farther west was that it would move the most upstream point actually reached by his surveyors at San Francisco Canyon closer to Chandler's final survey point on the river, thus reducing the apparent unsurveyed gap.

In any event, Michler's boundary maps ended up showing Lipan Crossing and San Francisco Canyon about ten miles west of their true longitudinal position.

Rapids below Lipan Crossing

Rapids are indicated on Michler's maps by stippled areas in the bed of the river. The locations shown are in good agreement with the location of present-day rapids. The first rapids was less than two miles below Lipan Crossing, an easy hour's walk below their camp. This rapids was at the mouth of Arroyo El Cíbolo, a large and extensive arroyo on the Mexican side whose headwaters began more than sixty miles to the southwest. Even though this major arroyo was near their camp, it is not shown on the boundary maps. The general lack of topographic detail along the bank of the river is a continuing weakness of the maps made during the boat survey and indicates that the party made a rapid descent in the boats, not recording the location of side canyons and spending very little time onshore.

They reached the second, more severe rapids on the morning of the first day, where they crashed the unwieldy flatboat into a rock wall, ripping off the entire front.[72] Today, satellite images of this rapids show a narrow chute crashing into the rock wall on the American bank.[73] Michler shows this rapids at the extreme western edge of his Boundary Map 16 but does not show Arroyo Zacate, whose apron of debris thrown out into the river channel forms the rapids (figure 42). Why they did not take the time to line the boats through this rapids is a puzzle. The rapids surprised them in spite of it being only three miles below their base at Lipan Crossing. Michler was negligent for not sending scouts down the river during the three weeks he and most of his party were at the base camp waiting on the surveyors working upstream. Without spending a single night away from camp, his scouts could have hiked ten miles down along the bank of the river and made a sketch map of potential river hazards.

The location of Zacate Rapids, seventy-one miles upstream from the mouth of the Pecos, reveals that the earlier claim of Lieutenants Smith and Michler that they had poled a flatboat eighty miles upstream from the mouth of the Pecos was excessive. There is no way a flatboat large enough to carry their supplies could pass this narrow rapids; however, poling even seventy-one miles above the Pecos was still an impressive feat.

The third rapids, at today's El Mesquite Crossing, was twenty-one miles downstream from Lipan Crossing and fifty-three miles above the Pecos and was formed by debris from Arroyo Viento Negro on the Mexican side.[74] The fourth, fifth, and sixth rapids were where Mesquite Canyon and two unnamed small canyons enter from the American side. There are no rapids today at the last three

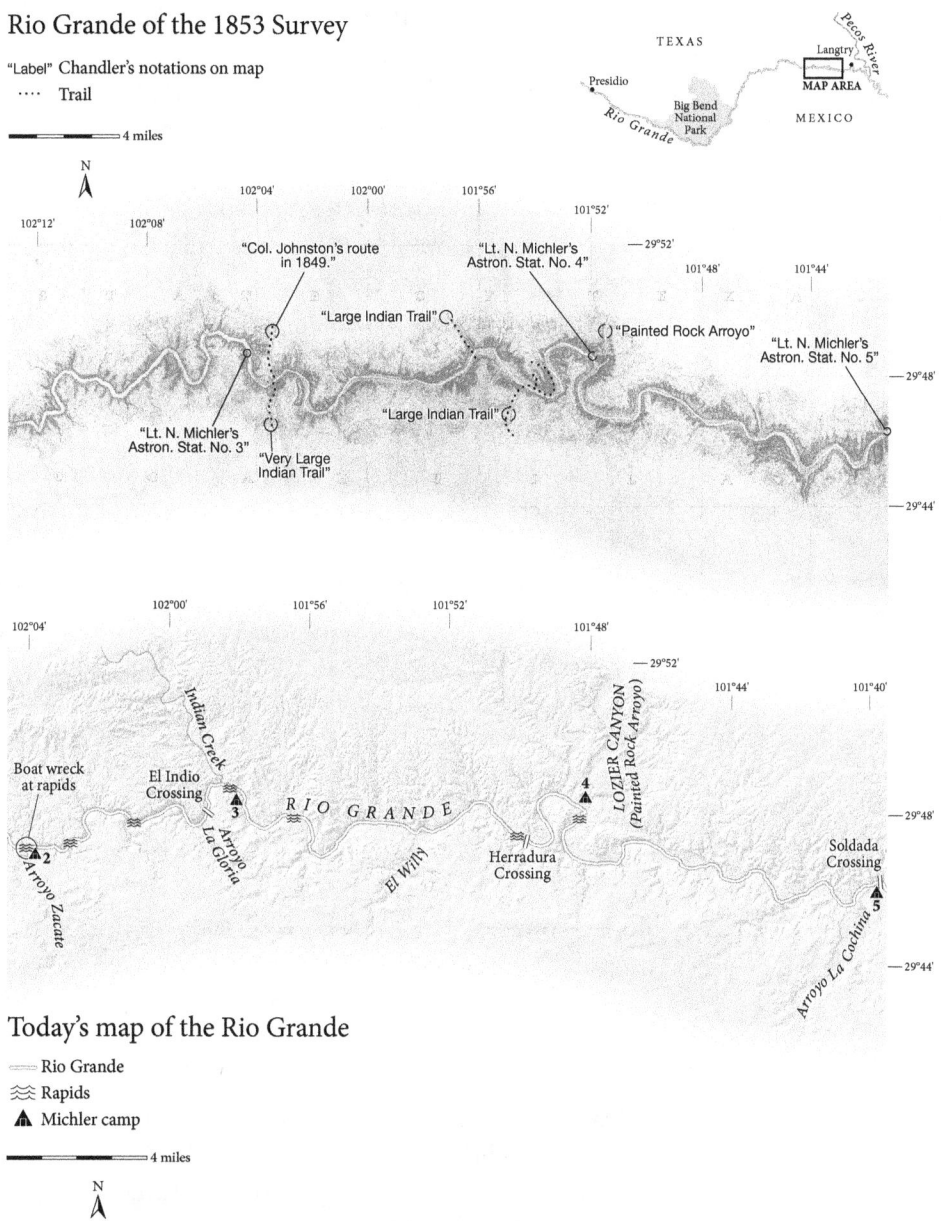

FIGURE 42. **River Trace Comparison: Lipan Crossing to Langtry.** A comparison of Boundary Map 16 with a modern map. The surveying for Map 16 was done from a boat floating down the river. The direction of the course of the river from one turn to the next was recorded by handheld compass, and distance was estimated by noting the elapsed time to float from one turn to another. The map is good in terms of reproducing the character and relative position of points along the river, but Michler's distances were uniformly overestimated by about 30 percent. Boundary Map 16, National Archives. Map by Carol Zuber-Mallison.

locations, but as all are close together, they could have been formed by rock debris thrown out into the river in a single flash flood.

The seventh rapids was at the mouth of what Michler called Painted Rock Arroyo, forty-eight miles above the Pecos. This is a major canyon on the American side, today called Lozier Canyon, and US Highway 90 crosses the canyon west of Langtry, Texas. Fifteen miles northwest of the bridge over the canyon is Meyers Springs, where Michler had stopped on his way to the Rio Grande. Johnston's 1850 map (see figure 36) also shows the trace of Lozier Canyon, and about ten miles up, the canyon shows a point marked "water," apparently meant to indicate Meyers Springs.

The eighth rapids is at today's Rock Crossing where the large Arroyo Carreta (small cart) enters from the Mexican side.[75] The last rapids shown on the boundary maps was at today's Soldado (soldier) Crossing at the mouth of Arroyo La Cochina (the sow), at the downstream end of Map 16, nine miles above the village of Langtry, Texas.[76]

No rapids were shown along the final thirty miles of the Rio Grande down to the mouth of the Pecos. In this section of the river, there were no large, sediment-carrying arroyos to throw debris out into the river to form a rapids.

The mapping of the junction of major tributary canyons with the Rio Grande must have been a low priority for the surveyors. These were usually not recorded on their maps. Michler's Map 15 did not show the large Langtry Creek and Eagle Nest Canyons near the later railroad village of Langtry, site of Judge Roy Bean's 1880s vintage "Law West of the Pecos" saloon and courthouse. A short distance downstream from the mouth of the Pecos, the surveyor Arthur Schott, in that portion of Map 15 that he surveyed, did not show the large Arroyo La Parida on the Mexican side or Seminole Canyon on the American side, now famous for its pictographs.[77]

Indian Trails Downstream from Lipan Crossing

Michler's maps showed Indian trails crossing the Rio Grande at three points during the boat survey. All were on Map 16, which was richer in detail than the adjoining boundary maps. This may be a result of greater attention to detail by Theodore H. Oehlschlager, the draftsman of that map.[78]

The first trail, at sixty miles above the Pecos, Michler labeled "Col. Johnston's route in 1849." The trail is shown to approach from the northwest and cross to the Mexican side, where it continues directly south and is labeled "Very Large Indian Trail." Michler's reason for locating and labeling this trail is unknown. We found no justification for locating a trail here or for crediting Johnston. The location was not favorable for a crossing. There were no arroyos intersecting the river to provide approach or exit trails, and no crossing is indicated here today on maps showing current Rio Grande crossings.[79] As for crediting Johnston, Johnston's 1849 reconnaissance map showed he did not come within fifty miles of this area, and the closest Indian trail shown on his later reconnaissance map of 1850 was ten miles farther west.[80]

Perhaps the trail should have been placed another four miles upstream at El Indio Crossing, where arroyos come down to the river from both the American and Mexican sides to provide favorable approach and exit routes, but that location still does not fit any trail mapped by Johnston.

The apparently erroneous trail position and label may have been taken from maps in the files of the Topographical Engineers when Michler was in the Washington, DC, office preparing his Boundary Map 16 in 1856. A *Map of Texas and Part of New Mexico* compiled by the Bureau of Topographical Engineers and published in 1857 showed a "Large Indian Trail" at the same location as that of Map 16 but credits Johnston's 1850 reconnaissance map.[81] The historical pattern suggests that the 1849 date and location for Michler's "Very Large Indian Trail" near the Pecos was an early mistake by mapmakers that took some time to get straightened out.

The second Indian trail and river crossing shown by Michler was fifty-three miles above the Pecos. It appears that the boat party recognized this crossing and correctly located it because it fits the topography and is located at today's Cinco de Mayo [Fifth of May] Crossing.

The third Indian trail Michler mapped, which he labeled "Large," reached the Rio Grande at forty-nine miles above the Pecos, just above the survey party's camp 4. The trail followed the bank on the American side for a mile before crossing to the Mexican side. This trail fits modern topographic maps as well as the location of today's Herradura (horseshoe) Crossing (see figure 42).

The boundary maps show no Indian trails or crossings along the last forty-five miles of river above the mouth of the Pecos, even though modern US Customs Service maps show four crossings in the upper part of this section, which lies upstream from Langtry, Texas.[82] Those same modern maps show no river crossings in the last thirty miles above the mouth of the Pecos as the river approaches the impounded waters of the Amistad Reservoir.

Michler would not have seen most Indian crossings because of his rapid descent of this section of the river. He reported that "for thirty miles above the Pecos [the Rio Grande] is one continued rapid; its average rate nearly six miles per hour." One has to wonder how Lieutenants Michler and Smith had poled a flatboat up these "rapids" in 1850.

Boundary Map 16 shows the large Painted Rock Arroyo, named Lozier Canyon today, coming down to the Rio Grande from the north to join it on the east side of a large, looping meander at forty-five miles above the Pecos (see figure 42). Michler's use of the name "Painted Rock Arroyo" made it clear that he understood that this arroyo connected, some miles to the north, with the spring (Meyers Springs) and its associated pictographs where he had earlier stopped on his way from King's Springs to the Rio Grande (see figure 35). The connection between Meyers Springs and Michler's Painted Rock Arroyo is further confirmed by a large-scale index map that accompanied Boundary Map 16 as part of the final set of boundary maps.[83]

Michler's Latitude Measurements

During the boat survey, Michler used a sextant to determine the latitude at camp each night except the first. The locations of each of those six camps are marked on Boundary Maps 15, 16, and 17, and the values are shown in a table in the final Emory Report.[84] When a modern map is used to locate the camps based on topography and the shape of the nearby river channel, Michler's latitude measurements are usually accurate to within 150 yards. This level of accuracy is consistent with Major Emory's note in his final report that said a single night's measurement with a sextant in experienced hands should be within 5 seconds of a degree (169 yards) of true latitude.[85] Michler did not make any latitude determinations during the twenty miles of land-based surveying his men conducted above Lipan Crossing before the party set off downriver. Perhaps he felt it would be redundant in light of the accurate traverse surveying his men were doing. Or maybe Michler's assistants, who did the work upstream from the Lipan Crossing base camp, did not know how to operate the sextant, and for Michler to do them himself would have entailed considerable trouble to stay overnight at some remote upstream camp to take readings after the sky was fully dark.

Arthur Schott's Survey Downstream of the Pecos River

The civilian surveyor Arthur Schott had mapped the Rio Grande downstream from the mouth of the Pecos in fall 1852. Thus, the eastern half of Boundary Map 15 is based on Schott's work, and he is shown in the map's title block as coauthor with Michler (figure 43). This was one of four boundary maps Schott authored that covered the area between Fort Duncan and the mouth of the Pecos River.

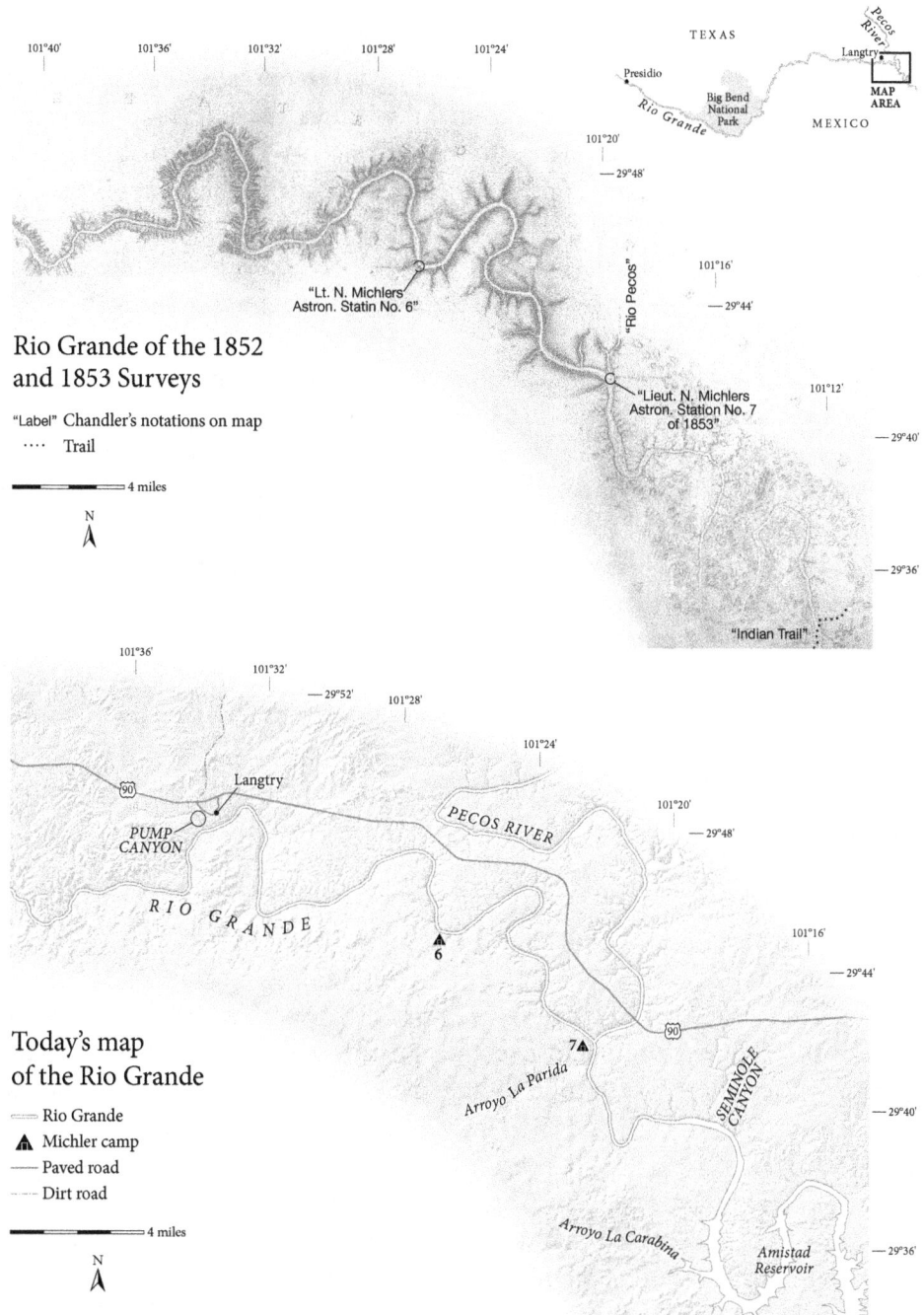

FIGURE 43. **River Trace Comparison: Langtry to beyond the Pecos River.** A comparison of Boundary Map 15 with a modern map for the area from Langtry, Texas, to a point twenty-five river miles beyond the Pecos. The western half of Map 15 was surveyed by Michler while floating in his boat and, like his Map 16, it is good in character but long in distance. The eastern half of Map 15 was surveyed by a party led by Arthur Schott in October 1852. Schott used careful onshore traverse lines and produced a map accurate in river channel detail and in distance. Boundary Map 15, National Archives. Map by Carol Zuber-Mallison.

Schott did a very good job on Map 15. The river trace, scale, general character of the terrain bordering the river, and detail within the channel are very good. He mapped two midchannel islands in the first twenty-five miles of river below the Pecos. There is, however, considerable discontinuity in the effective scale at the point on Map 15 where the rough surveying from Michler's boats meets the accurate overland traverse surveying of Schott. This is due to Michler's inflated distances just above the Pecos (+25%), while Schott's distances below the Pecos are close to correct (−8%).

No description of Schott's methods appears in the Emory Report, but his overall accuracy and detail indicate that he used a surveyor's compass or theodolite and surveyor's chain to carry traverse lines along the American bank of the river. The area he worked in was favorable for onshore work. Rounded limestone hills rise less than two hundred feet above the channel of the Rio Grande. Today, the waters of the Amistad Reservoir cover the original narrow channel and islands that Schott mapped in 1852.

On Map 15, Schott noted an Indian trail on the American side approaching the Rio Grande from the east at a point midway between the Pecos and Devils Rivers. While surveying near here in October 1852, Schott's party had been followed by an armed band of Lipan, causing the party to temporarily halt work and seek shelter at San Felipe Springs on the nearby San Antonio–El Paso Road.

Schott's Indian Encounter

Major Emory, at Fort Duncan in October 1852, wrote a general review of Indian problems in a letter to Secretary of the Interior Alexander Stuart. Emory said his party on the Rio Grande near the San Pedro River [Schott's party near Devils River] had been forced by Indian pressure to retire to the hills and seek aid. Arthur Schott, in an October 1 letter to Major Emory sent from his camp on the San Antonio–El Paso Road at San Felipe Spring (Del Rio, Texas), reported that when his survey party reached the mouth of the San Pedro River on September 30, he had been "followed by twenty-five well-armed and well-mounted Lipan Indians—the opposite bank seems to be entirely occupied by these wicked hunters." Emory's reply to Schott stated: "To withdraw is to invite attack—place yourself in a strong position and send for aid." Schott sought and received aid from the US Army at Fort

Clark, thirty miles to the east, and afterward made no further reports of Indian trouble.[1]

NOTE

1. San Pedro was the early name for the Devils River in Texas. Emory to Stuart, October 1, 1852, William H. Emory Papers, Beinecke Rare Book and Manuscript Division, Yale University, WA MSS S-1187, New Haven, CT (herafter cited as EP); Schott to Emory, October 1, 1852, EP; Lenard E. Brown, *Survey of the United States-Mexico Boundary, 1849–1855: Background Study* (Washington, DC: Office of Archaeology and Historic Preservation, Division of History, National Park Service, 1969), 143.

When Schott did his survey, the nearest reference station for longitude was at Emory's observatory at Fort Duncan, Texas. When Schott reached the most distant point of his survey at the mouth of the Pecos River, 116 river miles from the fort, his traverse-based determinations of longitude had gradually drifted 2.7 miles too far east, a small error in light of the distance from his starting point (see table 2). At the mouth of the Pecos River, the Michler and Schott Surveys were connected to a common point. Here, Michler accepted Schott's determination of longitude as the starting point of his determinations extending farther west.

Results of the Michler Survey

Michler's survey party produced a good set of maps for those parts of the Rio Grande they actually surveyed: the east half of Boundary Map 17, all of Map 16, and the west half of Map 15. In total, Michler surveyed the first ninety-four miles above the mouth of the Pecos, leaving unsurveyed thirty-four miles of river upstream from the mouth of San Francisco Canyon. There really was no way the party of wagons and wooden boats Michler had in the field could have surveyed inside the Lower Canyons of the Rio Grande. They could not have moved upstream from San Francisco Canyon because of the sheer canyons enclosing the river. Even if the party, through some miracle of navigation or luck, had initially come down to the Lower Canyons of the Rio Grande at the very spot where the Chandler Survey had ended, there would have been nothing they could have done. Their wagons could not move through the miles of massive canyons, and their three small boats would not carry enough supplies to last all the way through them. If the party had tried the boats, the unmanageable flatboat carrying most of its provisions would have quickly been destroyed in the first of many big rapids, the likes of which they did not see in their relatively easy descent through the smaller canyons below Lipan Crossing.

In the final report and maps Michler prepared, he did not admit the survey gap but glossed over it, showing on his map a relatively straight direction but generic meander pattern for the river. At the time, having a good boundary map through these wild unpopulated canyons may have seemed unimportant. He may even have been advised, in a private, "off the record" note from Emory, that he should not allow the dangerous canyons to jeopardize the completion of his survey down to the mouth of the Pecos. The Mexican surveyors produced no boundary maps in the Lower Canyons of the Rio Grande. They simply made a copy of the American maps for that area.

PART III

Wrapping It All Up

Later Surveys to Complete the Mapping of the Boundary

With the completion of the survey down to the Pecos River in August 1853, followed by the extension of the lower Rio Grande surveys all the way to the Gulf of Mexico by survey parties led by the civilians Arthur Schott and Charles Radziminski, all work along the river came to an end in September 1853. Major Emory's men had covered the thirteen hundred river miles of the Rio Grande boundary from El Paso del Norte to the Gulf of Mexico in less than two years and under budget. Emory left Texas in a good mood and returned to Washington, DC. The only negative was the loss of one man, assistant surveyor Thomas Jones, who drowned in July 1853 when a skiff under sail overturned on the lower Rio Grande below Reynosa, Mexico.[1]

At the end of 1853, only the disputed boundary west of El Paso del Norte remained to be surveyed. Emory had always maintained that a new treaty was needed for the disputed area because even the most favorable interpretation of the position of the boundary under the Treaty of Guadalupe Hidalgo would not provide an adequate route for a transcontinental railroad.[2] Emory's stance became the accepted view in Washington, and President Pierce directed the recently appointed US Minister to Mexico, James Gadsden, to seek a new treaty with Mexico that would both settle the conflict and secure additional lands needed for a transcontinental railroad.

Mexican president Antonio López de Santa Anna and Minister Gadsden signed the Gadsden Treaty (Gadsden Purchase) on December 30, 1853. Some changes were made as the treaty moved through the approval process in Congress, but by June 1854, all US and Mexican approvals were complete. The United States bought additional lands for $10 million, moving the boundary between the two countries far enough south to provide for a favorable route for a railroad near the 32nd parallel. Today the southern boundary lines of the states of New Mexico and Arizona follow the Gadsden Treaty boundary line (see figure 1).[3]

To survey the new Gadsden boundary, a new boundary commission, the fourth one, was formed in August 1854. Major Emory was named boundary commissioner and chief surveyor. In typical Emory fashion, he acted immediately, setting up two field parties to start from each end of the new boundary line. He sent Lieutenant Michler, assisted by Arthur Schott, E. A. Phillips, and John O'Donoghue, to the west end of the line near Fort Yuma on the Colorado River. Emory, with surveying assistants Lieutenant Charles Turnbull and the civilians M. T. W. Chandler, Charles Weiss, Maurice von Hippel, and others, was to start from the east end of the line on the Rio Grande near El Paso del Norte.[4]

Michler gathered his equipment and men and sailed from New York on September 20, going to Panama and then crossing overland on the primitive roads that were used prior to construction of the railroad or canal, and finally boarding a ship on the Pacific side that took him to San Diego via San Francisco. He arrived at Fort Yuma, near where he was to begin his survey, in December 1854. Since the new "initial point" at the west end of the boundary line specified in the Gadsden Treaty was 20 miles farther down the Colorado River than the earlier boundary, Michler, working with his Mexican counterpart, Captain Francisco Jiménez, determined the location of the new initial point using triangulation from the older upstream point at the junction of the Gila and Colorado Rivers. By mid-April, they had agreed on the location, erected an observatory, and set two monuments. Michler then began work on the new straight-line segment, the "azimuth line," that would run southeast from the Colorado River to connect to a turning point, where the boundary turned due east at 111 degrees longitude. Marking the azimuth line across 237 miles of the wild Sonoran Desert turned out to be a huge challenge for Michler and his Mexican counterpart. After running several scouting parties southeast along the line, as far as 45 miles from the Colorado River, and finding only deep sand and no water, they abandoned the effort to move directly southeast down the line. Instead, on May 5, 1855, they changed their plans. They decided to use existing primitive roads to detour around the desert, first moving up the Gila River, then east to Tucson in New Mexico Territory, and finally south to reach the turning point at the east end of the azimuth line where they would begin surveying northwest, up the azimuth line. The detour consumed almost two months, delaying any progress on the section of the line assigned to Michler.[5]

When Emory, who had been rapidly surveying the new boundary line west of the Rio Grande, reached the turning point at the east end of the azimuth line, he was disappointed to find no trace of Michler; indeed, he had heard nothing from Michler in over a year, so Emory sent an express rider to find Michler. When Michler sent a curt reply to Emory, along the lines of how the major should be aware of the problems of surveying in the desert, Emory, a strict and disciplined career soldier, lost his temper and started making plans to court-martial Michler.[6] Later, after meeting with Michler and hearing a full explanation of events, Emory reconsidered.

On June 26, Michler finally arrived at the turning point, where Emory's party had already set a monument for him to use as a starting point. It was there that he began surveying back up the line, moving northwest. Now aided by the desert rainy season, Michler, working with the Mexican surveyors, finished the line to the Colorado River on August 25. Cleanup work, calculations, and setting monuments lasted until mid-October. In the final set of boundary maps, Michler and his main assistant, Arthur Schott, would be shown as the authors of the six maps along the azimuth line.[7]

At last, all fieldwork on the United States–Mexico boundary was complete. Lieutenant Michler arrived back at San Antonio in late November 1855 and returned in January 1856 to the US Boundary Commission Office in Washington, DC, where he worked on the preparation of the final maps and reports.

The Final Report and Maps of the US Boundary Commission

The fieldwork of the boundary survey had taken place over seven years. For most of that time, the project was a political football in Washington, DC, kicked around by changing leadership in Congress, conflicts over slave versus free states, and sectional interests favoring alternate locations for a new transcontinental railroad. Four US presidents had been involved: James Polk, Zachary Taylor, Millard Fillmore, and Franklin Pierce.

In the early years, leadership of the US Boundary Commission was handed out based on political connections, not qualifications for the job. From the beginning in 1849, Major Emory's involvement provided the technical and organizational focus needed to keep the boundary survey moving forward. His role, limited at first, increased every year as it became clear to all that he could get the thing done in good fashion. Finally, in 1854, Emory had full control. He was both boundary commissioner, with control of the overall organization, and chief surveyor in control of all field operations. He quickly finished the fieldwork; authored the massive final congressional report; and, in closing the commission business, he and the Mexican boundary commissioner jointly signed each of the maps documenting the boundary.

At completion, the survey was recorded in two sets of documents: an immense three-book set of narrative, tables, and illustrations, and a set of fifty-four detailed strip-maps of the boundary line and the topography for a mile or two on either side of the line. These documents were a crucial step in bringing the new western lands into the consciousness of American citizens and making those lands a recognized part of the nation.

In January 1856, Emory rented office space and brought together his staff to complete the final documents of the US Boundary Commission. By the end of the summer, he had submitted the manuscript of his general report to the Secretary of the Interior and promised that appendices on botany and zoology would be ready by year's end.

Congress published volume 1 of the Emory Report in 1857, making fifteen thousand copies available. So many copies for an expensive document indicated demand was expected to be high. In 1859, Congress published the monumental, lavishly illustrated botany and zoology appendix as volume 2, in one thousand copies. The smaller number of copies reflected the expense of numerous color plates and the smaller audience expected for these more esoteric sections of the report. In 1987, the Texas State Historical Association published a new facsimile edition in a three-book set that included the complete Emory Report and the appendix.

The Emory Report was, essentially, a natural history encyclopedia for the new lands along the border. Emory knew that members of Congress and the public at large were less interested in the details of placement of the line and more interested in learning about the new lands that brought opportunity for westward expansion, including a favorable route for a transcontinental railroad.

Emory himself was more interested in exploration than in marking a boundary. In a sense, he used the job of marking the boundary as a way to enable the production of a scientific exploration report. This was not altogether unlike what Emory had heavily criticized Commissioner Bartlett for doing when Bartlett used his position as boundary commissioner to travel widely and then write

Part III: Wrapping It All Up

and publish a fine travelogue of the new western lands. The difference was that Emory also did his job of marking the boundary in good form, whereas Bartlett ignored that job.

From the outset, Emory had placed natural scientists on his surveying teams, recognizing the opportunity offered by the movement of his teams across thousands of miles of new lands being added to the United States. The unexplored, arid lands of the Far West were poorly known by Americans, almost all of whom lived in the forested lands east of the Mississippi. Encouraged by Emory, his surveying parties made large collections of plants, animals, rocks, minerals, and fossils, which he put into the hands of leading scientists to secure their expert evaluation and documentation for the final report. Although carrying only Emory's name, the report is a compilation of the work of many contributors on geography, geology, paleontology, botany, zoology, and metrology, as well as the customs of the Indians who inhabited the land.

Completed in the prephotography era, the report is abundantly illustrated with drawings and paintings to describe the new lands and the plants, animals, and Indians found along the boundary. In the general report (vol. 1), there are one hundred landscape drawings in black and white, nineteen geologic sections, and nine color plates of Indians in native dress. Numerous tables of distance along roads, distance along the Rio Grande, and latitude and longitude tables for points of interest are also included. In the paleontology section of the general report, there are twenty-one full-page plates, each with multiple fossils collected during the surveys and classified by experts. The separate appendix (vol. 2) has two parts, usually published as two books, one on botany and the other on zoology. These books compose an illustrated catalogue of the specimens collected during the survey, including plants, cacti, fish, reptiles, mammals, and birds. There are 270 artistic, full-page plates, including 25 color plates of birds.

The Emory Report is in reality an introduction to the new American lands along the border rather than a document to explain or justify the specific positioning of the line the surveyors marked, the methods they used in the process, or the monetary cost of the work. Only scattered comments on these latter subjects appear in the report. In designing the structure of his report, Emory followed the format of other successful western exploration reports published by Congress in the period from 1843 to 1848. These included works by fellow Topographical Engineer John C. Frémont, as well as Emory's own highly acclaimed earlier report of western exploration published in 1848. That report, *Notes of a Military Reconnoissance [sic] . . .* , had been based on the Mexican-American War campaign of General Stephen W. Kearny's Army of the West, which traveled across the Trans-Mississippi west to San Diego in 1846–47. Like Emory's later report, the Military Reconnaissance Report emphasized the natural history of the poorly known arid lands west of the 100th meridian, and in many ways was just a smaller version of the later report. Emory had been both Topographical Engineer and naturalist on the Kearny campaign, and he personally made the plant collections that he turned over to John Torrey and George Engelmann, who prepared the report's botany appendix. These are the same two men he engaged later for the botany appendix of the final Boundary Survey Report, or Emory Report. One of the most memorable aspects of Emory's earlier report was the inclusion of forty-eight delightful drawings of landscapes and Indians by the up-and-coming young artist John Mix Stanley, who was at the time employed by General Kearny as a draftsman attached to his Topographical Engineers.[8]

As an integral part of the boundary treaty, the boundary line was documented by a set of fifty-four maps. The US and Mexican commissions worked together at the boundary office in Washington, DC, from June 1856 to September 1857 to finalize and then jointly sign their approval of the maps. Forty-five maps are at a scale of 1:60,000 (approximately one inch equals one mile). Each map is thirty-six inches wide by twenty-three inches high and covers about thirty-four miles of border. There are nine slightly smaller maps at a scale of 1:30,000 that cover the southern boundary of California. These had been finished earlier, and all parties agreed not to change them to the match the scale of the later maps.

There were two sets of the fifty-four maps covering the boundary: a US Commission set, which remained in Washington, DC, and a Mexican Commission set taken to Mexico City. Both commissioners approved each map in each set, even though the maps are not identical. The US set consists of maps drafted by the staff of the US Boundary Commission in Washington, DC, and is based on US surveying or joint US and Mexican surveying. The Mexican set is made up of maps drafted by the Mexican Commission staff. Most of their maps are based on the work of Mexican surveyors or joint US and Mexican work. However, the Mexican Boundary Commission had to resort to copying some of the US maps to complete their full set of boundary maps. In the twenty-nine boundary maps that followed the Rio Grande from the Gulf of Mexico to El Paso del Norte, the Mexican Commission made complete or near-complete surveys for eleven boundary maps. These included eight maps from the mouth of the Rio Grande upstream to Laredo, Texas (Maps 1 through 8), and three maps along the upper Rio Grande: Map 22 downstream from Presidio del Norte and Maps 28 and 29 near El Paso del Norte. In addition, the Mexican Commission contributed some reconnaissance surveying for Maps 23 through 27 in the area between El Paso del Norte and Presidio del Norte, where the boundary line along the river channel was mapped by the US party led by von Hippel.

Of the eight boundary maps that span the greater Big Bend region from Presidio del Norte down to the mouth of the Pecos River (Maps 22 through 15), Mexican surveyors produced an excellent Map 22, but they copied the river trace from the US Commission for their Maps 21 through 15.

Original Intent for the Boundary Maps

The legal intention at the time for the fifty-four boundary maps was that they show, display, and fix the boundary at the time of the treaty. Thus, the maps were intended to be an integral part of the boundary treaty itself. If the river channels changed position along the Rio Grande or the Colorado River, the boundary would remain unchanged at the old position shown on the maps. In the straight-line sections of the boundary away from the rivers, the boundary was marked on the ground with stone or metal monuments whose locations were also shown on the maps. Once approved by both the US and Mexican Commissions, the monuments were considered to be on the true boundary line, even if they were later shown not to be accurately positioned.

Emory took steps to insulate the boundary maps from later attack on their accuracy. He ordered that all field survey records and preliminary maps made by the surveyors be destroyed so the maps contained in the final signed set would be the only ones of record. This step concealed sections where there were no field data to support the position of the boundary line, as well as locations arrived at by arbitrary assignments or compromises where data were in conflict. It is also likely that Emory purged from the written reports included in volume 1 any suggestion of uncertainty regarding the position of the line, as no such doubts appear.

In spite of his precautions, problems related to ambiguity over the exact location of the boundary arose almost immediately. Most of the boundary is along the Rio Grande or Colorado River. A river is a living thing, and a river channel in a floodplain can and will change overnight. On land away from the rivers, monuments can be destroyed, lost, or poorly located. Today the boundary between the United States and Mexico and the waters that move along its rivers are managed by an ongoing, joint Mexico–United States organization—the International Boundary and Water Commission (IBWC)—which was established in 1889.[9]

In practice, the boundary maps turned out to be of limited use in resolving border issues. With early delays in publication due to cost and later lack of interest, the fifty-four-map set was never published. They remain at the National Archives in College Park, Maryland, where, coated with a thick layer of varnish, they now have an attractive orange patina. Photographic copies of some of the maps have been published in historical books and articles, usually reduced to one page in size and not capable of showing the rich detail of the full-size maps.

Summary

In the Treaty of Guadalupe Hidalgo signed at the end of the Mexican-American War, a new United States–Mexico boundary extending from the Gulf of Mexico to the Pacific Ocean was to be surveyed by a joint effort of both countries. The Rio Grande defined that boundary across Texas, and the most remote part of it was the 337 miles of the Rio Grande across the greater Big Bend region from Presidio del Norte (Ojinaga, Chihuahua–Presidio, Texas) to the mouth of the Pecos River. Two American field parties surveyed this frontier section of the boundary: the 1852 Chandler party began at Presidio del Norte and worked 209 miles down the river to the start of the Lower Canyons of the Rio Grande, and the 1853 Michler party carried the survey 94 miles down the Rio Grande from the mouth of San Francisco Canyon to the mouth of the Pecos River. Separating these two surveys was an unsurveyed gap of 34 miles of the boundary along the Rio Grande in the heart of the Lower Canyons.

The two field parties documented their work with eight detailed maps at a scale of 1:60,000, about one inch to the mile. A comparison of these maps with modern topographic maps and satellite images provides insight into the difficulty of their task and the methods they used to respond to the challenges presented by the sheer walls and rapids through the unexplored canyons. The recently discovered daily journal of Charles C. Parry, a member of the Chandler party, allows us to follow that party each day, revealing when and where they went, where they did not go, sections they carefully surveyed, sections they rushed through, and sections they skipped over entirely.

The surveyors started at Presidio del Norte. Here there was good access to the bank of the river, which extended for twenty-nine miles down to the first canyons. They walked down the low banks and used their instruments for accurate traverse surveys, which produced excellent maps of this section of river.

Part III: Wrapping It All Up

The next section of river downstream was twenty-two miles of canyons and rapids in the Upper Canyons of the Rio Grande. With the canyons blocking access along the river, Chandler sent his army escort and mule train carrying provisions on a seven-day overland detour through Mexico to rendezvous with him at a river crossing below the canyons, while his surveyors, in two wooden boats and two smaller inflatable rubber boats, floated through the canyons, keeping a record of the direction of the river channel and the time it took to float from one bend to the next as a means to estimate distance. On the second day in the canyons, the surveyors ran into a dangerous rapids and lost both of their large wooden boats, which carried their provisions and camp gear. They salvaged a bag of beans and some water-soaked flour. Now with only the two smaller boats and short of food, they moved rapidly downstream to meet the mule train at the river crossing. In spite of their rapid descent, the surveyors produced a good map of this section of the boundary.

The survey party met the mule train at the river crossing, and while waiting there for part of the train to return to Presidio del Norte to secure provisions to replace those lost when the boats were wrecked, a large raiding party of Comanche from Texas came down to the crossing on their way to interior Mexico. After some initial tension, there was a powwow and an exchange of gifts, and then the Comanche crossed the river and continued into Mexico.

In the eleven-mile section from the river crossing down to the entrance of the massive Santa Elena Canyon, there was good access to the banks of the river, and the surveyors used onshore traverse lines to make an excellent map of the boundary.

The Chandler party camped at the mouth of Santa Elena Canyon and scouted the dangerous Rock Slide Rapids, which lay about one mile inside. Chandler decided to detour around the rapids rather than risk the lives of his men. Before beginning the detour, the surveyors hiked across the high mesa overlooking the canyon to reach a point just above the canyon exit to record compass bearings to distant landmarks, which allowed them to calculate the location of the river exit by triangulation. Then, based on a distant view from the mesa on the Mexican side, they drew a rough sketch of the course of the river between the entrance and exit points.

To detour around the seven miles of river inside Santa Elena Canyon, the surveyors traveled along fifty-six miles of overland trails to rejoin the Rio Grande downstream from the canyon in an area of wide floodplains. With good access to the river for the next forty-four miles down to the entrance to Mariscal Canyon, the surveyors used tripod-mounted instruments and light surveyor's chain to record traverse lines and make an excellent map of this long section of the Big Bend of the river lying south of the Chisos Mountains. An exception to the otherwise accurate map is an eleven-mile section of the river trace at the western margin of Map 20, which was compressed to four miles. This greatly distorted the mapped trace of the river across the eleven miles but was apparently done by the makers of the final set of maps in Washington, DC, in order to shift all downstream maps to the north and west to achieve a better fit of all maps lying farther downstream.

The next section of river was the eighteen-mile passage of the twin canyons of Mariscal and San Vicente. The mule train had to detour around the canyons while the surveyors pressed through in rubber boats. As they had done at Santa Elena, they used triangulation to determine the location of the canyon exit, then sketched in the river track from notes made during their rapid descent through the canyons.

Once past San Vicente Canyon, they entered a more open area where they made a very good map using traverse surveying onshore. They passed ruins of Presidio San Vicente on the Mexican side, which had been abandoned about seventy years earlier, and continued through the small Hot Springs Canyon just above today's Rio Grande campgrounds of Big Bend National Park, then on to Boquillas Canyon where the Rio Grande has carved its course through the towering limestone cliffs of the Sierra del Carmen range.

At the entrance to Boquillas Canyon, the surveyors started through the seventeen-mile canyon in rubber boats, while the army escort and mule train, carrying their food and shelter, made a thirty-four-mile rocky detour to meet them at the canyon exit. As before, they determined the location of the canyon exit by triangulation and sketched in the river trace within the canyon.

Beyond Boquillas Canyon they entered a forty-three-mile section of the Rio Grande that was a scenic mix of floodplains, low banks, and short but steep canyons along the river bordering today's Black Gap Wildlife Management Area. Here they surveyed onshore using traverse lines to produce the most accurate of the five boundary maps made by the Chandler party. This map is especially rich in its detail of topography near the river and the trace of numerous Indian trails. It is counterintuitive that Chandler's finest map was his last map, made when his men were at the ragged edge of their endurance and out of touch with the food and shelter carried by their mule train.

Chandler was forced to abandon further surveying down the river when he reached the massive Lower Canyons of the Rio Grande near today's Reagan

Canyon area. The uninterrupted sequence of towering canyons would not allow his surveyors to both work along the river and stay in daily contact with the supplies and shelter carried by the mule train. After a final harrowing experience when the surveyors went without food or shelter for three days, the entire Chandler party left the Rio Grande and walked more than three hundred miles across interior Mexico to the US Army post on the lower Rio Grande at Fort Duncan, Eagle Pass, Texas.

In spring 1853, five months after Chandler aborted his survey, Major Emory ordered Lieutenant Michler to go to the point on the Rio Grande where the Chandler party had stopped surveying and continue the survey downstream to the mouth of the Pecos River. Michler's thorniest problem was figuring out where to start. Neither Chandler nor Michler had a reasonably accurate fix on the longitude and latitude where Chandler had stopped. Chandler's raw field records had not yet been converted to a map by the time Michler began his survey. The consensus of the Topographical Engineers was that Chandler had ended his survey about one hundred river miles upstream from the mouth of the Pecos River. Michler attempted to reach the point on the river where the Chandler party had stopped but was forced to alter his route due to the realities of available trails, scarce water supply, and precipitous canyons. At the start, Michler ended up striking the Rio Grande at an Indian crossing too far downstream. Referring to it as Lipan Crossing, he set up a base camp and sent his surveyors upstream to conduct traverse lines along the hills overlooking the river while moving toward Chandler's stopping point. The work progressed well enough until they reached a point twenty miles above their base camp where they were blocked by a deep side canyon that intersected the Rio Grande.

Looking farther upstream from that point, they saw the height and steepness of the canyons rapidly increasing. They had reached the limit of day trips out of their base camp and had no way to move the wagon-based camp farther upstream. They aborted the upstream survey without reaching the point on the river mapped by the Chandler party in 1852. Michler's men produced an excellent map of the twenty miles lying between their base camp and the side canyon that finally blocked them.

Michler's failure to reach the point where Chandler had stopped resulted in an unsurveyed gap, which Michler thought, at the time, was quite small. However, when he later plotted his field surveying records back in Washington, DC, a gap of fifteen air-miles was indicated between Chandler's most downstream survey point and Michler's most upstream point. To fill in the unsurveyed gap on his Boundary Map 17, Michler sketched a meandering river channel, which totaled twenty miles of river to allow for the distance added by a meandering course. Michler did not admit the existence of a gap in his final reports to Emory or on his boundary maps. Emory certainly was aware of the gap but did not want the final maps or reports to reveal any uncertainty as to the location of the boundary line.

The twenty-mile trace of the Rio Grande that Michler sketched across the unsurveyed gap on his Boundary Map 17 was pure fantasy. The actual river distance across the gap was thirty-four miles, and his men did not set foot on the bank or traverse the river in a boat along any portion of it. It was as if Major Emory had advised his men "off the record" not to exhaust their resources trying to trace the river inside hostile canyons. This might have been rationalized on several grounds: the river channel was carved in solid rock and would not change for centuries, thus there was no need to document the trace now; there was no foreseeable economic interest in the canyons—no agriculture, ranching, or mining; surveying the canyons would take too much time, putting in jeopardy the completion of the entire boundary survey; the canyon rapids were too dangerous and would risk the lives of the men. The Mexican surveyors spent no time surveying the deep canyons of the Rio Grande either. They made their final boundary maps of that area by copying the American maps.

To survey the Rio Grande downstream from their Lipan Crossing base camp, Michler used wooden boats he had brought disassembled in wagons. He surveyed by recording the direction of the river and the minutes of travel while floating from one bend to the next.

Later, when Michler converted his notes to a map, he overestimated the distance traveled by his boats by an average of 29 percent. He either overestimated the speed of his boats in his original notes, or he arbitrarily increased his estimates later when he prepared his boundary maps to make it appear that his surveyors had reached a point farther upstream. Because the distance error during the boat survey is evenly spread, the "relative" distances of points are undisturbed. Thus, the relative shape and size of the meanders of the river appear correct, and after adjusting for the inflated distances, a useful set of maps can be produced.

Overall, the eight boundary maps produced by the pioneering expeditions of Chandler and Michler were excellent where they had access to the banks of the river to conduct instrument-based traverse surveys. The entrance and exit locations of canyons were determined by triangulation and are also good; however, the river traces inside the canyons range from good in the Upper Canyons near Presidio del Norte, to fair in the Big Bend area, to nonsense in the Lower Canyons. The canyons were definitely a low priority for the surveyors; they rushed through them in their boats or detoured around them. Their surveying of the canyons consisted of making good location determinations at the entrances and exits and sketching the river in between.

In terms of general quality, the boundary maps produced by the low-profile civilian surveyor M. T. W. Chandler were superior to those of the Army Topographical Engineer Lieutenant Michler, but Michler did have to deal with the more challenging terrain of the Lower Canyons of the Rio Grande.

Indian Encounters

The stealing of mules, horses, and cattle by Indians was a constant problem for the US Boundary Commission. It was most serious in 1851 and early 1852 when they had large herds at their Frontera office near El Paso del Norte and at the Santa Rita Copper Mines farther west in New Mexico. On one occasion, Apache took fifty mules and ninety-four beeves from herds at the latter location. While the threat of Indians directly attacking the men of surveying parties was ever present, especially for the Chandler party, whose survey crossed two heavily used Comanche trails into Mexico, the only loss of life in an Indian attack against men of the US Boundary Commission in seven years of operations took place on October 18, 1852, when one Mexican herder employed by Commissioner Bartlett's small party of wagons was killed by Comanche on the road between El Paso del Norte and Chihuahua City when the party was on the way across Mexico to meet Major Emory on the lower Rio Grande.

For surveyors operating in the field, only four encounters with Indians were reported. In September 1852 while camped at the Rio Grande crossing at today's Lajitas, Texas, the Chandler party encountered a band of fifty Comanche on their way from the High Plains of Texas to raid the interior of Mexico. After a few tense moments, which included the forming up of the twenty-two well-armed soldiers of Chandler's army escort, a meeting with the chief led to an exchange of gifts and the Indians crossing the river and continuing on their way.

Also in September, but 160 miles to the east, Arthur Schott's party, which was surveying up the Rio Grande toward the Pecos River, reported being hounded for days by twenty-five armed Lipan Indians before the surveying party moved away from the river to a secure camp at San Felipe Springs (Del Rio, Texas), where it sought support from nearby Fort Clark. Schott reported no further problems after that (see also pages 192–93).

In November 1852, during their trek across interior Mexico to reach Fort Duncan on the Lower Rio Grande, the Chandler party unexpectedly came upon and alarmed the camp of Seminole Chief Wild Cat near the town of Santa Rosa (Múzquiz), Coahuila. After a meeting with the chief to explain their sudden appearance, and a gift of a beef to the camp, the party continued its journey. In July 1853, when Michler's surveying party was camped for a month seventy-four miles upstream from the Pecos at Lipan Crossing, he reported: "The Lipans often visited us here and made themselves useful as guides."[10]

Conclusions

The men of the 1852 and 1853 Chandler and Michler boundary surveys deserve much credit for what they accomplished in a short time while working under the severe conditions of the unexplored Rio Grande frontier. Even today, this section of river is essentially uninhabited. There is no bridge crossing the river and no river village on either side larger than one hundred people along the entire four hundred river miles between the present twin border cities of Presidio, Texas/Ojinaga, Chihuahua, and Del Rio, Texas/Ciudad Acuña, Coahuila.

The United States–Mexico Boundary Survey was a landmark event in the Manifest Destiny era of rapid western expansion before the Civil War. These were exciting times. I hope that this account, which shares some details of the day-to-day experiences and accomplishments of the explorers on the front lines, has allowed the reader to appreciate some of the excitement as well as the challenges the surveyors experienced.

Epilogue
The Men of the Boundary Survey

JOHN RUSSELL BARTLETT (1805–1886)

In December 1852, when the second boundary commission ran out of funds and was disbanded at Ringgold Barracks on the lower Rio Grande, John Russell Bartlett's role in the boundary surveys ended, and he returned home to Providence, Rhode Island. He prepared for publication the extensive private journal he had kept during his three years of travel as head of the commission. The two volumes of his *Personal Narrative of Explorations and Incidents in Texas, New Mexico, California, Sonora, and Chihuahua, . . . during the Years 1850, '51, '52, and '53* were published in New York in 1854 and included many illustrations. It is one of the very best accounts of early travel in the US Far West.

Bartlett served as Secretary of State of Rhode Island from 1855 to 1872 and later wrote an important book on American linguistics. He married Eliza Allen Rhodes in 1831, and they had four daughters and three sons. Eliza died in 1853, not long after Bartlett returned from the boundary survey; he remarried in 1863. Bartlett maintained a lifelong interest in linguistic and intellectual endeavors and later in life became the librarian for the John Carter Brown Library. He died in Providence at the age of eighty.[1]

William Hemsley Emory (1811–1887)

When work at the US Boundary Commission offices in Washington, DC, came to an end in September 1857, Major Emory was available for a new army assignment. At the request of his boyhood friend former Secretary of War and then Senator Jefferson Davis, Emory was transferred to a cavalry regiment at Fort Riley, Kansas Territory, where Indian trouble was increasing. Shortly afterward, his unit was moved south to Fort Arbuckle in the Indian Territory. When the Civil War began in 1861, Emory was traveling back to his unit at Fort Arbuckle from a visit to Washington, DC. As the son of a wealthy, slave-holding family in rural Maryland, his first reaction was to tender his resignation from the Federal Army; but, after mailing his letter, he changed his mind, returned to his post, and in the absence of orders, led his men north to the more secure Fort Leavenworth in Kansas Territory. Impressed with his initiative, his higher-ups promoted Emory to lieutenant colonel and shortly to full colonel. In March 1862, Emory was moved up to brigadier general of volunteers and sent to join General George B. McClellan's Army of the Potomac. After the Peninsula Campaign and a short stint in New Orleans, he was promoted to major general and assigned to Washington, DC, where he won acclaim for his actions in support of General Phil Sheridan's campaign in the Shenandoah Valley of Virginia.[2]

In the troop reductions after the war, Emory was mustered out of the volunteers but retained his commission in the regular army. At first, he commanded the Department of Washington and later the Department of the Platte in Nebraska. In 1871, he was assigned to the Department of the Gulf in New Orleans, where harsh conditions during reconstruction had led to constant political conflict. Not happy with events in New Orleans, General Sheridan relieved Emory from command and took over the department himself in early 1875. Later that year, President Grant, apparently thinking Emory was treated too harshly, assigned him to the position of president of the Army Retirement Board in Washington. Emory retired with a promotion to major general in 1876 after forty-three years of service.[3]

In 1838, Emory married Matilda Wilkins Bache, a great-granddaughter of Benjamin Franklin. They maintained a home in Washington, DC, during Emory's long absences. The Emorys had ten children. The oldest son was an aide to General George Meade during the Civil War, and another son became a rear admiral in the US Navy. Emory died at his home in Washington, DC, in 1887 and is buried in the Congressional Cemetery on Capitol Hill in Washington, DC.[4]

Emory was the glue that kept the boundary survey moving forward during the nine years of its on-off existence. He was a strict, disciplined, and take-charge soldier-scientist. His interest in, support of, and capacity for scientific work are on full display in the monumental volumes of the US Boundary Commission's final report (the Emory Report).

Marine Tyler Wickham Chandler (1819–1868)

After the 1852 survey was aborted, Marine Tyler Wickham Chandler had returned to Washington, DC, and was working at the US Boundary Commission Office. In August 1854, Emory named him to assist in surveying the new Gadsden Treaty boundary that began near El Paso del Norte and extended west. By November 1855, Chandler had finished that work and was back in Washington helping complete the final maps and reports for the 1852 survey. He worked there until the office closed in September 1857.[5]

Emory's description of the untimely end of Chandler's 1852 surveying party indicated he was not satisfied with Chandler's leadership and the "unmilitary" way the field party had ended. In one letter, he reported that the party "brokedown," and in the final report, he wrote: "No disaster, except the suspension of the work of Mr. Chandler's party, which was wrecked in the Cañon of the Rio Bravo." Perhaps this explains why Emory did not ask Chandler to lead another field party, assigning him only office work, except for the one assignment as an assistant on the Gadsden line survey.[6]

Little is known of Chandler after his work on the boundary survey. He died of an unknown cause in June 1868 at Canaviares, Brazil, at age forty-nine while serving as Surveyor General of Brazil. No trace of him exists in the 1860 federal census, Civil War military records, or the 1860–65 Philadelphia city directories, all of which suggests he went to Brazil shortly after working for the boundary commission.[7]

Chandler earned a master's degree from the University of Pennsylvania and had worked for the city of Philadelphia as an engineer and surveyor. While living in Philadelphia, he became a member of the First Troop of the Philadelphia City Cavalry. He was member number 538 of this group of gentlemen from 1845 to 1850. The First Troop had been formed in 1774, and its members served in the Revolutionary War, the War of 1812, and the Civil War. They formed the honor guard at Abraham Lincoln's burial.[8]

Little else is known about Chandler's personal life. In 1874, when the First Troop put together a photo gallery of past members for their one-hundredth anniversary, they secured an undated photograph of M. T. W. Chandler that appears to have been taken sometime between 1860 and 1868 (see figure 4). His August 1854 passport renewal indicates that he was 5 foot 6 inches tall, had dark-gray eyes, dark-brown hair, and an oval face.[9]

Charles Christopher Parry (1823–1890)

When surveying in the field ended in 1852, Charles Christopher Parry took his notes and collections of plants, fossils, and rocks and reported to Major Emory in Washington, DC. For the next year, he worked at the US Boundary Commission office, writing sections of the final report on geology, botany, and geography. In all, Parry wrote six sections, including general descriptions of the country and sections on geology in volume 1, and the introduction to the expansive "Botany of the Boundary" in volume 2, which was authored by his friend and mentor John Torrey, who had been a professor at Columbia College, Princeton College, and West Point. Plant collections Parry made in the field formed an important part of the specimens described and illustrated.[10]

Parry returned home to Davenport, Iowa, in 1853, where he married Sarah Dalzell, resumed his medical practice, and worked on his botany collections. In the summer of 1854, Emory offered him a medical-science position in the field party to survey the Gadsden boundary line, but Parry declined. Parry and his wife had a daughter, Eliza, who was born in 1855. Sarah died in 1858, and in 1859, Parry married Emily Preston of Eastford, Connecticut. Parry's daughter Eliza died in 1865.[11]

In the summer of 1861, Parry went to Colorado to explore and collect high-altitude plants in the Pike's Peak area, the first of many trips he made from Davenport to the Rockies. He returned in 1864, working in the Long's Peak and Middle Park areas northwest of Denver. He continued to visit and collect plants in the Rockies for the next decade. Parry's pioneering work in Colorado earned him the title "The King of Colorado Botany." To document his high-altitude plant collections, Parry carried a barometer with him, and as a result, documented the height of many prominent peaks at a time when their elevations had been unknown. He proposed names for some of the high peaks in Colorado, naming them after fellow naturalists Gray, Torrey, Guyot, James, Audubon, and Engelmann. The US Geological Survey named Parry Peak in his honor. On the same ridge with Parry Peak is Mount Eva, which some mountain guidebooks say Parry named for his wife, but this seems unlikely since it does not fit Parry's private lifestyle, his use of naturalists' names elsewhere, and the fact that his wives' names were Sarah and Emily.[12]

In 1867, two years before John Wesley Powell's historic boat expedition through the Grand Canyon, Parry became involved in a public debate about whether or not the Colorado River through the Grand Canyon was a navigable stream. At the time, Parry was employed by the Kansas Pacific Railroad, which was building a new line across Kansas and seeking congressional support to extend the line southwest to cross the Continental Divide south of the Colorado Rockies along the 35th parallel and near the Grand Canyon. The proximity of a navigable Colorado River would greatly support the route proposed by the Kansas Pacific. The strong consensus at the time was that the Colorado was not navigable inside the Grand Canyon, yet in September 1867, a lone trapper named James White, starving, nearly naked, and confused, arrived on a raft at a Mormon village on the river, sixty-five miles downstream from the exit of the Grand Canyon, to report that he had just passed through the canyon in fourteen days.

In January 1868, the Kansas Pacific Railroad sent Parry to interview James White. In spite of White's sketchy and confused account, Parry believed his story and wrote a report to the Kansas Pacific and later wrote newspaper articles supporting White's claim of a first passage through the canyon. A successful passage using a simple raft indicated to Parry that the river was indeed navigable. Two years later, when Powell completed the first documented passage through the Grand Canyon, the number and severity of rapids he encountered made it clear that the river was not navigable for boats moving upstream, and Parry suffered some loss of credibility in the scientific community. It appears Parry's judgment was clouded by his desire to tell his superiors at the Kansas Pacific Railroad what they wanted to hear. Today, many observers say that while it is very unlikely, it is just possible that in a time of very high water, White made the first passage.[13]

In 1869, with the strong support of John Torrey, Parry became the first person to hold the position of Chief Botanist for the Department of Agriculture in Washington, DC, a post he held until late 1871 when he fell victim to "political house cleaning" by the incoming administration of Ulysses S. Grant. The botanist George Vasey, a bitter rival of Parry and a close friend of the then influential John W. Powell, replaced Parry. Returning to Davenport, Parry continued his western botanical expeditions through 1878, including trips to the Wind River and Yellowstone areas of Wyoming, central Utah, and the Mexican state of San Luis Potosí. In his final years, Parry made botanical excursions to coastal

California and to the famous Kew Botanical Gardens in London. He died at his home in Davenport in 1890.[14] Today his considerable papers, including his daily journal kept during the 1852 Chandler Survey, are held in the Parks Library at Iowa State University in Ames.[15]

Duff Cyrus Green (1828–1865)

Duff Cyrus Green had lingering health problems with scurvy and rheumatism after the ordeal of the 1852 Chandler Survey. In 1853, he was back home in Greene County, Alabama, on sick leave from the US Army. In 1855, he married Rebecca Pickens, and in December 1856, he resigned his army commission. The 1860 federal census for Greene County (near Eutaw, Alabama) shows that he and Rebecca had two children, and he was a cotton broker. At the start of the Civil War in 1861, he "joined the rebellion" and later was promoted to brigadier general and held the post of Quartermaster General of Alabama. He was captured during the fall of Mobile, Alabama, in 1865, and after the end of the war, he was pardoned shortly before he died in November 1865 at the age of thirty-seven. He was buried near his home in Eutaw, Alabama.[16]

Nathaniel Michler (1827–1881)

Nathaniel Michler, a career soldier, continued his army service after his work on the boundary survey. In 1857 and 1858, by then a first lieutenant and accompanied by his longtime civilian assistant Arthur Schott, he investigated a potential route for a Panama canal near the Atrato River in eastern Panama. During the Civil War, Captain Michler first served in the federal Armies of the Ohio and the Cumberland, and then, in 1863, he was transferred to the Army of the Potomac to resurvey Harper's Ferry. He and his men built defensive works for the major battles of The Wilderness, Spotsylvania, Cold Harbor, and Petersburg. He quickly moved up in rank, and in April 1865, was brevetted brigadier general for his service during the war.

Back in Washington, DC, after the war, Michler held several important and high-profile posts, including superintendent for public buildings and officer in charge of surveying the Potomac River. During 1878–80, he served on the staff of the US ambassador to Vienna, Austria. Returning to the United States, he was superintendent for river and harbor improvements for New York, New Jersey, and Vermont in 1880 and 1881.

Michler married Fannie Kirkland shortly after graduating from West Point in 1848. They had four sons, but Fannie died in 1857. He married Sallie A. Hollingsworth in San Francisco in 1861, and she survived him. Michler, still in the service, died of kidney failure in 1881 at Saratoga Springs, New York, at age fifty-four, and was buried near his family home in Easton, Pennsylvania. Some of Michler's surveying equipment had been reported to be on display at the Chamizal National Memorial in downtown El Paso, Texas, but an inspection of those instruments by this author shows they are of 1880 or later vintage.[17]

Edward Ingraham (1830–1862)

Edward Ingraham's job as assistant surveyor for Michler ended in August 1853, and that appears to have been his last work for the US Boundary Commission. He may have done a few weeks of cleanup work in 1853, assisting the surveyors Schott or Radziminski on the lower Rio Grande, but all work on the river was complete in September. In a February 1854 letter to his friend Clint Gardner, who was Major Emory's clerk and the same age as Ingraham, he said he was traveling with his father on the way to the family plantation at Grand Gulf, Mississippi. Ingraham said he was not sure what he was going to do next, but that he had been treated "meanly" by Michler and did not wish to work for him again.[18] In August 1854, when Emory formed an organization to survey the new Gadsden Treaty line, Ingraham was not listed among the staff.[19]

In June 1856, when he was twenty-six, Ingraham joined the 1st Cavalry of the US Army as a second lieutenant, likely recommended by his maternal uncle Captain George Meade and by Major Emory. In 1857, Ingraham assisted Colonel Joseph E. Johnston with the survey of the south boundary of the Kansas Territory, and he later served at various cavalry posts in the Kansas and Indian Territories from 1857 to 1861, at the same time that Emory was also serving in that area. At the outset of the Civil War, Ingraham resigned from the army to join the Confederate cause. His years growing up on the family plantation in Mississippi had more impact on his view of the conflict than did his birth in Pennsylvania or the influence of his uncle, the Union Army's soon-to-be Brigadier General George Meade. Ingraham was selected to lead Company A, 1st Regular Confederate Cavalry, reporting to Colonel Earl Van Dorn in San Antonio, Texas. Early in 1862, Company A was ordered east to assist Van Dorn, then a major general, who had been transferred to Memphis, Tennessee. In April, Ingraham was promoted to major, and in May, while serving on Van Dorn's staff, he was killed near Corinth, Mississippi, 250 miles northeast of his family's Mississippi River plantation. One year later, Ingraham's older brother, also a Confederate soldier, was killed at the battle of Chancellorsville in Virginia; their younger brother had died of yellow fever in 1860. In 1866, Edward's parents secured approval to reinter the three brothers in the Ingraham family plot at All Saints' Church in Philadelphia, Pennsylvania. Apparently, Edward never married.[20]

Christoph Conrad Stremme (1807–1877)

After the 1853 survey ended, Christoph Conrad Stremme was employed as a draftsman in the Texas General Land Office (TXGLO) in Austin from 1854 to 1874. In addition to drafting, he prepared architectural plans for several new state government buildings in Austin, including one for the General Land Office and one for the State Lunatic Asylum (later the Austin State Hospital). In 1860, Stremme began experimenting with photography to preserve and duplicate maps in the TXGLO files. He acquired a large format camera from Germany and established what became the Photographic Bureau of the TXGLO. Stremme was also an inventor and had filed in the Patent Office inventions on stoves, chimneys, a lamp, a cartridge case, and an air ventilator for a hat.[21]

A personal letter to Stremme from his friend Swante Palm (aka Swen Jaensson), a Swedish immigrant and renowned Austin book collector, reveals that Stremme made the landscape drawings used by Michler to illustrate his 1853 survey along the Rio Grande. In the letter, Palm relates a conversation with Stremme when the two were looking over the landscape drawings in Palm's personal copy of the Emory Report. Stremme pointed to landscapes he sketched during the survey, noting that he had made them and others that did not appear in the report. This letter was found in Palm's copy of the Emory Report when, after his death, Palm gave his library of twelve thousand books to the University of Texas.[22] A recent examination of Palm's copy of the Emory Report by this author found no other correspondence.

Stremme lived in Austin until his death from heart disease in 1877, and he was buried in an unmarked grave at Oakwood Cemetery in the family plot of a friend.[23]

APPENDIX A

Colonel Langberg's 1851 Expedition

FOLLOWING LANGBERG's route from the village of San Carlos (Manuel Benavides) to the site of the abandoned Presidio San Vicente, as shown in figure 6, one can see that he first moved southeast, crossed Arroyo San Antonio at twelve miles, continued past Palos Blancos water hole at twenty miles, and camped for water after thirty-six miles near a marsh in the Arroyo Altares. Here he turned northeast and followed a Comanche trail running alongside the arroyo for twelve miles to a ford he called "Vado Chisos" (Chisos Crossing, directly south of the Chisos Mountains of today's Big Bend National Park).[1]

To reach the ruins of the old Presidio San Vicente farther downstream on the Mexican side of the Rio Grande and eighteen miles to his northeast, Langberg first had to detour around the precipitous Mariscal and San Vicente Canyons, which blocked a direct approach. From his camp at Chisos Crossing, Langberg crossed to the American side and followed the heavily traveled Comanche Trail north, then, leaving that trail, he turned east around the plunging north end of Mariscal Mountain, where the Mariscal Mine would later be. He then turned southeast down to the San Vicente crossing, a twenty-two-mile overland detour from his camp.[2] He noted that the crossing to San Vicente was "quite difficult," as the river was wider and deeper than at Chisos Crossing. Langberg camped at the old Presidio site, sixty-nine trail miles from his start at San Carlos.

On leaving San Vicente, he started northeast to take advantage of a trail closer to the river, as evidenced by the direction of the trail labeled "to Santa Rosa" on

Chandler's Boundary Map 20. Chandler must have copied this trail location from Langberg's map. After traveling twenty-four miles in two days—first northeast then southeast—Langberg camped at springs he called La Salada or Jabalí. The springs were probably at or near the present settlement of Jaboncillos, which is seventeen miles south of today's Mexican village of Boquillas on the Rio Grande. Langberg said La Salada was north of a well-known Indian watering place he called Las Piedras, which today is called San José de las Piedras. The small but reliable Piedras spring is at the southern foot of a high volcanic mountain—the Cerro de San José, which reaches an elevation of 5,315 feet and is visible from the site of Jaboncillos, which sits in an open area, away from nearby hills and 150 feet higher than the main arroyo. Langberg said he could see Santiago Peak, seventy miles to the north-northwest, and the Chisos Mountains, eighty miles to the west-northwest; both are major landmarks of the Big Bend National Park area. He also said he could see the "Serranía de Pico Etéreo" lying east of El Carmen [Sierra del Carmen] to his front. He must have meant he could see a part of the range of mountains associated with Pico Etéreo because his view of the Pico Etéreo pinnacle itself, twenty-nine miles to the northeast, was blocked by intervening higher culminations of the Sierra del Carmen, only ten miles east of his camp.[3]

Leaving La Salada, Langberg continued south, and in the low-lying desert flats west of Sierra de La Encantada he came upon wagon tracks headed west toward the Piedras spring. These were the tracks of a group of Forty-Niner gold seekers, who, two years earlier in the summer of 1849, had traveled west between the towns of Santa Rosa, Coahuila, and San Carlos, Chihuahua. Their wagons had a very rough time, evidenced by the bits and pieces of debris along their route, but they lost only two wagons along the 250 miles they traveled on the primitive trail. It is not known how many wagons they started with in Santa Rosa, but a diary of one of the travelers reported that there were eighty-four men in the wagon train. The diarist traveled with a group of seven men who camped and ate together, with four men riding horses and three in a wagon. Some of the subgroups were referred to as "the wagons," and the entire outfit was referred to as "our wagon train." A reasonable guess is that they had fifteen to twenty wagons on the trail between Santa Rosa and San Carlos.[4]

Forty-five miles south of the La Salada springs, Langberg went over the pass on the flank of La Encantada (Sierra de La Encantada), near today's high mountain pass on Mexican Highway 53. The heaviest Forty-Niner wreckage was in the pass where a wagon had gone off the trail and crashed to the rocks below. With minor variations, Langberg backtracked along the gold seekers' wagon tracks from this pass to the town of Santa Rosa.

Once through the pass, Langberg continued south-southeast another 56 miles to the point where Arroyo de Santa Ana enters Cañón de Alameda. He turned east, traveled 20 miles in the canyon, and then left the canyon and the Forty-Niner wagon route. He then turned south to go over a minor pass and arrived at the deep, clear waters of Río Sabinas, upstream from today's Kickapoo village. After resting at this beautiful camp, Langberg went directly southeast 20 miles across the flats to the old town of Santa Rosa, today's Múzquiz, Coahuila. Unlike the later Chandler party, Langberg did not encounter the Seminole band of Chief Wild Cat, which did not arrive on the Río Sabinas until early 1852. At Santa Rosa, Langberg had traveled 240 miles in sixteen days from San Carlos.[5]

From Santa Rosa, Langberg traveled northeast about one hundred miles on established trails: first to San Fernando (now Zaragoza, Coahuila) and then to Piedras Negras on the Rio Grande opposite Fort Duncan at Eagle Pass, Texas. At Piedras Negras, Langberg departed from the route of the Forty-Niners and the later Chandler party to go sixteen miles upriver to his primary destination of Colonia de Monclova Viejo.

The Colonia was on the right bank of the Río Rodrigo near its junction with the Rio Grande at the present village of El Moral. Langberg mentioned that the ruins of the old Presidio Monclova Viejo, which had been established in 1773, were 1.25 leagues (3.3 miles) west of the Colonia. He noted that the walls of the old presidio enclosure were still standing and occupied a "140 vara square" (390 feet on a side). Today, on Google Earth satellite imagery, the enclosure walls are revealed by the dark shadows they cast. The trace of the bastions, which Langberg called "customary protruding angles," can be seen today in the lineation of mesquite trees that extend out 150 feet from the main walls.

The location of the ruins on the north bank of Río San Rodrigo, at 5.7 kilometers west of today's town plaza of El Moral, at the site of the old Colonia, agrees well with Langberg's distance from the Colonia.[6]

APPENDIX B

1855 Mexican Triangulation Stations near Presidio del Norte

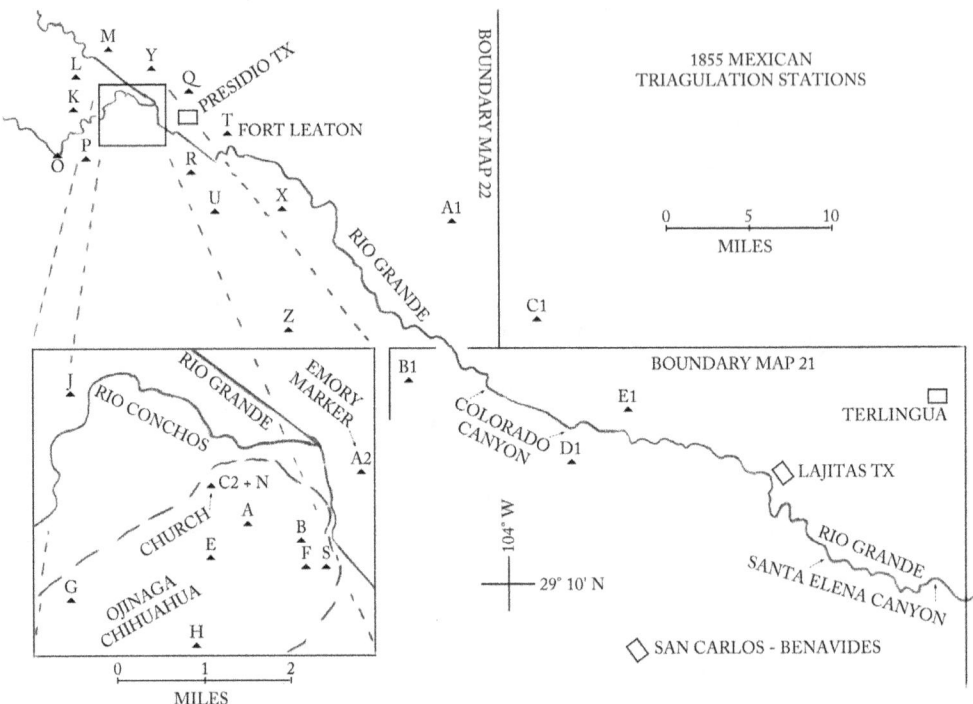

FIGURE 44. **1855 Mexican Triangulation Stations near Presidio del Norte.** Station locations determined by surveyor Kent Neal McMillan. Field work for the triangulation stations was done by Mexican boundary surveyors working out of Presidio del Norte in late 1854 and early 1855. Map by Morgan Morrison. (*Key on facing page.*)

222

Station	Estimated NAD83 Latitude (N)	Position Longitude (W)	Location and Remarks*
A2	29°34′06.6″	104°23′18.1″	Emory's Observatory (in US)
A	29°33′39.0″	104°24′35.2″	On Baseline N-S (in Ojinaga)
B	29°33′20.0″	104°23′58.3″	On Baseline N-S (in Ojinaga)
E	29°33′16.0″	104°24′59.3″	Offset from Baseline N-S (in Ojinaga)
F	29°33′09.8″	104°23′54.5″	Offset from Baseline N-S (in Ojinaga)
G	29°32′54.8″	104°26′34.0″	Rancho de la Cruz (in Ojinaga)
H	29°32′23.0″	104°25′09.3″	Road to Chihuahua (in Ojinaga)
J	29°34′40.6″	104°26′37.6″	Rancho de San Francisco (4 km N of Ojinaga)
K	29°33′40.2″	104°28′34.1″	High Hill on the Left Bank of the Río Conchos
L	29°35′21.3″	104°28′22.9″	Hill of the Palmas, Right Bank of the Río Bravo (N of Conchos)
M	29°36′48.3″	104°26′26.1″	Hill on Right Bank of the Río Bravo (in US, 6 km N of Ojinaga)
N	29°33′52.3″	104°25′00.8″	North End of Baseline at the Church of the Presidio (Ojinaga)
O	29°31′24.3″	104°29′31.8″	Blue Hill on the Right Bank of the Río Conchos (W Ojinaga)
P	29°32′03.6″	104°27′56.5″	Rancho del Divisadero (SW of Ojinaga)
Q	29°34′31.5″	104°21′30.3″	Red Hill on Left Bank of the Río Bravo (in US)
R	29°31′37.0″	104°21′38.9″	Hill on the Right Bank of the Río Bravo (SE of Ojinaga)
S	29°33′10.4″	104°23′39.9″	South End of the Baseline on Loma Vado de Cabezas (SE of Ojinaga)
T	29°32′30.1″	104°19′16.8″	El Fortín (in US, just E of Fort Leaton)
U	29°28′52.2″	104°19′59.6″	Barranco del Saucillo (14 km S of Ojinaga)
X	29°29′37.0″	104°15′51.4″	Red Hill (Cerro El Centinela)
Y	29°35′42.8″	104°23′48.0″	Hill at La Junta de los Ríos (US, 3 km N of Ojinaga)
Z	29°22′47.7″	104°15′25.7″	Sierra San José (9 km W of El Mulato)
A1	29°28′15.8″	104°05′32.7″	Bofecillos Peak (in US, 10 km E of Redford)
B1	29°20′51.2″	104°08′11.1″	Hill of the Álamos (S of Mulato)
C1	29°23′15.3″	104°00′31.9″	2nd Peak of Bofecillos (in US, N of Colorado Canyon)
D1	29°16′39.0″	103°58′35.8″	Cerro Salazar (SE of Colorado Canyon)
E1	29°19′11.3″	103°55′13.9″	Mesa de San Juan (in US, 16 km NW of Lajitas)

* All stations are in Mexico except as noted otherwise. The above positions are estimates based on a reconstruction of the triangulation network computed by the Texas surveyor Kent Neal McMillan, RPLS, in 2018, working from the data presented in tables in Manuel Orozco y Berra, *Apuntes para la historia de la geografía en México* (Mexico City: Francisco Díaz de León, 1881), 465–70, as the work of Manuel Fernández, Francisco Herrera, and Miguel Iglesias, sent to Presidio del Norte in 1855 by Mexican Boundary Commissioner José Salazar Ylarregui. McMillan's reconstruction was based on that published data, reconciling a few apparent mistakes in a manner he thought most likely consistent with the methods used in the triangulation and the difficult circumstances of its execution.

APPENDIX C

The First Documented Boat Passage through Santa Elena Canyon

In September 1852, when Chandler was faced with the choice of going through or going around Santa Elena Canyon, there had been no documented passage of a boat through the canyon, and the Mexican guide from the nearby village of San Carlos knew of none. The first passage was ultimately made on January 7 and 8, 1882, by a Presidio County surveying party led by John T. Gano. That party was made up of five surveyors, including Gano, Edward L. Gage, and Eanes M. Powell, and was escorted by five Texas Rangers led by Captain Charles L. Nevill. Both surveyors and rangers were based at the town of Fort Davis, which was the county seat of Presidio County until 1885. Captain Nevill described the trip in a letter to his father, Z. L. Nevill, that was published in the *Austin Daily Statesman* in 1882.[1] Nevill said they left Presidio in four wooden boats on December 13, 1881, and expected to travel 264 miles of river to survey down to the southeast corner of Presidio County. That corner of the county was defined as the junction of San Francisco Creek and the Rio Grande, but the location of that junction was poorly known prior to Gano's survey.

The estimate of 264 miles along the river, which I assume was made by Gano, turned out to be reasonably close to today's distance of 243 miles. Gano had little on which to base his prior estimate for the location of the corner of the county. In 1876, a county map of Texas showed San Francisco Creek and the east corner of Presidio County but located the intersection about 20 miles too far west. The official 1857 boundary maps of Chandler and Michler would not have helped Gano, because Chandler did not reach San Francisco Creek, and Michler's Map 17, which included the area at the mouth of San Francisco Creek, did not reflect that the ordinary-looking dry canyon Michler mapped was indeed the mouth of San Francisco Creek, because he was not aware of this fact. John Gano's map of eastern Presidio County prepared in March 1882, after he finished his survey along the river, was the first map to name and display the correct location of the mouth of San Francisco Creek at 243 river miles downstream from Presidio del Norte.[2]

On their way down the Rio Grande below Presidio, the Gano party reached the entrance to Santa Elena Canyon, which Nevill called "The Grand Canyon," on January 4, 1882. They scouted the Rock Slide Rapids the next day, and on January 6, the boats entered the canyon. Nevill and a group of men "not comfortable with swimming" chose to hike overland to the canyon exit, traveling across the mesa south of the canyon. They likely used the same trail high above the river on the Mexican side that Chandler's surveyors had used in 1852. Nevill watched from the cliffs above while the men on the river below worked a day and a half to carry the boats across the narrow rock ledges above the rapids. Nevill's party hiked ten miles along a circuitous trail to cross the mesa above the canyon and then scrambled down the fifteen-hundred-foot-high cliffs to the river to cover the five-mile direct distance from the Rock Slide Rapids. Nevill arrived at the canyon exit at the same time as the boats on January 9. He and his comrades had been without food for three days.

After passing Santa Elena Canyon, the Nevill narrative is brief. On January 16, he said he "came upon four Indians." This was a period in which the Texas Rangers were in an open war with the Apache and Comanche in the greater Big Bend area. Walter Prescott Webb, in his 1935 classic, *The Texas Rangers*, reported that Nevill had three encounters with hostiles along the river. The first, on the sixteenth, probably at Boquillas Canyon, started with an exchange of rifle fire when the rangers suddenly appeared in boats. While the total number of Indians was not reported, four were seen escaping into Mexico, and they left nine horses in their camp. Fearing the horses would be used in future Indian raids on area ranches and having no way to transport them, Nevill's men blindfolded the horses and killed them with an axe to save ammunition, which was in limited supply due to earlier losses when their boats had overturned in rapids. This event may be the source of the name of the mountains northeast of Boquillas: Sierra del Caballo Muerto (Dead Horse Mountains), but Arthur Stiles, who supervised the original 1903 topographic maps in the area for the US Geological Survey, told Ross Maxwell, the first superintendent of Big Bend National Park, that he named the mountains Caballo Muerto because his favorite saddle horse was killed in a fall in these mountains.

Two days later, the boatmen caught sight of eight Indians crossing into Texas, but they remained at a distance beyond rifle shot and later disappeared. The next day, the nineteenth, they came upon a large but abandoned Indian camp at the mouth of Maravillas Creek.[3]

Nevill recounts that, by prior arrangement, he met a support party of Texas Rangers and horses at the mouth of Maravillas Creek, in today's Black Gap Wildlife Management Area, sixty-four miles short [actually fifty-five miles] of the Gano party's final destination. Apparently Nevill had set up this rendezvous to bring additional supplies to the party and provide an escape if needed. In any event, he later reported to his commanding officer that he had continued to scout for Indians as the party floated downriver to the eastern limit of Presidio County at the mouth of San Francisco Creek, but had no further encounters with Indians.

John Gano's detailed map, the first to accurately show the trace of the river through the Lower Canyons of the Rio Grande, proved he traveled along the Rio Grande to the mouth of San Francisco Creek. Additional information on Gano's map can be found in part II and in figure 39. Gano ended his surveying work at San Francisco Creek, but here the party was still surrounded by precipitous canyon walls. Neither Gano nor Nevill describe their return trip to Fort Davis, but they must have descended the river another 20 miles to reach the low banks of the river at Shafter Crossing (Michler's Lipan Crossing), where, one can assume, Nevill had arranged for Texas Rangers with horses to meet them. From Shafter Crossing they likely rode 20 miles north to join the primitive east-west military road and then turned west. After a ride of about 160 miles, they would have reached Fort Davis via Maxon Springs; Fort Peña, Colorado (near later Marathon, Texas); and Burgess Springs (at later Alpine, Texas).[4]

Other river runners successfully took boats across the Rock Slide Rapids of Santa Elena Canyon in the late 1880s and 1890s. The best known of these was the October 1899 passage by the party of the USGS geologist Robert T. Hill. Hill's account "Running the Cañons of the Rio Grande" appeared in the popular *Century Magazine* in 1901. Hill and companions portaged on the rocks above the Rock Slide in three days. An experienced Rio Grande trapper, James MacMahon, who lived in Del Rio at the time, was hired by Hill to serve as guide, and MacMahon built the three wooden boats used by the expedition. MacMahon told Hill that three trappers had gone through Santa Elena Canyon in 1887. One trapper was drowned at the Rock Slide, and MacMahon found the trapper's body when he and another man named Pafford went through the Rock Slide in 1888. MacMahon went through again in 1890 with a fellow trapper named Carr, and again in 1894 with a man named Strickland. After the trapper died in the first passage, it is assumed the other parties portaged over the rocks above the rapids, as it is known the Gano and Hill parties did.[5]

On June 11, 1901, an International Boundary and Water Commission (IBWC) reconnaissance party of six—two US engineers, one Mexican engineer, a representative of the US DOJ, a USGS hydrologist, and a cook—portaged their two sixteen-foot-long skiffs above the Rock Slide Rapids. The party had started on May 7 from Marcial, New Mexico, a railroad and river town about two hundred river miles upstream of El Paso, Texas. Marcial was destroyed by a flood in 1929, and today only the graveyard can be identified on satellite images (at 33°42′ N).

The party was directed to record during the seasonal spring flood the diversion of river waters by local irrigation canals and the width and length of all floodplains along the river. The final destination was Laredo, Texas, on the Lower Rio Grande about eleven hundred river miles below Marcial. On July 13, when the party was only one hundred miles from Laredo, both skiffs capsized in the Las Islitas rapids near Guerrero, Coahuila, and the leader of the expedition, thirty-one-year-old engineer Paul Davis Cunningham, was drowned. His body was recovered the next day and returned to his home in Tennessee. Under the leadership of the US engineer J. D. Dillard, the party then completed the survey down to Laredo.[6]

APPENDIX D

Chronology

2 Feb. 1848	Treaty of Guadalupe Hidalgo signed in Mexico City
4 July 1848	Revised treaty formally proclaimed in Washington, DC
16 Jan. 1849	President James Polk appointed John Weller Boundary Commissioner; Andrew B. Gray Chief Surveyor; Major William Emory Chief Astronomer
20 May 1849	Forty-Niners destroyed a wagon crossing Encantada Pass, Coahuila
1 June 1849	Major Emory arrived in San Diego to begin survey
2 Dec. 1849	Emory forced to stop California surveying work due to lack of funds
18 Dec. 1849	John Weller removed as Boundary Commissioner
3 Feb. 1850	US and Mexican Commissions agreed to stop California effort and meet on the first Monday of November at El Paso del Norte
4 May 1850	President Zachary Taylor appointed John Bartlett Boundary Commissioner
13 Aug. 1850	Bartlett left the East Coast for El Paso del Norte
Late Oct. 1850	Emory left San Diego for Washington, DC
13 Nov. 1850	Bartlett's advance party arrived in El Paso del Norte
9 Dec. 1850	Bartlett's main party with M. T. W. Chandler arrived in El Paso del Norte
4 Mar. 1851	Parry returned to Washington, DC, from San Diego
Apr. 1851	Bartlett moved US Boundary Commission offices to Santa Rita Copper Mines

24 Apr. 1851	Marker set on Rio Grande at point of Bartlett–García Conde Compromise
16 May 1851	Bartlett party left the Santa Rita Copper Mines office to travel into Mexico
14 July 1851	Lieutenant Hardcastle finished work on the California line and departed for Washington, DC
19 July 1851	Chief surveyor A. B. Gray arrived at the Santa Rita Copper Mines office and challenged the Bartlett–García Conde Compromise
13 Sep. 1851	Emory ordered to El Paso del Norte to take charge of the survey
3 Oct. 1851	Mexican Colonel Langberg started east from San Carlos, via Chisos Crossing, Presidio San Vicente, Encantada Pass, and Santa Rosa
24 Nov. 1851	Emory, Michler, Parry, Schott, and others reached El Paso del Norte
19 Dec. 1851	Mexican Commissioner García Conde died; replaced by José Salazar Ylarregui
20 Dec. 1851	Emory sent Michler and Schott to Fort Duncan on the lower Rio Grande
Jan. 1852	Chandler left El Paso del Norte on leave of absence to New Orleans
Jan. 1852	Emory ordered Maurice von Hippel to lead a survey party down the Rio Grande below El Paso del Norte
15 May 1852	Von Hippel reached Presidio del Norte; requested funds to pay his men
6 June 1852	Colonel Craig, head of army escort, killed by deserters in California
11 June 1852	Emory's party left El Paso area to go downriver to Presidio del Norte
8 July 1852	Emory, Parry, et al., arrived at Presidio del Norte and set up an observatory
22 July 1852	Von Hippel resigned rather than continue survey farther downriver
2 Aug. 1852	Lieutenant Green went to El Paso for supplies and men for the army escort

The 1852 Chandler Survey

8 Aug. 1852	Chandler returned to Presidio; ordered by Emory to extend Rio Grande survey down to the mouth of the Pecos River
16 Aug. 1852	Chandler's men started surveying along the river banks downstream of Presidio del Norte
17 Aug. 1852	Near El Paso, Lieutenant Green unexpectedly met Commissioner Bartlett, just arrived overland from San Diego
24 Aug. 1852	Chandler surveyors finished surveying the boundary above the Upper Canyons of the Rio Grande
26–29 Aug. 1852	Parry explored Upper Canyons of the Rio Grande

Chronology

31 Aug. 1852	Emory party left Presidio del Norte for Fort Duncan, TX
2 Sep. 1852	Green returned to Presidio del Norte from El Paso del Norte area
8 Sep. 1852	Parry signed contract with Green to be surgeon for army escort
13 Sep. 1852	Green started escort overland; Chandler started boats downriver
14 Sep. 1852	Chandler lost wooden boats and most provisions in Rancheria Rapids
15 Sep. 1852	Chandler found one overturned wooden boat in good condition
18 Sep. 1852	Chandler party reached Comanche Crossing (Lajitas, TX)
20 Sep. 1852	Lieutenant Green's escort and mule train reached Comanche Crossing
23 Sep. 1852	Comanche raiding band arrived at Comanche Crossing
23 Sep. 1852	Emory's party arrived at Fort Duncan from Presidio del Norte
28 Sep. 1852	Chandler and Green departed camp at Comanche Crossing
29 Sep.–2 Oct. 1852	All men of survey party in camp at entrance to Santa Elena Canyon
3 Oct. 1852	Chandler and Green started detour around Santa Elena Canyon
6–7 Oct. 1852	All camped on the river 14 miles below Santa Elena Canyon
9–10 Oct. 1852	All camped at Chisos Crossing of the Rio Grande
13–14 Oct. 1852	Green camped at exit of San Vicente Canyon
16–20 Oct. 1852	All camped near entrance to Boquillas Canyon
18 Oct. 1852	Bartlett attacked by Comanche while traveling across Mexico
21–22 Oct. 1852	Green's mule train and Parry detoured around Boquillas Canyon
22–23 Oct. 1852	All camped at exit of Boquillas Canyon
26–27 Oct. 1852	All crossed Rio Grande into Mexico (La Linda, Coahuila)
28–29 Oct. 1852	Green's mule train detoured around Temple Canyon
30 Oct–4 Nov. 1852	All camped at Hot Springs Rapids on the Rio Grande
4 Nov. 1852	Chandler and Parry wrote to Emory; survey abandoned; Abbott and companions started down Rio Grande in last rubber boat
5–12 Nov. 1852	Chandler party began trek across Mexico; first to Encantada Pass
12 Nov. 1852	Major Emory left Fort Duncan to go downriver to meet Bartlett
13–18 Nov. 1852	Chandler's trek continued from Encantada Pass to Santa Rosa, Coahuila
14 Nov. 1852	Abbott arrived at Fort Duncan in rubber boat after 10 days on river
18 Nov. 1852	Chandler party encountered Chief Wild Cat camp near Santa Rosa
19–24 Nov. 1852	Chandler party on the road from Santa Rosa to Fort Duncan
25 Nov. 1852	Chandler sent letter to Emory reporting arrival at Fort Duncan

The 1853 Michler Boundary Survey

22 Dec. 1852	Emory and Bartlett met at Ringgold Barracks; survey disbanded
Feb. 1853	Emory and Bartlett arrived in Washington, DC, area
Mar. 1853	New boundary commission organized: Robert B. Campbell, Commissioner; Major Emory, Chief Astronomer and Surveyor
4 Apr. 1853	Emory ordered Lieutenant Michler to survey unfinished section between point reached by Chandler and mouth of the Pecos
May 1853 (approx.)	Michler left San Antonio with his party to start 1853 survey
June 1853 (approx.)	Michler arrived at King's Springs 50 miles west of Pecos Spring
Mid-July 1853 (approx.)	Michler arrived on the Rio Grande at Lipan Crossing to begin survey
2 Aug. 1853 (approx.)	Michler terminated upstream survey at San Francisco Canyon
6 Aug. 1853	Michler began surveying downriver from Lipan Crossing (in 3 boats)
13 Aug. 1853	Michler arrived at Pecos River to complete surveying work
18–19 Aug. 1853	Michler arrived at Fort Duncan; reported his survey complete

Finishing the Boundary Surveys

Sep. 1853	All surveying along the Rio Grande completed
30 Dec. 1853	Gadsden Purchase signed in Mexico City
15 Aug. 1854	Emory appointed Boundary Commissioner to mark the Gadsden line
Oct. 1855	All surveying work on the Gadsden Line completed
June 1856	Mexicans and Americans meet in Washington, DC, to finish and sign boundary maps
29 July 1856	Emory's final boundary survey report sent to Secretary of the Interior
30 Sep. 1857	Joint Boundary Commission office in Washington, DC, closed
1857	Emory Report volume 1 published by Congress
1859	Emory Report volume 2, botany and zoology sections, published by Congress

APPENDIX E

Glossary

álamo: Spanish word for a cottonwood tree.
alluvial terrace: Flat or gently sloping deposits of sand and gravel flanking a stream; formed by the stream during an earlier time when it occupied an older and higher floodplain.
anticline: A fold in rock layers in which the rocks on the two sides of the fold incline (dip) away from each other.
arroyo: A usually dry creek, wash, or gully that floods after a heavy rain.
basalt: A fine-grained dark-colored igneous rock.
bearing: The direction to a distant object in terms of degrees on the compass. Magnetic bearing is stated in degrees relative to magnetic north as shown by a magnetic needle. True bearing is stated relative to true north.
cerro: Spanish word for hill.
class of rapids: see rapids, classification of
Cretaceous: A unit of geologic time; covering the range from 66 to 145 million years before the present day.
cuesta: Spanish word for an asymmetrical ridge with one slope gentle and extensive and the other slope narrow but very steep.
declination: The difference in degrees between magnetic north and true north; it varies with location and time. Declination in the Big Bend area was 10 to 11 degrees east of true north in the mid-1800s, but today it is about 7 degrees east.
dike: A thin but extensive layer of igneous rock, usually vertical or very steep, and cutting across other relatively flat-lying rock formations.

dip: The angle at which a bed of rock is inclined to the horizontal.

escarpment: A topographic feature composed of a long line of cliffs or steep slope that forms a boundary between two relatively flat areas.

fault: A line of fracture or linear narrow zone of multiple fractures in rocks where the rocks on one side of the fault line have been displaced horizontally or vertically relative to the other side.

flatboat: A rectangular-shaped boat with a flat bottom chiefly used to float cargo downstream. Michler's flatboat was likely small and open, since he had carried it in a wagon and it was intended to serve only his small boat party; perhaps it was on the order of 5 feet wide and 14 feet long.

graben: A linear block of the earth's crust that has been displaced downward along two faults that lie on either side of the block; in other words, a depressed block of land bordered by two faults.

hogback: A narrow ridge or linear series of ridges with steep flanks, usually dipping 45 to 80 degrees; usually formed from the erosion of steeply dipping layers of sedimentary rocks.

igneous rock: Rock formed when molten magma cools and solidifies. See also basalt.

India rubber: A natural rubber. India was the major source of the raw material in the mid-nineteenth century.

latitude: North-to-south geographic position on the earth's surface, measured in degrees north or south from the equator, with zero being the equator, 90 degrees north being the north pole, and 90 degrees south being the south pole.

line a boat: A method of passing a rapids by unloading a boat's cargo and lowering it through the rapids while holding it with a rope as you walk along the shore.

longitude: East-to-west geographic position on the earth's surface, measured in degrees from the meridian at Greenwich, England, which is zero longitude, to 180 degrees west or 180 degrees east, which is the meridian on the opposite side of the earth from Greenwich.

mesa: A flat-topped hill bordered on at least one side by a cliff or steep slope.

mortar hole: A round hole in bedrock made by Indians grinding seeds with a wooden pestle. These distinctive artifacts are common near springs and tinajas and are about five inches in diameter and one to two feet deep.

outcrop: An exposure of a rock unit at the earth's surface.

pico: Spanish word for peak.

portage a boat: To carry a boat onshore to detour around falls or rapids.

presidio: A Spanish fort, usually with a church and garrisoned by soldiers.

puerto: Spanish word for a mountain pass.

rapids, classification of:
- Class I: Fast-moving water with riffles and small waves. The few obstructions are easy to avoid. Not much training is needed and there is little risk to swimmers.
- Class II: Novice boat control for wide, clear channel; rocks easily avoided.
- Class III: Intermediate boat control, waves can swamp a canoe, moves around rocks required. Scouting in advance suggested.
- Class IV: Intense rapids requiring experienced, precise boat handling; rocks and/or narrow chutes. Scouting required. Consider portage around or lining through.

sextant: A handheld precision instrument with a sighting telescope used to measure the angle of elevation of moon, sun, or stars above the horizon and thus determine the latitude of the location of the observer.

sierra: Spanish word for a chain of mountains.

skiff: A small boat, usually for one to four passengers, with a flat bottom and flat stern but a pointed bow.

slot canyon: A small and very narrow but very deep canyon in solid rock; may be ten to fifteen feet wide but hundreds of feet deep. Common in deserts when rapid erosion during flash floods can cut a notch through a solid rock wall.

surveyor's chain: A light chain of foot-long wire links, usually fifty or one-hundred feet in total length. This was the usual tool for measuring distance on the ground in land surveying in the nineteenth century (see figure 7).

surveyor's compass: A large (five- to eight-inch diameter) precision compass mounted on a tripod; it has spirit levels and a gunsight to point to a distant landmark or object; capable of measuring direction to fractions of a degree (see figure 7).

Tertiary: An interval of geologic time from approximately 2.6 to 66 million years before the present day.

theodolite: A precise yet compact surveying instrument used to measure both horizontal and vertical angles. Mounted on a tripod, it has a telescope, compass, spirit levels, and highly accurate scales marked along the metal case of the compass and telescope that can achieve an accuracy of readings of about a minute of a degree (1/60th of a degree) of rotation of the compass or the telescope (see figure 7).

tinaja: Spanish word for bowl. A moderate to large bowl-shaped depression in rock that holds water in an otherwise dry creek bed.

traverse: In surveying, a series of connected straight lines that join survey stations. Traversing is the act of measuring the direction and distance of each of these lines in order to accurately map the location of each station along the lines.

triangulation: A surveying technique used to determine the position of difficult-to-reach stations without actually going to the station. Triangulation uses the axioms that the three angles of a triangle must add up to 180 degrees, thus measuring two angles tells you all three; and, knowing all angles, measuring the length of just one side tells you the length of all sides (see figure 8).

***vado*:** Spanish word for a river crossing or ford.

Notes

Abbreviations

BBNP	Big Bend National Park, Texas
BBRSP	Big Bend Ranch State Park, Texas
BGWMA	Black Gap Wildlife Management Area, Texas
DGR	Duff Green Report, Ronnie C. Tyler, "Exploring the Rio Grande: Lt. Duff C. Green's Report of 1852," *Arizona and the West* 10, no. 1 (1968): 43–60
EP	William H. Emory Papers, Beinecke Rare Book and Manuscript Division, Yale University, WA MSS S-1187, New Haven, CT
ER	William H. Emory, *Report on the United States and Mexican Boundary Survey*, 34th Cong., 1st sess., 1857, Vol. 1, HED 135; 1859, Vol. 2, SED 108. All page references are to volume 1, part 1, unless otherwise specified.
HED	House Executive Document, US Congressional publication
HOT	*Handbook of Texas Online*, Texas State Historical Association, tshaonline.org
IBWC	International Boundary and Water Commission
LRHA	Letters Received, Headquarters of the Army
PJ	Parry Journal ("Field Notebook and Journal: Botany and Geology: U.S. Boundary Commission 1852"), Charles Christopher Parry Papers, MS 290, Parks Library, Iowa State University, Ames, Iowa
RG	Record Group
SED	Senate Executive Document, US Congressional publication
SHQ	*Southwestern Historical Quarterly*, Texas State Historical Association
TSA	Texas State Library and Archives Commission, Austin, Texas
TXGLO	Texas General Land Office, 1700 North Congress Avenue, Austin, Texas

USCS   United States Customs Service
USGS   United States Geological Survey
UT-BCAH   Briscoe Center for American History, University of Texas at Austin
UT-BEG   Bureau of Economic Geology, University of Texas at Austin
UT-PCL   Perry-Castañeda Library (Main), University of Texas at Austin

Introduction

1. William H. Emory, "Report on the United States and Mexican Boundary Survey," 34th Cong., 1st sess., 1857, HED 135, Vol. 1, xv; hereafter referred to as Emory Report or ER. A marine league equals 3 nautical miles and approximately 3.45 statute miles.
2. Lenard E. Brown, *Survey of the United States-Mexico Boundary, 1849–1855: Background Study* (Washington, DC: Office of Archaeology and Historic Preservation, Division of History, National Park Service, 1969), 4.
3. Emory's report, published in 1848 as Senate Executive Document No. 7, contained 416 pages, including 126 pages of Emory's daily journal; 33 pages of plant classifications collected by Emory and described by John Torrey of Princeton and George Engelmann of Saint Louis; and 225 pages of tables of meteorology, geographical positions, and astronomical observations. Also included were twenty-six page-size lithographs of natural history, some by the artist John Mix Stanley, plus fourteen page-size lithographs of plant drawings. Maps in a pocket included one large (30 × 72 inches), folded map of the detail of the route from Leavenworth to San Diego, and three small sketch maps of local areas. Another version of 10,000 copies of Emory's "Notes" was published as House Executive Document No. 41. It included reports by other members of Emory's team and ran to 615 pages.
4. L. David Norris, James C. Milligan, and Odie B. Faulk, *William H. Emory, Soldier-Scientist* (Tucson: University of Arizona Press, 1998), 82.
5. Ibid., 83.
6. Brown, *Survey of the United States-Mexico Boundary*, 9.
7. Norris, Milligan, and Faulk, *William H. Emory*, 107. Only Bartlett and his chief surveyor Gray received $3,000; the next-highest salary was $1,500 for Bartlett's friend John M. Bigelow and Bartlett's brother, George Bartlett.
8. University of Pennsylvania Alumni Archives, alumni card file for M. T. W. Chandler.
9. ER, 10.
10. Norris, Milligan, and Faulk, *William H. Emory*, 50–51.
11. Edward S. Wallace, *The Great Reconnaissance: Soldiers, Artists, and Scientists on the Frontier, 1848–1861* (Boston: Little Brown, 1955), 12.
12. Norris, Milligan, and Faulk, *William H. Emory*, 88.
13. Wallace, *The Great Reconnaissance*, 15.
14. A. Ray Stephens, *Texas: A Historical Atlas* (Norman: University of Oklahoma Press, 2010), 133.

15. Arriving late to force another person to wait sends the message that your time is more valuable and demonstrates your power over the other person—personal observation of the author after thirty-two years of working for a major corporation.
16. Joseph R. Werne, *The Imaginary Line: A History of the United States and Mexican Boundary Survey, 1848–1857* (Fort Worth: Texas Christian University Press, 2007), 30. The west end of the California line was agreed to on October 10, and the east end on November 30, 1849. It would take another year to mark the boundary line between the two end points.
17. John Disturnell, *Mapa de los Estados Unidos de Méjico* (New York: J. Disturnell, 1847); also known as "The Treaty Map." Scale: 1:4,430,000.
18. Disturnell's reference town of "Paso" was the Mexican village of El Paso del Norte, which was south of the Rio Grande on the trail from Chihuahua City to Santa Fe. There was no town on the American side. Emory's map with his 1857 report labeled the Mexican town "El Paso." Today the Mexican city south of the river is Ciudad Juárez, named in 1888 for the Mexican hero Benito Juárez, and across the river on the American side is the city of El Paso, Texas. I have used El Paso del Norte for the 1850s Mexican town, and Ciudad Juárez, Mexico, and El Paso, Texas, for the modern twin cities.
19. In the 1850s, the proper location for a first transcontinental railroad was a hot topic both in the US Congress and in the states across which the railroad might be built. Southern slave states wanted a route near the 32nd parallel across Texas to the San Diego area. Northern nonslave states wanted a route farther north across Nebraska and Wyoming to San Francisco. Therefore, the southern states were very interested in making sure the United States–Mexico boundary was drawn far enough south to take advantage of a possible route running across the relatively flat terrain west of El Paso del Norte. In the Mexican-American War, Major Emory had served as an Army Topographical Engineer on the staff of General Kearny, whose Army of the West explored a possible southern route as it marched from Santa Fe to San Diego in 1846.
20. Gray had worked with Emory on the boundary line near San Diego and did not arrive back in Washington, DC, until December 1, 1850. There he "suffered a severe illness" and did not arrive in El Paso del Norte until long after Bartlett had moved the commission office to the Santa Rita mines in Nuevo México, where Gray arrived on July 19, 1851, and immediately challenged the compromise agreement and Whipple's authority to sign for him; 33rd Cong., 2nd sess., 1855, SED 55, 1–50.
21. Today the Gadsden Treaty line coincides with the southern boundary of the states of New Mexico and Arizona. It begins only three miles north of the old town of El Paso del Norte.
22. It appears Bartlett moved the office west to extend work on the survey in the less controversial section of the boundary running down the Gila River, since the location of the starting point on the Rio Grande that he had agreed to in his compromise with García Conde had not been approved in Washington, DC. The real reason likely was that Bartlett had been in El Paso del Norte for a month and wanted to see new country farther west.

23. Brown, *Survey of the United States–Mexico Boundary*, 21.
24. The root causes of the survey delays were lack of funds from Washington and the ongoing conflict over the Bartlett–García Conde Compromise, but Bartlett's absence was a contributing factor.
25. Colonel John James Abert had founded the Army Corps of Topographical Engineers in 1838 and remained its leader until he retired in 1861. See William H. Goetzmann, *Army Exploration in the American West, 1803–1863* (New Haven, CT: Yale University Press, 1959), 11, 432.
26. Stuart to Emory, November 4, 1851. William H. Emory Papers, WA MSS S-1187, Beinecke Rare Book and Manuscript Library, Yale University, New Haven, CT; hereafter referred to as EP.
27. Andrew Denny Rodgers III, *John Torrey: A Story of North American Botany* (Princeton, NJ: Princeton University Press, 1942), 221.
28. Emory was born on his family's large planation in Maryland. His boyhood friends and West Point classmates, who later became leaders of the Confederacy in the Civil War, were Joseph E. Johnston and Jefferson Davis. The noted South Carolina statesman John C. Calhoun was responsible for Emory's appointment to West Point (Norris, Milligan, and Faulk, *William H. Emory*, 2). Emory became a supporter of a southern route for the first transcontinental railroad after his extensive topographical work for General Kearny's Army of the West when it traveled the route from Santa Fe to San Diego in 1846. In 1847, Emory indicated his support for a southern route in a report to the cabinet of President Polk (ibid., 154). After his work on the US Boundary Commission, Emory received a promotion and a new assignment to a cavalry post at the order of Secretary of War Jefferson Davis. When the Civil War began, Emory sent a letter of resignation to Washington, DC, but he quickly withdrew it and later became a general in the Federal Army.
29. Norris, Milligan, and Faulk, *William H. Emory*, 115.
30. Ibid., 131.
31. Brown, *Survey of the United States–Mexico Boundary*, 21; US Congress, "Report of the Secretary of the Interior made in compliance with a resolution of the Senate calling for information in relation to the commission appointed to run and mark the boundary between the United States and Mexico," 32nd Cong., 1st sess. 1852, SED 119, Letter of January 10, 1852, from A. B. Gray to Secretary Stuart, 305.
32. Brown, *Survey of the United States–Mexico Boundary*, 27. While Bartlett's work as a boundary commissioner may have left something to be desired, he did publish his writings about his travels, which provided insight into the area: John Russell Bartlett, *Personal Narrative of Explorations and Incidents in Texas, New Mexico, California, Sonora, and Chihuahua, connected with the United States and Mexican Boundary Commission, during the Years 1850, '51, '52, and '53*, 2 vols. (New York: D. Appleton, 1854).
33. "Some of the men had not been paid in eighteen months," ER, 12.
34. Emory and Magoffin became friends in 1846 when Magoffin and his wagons joined Emory's army caravan as it moved west along the Santa Fe Trail; Norris, Milligan, and Faulk, *William H. Emory*, 109.

35. We know von Hippel used boats and a mule train because Parry noted that one of the wooden boats later used by Chandler had traveled the Rio Grande all the way from El Paso del Norte where von Hippel had begun, and because von Hippel reported to Emory that he needed to pay off his packers after they were discharged near Presidio del Norte. ER, pt. 2, 57; Norris, Milligan and Faulk *William H. Emory*, 123; von Hippel to Emory, Camp near Presidio del Norte, May 15, 1852, box 5, EP.
36. ER, 85.
37. Von Hippel to Emory, May 15, 1852, box 5, EP.
38. In August 1852, Parry made a reconnaissance and recorded distances along the Rio Grande in his daily journal. This allows us to estimate how far down the river Thompson would have traveled and returned in five days.
39. Von Hippel to Emory, July 22, 1852, box 5, EP.
40. George Clinton Gardner, *Fiasco: George Clinton Gardner's Correspondence from the U.S.-Mexico Boundary Survey, 1849–1854*, ed. David J. Weber and Jane Lenz Elder (Dallas: SMU Press, 2010), 231. The location of Emory's observatory is shown on Chandler's Boundary Map 22 (see figures 10 and 13). Today, the marker that Emory placed at the site has been carried away by flash floods along Cibola Creek. The site is thought to be at a point 0.6 miles northeast of today's international bridge over the Rio Grande. Modern surveying maps often label the spot as RP 27A.

Part I: The 1852 Chandler Surveying Party

1. Emory to Chandler, August 8, 1852, EP.
2. Gardner, *Fiasco*, 232.
3. Nancy Miller, University of Pennsylvania Archives, email message to author, August 20, 2012.
4. Bartlett, *Personal Narrative*, 2:595.
5. ER, 249.
6. Chandler to Bartlett, July 24, 1851, and July–September 1851, John Russell Bartlett Collection, Brown University, Providence, RI.
7. Gardner, *Fiasco*, 177.
8. Ibid., 200.
9. 32nd Cong., 1st sess., 1852, SED 121, 201.
10. Parry Journal ("Field Notebook and Journal: Botany and Geology: U.S. Boundary Commission 1852"), Charles Christopher Parry Papers, MS 290, Parks Library, Iowa State University, Ames, Iowa, 1–167; hereafter cited as PJ.
11. Biographical note, PJ.
12. Rodgers, *John Torrey*, 193.
13. Ibid., 223.
14. Ibid.

15. ER, 1:81, 82, 83; 2:55, 59.
16. ER, 2:49–61.
17. The Papers of Charles Christopher Parry 1823–1890, Special Collections, MS 290, Parks Library, Iowa State University, Ames, Iowa.
18. Paula Rebert, *La Gran Línea: Mapping the United States–Mexico Boundary, 1849–1857* (Austin: University of Texas Press, 2001), 54.
19. Duff Green Report, in Ronnie C. Tyler, "Exploring the Rio Grande: Lt. Duff C. Green's Report of 1852," *Arizona and the West* 10, no. 1 (1968): 43–60, 51; hereafter referred to as DGR.
20. Ibid.
21. Parry to Emory, November 4, 1852; and Schott to Emory, undated but after November 25, 1852, EP.
22. September 12, 1852, PJ, 12.
23. DGR, 51; Bartlett, *Personal Narrative*, 2:136.
24. DGR, 54.
25. W. D. Smithers, *Chronicles of the Big Bend: A Photographic Memoir of Life on the Border* (Austin: Texas State Historical Association, 1999), 22.
26. Bartlett, *Personal Narrative*, 2:605.
27. Gardner, *Fiasco*, 213.
28. August 16, 1852, PJ.
29. Gouverneur K. Warren, "Memoir to Accompany the Map of Territory of the United States from the Mississippi River to the Pacific Ocean," in vol. 2 of *Reports of Explorations and Surveys to Ascertain the most Practicable and Economical Route for a Railroad from the Mississippi River to the Pacific Ocean*. 33rd Cong., 2nd sess., 1859, Vol. 2, SED 78, 62.
30. PJ, 30.
31. ER, 2:57.
32. October 30–November 4, 1852, PJ.
33. Parry to Emory, Camp on the Rio Grande, November 4, 1852; and Parry to Emory (unsigned), Eagle Pass, November 14, 1852, EP.
34. George W. B. Evans, *Mexican Gold Trail: Journal of a Forty-Niner*, ed. Glenn S. Dumke (San Marino, CA: Huntington Library, 1945); Samuel Maverick, *Samuel A. Maverick, Texan*, ed. Mary Rowena [Rena] Maverick Green (San Antonio: Privately printed, 1952); Solveig A. Turpin and Herbert H. Eling Jr., eds., *Dust, Smoke, and Tracks: Two Accounts of Nineteenth-Century Mexican Military Expeditions in Northern Coahuila and Chihuahua: Colonel Emilio Langberg, 1851, and Major Blas Flores, 1880–1881* (Alpine, TX: Sul Ross University, Center for Big Bend Studies, 2009).
35. Ronnie C. Tyler, *The Big Bend: A History of the Last Texas Frontier* (Washington, DC: US Government Printing Office, 1975), 262n13; Solveig A. Turpin, phone conversation with author, January 2013.
36. Turpin and Eling, *Dust, Smoke, and Tracks*, 5–30.
37. The junction of the routes is clear from the descriptions of the Encantada Pass in the journals of Evans, *Mexican Gold Trail*, 60; Turpin and Eling, *Dust, Smoke, and Tracks*, 13; PJ, 125.

38. ER, 245. At his observatory across the river from Presidio del Norte, Major Emory determined latitude by Zenith Telescope and longitude by the moon's culminations. At Fort Duncan, Lieutenant Michler determined the latitude by sextant, and Major Emory, the longitude by moon's culminations. In 1853, Michler also made latitude determinations by sextant at overnight camps as he floated down the Rio Grande for 76 miles from his Lipan Crossing camp to the mouth of the Pecos River. Michler's sextant locations, while accurate, had marginal value without an accompanying longitude determination, because the river flows in an easterly direction, and latitude changes were small from camp to camp.
39. James D. Graham, *Report of the Secretary of War, in Compliance with a Resolution of the Senate, the Report of Lieutenant Colonel Graham on the Subject of the boundary line between the United States and Mexico.* 32nd Cong., 1st sess., 1852, SED 121, 95–98, 149. Letter of Colonel James D. Graham [chief astronomer] to John R. Bartlett [boundary commissioner], August 6, 1851, Santa Rita Copper Mines, New Mexico Territory:

It is considered that the surveys down the Rio Grande and Gila need not be attended with triangulation. Although the most accurate, this is, at the same time[,] an expensive and slow mode of proceeding and is not necessary to satisfy accomplishment of the object committed to the joint commission. It will be sufficient if the shores of these streams are laid down by simple traverse work with small light theodolite and [or] surveyors compass and the measurements made with the chain. The run of the work to be corrected by determinations of latitude and longitude from astronomical observations at suitable points.

Graham's instrument inventory included two theodolites reading to 30 seconds of a degree; four small theodolites made to order for Graham and reading to a minute of a degree; eight surveyor's compasses made to order for Graham, all the above on tripods; and fourteen sets of surveying chain of 50- or 100-foot lengths to measure distance on the ground. A smaller number of instruments appropriate for astronomical observations included two large transits and one large altitude and azimuth instrument, a leveling instrument, three chronometers, eight barometers, etc.

Report of the Secretary of the Interior Made in Compliance with a resolution of the Senate calling for information in relation to the commission appointed to run and mark the boundary between the United States and Mexico. 32nd Cong., 1st sess., 1852, SED 119, 240. Letter of Lieutenant A. W. Whipple [acting astronomer and surveyor] to T. Thompson [asst. surveyor of a Gila River party], April 26, 1851, Doña Ana, New Mexico:

The basis of your operations will be the line of the survey of the river. Angles and courses will be measured by the various methods, which the nature of the country will render most convenient and correct. The distance over precipice or other obstacle not easily chained may be determined by hasty triangulation.—You will also please from time to time, take angles in bearings to distant mountain peaks and other prominent features of the country.

PJ, 55; ER, 83. Parry noted in his journal that a reconnaissance party of surveyors had hiked across the high mesa above Santa Elena Canyon to reach a point high above the canyon exit and "had brought the survey up to this point by triangulation." Chandler, in his proposal to name Mount Emory [Emory Peak], observed: "From many places on the line it [Emory Peak] was taken as a prominent point on which to direct the instrument." "On the line" is taken to mean his survey traverse line, and "direct the instrument" [theodolite] was a usual step in triangulation.

40. EP; PJ, 1–167; DGR, 43–60; ER, 80–85; ER, 2:49–61.
41. The course of the river in 1852 was not the same as it is today. After a 1970 treaty agreement, about five miles of the river below Presidio, Texas, were "channelized" in straight-line segments to keep it from meandering back and forth across the international boundary. The current channel cuts off some old meanders and shortens the river by about one mile.
42. DGR, 51.
43. Oscar S. Rodríguez, "El Mulato, Chihuahua: A Continuing Light in the Desert" (paper presented at the Twenty-Third Annual Conference of the Center for Big Bend Studies, Sul Ross University, Alpine TX, November 12, 2016).
44. PJ, 13; ER, 2:5.
45. ER, 81. In the past, the well-known drawings in the Emory Report have often been credited to other men and not to Parry.
46. ER, 2:52.
47. ER, 2:53.
48. PJ, 18.
49. The following sources of images of the original 1857 boundary maps were used by the author: Rebert, *La Gran Línea*, 154; Rebert shows a page-size image of Mexican Boundary Map 22. The author also engaged a contractor to take digital photographic images of the original US Boundary Maps 15 through 22 held in the National Archives. Finally, a digital copy of Mexican Map 21 was provided courtesy of Mapoteca Manuel Orozco y Berra Museum in Mexico City. In the Gadsden Purchase of 1854, the United States agreed to pay the Mexican government ten million dollars for a thirty-thousand-square-mile strip of land that would extend the southern margins of the later states of New Mexico and Arizona farther south to provide for a possible route of a transcontinental railroad.
50. Manuel Orozco y Berra, *Apuntes para la historia de la geografía en México* (Mexico City: Francisco Díaz de León, 1881), 465–67. The longitude calculations are courtesy of the Austin, Texas, surveyor Kent McMillan, from the Spanish triangulation data in the Orozco y Berra book. Translation from Spanish to English of the Orozco y Berra text on page 465 was made by a member of the staff at the Benson Latin American Library at the University of Texas, Austin; Werne, *The Imaginary Line*, 126; Rebert, *La Gran Línea*, 155.
51. Ralph Wright, *Field Survey Notes of June 27, 1857*, Presidio County, Abstract no. 2109, Survey Tract 13, Texas General Land Office (TXGLO); US Army Corps of Engineers, *Tactical Map, Presidio Sheet*, 1:62, 500, 1932.

52. Wm. H. C. Whiting, "Journal of a Reconnaissance from San Antonio de Bexar to El Paso del Norte, 1849," in Philip St. George Cooke, William Henry Chase Whiting, and François Xavier Aubry, *Exploring Southwestern Trails, 1846–1854*, ed. Ralph P. Bieber (Philadelphia: Porcupine, 1974), 286.
53. Gardner, *Fiasco*, 234.
54. ER, 1:88; Gardner, *Fiasco*, 234; Roy L. Swift, *Three Roads to Chihuahua: The Great Wagon Roads That Opened the Southwest, 1823–1883* (Austin: Eakin Press, 1988), 3, 9, 33–42.
55. From Presidio del Norte the trail went east to Fort Leaton, north up Alamito Creek, and then left the creek to go east over Paisano Pass, down to a valley near where the town of Alpine sits today, then northeast to join the main San Antonio Stage Road at Leon Springs, eight miles west of Fort Stockton, Texas. At Leon Springs where the old "salt trail" continued north to Horsehead Crossing, Emory turned east on the San Antonio road to Comanche Springs (Fort Stockton, Texas) and east to Escondido Springs. He followed that wagon road toward San Antonio for three hundred miles until he left it at Fort Inge (Uvalde, Texas) to turn southwest to Fort Duncan (Eagle Pass, Texas).
56. PJ, 26, 103; correspondence in the Parry Papers, file number Qk 31, 248c, Special Collections, Parks Library, Iowa State University, Ames, Iowa. This is Parry's copy of the agreement with Lieutenant Green for Parry to serve as surgeon for the Chandler party. Parry's friend assistant surveyor Thomas Thompson was a witness.
57. DGR, 53.
58. PJ, 14.
59. This author's observation based on Chandler's Boundary Map 21.
60. DGR, 53. Although Green gives no detail, the unfortunate event was likely due to a combination of factors: inexperience on the part of the newly hired group of packers, both in securing the packs to the mules and in their slow reaction to problems when they first started; and a nervous first-hard-day response of the mules after being idle for a month or more.
61. To "line" is to lower a boat in the water while walking along the bank with a rope tied to the boat. To "portage" means to carry the boat overland by hand.
62. Robert T. Hill, "Running the Cañons of the Rio Grande," *Century Magazine*, January 1901, 377.
63. PJ, 31–37. Parry documented a rapid descent of the river, covering twenty-five miles in three days.
64. PJ, 33.
65. Louis F. Aulbach and Linda C. Gorski, *The Upper Canyons of the Rio Grande: Presidio to Terlingua Creek, including Colorado Canyon and Santa Elena Canyon* (Houston: Wilderness Area Map Service, 2000), 65.
66. David Alloway, *El Camino Del Rio—The River Road—FM 170 from Study Butte to Presidio and through Big Bend Ranch State Park* (Austin: Texas Parks and Wildlife Department, 1995), 17.

67. Ibid., 16; William MacLeod, *River Road Vistas: A Journey along the River Road* (Alpine: Texas Geological Press, 2008), 95. See also Texas Parks and Wildlife, *Contrabando Movie Set at Big Bend Ranch State Park*, video, https://www.youtube.com/watch?v=SJ7pKe4u-c4.
68. The scene he sketched is easily recognizable today as a view of the isolated spire, which reaches an elevation of 3,090 feet.
69. At the author's request, a download of a high-quality digital image of Mexican Boundary Map 21 was provided courtesy of the Mapoteca Manuel Orozco y Berra Museum in Mexico City.
70. DGR, 54.
71. PJ, 39, 40.
72. Joaquín Rivaya-Martínez, ed. and trans., "The Captivity of Macario Leal: A Tejano among the Comanches, 1847–1854," *SHQ* 117, no. 2 (April 2014): 382.
73. Ralph A. Smith, "The Comanche Bridge between Oklahoma and Mexico," *Chronicles of Oklahoma* 39, no. 1 (1961): 55.
74. PJ, 39.
75. ER, 86.
76. DGR, 55; Wayne R. Austerman, *Sharps Rifles and Spanish Mules: The San Antonio–El Paso Mail, 1851–1881* (College Station: Texas A&M Press, 1985), 26.
77. Orozco y Berra, *Apuntes para la historia de la geografía*, 465.
78. Rodgers, *John Torrey*, 221. Emory's encouragement of botanical collections and the relationships of Emory, Parry, and the Columbia College botanist John Torrey are illustrated by the following quote from a letter by Torrey to Asa Gray (botanist) in September 1851: "He [Emory] told me to send down—Parry [to join Emory in New York to depart for El Paso del Norte via New Orleans]. Parry will collect plants as before." Evidence of Emory's interest in botany includes these facts: Emory collected his own plants during his 1846 expedition with General Kearny and sent them to the Columbia botanist John Torrey for analysis; Emory sent a letter to Parry in 1850 in San Diego to come to DC and bring his plants; Parry, in a note to Emory when the Chandler party walked across Mexico, said he was not taking the rubber boat with Abbott out of concern over losing his plants; Emory, in a note to Parry at the end of the Chandler Survey at Fort Duncan in December 1852, said: "Come to DC and bring your plants."
79. Hill, "Running the Cañons of the Rio Grande," 378.
80. Aulbach and Gorski, *Upper Canyons of the Rio Grande*, 26.
81. PJ, 55.
82. True bearing from the peak near camp to the cliff overlooking the canyon exit on Google Earth is 97 degrees, at a distance of 6.0 miles, whereas Chandler's Map 21 shows 99 degrees, 5.9 miles, which may be exactly correct, since we do not know the precise spot where the surveyor was standing near the exit.
83. ER, 2:5.
84. PJ, 52.

85. PJ, 50.
86. Thompson to Chandler, October 1, 1852, Camp near San Carlos, EP.
87. ER, 82.
88. ER, 2:57.
89. Duff Green [at Fort Duncan] to Colonel Samuel Cooper, December 16, 1852, LRHA, RG 108, National Archives.
90. James E. Ivey, *Presidios of the Big Bend Area*, Professional Paper No. 31 (Santa Fe, NM: Southwest Cultural Resources Center, National Park Service, 1990). In a presentation at a conference in San Antonio, Texas, in November 2018, Emiliano Gallaga Murrieta reported a new study of the Presidio San Carlos. The abstract, titled "The Presidio San Carlos, a Remote Outpost in the Nueva Viscaya Region," and presentation slides can be seen online at https://jtah.org/special-publications/.
91. PJ, 60.
92. PJ, 61.
93. Turpin and Eling, *Dust, Smoke, and Tracks*, 6; Evans, *Mexican Gold Trail*, 73.
94. PJ, 66.
95. The meaning of *anguila* in this context is not agreed upon. The word means "eel" in Spanish but may be a corruption of *águila*, the word for eagle, or may have other origins. Richard Bruhn, "Mesa de Anguila," *Handbook of Texas Online* (hereafter cited as *HOT*), accessed January 23, 2020, http://www.tshaonline.org/handbook/online/articles/rjm45.
96. Turpin and Eling, *Dust, Smoke, and Tracks*, 6; Google Earth image shows the tinaja at 28°57'46" north; 103°32'45" west; at the head of Arroyo Canastillas and one hundred yards from an old concrete water tank.
97. ER, 83.
98. Rebert, *La Gran Línea*, 54.
99. PJ, 68.
100. Rebert, *La Gran Línea*, 193. There were no Mexican surveys of Boundary Maps 9 through 20, and the Mexican mapmaker traced the US maps. A comparison of US and Mexican Maps 21 and 22 by the author indicates an excellent Mexican survey was done across the southern three-quarters of Map 22. The Mexican Map 21 was a copy of the US map of Chandler, except for the first few miles of river trace where a generalized river trace is sketched in to allow a connection with the accurate position of the river on the adjoining Mexican Map 22.
101. ER, 83.
102. PJ, 69.
103. DGR, 56.
104. Names used for the crossing include: Paso de los Chisos, on a copy of an 1805 map, untitled and unsigned in Thomas C. Alex, *Big Bend National Park and Vicinity* (Charleston, SC: Arcadia, 2010), 12; los Chisos in 1851, in Turpin and Eling, *Dust, Smoke, and Tracks*, 9; Vado de Fleche in 1852, DGR, 56; El Vado Chisos in 1961, in Ralph Smith, "The Comanche Bridge between Oklahoma and Mexico, 1843–1844," *Chronicles of Oklahoma* 39, no. 1 (1961):

54; Paso de Chisos in 1966, in Oscar W. Williams, *Pioneer Surveyor, Frontier Lawyer: The Personal Narrative of O. W. Williams, 1877–1902*, ed. S. D. Myres (El Paso: Texas Western College Press, 1966), 270; Paso del Chisos in 1968, in Ross A. Maxwell, *The Big Bend of the Rio Grande: A Guide to the Rocks, Landscape, Geologic History, and Settlers of the Area of Big Bend National Park* (Austin: Bureau of Economic Geology, University of Texas at Austin, 1968), 49; Chisos Ford in 1979, in Tyler, *The Big Bend*, 65; Vado de Chisos in 2008, in International Boundary and Water Commission (IBWC), *2008 Rio Grande Boundary Maps: Reed Camp/Vado de Chisos Map 124*.

105. Turpin and Eling, *Dust, Smoke, and Tracks*, 9.
106. Ibid. The original document from which the landscape copy was taken is "Itinerario de la Expedición San Carlos a Monclova El Viejo hecho por el Coronel D. Emilio Langberg, 1851," in the Luis Alberto Guajardo Papers, Western Americana Division, Beinecke Library of Rare Books and Manuscripts, Yale University, New Haven, CT.
107. R. A. Smith, "The Comanche Bridge," 56.
108. At the time there was only a ranch and a scatter of other buildings on the Texas side. However, a person in San Antonio would have referred to the El Paso del Norte area as "El Paso." For example, in 1848, the new wagon road from San Antonio was called "The El Paso Road." Officially there was no El Paso, Texas, until 1859, when a plat of the town was drawn and named El Paso.
109. Richard (Dick) Howard guided expeditions across the Big Bend such as the Hays-Highsmith Expedition in 1848 and those of officers of the Army Topographical Engineers office in San Antonio, including Lt. W. H. C. Whiting in 1849, and Col. Joseph E. Johnston in 1849 and 1850.
110. Maverick, *Samuel A. Maverick, Texan*, 330–42. Maverick's journal records the journey as first north to Fredericksburg, back south to Las Moras Springs (Brackettville, Texas), west to and then north up the Devils River, west across the Pecos River, south down to the Rio Grande, then west through the canyon country on the American side of the river by traveling west but remaining far enough from the river to avoid massive canyons, then finally reaching the Persimmon Gap area of today's Big Bend National Park.
111. Ibid., 337.
112. IBWC, Areal Geologic Map, Fresno Creek to Talley's Ranch, Map 206, 1951, 1:50,000. Digital copy download courtesy of UT-BEG.
113. John C. Hays, "Report of Col. Hays [to Peter Bell]," *Corpus Christi Star*, January 20, 1849. https://texashistory.unt.edu/ark:/67531/metapth80212/m1/1/?q=John C. Hays.
114. Swift, *Three Roads to Chihuahua*, fly leaf map and page 57.
115. Louis F. Aulbach, *The Great Unknown of the Rio Grande: Terlingua Creek to La Linda, including Boquillas Canyon and Mariscal Canyon* (Houston: Louis F. Aulbach, 2007), 12, 49, 51.
116. Oscar W. Williams, *O. W. Williams' Stories from the Big Bend*, ed. S. D. Myres (El Paso: Texas Western College Press, 1965), 24.

117. US Geological Survey and US Customs Service, *Reed Camp 1982*, photomap along the border, 1:25,000 (Austin: University of Texas Perry-Castañeda Library Map Collection, http://www.lib.utexas.edu/maps/us_mexico_border/; accessed May 11, 2014).
118. IBWC, *2008 Rio Grande Boundary Maps: Reed Camp/Vado de Chisos Map 124*, 2008, 1:25,000.
119. ER, 8.
120. PJ, 74.
121. Ibid.
122. Chandler's Boundary Map No. 20.
123. Aulbach, *The Great Unknown of the Rio Grande*, 65. Aulbach provides a review of the life of Francis Rooney. To visit the site, see Jon R. Pearson, *Road Guide to Backcountry Dirt Roads of Big Bend National Park* (Big Bend Natural History Association, 1980), 18. Today "Rooney's Place" is marked by the remains of small rock buildings fifty feet above and one hundred yards from the bank of the river.
124. PJ, 77.
125. PJ, 78.
126. Robert T. Hill, *Field Notebook of 1899 Rio Grande Exploration from Presidio to Langtry*. Accession no. 815, Big Bend Region River Book, Author: R. T. Hill, Index no. RTH-15, Locality: H-15, Texas, year 1899, US Geological Survey, Denver, CO., 62–70.
127. Nancy Alexander, *Father of Texas Geology: Robert T. Hill* (Dallas: SMU Press, 1976), 68.
128. ER, 2:59; Parry's description of the formations dipping northeast and of convolute fossils indicate an outcrop of the Cretaceous Boquillas Formation. Parry and Chandler referred to the Sierra del Carmen mountain range as "Sierra Carmel." This was consistent with American usage during most of the 1800s, during which time the Mexicans used Sierra del Carmen. The highly regarded 1881 edition of Stielers Hand Atlas of the United States showed Sierra Carmel. In 1899, the geologist R. T. Hill used Sierra del Carmen in his *Century Magazine* article about floating the Rio Grande. Modern US maps show Sierra del Carmen.
129. PJ, 80; San Vicente Presidio is located at 29°06'24" north; 103°01'30" west; for more information, see Ivey, *Presidios of the Big Bend Area*.
130. Turpin and Eling, *Dust, Smoke, and Tracks*, 10.
131. PJ, 81.
132. J. O. Langford, *Big Bend, A Homesteaders Story* (Austin: University of Texas Press, 1952), 98. The water temperature today of Langford's Hot Spring is 105 degrees F. The homesteader J. O. Langford and his family settled at the spring in 1909, and later built a bathhouse for the occasional tourist or river-runner. The Langford family lived here, off and on, until 1942. As late as 1976 these springs, also called Boquillas Hot Springs, had a flow of 300,000 gallons a day, but it is much less today. Gunnar Brune, *Springs of Texas*. 2nd ed. (College Station: Texas A&M Press, 2002), 1:86. See the pictographs at: https://www.nps.gov/bibe/learn/historyculture/hotsprings.htm.
133. PJ, 87.

134. ER, 42.
135. Maxwell, *The Big Bend of the Rio Grande*, 106. Maxwell's map shows the Straw House ruin on the American side, several hundred feet from the river at 102°55′32″ west.
136. ER, 2:60. Parry's description of Pico Tena makes it clear it is today's Pico Etéreo; Franklin K. Daugherty, "Geology of the Pico Etéreo Area, Municipio de Acuña, Coahuila, Mexico" (PhD diss., University of Texas, 1959), 2. Daugherty states that Parry's Pico Tena is Pico Etéreo.
137. Turpin and Eling, *Dust, Smoke, and Tracks*, 12; Alex, *Big Bend National Park and Vicinity*, 12.
138. Chandler's Boundary Map 19.
139. See figure 2.
140. PJ, 92.
141. PJ, 93.
142. Author's personal observation of Pico Etéreo from a distance and direction similar to Parry's 1852 view.
143. Distances taken from Chandler's Map 19 and the online satellite image from Google Earth.
144. Rebert, *La Gran Línea*, 200. Chandler's Boundary Map 19 was drawn by M. C. Grilzner.
145. PJ, 94.
146. E. N. Brandt, *Chairman of the Board: A Biography of Carl A. Gerstacker* (East Lansing: Michigan State University Press, 2003), 1967.
147. DGR, 57.
148. ER, 85; PJ, 95.
149. Hill, "Running the Cañons of the Rio Grande," 384.
150. Visit to BGWMA by author on October 17, 2013.
151. R. T. Hill, "Running the Canyons of the Rio Grande, Part 5," *Dallas Morning News*, September 16, 1934.
152. ER, 84.
153. Areal Geologic Map, Talley's Ranch to Reagan Canyon, 1951, IBWC Map A-203.1, in files of UT-BEG, Austin, TX.
154. PJ, 97.
155. W. C. Jameson, *Border Bandits, Border Raids* (Helena, MT: Lone Star Books, 2017), 39–50. John M. Flynt came to the Big Bend area in the mid-1880s and formed a small band of outlaws that operated out of temporary camps in the meadows along the Rio Grande downstream from Maravillas Creek. On September 2, 1891, at a horseshoe bend twelve miles northwest of Langtry, Texas, and sixty-five miles northeast of their camp at the meadows, Flynt and four or five companions stopped the San Antonio–El Paso train by placing large boulders on the tracks and robbed the Wells Forgo mail car. Texas Rangers led by Captain John Jones arrived at the robbery site and tracked the bandits for a month, following them across the Rio Grande into Mexico and back before losing their trail. In October, the outlaws were reported to be at a general store on Devils River on the Lower San Antonio–El Paso Road. The Rangers picked up the trail and followed them north up the road past Howards Well (Spring) and the site of Fort Lancaster, finally catching them

near the Pecos south of the later site of Iraan, Texas, on October 16. In a running gunfight, Flynt and one other outlaw were killed, and two were captured and sentenced to ten years in federal prison.

156. PJ, 98.
157. The mule train was now nine miles east of their prior camp on the Rio Grande. See USGS topographic map *Dove Mountain*, 1985, 1:100,000.
158. PJ, 99, 106. Parry's "Point Mountain" (point of the mountain) location is shown in figure 31. Camp #31 was 3/4 mile west of Point Mountain.
159. PJ, 99.
160. Chandler to Emory, Camp on the Rio Grande, November 4, 1852, EP. Chandler reports that some of his men had been without food for seventy-eight hours.
161. DGR, 57.
162. PJ, 98; Parry's route description allows us to be sure they are traveling east in the Arroyo Ceferino.
163. DGR, 58.
164. Distances measured on the satellite image from Google Earth online.
165. The Chandler party wrecked the two large wooden boats on September 14, 1852, soon after leaving Presidio del Norte. They recovered one on September 16 but abandoned it on October 2. PJ, 30; ER, pt. 2, 57.
166. USGS map, *Dove Mountain*, 1985, 1:100,000.
167. PJ, 103.
168. To determine Parry's location, one needs only a modern map showing the prominent landmarks he observed, a simple protractor to measure angles in degrees, a straight edge to draw a line, and a list or map showing the small angular difference (declination) in degrees between true north and magnetic north as indicated by a compass for this area in 1852. To plot Parry's location, first add 11 degrees of bearing to his directions to account for the compass declination in 1852. Then, to be able to draw lines from the landmark to Parry, reverse the directions noted by Parry by subtracting 180 degrees. These steps allow the drawing of bearing lines from Pico Cerda toward Parry's location of 21 degrees east of true north and 6 degrees east of true north from Pico Etéreo. The two lines intersect at Parry's calculated location. This indicates a location about one mile west of where I believe he was standing on a three-thousand-foot-high mountain less than a mile southwest of his camp but accessible by scrambling up a ravine. This level of accuracy within two degrees of being dead-on is unexpected, considering Parry used a pocket compass and only recorded his bearings in multiples of five degrees.
169. Gómez reported that Chandler stopped surveying at the entrance to Boquillas Canyon, 149 miles downstream from Presidio del Norte. Goetzmann thought he stopped 12 miles inside Boquillas Canyon, and Tyler suggested he stopped "in Boquillas Canyon"; but Chandler surveyed well past Boquillas Canyon into the Lower Canyons of the Rio Grande below Reagan Canyon to a point 209 miles below Presidio del Norte. Arthur R. Gómez, *A Most*

Singular Country: A History of Occupation in the Big Bend (Washington, DC: National Park Service, 1990), 61; William H. Goetzmann, "Science Explores the Big Bend, 1852–1853," *Password* 3, no. 2 (1958): 64; Tyler, *The Big Bend*, 96.
170. Hill, "Running the Cañons of the Rio Grande," 384; Hill, *Field Notebook of 1899*, 98.
171. Chandler to Emory, November 4, 1852, and Parry to Emory November 4, 1852, EP. Portions of both the Chandler and Parry letters are reproduced in Brown, *Survey of the United States-Mexico Boundary, 1849–1855* (Washington, DC: Office of Archaeology and Historic Preservation, Division of History, National Park Service, 1969), 60–61.
172. Ibid.
173. PJ, 101.
174. Chandler to Emory, Camp on the Rio Grande, November 4, 1852, EP.
175. The uniform and generic meander pattern shown on Michler's Boundary Map 17 extends downstream across a thirty-four-mile unsurveyed section of river, starting at the point where Chandler's men ended their record of mapping the river and proceeding down to the mouth of San Francisco Canyon where Michler's surveying began.
176. DGR, 60.
177. Parry to Emory, Camp on the Rio Grande, November 4, 1852, EP.
178. Schott to Emory, from Ft. Duncan, no date (probably on November 15 but must be on or shortly after November 14 when Abbott arrived at Fort Duncan), EP.
179. PJ, 106. See also note 158.
180. Charles I. Smith, *Lower Cretaceous Stratigraphy, Northern Coahuila, Mexico*. Report of Investigations No. 65 (Austin: Bureau of Economic Geology, University of Texas, 1970), 10.
181. PJ, 106. Noting Parry's 30-degree angle between his earlier bearings to Pico Etéreo and Pico Cerda and his later angle of only 15 degrees between these two landmarks, it is clear that he has moved closer to them. A calculation using his bearings and his description of his route indicates he had moved fourteen air miles closer to Pico Etéreo.
182. See figure 31 for a comparison of Parry and Green sketch maps of the route they followed when they left the Rio Grande to walk across the interior of Mexico to Fort Duncan.
183. PJ, 110.
184. PJ, 109.
185. PJ, 112; DGR, 60.
186. PJ, 117.
187. PJ, 119.
188. PJ, 121.
189. PJ, 123.
190. An online Google search for "Cuesta de Malena" reveals photographs of the igneous rock towers of this scenic landmark.
191. DGR, map B; "tinaja" is Spanish for earthen jar and is used to describe a bathtub-like depression eroded in solid rock along an otherwise dry ravine.

192. Evans, *Mexican Gold Trail*, 57; see Langberg's itinerary in Turpin and Eling, *Dust, Smoke, and Tracks*, 14; PJ, 125; Blas Flores, "Review of Campaigns," in *Dust, Smoke, and Tracks*, 86.
193. Turpin and Eling, *Dust, Smoke, and Tracks*, 29n28.
194. Ibid., 13.
195. Abbott's departure from Hot Springs camp is noted in Chandler to Emory, Camp on the Rio Grande, November 4, 1852, EP. Emory on his way to meet Bartlett is found in Emory to Chandler, On the road to Loredo [*sic*], November 13, 1852, EP. Abbott's arrival at Fort Duncan can be found in an unsigned note from Eagle Pass to Emory, November 14, 1852, EP. Portions of the three letters above are shown in Brown, *Survey of the United States-Mexico Boundary*, 60–61.
196. Matt Walter, "Love on the Rio Grande: The 1850 Exploration by Captain Love," *Journal of Big Bend Studies* 19 (2007): 35–45.
197. Paul Horgan, *Great River: The Rio Grande in North American History*, 2 vols. (New York: Rinehart, 1954), 2:821.
198. Hill, *Field Notebook of 1899*, 100.
199. Turpin and Eling, *Dust, Smoke, and Tracks*, 14.
200. PJ, 128.
201. PJ, 125.
202. PJ, 131.
203. Turpin and Eling, *Dust, Smoke, and Tracks*, 15.
204. DGR, Map B.
205. Ranches are seen on Google Earth satellite images, accessed May 5, 2017.
206. PJ, 135.
207. PJ, 137.
208. Turpin and Eling, *Dust, Smoke, and Tracks*, 16.
209. Donald A. Swanson, "Coacoochee (Wild Cat)," *HOT*, accessed June 15, 2013.
210. Kevin Mulroy, *Freedom on the Border: The Seminole Maroons in Florida, the Indian Territory, Coahuila, and Texas* (Lubbock: Texas Tech University Press, 1993), 55–84.
211. Ibid., 70.
212. Varied current photos of the Comunidad Negros Mascogos area are available at https://mexico.pueblosamerica.com/foto/negros-maskogos-nacimiento.
213. Mulroy, *Freedom on the Border*, 73.
214. Michael L. Tate, "Black Seminole Scouts," *HOT*, accessed June 15, 2013.
215. Ibid.
216. Christopher M. Nunley, "Kickapoo Indians," *HOT*, accessed June 15, 2013.
217. Turpin and Eling, *Dust, Smoke, and Tracks*, 16.
218. Photo of the small park as seen on Google Earth, accessed October 4, 2013.
219. DGR, 59.
220. Ibid. Green said his camp was on "Rio Allamo" (*sic*), but that stream was twenty-five miles to the east, and he was on the Río Sabinas. His attached sketch map correctly shows he

was on the Río Sabinas, but he shows that stream farther south, flowing into the Álamos rather than the actual pattern of the Álamos flowing into the Sabinas.
221. DGR, 60.
222. PJ, 147.
223. PJ, 149; Samuel Chamberlain, *My Confession: Recollections of a Rogue*, annotated and introduced by William H. Goetzmann (Austin: Texas State Historical Association, 1996), 76n160.
224. PJ, 150.
225. PJ, 152.
226. PJ, 154.
227. PJ, 156.
228. PJ, 158.
229. PJ, 159.
230. [Unsigned note from Eagle Pass, likely from Michler or Schott] to Emory, November 14, 1852, EP.
231. Thomas T. Smith, *The Old Army in Texas: A Research Guide to the U.S. Army in Nineteenth-Century Texas* (Austin: Texas State Historical Association, 2000), 95.
232. Brown, *Survey of the United States-Mexico Boundary*, 62. This page shows a copy of a letter from Chandler at Fort Duncan to Emory, November 25, 1852.
233. Bartlett to Emory, Ringgold Barracks, December 22, 1852, folder V, EP.
234. Virgil E. Barnes, *Geologic Atlas of Texas* (Austin: Bureau of Economic Geology, University of Texas), "Crystal City-Eagle Pass Sheet" (1976).
235. PJ, 167.
236. Emory to Bartlett, December 20, 1852, 33rd Cong., Special sess., 1853, SED 6, 49.
237. Norris, Milligan, and Faulk, *William H. Emory*, 133.
238. Gardner, *Fiasco*, entire book.
239. Bartlett, *Personal Narrative*.

Part II: The 1853 Michler Survey

1. William H. Goetzmann, *Army Exploration in the American West, 1803–1863* (New Haven, CT: Yale University Press, 1959), 194.
2. ER, 75.
3. Vintage maps showed only a general course for the river and no names downstream from San Vicente. The river was shown to flow north, gradually turning east to reach the mouth of the Pecos in about a hundred miles. See John Arrowsmith's *Map of Texas, Compiled from Surveys Recorded in the Land Office of Texas* (London: Soho Square, 1844).
4. Michler's flatboat was not described, but it was likely a rectangular boat with a flat bottom, designed for floating downstream and carrying cargo. Michler's smaller, more agile skiffs likely had flat bottoms and sterns but pointed bows. In a February 14, 1853, letter to

Boundary Commissioner John Bartlett, Major Emory included a line-item estimate of the cost of completing the boundary survey above the mouth of the Pecos (later to be assigned to Michler), in which he listed eight India rubber boats for a total cost of $1,000. Shortly thereafter, in early April, and likely before these rubber boats could be acquired or built in San Antonio, Texas, Lt. Michler was ordered to conduct the survey above the Pecos. See *Report of the Secretary of the Interior, communicating, in further compliance with a resolution of the Senate, certain papers in relation to the Mexican Boundary Commission*, 33rd Cong., Special sess., March 1853, SED 6, 56.

5. Goetzmann, *Army Exploration*, 237.
6. "Nathaniel Michler, 1827–1881," US Corps of Topographical Engineers. http://www.topogs.org/b_michler.html, accessed December 7, 2016 but no longer available.
7. ER, 80.
8. ER, 15.
9. Richard B. McCaslin, "United States Regulars in Gray," *SHQ* 118, no. 1 (July 2014): 29; Rebert, *La Gran Línea*, 22. A "computer" was responsible for performing the computations needed to convert the large volume of numerical notes coming from celestial observations for longitude and latitude, as well as field surveying notes. The field records of surveyors were pages of numbers for direction and distance that needed to be converted to straight lines on a map to display the survey lines. Also, celestial observations were numbers that needed to be converted to longitude or latitude location using reference tables.
10. McCaslin, "United States Regulars in Gray," 18; Freeman Cleaves, *Meade of Gettysburg* (Norman: University of Oklahoma Press, 1960), 18.
11. ER, 11.
12. ER, 15; Gardner, *Fiasco*, 257, 261, 272, 319.
13. ER, 75–79; Bill Green, "A Preliminary Report on Christoph Conrad Stremme (1807–1877)." 04/27/1989, Texas General Land Office Archives, 1700 North Congress Ave., Austin, Texas.
14. William H. Goetzmann, "Science Explores the Big Bend, 1852–1853," *Password* 3, no. 2 (1958), 65. Goetzmann quoted from a letter by the surveyor Arthur Schott to Major Emory stating that Abbott had made a sketch map of the course of the Rio Grande, including the section of river from Chandler's final camp to the Pecos River; among the incidents for my supposition on Michler are his 1855 disrespectful note to Major Emory, which almost got him a court martial (Norris, Milligan, and Faulk, *William H. Emory*, 150) and the complaint of Ed Ingraham (a surveyor in Michler's 1853 party) that he had been treated "meanly" by Michler (Gardner, *Fiasco*, 331).
15. ER, 80.
16. Emory to Bartlett, December 20, 1852, and February 14, 1853, 33rd Cong., Special sess., March 1853, SED 6, 42, 49, 50, 56. Major Emory estimated that twenty men being paid $40 a month would be required for the survey of the Rio Grande to be conducted upstream of the Pecos River. This $40 rate indicates that these men were laborers, camp helpers, cooks, herders, and boatmen, based on a list of the money owed each of the

forty-four men in these employment categories that was attached to Emory's letter of December 1852.

17. Chandler did not leave Fort Duncan on the Rio Grande for the long trip to Washington, DC, via San Antonio, Texas, until December 30, 1852, and in addition, the US Boundary Office in Washington, DC, which had been closed for a year, did not reopen until March 1853. Rebert, *La Gran Línea*, 46.

18. Chandler, Camp on the Rio Grande, to Emory, November 4, 1852, EP. Since Michler had only a very rough idea of where the Chandler Survey had ended and where to start his survey, he must have had a flexible plan to react to conditions as they unfolded. His actions suggest that his general plan was to find a route suitable for his wagons to reach the river at a point about seventy miles directly west of the mouth of the Pecos, then survey up the river to move toward Chandler's final point. If he ran short of time or provisions, he planned to use the boats to survey quickly down to the Pecos River and then use the boats to reach Fort Duncan.

19. Joseph E. Johnston et al., *Sketch of Reconnoissances [sic] of the Valley of the Rio Grande, April to September, 1850*, photocopy in Archives of the Big Bend, 976.44 J73S, Bryan Wildenthal Memorial Library, Sul Ross State University; original in National Archives, RG 77, Q-26.

20. A copy of a telegraph message from Edward Ingraham in New Orleans, Louisiana, to Major Emory in Washington, DC, in January 1853 confirms that Major Emory could send telegrams from Washington to New Orleans. Gardner, *Fiasco*, 319. I estimate it would take a week for a sailing ship to transport Emory's orders the 600 miles from New Orleans to Indianola, Texas, and another week for the 150 miles by horse to San Antonio.

21. Michler's route along the Lower El Paso Road passed through Fort Clark, now at Brackettville, Texas; continued west to San Felipe Springs, now Del Rio, Texas; over the first crossing of Devils River to head north up the river; then northwest overland to Howards Springs and Live Oak Creek; then across the Pecos near the future site of Fort Lancaster; and up the west bank to Pecos Springs.

22. ER, 75; Goetzmann, "Science Explores the Big Bend," 65.

23. Vincent Virga and Don Blevins, *Texas: Mapping the Lone Star State through History: Rare and Unusual Maps from the Library of Congress* (Guilford, CT: Globe Pequot, 2010), 44.

24. ER, 75.

25. Brune, *Springs of Texas*, 362, 422.

26. Sanderson Sheet, Military Map, 1917, https://legacy.lib.utexas.edu/maps/topo/texas/txu-pclmaps-topo-tx-sanderson-1917.jpg, accessed November 17, 2016.

27. ER, 75.

28. Johnston et al., *Sketch of Reconnoissances [sic] of the Valley of the Rio Grande*.

29. ER, 76.

30. Brune, *Springs of Texas*, 424. See the pictographs online at https://mirrormagic.com/?s=meyers+spring+rock+art.

31. ER, 76.

32. Paul H. Carlson, *Pecos Bill: A Military Biography of William R. Shafter* (College Station: Texas A&M University Press, 1989), 90–93. Lt. Colonel Shafter, based at Fort Duncan, led an expedition of cavalry and Seminole Scouts that crossed here into Mexico June 7, 1876, traveled southwest about fifty miles to the foothills of Sierra del Carmen but found only old Indian camps, and returned to the crossing on June 18. ER, 75.
33. Smith to Johnston, January 6, 1851, RG 77, Topographical Engineers, LRHA.
34. ER, 75.
35. ER, 77.
36. ER, 76.
37. The headlands increase in height upstream because the resistant Cretaceous limestone beds, which form the headlands, dip gently downstream (thus rise upstream) at a rate of about 150 feet per mile.
38. ER, 77.
39. IBWC, unpublished map A-224, 1951, UT-BEG.
40. W. R. Livermore and F. E. Butterfield, *Military Map of the Rio Grande Frontier: Prepared from Original Surveys, County Maps, Reports of Officers etc.* (1881), UT-BCAH, map MLC 151–64, Austin, Texas. https://www.cah.utexas.edu/db/dmr/gallery_lg.php?s=24&gallery=maps
41. John T. Gano, *Map of the Extreme South-East Part of Presidio County*, Brewster County Sketch file, Map no. 10985, 1882 (Austin: Texas General Land Office Archives).
42. Captain Charles Nevill to Z. L. Nevill, *Austin Daily Statesman*, February 25, 1882; Nevill to Adj. Gen. W. H. King, Texas State Archives, box 401, folder 13.
43. November 14, 1852, Eagle Pass, author unknown (probably Arthur Schott), EP.
44. ER, 76.
45. USGS and USCS, *Shafter Hills,* Map no. 138, 1982. United States–Mexico Border Color Image Map Series, www.lib.utexas.edu/maps/us_mexico_border/, accessed December 7, 2016.
46. Louis F. Aulbach, and Joe Butler, *The Lower Canyons of the Rio Grande: La Linda to Dryden Crossing—Maps and Notes for River Runners* (Houston: The Wilderness Area Map Service, 2005), 87–97.
47. USGS AND USCS, *Shafter Hills*, Map no. 138, 1982.
48. ER, 76. Michler to Emory, Washington, March 10, 1856.
49. ER, 78.
50. Author's personal observation: igneous rocks occur at the river's edge just west of the ruins of Johnson's Ranch in Big Bend National Park, and scattered igneous exposures cap the higher hills about a mile from the river in the Black Gap Wildlife Management Area just northeast of Big Bend National Park.
51. ER, 85. Chandler's letter dated December 1852 was altered before publication of the ER to include the "125 miles" statement. Chandler had no way to know that distance until all maps were completed in Washington, DC, in 1856.

52. ER, 77, 78. Michler reported the distance along the river from the Pecos to San Francisco Canyon as 105 miles, but the actual distance was 94 miles. He was 11 miles too long. Michler reported the distance from San Francisco Canyon up the river to his initial point was 20 miles, but it was 34 miles. He was 14 miles too short. Michler's $105+20=125$ compares to actual distances of $94+34=128$ miles.
53. The title block of Boundary Map 17 shows only Michler as the author, even though Chandler's surveyors mapped about seven miles of the river trace displayed on Michler's map and then camped on the river fifteen miles inside the area covered by Michler's Map 17.
54. PJ, 105. Parry's handheld magnetic compass bearing to Pico Etéreo and Pico Cerda and his description of the site indicate that he stood on a hilltop one mile southwest of their Hot Springs camp. The sketched-in trace of the Rio Grande shown on Michler's Map 17 passes five miles north of the location of Chandler's last camp on the river bank at Hot Springs Rapids.
55. Lenard E. Brown, *Survey of the United States-Mexico Boundary, 1849–1855: Background Study* (Washington, DC: Office of Archaeology and Historic Preservation, Division of History, National Park Service, 1969), 59; Chandler to Emory, Camp on the Rio Grande, November 4, 1852, EP.
56. Parry to Emory, Camp on the Rio Grande, November 4, 1852, EP.
57. Goetzmann, "Science Explores the Big Bend," 65.
58. Fort Duncan was established in 1849 and by 1853 had five companies under Major T. Morris. The US Boundary Commission had an office and an observatory at the fort to determine longitude and latitude. Thomas T. Smith, *The Old Army in Texas*, 96. Michler likely spent only a few days at Fort Duncan before returning to San Antonio, where his wife likely awaited him and where he was on September 29 when Emory ordered him to Washington, DC. Gardner, *Fiasco*, 324.
59. ER, 77.
60. Ibid.
61. ER, 79.
62. Table E, ER, 245; Michler to Emory, from Fort Duncan, August 18, 1853; Gardner, *Fiasco*, 324n102; box 6, folder 55, EP.
63. ER, 78.
64. ER, 245.
65. Table E, ER, 245.
66. ER, 79.
67. ER, 78.
68. Smith to Johnston January 6, 1851, RG 77, Topographical Engineers LRHA.
69. Michler to Emory, August 18, 1853, EP; Gardner, *Fiasco*, 324n102.
70. ER, 78. Michler also said the average current was six mph, which seems high when compared to the two mph his boat averaged when not surveying en route from the mouth of the Pecos River to Fort Duncan, Texas.
71. Johnston et al., *Sketch of Reconnoissances [sic] of the Valley of the Rio Grande*.

72. ER, 80.
73. Google Earth image, http://google.com/earth, accessed December 5, 2016.
74. USGS and USCS, *Palma Canyon*, Map no. 140, 1983, UT-PCL, Map Library online.
75. Ibid., *Lozier Canyon*, Map no. 141.
76. Ibid.
77. Ibid., Maps 142 and 145; Seminole Canyon Texas State Park.
78. Oehlschlager drew ten of the maps in the set of fifty-four final boundary maps, including Map 16 for Michler and Map 21 for Chandler, both of which are rich in detail; Rebert, *La Gran Línea*, 201.
79. USGS and USCS, *Lozier Canyon*, Map no. 141.
80. Joseph E. Johnston et al., *Reconnoissances[sic] of Routes from San Antonio de Bexar to El Paso del Norte, 1849*, 31st Cong., 1st sess., July 1850, SED 64; the map: *Sketch of Reconnoissances [sic] of the Valley of the Rio Grande*.
81. US War Department, Topographical Engineers, *Map of Texas and Part of New Mexico*, 1857. This is generally regarded as the best pre–Civil War military map of Texas and can be seen on many websites online by searching under the title. Copies are for sale at National Park stores in BBNP and Fort Davis National Historic Site, Texas.
82. USGS and USCS, *Lozier Canyon*, Map no. 141.
83. Index Map no. 2, *Rio Bravo Del Norte Section of Boundary Between the United States and Mexico—Surveyed in 1852–53, Agreed upon by the Joint Commission under the Treaty of Guadalupe Hidalgo*, 1857; see copy at Library of Congress online: https://www.loc.gov/resource/g3701f.ctb00345.
84. ER, 245.
85. There are 60 minutes in a degree and 60 seconds in a minute.

Part III: Wrapping It All Up

1. Gardner, *Fiasco*, 286.
2. Norris, Milligan, and Faulk, *William H. Emory*, 143.
3. Ibid.
4. ER, 24.
5. ER, 118.
6. Norris, Milligan, and Faulk, *William H. Emory*, 1, 149, 150.
7. ER, 124.
8. William H. Emory, *Notes of a Military Reconnoissance [sic] from Fort Leavenworth, in Missouri, to San Diego, in California, in 1846–47*, 30th Cong., 1st sess., 1848, SED 7.
9. See the IBWC website at https://www.ibwc.gov/home.html; accessed December 9, 2016.
10. Bartlett, *Personal Narrative*, 2:412–14; Brown, *Survey of the United States-Mexico Boundary*, 142–44; PJ, 39; Schott to Emory, Camp on Arroyo San Felipe, October 1, 1852, EP; DGR, 59; ER, 77.

Epilogue: The Men of the Boundary Survey

1. Odie B. Faulk, "Bartlett, John Russell," *HOT*, accessed April 2, 2019, http://www.tshaonline.org/handbook/online/articles/fba93. Uploaded on June 12, 2010. Published by the Texas State Historical Association.
2. Norris, Milligan, and Faulk, *William H. Emory*, 208–47.
3. Ibid., 248–302.
4. Ibid., 4, 302; Guide to the Emory Papers, Yale University Beinecke Rare Book and Manuscript Library, New Haven, CT.
5. Rebert, *La Gran Línea*, 54.
6. ER, 12.
7. Nancy Miller, University of Pennsylvania Archives, email message to author, August 20, 2012, in reply to request for information on M. T. W. Chandler, image of Alumni card file, University of Pennsylvania, Philadelphia.
8. Michael M. Phillips, "Philadelphia Is Looking for a Few Good Gentlemen," *Wall Street Journal*, October 15, 2014. Today the First Troop is still active but has morphed into a small National Guard unit. Some of its members have deployed to Bosnia, Kuwait, and Iraq. By early 2014, the total member count since 1774 had reached 2,438.
9. United States Passport Applications, 1795–1925, http://familysearch.org., accessed December 12, 2016. "United States Passport Applications, 1795–1925," database with images, *FamilySearch* (https://familysearch.org/ark:/61903/1:1:Q295-JS51: March 14, 2016), M T W Chandler, August 17, 1854; citing Passport Application, United States, source certificate #, Passport Applications, 1795–1905, 48, NARA microfilm publications M1490 and M1372 (Washington, DC: National Archives and Records Administration, n.d.); FHL microfilm 1,432,548.
10. ER, 1–24, 49–61; ER, 2:1, 9–26.
11. William A. Weber, *King of Colorado Botany: Charles Christopher Parry, 1823–1890* (Boulder: University Press of Colorado, 1997). Charles Parry and Sarah and Eliza are buried in Oakville Memorial Gardens, Davenport, Iowa. http://findagrave.com, accessed July 21, 2017.
12. "Mount Eva," https://www.summitpost.org/mount-eva/154728, accessed May 19, 2017.
13. Don Lago, *The Powell Expedition: New Discoveries about John Wesley Powell's 1869 River Journey* (Reno: University of Nevada Press, 2018), 21–56.
14. Charles H. Preston, "Biographical Sketch of Dr. C. C. Parry," *Proceedings of the Davenport Academy of Natural Sciences* 6 (1897): 35–45; Charles C. Parry, "On Depositing the Parry Botanical Collection," *Proceedings of the Davenport Academy of Natural Sciences* 2 (1878): 279–82.
15. Charles Christopher Parry Papers, 1823–90, Special Collections Department, Parks Library, MS 290, Iowa State University, Ames, Iowa.

16. Duff Cyrus Green, http://findagrave.com, accessed June 10, 2014.
17. Frank Wagner, "Michler, Nathaniel," *HOT*, https://tshaonline.org/handbook/online/articles/fmi88, accessed May 12, 2014. Uploaded June 15, 2010. Published by the Texas State Historical Association; William H. Goetzmann, *New Lands, New Men: America and the Second Great Age of Discovery* (New York: Viking Penguin, 1986), 342; records for Nathaniel Michler from Family Search, http://familysearch.org, accessed March 14, 2017.
18. Gardner, *Fiasco*, 330.
19. ER, 24.
20. Richard B. McCaslin, "United States Regulars in Gray: Edward Ingraham and Company A, 1st Regular Confederate Cavalry," *SHQ* 118, no. 1 (July 2014): 24–45.
21. Bill Green, "A Preliminary Report on Christoph Conrad Stremme (1807–1877)," April 27, 1989, archives of TXGLO; Alex Chiba, "Christoph Conrad Stremme," https://medium.com/savetexashistory/christoph-conrad-stremme, accessed March 15, 2017; "The Photographic Bureau," http://medium.com/save/texas/history/the-photographic-bureau, accessed March 15, 2017. Although these articles are no longer available, readers may wish to consult Texas General Land Office, "Christoph Conrad Stremme: German Polymath and Pioneer," https://medium.com/save-texas-history/christoph-conrad-stremme-german-polymath-and-pioneer-4fc213ffa92a, and "The Photographic Bureau: 19th Century Innovation at the GLO," https://medium.com/save-texas-history/the-photographic-bureau-19th-century-innovation-at-the-glo-bb683b1421f6.
22. Alfred E. Rogers, "Jaensson, Swen [Swante Palm]," *HOT*, https://tshaonline.org/handbook/online/articles/fja41 accessed March 15, 2017. Uploaded June 15, 2010. Published by the Texas State Historical Association.
23. Green, "A Preliminary Report." Stremme was buried in section 1, lot 66.

APPENDIX A: COLONEL LANGBERG'S 1851 EXPEDITION

1. Turpin and Eling, *Dust, Smoke, and Tracks*, 8.
2. Pearson, *Road Guide to Backcountry Dirt Roads*, 16.
3. Turpin and Eling, *Dust, Smoke, and Tracks*, 9–12.
4. Evans, *Mexican Gold Trail*, 50–54.
5. Turpin and Eling, *Dust, Smoke, and Tracks*, 14–16.
6. Ibid., 21; John Stockley, "Monclova Viejo," paper presented at National Park Service conference on San Antonio Missions, San Antonio, TX, 1989. Stockley described the location as 3 kilometers west of the mouth of Río San Rodrigo. Satellite view shows it is about 6 kilometers southwest of the mouth. (One kilometer is 0.62 miles.) See also John Stockley, "Update on Monclova Viejo Based on Langberg's Diaries," paper presented at the Third Annual Conference of the Center for Big Bend Studies, Sul Ross State University, Alpine, TX, 1996.

Appendix C: The First Documented Boat Passage through Santa Elena Canyon

1. Charles Nevill to Z. L. Nevill, in *Austin Daily Statesman*, February 25, 1882.
2. John T. Gano, "Map of the Extreme South-East Part of Presidio County," (1882) TXGLO Brewster County sketch file, NS-1, map no. 10985; Mitchell, "County Map of the State of Texas," *Mitchell's Modern Atlas* (1876) J. H. Butler and Company, Philadelphia.
3. Walter P. Webb, *The Texas Rangers: A Century of Frontier Defense* (Austin: University of Texas Press, 2000), 410; Ross Maxwell, *Big Bend Country: A History of Big Bend National Park* (Big Bend, TX: Big Bend Natural History Association, 1985), 18; Lt. C. L. Nevill to Adj. Gen. W. H. King, February 4, 1882, Texas State Archives, box 401, folder 13, Adj. Gen. Office Transcripts, Austin, TX.
4. John T, Gano, *Map of the Extreme South-East Part of Presidio County*, Brewster County Sketch file, Map no. 10985, 1882 (Austin: Texas General Land Office Archives); W. R. Livermore, *Military Map of the Rio Grande Frontier: 1883*. Shafter Crossing was named for Colonel Wm. R. Shafter, who, accompanied by his Black Seminole Scouts, crossed here in June 1876 in pursuit of Indians who had raided Texas ranches. Paul H. Carlson, *Pecos Bill: A Military Biography of William R. Shafter* (College Station: Texas A&M Press, 1989). If Nevill and Gano had made their return trip to Fort Davis a year later (1883), they might have ridden horses only twenty miles north of Shafter Crossing to the new railroad tracks at Dryden Station, loaded the horses on the train to Alpine, Texas, then ridden another twenty miles north to Fort Davis. Julia Cauble Smith, "Dryden, Texas," *HOT*, https://tshaonline.org/handbook/online/articles/hnd46, accessed July 30, 2017.
5. Robert T. Hill, "Running the Cañons of the Rio Grande," *Century Magazine* 61, no. 3, January 1901; R. T. Hill, handwritten notebook, copy in Hill's papers, Dallas: SMU, DeGolyer Library. Special Collections, 34; R. T. Hill, "Running the Canyons of the Rio Grande," *Dallas Morning News*, August 5, 19, 26, and September 2, 16, 23, 1934. The men whom MacMahon identified by last name only are assumed to have been trappers.
6. US Department of State, *Proceedings of the International Boundary Commission, United States and Mexico, Treaties of 1884 and 1889, Equitable Distribution of the Waters of the Rio Grande* (Washington, DC, Government Printing Office, 1903), 2:405–16; Paul Davis Cunningham died July 13, 1901, https://www.findagrave.com, accessed December 15, 2018.

Bibliography

GOVERNMENT REPORTS, THESES, AND MANUSCRIPTS

Daugherty, Franklin W. "Geology of the Pico Etéreo Area, Municipio de Acuña, Coahuila, Mexico." PhD diss., University of Texas at Austin, 1959.

Echols, William H. *Diary of a Reconnoissance [sic] of the Country Between the El Paso Road and the Rio Grande River.* 36th Cong., 2d sess., 1861, S. Ex. Doc. 1.

Emory, William H. *Notes of a Military Reconnoissance [sic], from Fort Leavenworth, in Missouri, to San Diego, in California.* 30th Cong., 1st sess., 1848, S. Ex. Doc. 7.

———. *Report on the United States and Mexican Boundary Survey, Made under the Direction of the Secretary of the Interior.* 34th Cong., 1st sess., 1857, Vol. 1, H. Ex. Doc. 135; 1859, Vol. 2, S. Ex. Doc. 108. Cited as ER.

———. "William Hemsley Emory Papers: 1823–1886." WA MSS S-1187. Beinecke Rare Book and Manuscript Library, Yale University, New Haven, CT.

Frémont, John C. *Report of the Exploring Expedition to the Rocky Mountains in the Year 1842, and to Oregon and North California in the Years 1843–44.* 28th Cong., 2nd sess., 1845, S. Ex. Doc. 174, OCLC 563061.

Graham, James D. *Report of the Secretary of War, in Compliance with a Resolution of the Senate, the Report of Lieutenant Colonel Graham on the Subject of the boundary line between the United States and Mexico.* 32nd Cong., 1st sess., 1852, S. Ex. Doc. 121.

Green, Bill. "A Preliminary Report on Christoph Conrad Stremme (1807–1877)." 04/27/1989, Texas General Land Office Archives, 1700 North Congress Ave., Austin, Texas. Includes a letter of Aug. 22, 1864, from Swante Palm to C. C. Stremme.

Green, Duff C. "Letter to Colonel Samuel Cooper, December 16, 1862." G-40-1853, Letters Received, Headquarters of the Army (hereafter LRHA), Record Group 108, National Archives Building, Washington, DC.

Hill, Robert T. *Field Notebook of 1899 Rio Grande Exploration from Presidio to Langtry*. Accession no. 815, Big Bend Region River Book, Author: R. T. Hill, Index no. RTH-15, Locality: H-15, Texas, year 1899, US Geological Survey, Denver, CO. The *Field Notebook* comprises two notebooks, each measuring about 5 × 7.5 inches, with a total of 102 pages. The DeGolyer Research Library, Southern Methodist University, Dallas, TX, has a photocopy of the *Field Notebook* in their papers of R. T. Hill.

Hughes, George W. *Report of the Secretary of War, communicating, in compliance with a resolution of the Senate, a map showing the operations of the Army of the United States in Texas and the adjacent Mexican States on the Rio Grande; accompanied by astronomical observations, and descriptive and military memoirs of the country*. 31st Cong., 1st sess., 1849, S. Ex. Doc. 32.

Ivey, James E. *Presidios of the Big Bend Area*. Professional Papers No. 31. Santa Fe, NM: Southwest Cultural Resources Center, National Park Service, 1990.

Johnston, Joseph E. *Report of the Reconnaissance of Routes from San Antonio de Bexar to El Paso del Norte in 1849*. 31st Cong., 1st sess., 1850, S. Ex. Doc. 64.

Langberg, Emilio. "Expedición del Coronel Emilio Langberg de San Carlos, Chihuahua a Monclova Viejo 1851." Transcript in the collection of Luis López Elizondo Musquiz, from Luis Alberto Guajardo Papers, Beinecke Rare Book Library, Yale University, New Haven, CT.

Nevill, Charles. "Letter to Adj. General W. H. King, Feb. 4, 1882." Box 401, Folder 13: Transcripts of Adj. Gen. Office. Austin: Texas State Library and Archives Commission.

Parry, Charles C. "Field Notebook and Journal, Botany and Geology, U.S. Boundary Commission 1852, Texas and Mexico: The Papers of Charles Christopher Parry (1823–1890)." Special Collections, MS-290, Parks Library, Iowa State University, Ames, Iowa.

US Congress. Listed below in order of publication date are nine selected congressional reports that include lists of equipment and personnel and extensive correspondence relative to the Boundary Survey in the years 1849 through 1855.

———. *Report of the Secretary of the Interior, in answer to a resolution of the Senate for information in relation to the operations of the Commission to Run and Mark the Boundary between the United States and Mexico*. 31st Cong., 1st sess., 1850, S. Ex. Doc. 34.

———. *Reports of the Secretary of War with Reconnaissance of Routes from San Antonio to El Paso*. 31st Cong., 1st sess., 1850, S. Ex. Doc. 64.

———. *Report from the Secretary of War enclosing a report from the Colonel of Topographical Engineers with a map showing the operations of the Army in Texas and Mexican States on the Rio Grande*. 31st Cong., 1st sess., 1850, S. Ex. Doc. 73.

———. *Report of the Secretary of the Interior made in compliance with a resolution of the Senate calling for information in relation to the commission appointed to run and mark the boundary between the United States and Mexico*. 32nd Cong., 1st sess., 1852, S. Ex. Doc. 119. This congressional report and Doc. 121 shown below include, in total, over one hundred letters written between 1850 and 1852 by Commissioner Bartlett and over ninety letters written by Lieutenant Colonel Graham, the chief surveyor until December 1851.

———. *Report of the Secretary of War, communicating, in compliance with a resolution of the Senate, the Report of Lieutenant Colonel Graham on the Subject of the Boundary Line between the United States and Mexico.* 32nd Cong., 1st sess., 1852, S. Ex. Doc. 121.

———. *Report of the Secretary of the Interior, communicating, in compliance with a resolution of the Senate, a report from Mr. Bartlett on the subject of the Boundary Line between the United States and Mexico.* 32nd Cong., 2nd sess., 1853, S. Ex. Doc. 41.

———. *Report of the Secretary of the Interior, communicating, in further compliance with a resolution of the Senate, certain papers in relation to the Mexico Boundary Commission.* 33rd Cong., Special sess., 1853, S. Ex. Doc. 6.

———. *Report of the Secretary of the Interior in compliance with a resolution of the Senate of January 22, communicating a report and map of A. B. Gray relative to the Mexican Boundary.* 33rd Cong., 2nd sess., 1853, S. Ex. Doc. 55.

———. *Report of the United States and Mexican Boundary Survey made under the direction of the Secretary of the Interior.* 34th Cong., 1st sess., 1857, Vol. 1, H. Ex. Doc. 135; 1859, Vol. 2, S. Ex. Doc. 108 ("The Emory Report").

US Department of State. *Proceedings of the International Boundary Commission, United States and Mexico, Treaties of 1884 and 1889, Equitable Distribution of the Waters of the Rio Grande.* 2:405–16. Washington, DC: Government Printing Office, 1903.

Warren, Gouverneur K. "Memoir to Accompany the Map of Territory of the United States from the Mississippi River to the Pacific Ocean." In vol. 2 of *Reports of Explorations and Surveys to Ascertain the most Practicable and Economical Route for a Railroad from the Mississippi River to the Pacific Ocean.* 33rd Cong., 2nd sess., 1859, Vol. 2, S. Ex. Doc. 78.

Whipple, Amiel W. "Explorations for a Railroad Route near the Thirty-Fifth Parallel from the Mississippi River to the Pacific Ocean." In *Reports of Explorations and Surveys to Ascertain the most Practicable and Economical Route for a Railroad from the Mississippi River to the Pacific Ocean.* 33rd Cong., 2nd sess., 1856, H. Ex. Doc. 91.

Willeford, Glenn. "A History of Johnson's Ranch and Trading Post on the Rio Grande." Master's thesis, W698h, Sul Ross State University, Alpine, TX, 1993.

Wright, Ralph. *Field Survey Notes of June 27, 1856.* Presidio County, Abstract no. 2109, Survey Tract 13, Texas General Land Office Archives Online. http://www.glo.texas.gov/ncu/SCANDOCS/archives_webfiles/arcmaps/webfiles/landgrants/PDFs/1/5/6/156164.pdf, accessed April 18, 2014; the survey notes refer to an "Emory Marker."

Maps

Archival

Carrington, F. de L. *Map Accompanying Scout Made by 2nd Lt. Carrington, Sept. 1881: Chief Engineer Office, San Antonio, Texas.* Map no. 65407. Austin: Texas General Land Office Archives.

Fernández, Manuel, Francisco Herrera, and Miguel Yglesias. *Línea divisoria entre México y los Estados Unidos*. 1857. This is Mexican Boundary Map 21, in the archives of Mapoteca Manuel Orozco y Berra, Mexico City.

Gano, John T. *Map of the Extreme South-East Part of Presidio County*. Brewster County Sketch file, Map no. 10985, 1882. Austin: Texas General Land Office Archives.

International Boundary and Water Commission. *Geologic Strip Maps along the Rio Grande: Lajitas to Del Rio, 1950–1955*. Brewster County File, scale 1:50,000. Austin, Texas: Bureau of Economic Geology, University of Texas.

———. *2008 Rio Grande Boundary Maps: Reed Camp/Vado de Chisos Map 124*. Color aerial photo base at 1:25,000. ftp://anonymous:anonymous@63.96.218.8/RG_MAPS_2008/Page40_124 _Reed%20Camp.jpg, accessed June 6, 2014.

Johnston, Joseph E., W. F. Smith, F. T. Bryan, and N. H. Michler. *Reconnoissances [sic] of Routes from San Antonio de Bexar to El Paso del Norte, 1849*. 31st Cong., 1st sess., July 1850, S. Ex. Doc. 64, 26–29. Map no. 1529. See the map online at Texas State Library and Archives, Austin, https://www.tsl.texas.gov.

Johnston, Joseph E., W. F. Smith, M. L. Smith, [F. T.] Bryan, [N. H.] Michler, R. A. Howard, and J. F. Minter. *Sketch of Reconnoissances [sic] of the Valley of the Rio Grande, April to September, 1850*. Photocopy, Archives of the Big Bend, 976.44 J73S, Bryan Wildenthal Memorial Library, Sul Ross State University, Alpine, TX. Original, National Archives, RG 77, Q-26.

Livermore, W. R., and F. E. Butterfield. *Military Map of the Rio Grande Frontier: Prepared from Original Surveys, County Maps, Reports of Officers etc.* (1881). UT-BCAH, map MLC 151–64, Austin, Texas. https://www.cah.utexas.edu/db/dmr/gallery_lg.php?s=24&gallery=maps.

US Army Corps of Engineers. *Tactical Map, Presidio Sheet*. 1:62,500, 1932. Austin: University of Texas Perry-Castañeda Library Map Collection, https://legacy.lib.utexas.edu/maps/topo /texas/txu-pclmaps-topo-tx-presidio-1932.jpg, accessed June 6, 2017.

US Boundary Commission. *Boundary between the United States and Mexico*. Map nos. 15 through 22, scale 1:60,000, 1857. Record Group 76, Map Records, Entry 417, National Archives at College Park, College Park, MD.

US Geological Survey and US Customs Service. *Reed Camp 1982*. United States–Mexico Border Color Image Map Series, 1:25,000. Austin: University of Texas Perry-Castañeda Library Map Collection, https://legacy.lib.utexas.edu/maps/us_mexico_border/txu_oclc_15606487 _124.jpg, accessed May 11, 2014.

US War Department, Topographical Engineers. *Map of Texas and Part of New Mexico*. Compiled in the Bureau of Topographical Engineers, 1857. This is regarded as the best pre–Civil War military map of Texas. https://www.loc.gov/item/2015591074/.

Warren, G. K., A. A. Humphreys, and Julius Bien. *Map of the Military Dep't of Texas: Being a Section of the Map of the Territory of the U.S. from the Mississippi River to the Pacific Ocean*. Office of Exploration and Surveys, War Dept., 1859. Washington, DC: Library of Congress, http://www.loc.gov/item/2003627041, accessed November 16, 2014.

Bibliography

Published

Arrowsmith, John. *Map of Texas, Compiled from Surveys Recorded in the Land Office of Texas.* London: Soho Square, 1844.

Barnes, Virgil E. *Geologic Atlas of Texas.* Thirty-eight sheets each at a scale of 1:250.000. Austin: Bureau of Economic Geology, University of Texas. See "Crystal City-Eagle Pass Sheet" (1976); "Del Rio Sheet" (1977); "Emory Peak-Presidio Sheet" (1979).

Disturnell, John. *Mapa de los Estados Unidos de Méjico.* Scale: 1:4,430,000. New York: J. Disturnell, 1847. Known as "The Treaty Map."

Flawn, Peter T. *Geologic Map of the Big Bend National Park, Brewster County, Texas.* 1:62,500. Austin: Bureau of Economic Geology, University of Texas, 1966. Included in pocket of the book by Ross Maxwell, *The Big Bend of the Rio Grande*, Bureau of Economic Geology Guidebook 7. Austin: Bureau of Economic Geology, University of Texas, 1968.

McKnight, John F. *Geologic Map of Bofecillos Mountains Area, Trans-Pecos, Texas.* Quadrangle Map 37. Austin: Bureau of Economic Geology, University of Texas, 1970.

Mitchell, S. Augustus. *County Map of State of Texas*, In *Mitchell's Modern Atlas*, 64–65. Philadelphia: J. H. Butler, 1876.

National Geographic. *Texas Topographic Maps.* On CD-ROM. San Francisco: Nat. Geo. Holdings, 2000.

St. John, D. E. *Geology of Black Gap Area, Brewster County, Texas.* Quadrangle Map 30. Austin: Bureau of Economic Geology, University of Texas, 1966.

Stephens, A. Ray. *Texas: A Historical Atlas.* Norman: University of Oklahoma Press, 2010.

Turner, K. J., M. E. Berry, W. R. Page, et al. *Geologic Map of Big Bend National Park, Texas.* USGS Scientific Investigations map 3142, scale of 1:75,000, 84 pp., 2011.

US Government Defense Mapping Agency. *La Morita Mexico.* Joint Operations Graphic Aeronautical Map NH-13-12, scale of 1:250,000. Bethesda, MD: Defense Mapping Agency, 1992.

Published Sources

Books

Alex, Thomas C. *Big Bend National Park and Vicinity.* Charleston, SC: Arcadia, 2010.

Alexander, Nancy. *Father of Texas Geology: Robert T. Hill.* Dallas: SMU Press, 1976.

Alloway, David. *El Camino Del Rio—The River Road—FM 170 from Study Butte to Presidio and through Big Bend Ranch State Park.* Austin: Texas Parks and Wildlife Department, 1995.

Aulbach, Louis F. *The Great Unknown of the Rio Grande: Terlingua Creek to La Linda, including Boquillas Canyon and Mariscal Canyon.* Houston: Louis F. Aulbach, 2007.

Aulbach, Louis F., and Joe Butler. *The Lower Canyons of the Rio Grande: La Linda to Dryden Crossing—Maps and Notes for River Runners.* Houston: Wilderness Area Map Service, 2005.

Aulbach, Louis F., and Linda C. Gorski. *The Upper Canyons of the Rio Grande: Presidio to Terlingua Creek, including Colorado Canyon and Santa Elena Canyon*. Houston: Wilderness Area Map Service, 2000.

Austerman, Wayne R. *Sharps Rifles and Spanish Mules: The San Antonio–El Paso Mail, 1851–1881*. College Station: Texas A&M University Press, 1985.

Bartlett, John R. *Personal Narrative of Explorations and Incidents in Texas, New Mexico, California, Sonora, and Chihuahua, connected with the United States and Mexican Boundary Commission, during the Years 1850, '51, '52, and '53*. 2 vols. New York: D. Appleton, 1854.

Brandt, E. N. *Chairman of the Board: A Biography of Carl A. Gerstacker*. East Lansing: Michigan State University Press, 2003.

Britten, Thomas A. *The Lipan Apaches*. Albuquerque: University of New Mexico Press, 2009.

Brown, Lenard E. *Survey of the United States-Mexico Boundary, 1849–1855: Background Study*. Washington, DC: Office of Archaeology and Historic Preservation, Division of History, National Park Service, 1969.

Brune, Gunnar. *Springs of Texas*. Vol. 1. 2nd ed. College Station: Texas A&M University Press, 2002.

Carlson, Paul H. *Pecos Bill: A Military Biography of William R. Shafter*. College Station: Texas A&M University Press, 1989.

Casey, Clifford B. *Mirages, Mysteries and Reality: Brewster County, Texas, the Big Bend of the Rio Grande*. Hereford, TX: Pioneer, 1972.

———. *Soldiers, Ranchers and Miners in the Big Bend*. Washington, DC: Office of Archeology and Historic Preservation, Division of History, National Park Service, 1969.

Chamberlain, Samuel. *My Confession: Recollections of a Rogue*. Annotated and introduced by William H. Goetzmann. Austin: Texas State Historical Association, 1996.

Cleaves, Freeman. *Meade of Gettysburg*. Norman: University of Oklahoma Press, 1960.

Dobie, Dudley R. *Adventures in the Canyon, Mountain and Desert Country of the Big Bend*. San Marcos, TX: Privately printed, 1952.

Egan, Ferol. *Frémont: Explorer for a Restless Nation*. Garden City, NJ: Doubleday, 1977.

Evans, George W. B. *Mexican Gold Trail: Journal of a Forty-Niner*. Edited by Glenn S. Dumke. San Marino, CA: Huntington Library, 1945.

Foreman, Grant, ed. *A Pathfinder in the Southwest: The Itinerary of Lieutenant A. W. Whipple during His Explorations for a Railway Route from Fort Smith to Los Angeles in the Years 1853–1854*. Norman: University of Oklahoma Press, 1941.

Frémont, John C. *Narratives of Exploration and Adventure*. Edited by Allan Nevins. New York: Longmans-Green, 1956.

Froebel, Julius. *Seven Years' Travel in Central America, Northern Mexico, and the Far West of the United States*. London: Richard Bentley, 1859.

Gardner, George Clinton. *Fiasco: George Clinton Gardner's Correspondence from the U.S.-Mexico Boundary Survey, 1849–54*. Edited by David J. Weber and Jane Lenz Elder. Dallas: SMU Press, 2010.

Gerald, Rex E. *Spanish Presidios of the Late Eighteenth Century in Northern New Spain*. Santa Fe: Museum of New Mexico Press, 1968.

Goetzmann, William H. *Army Exploration in the American West, 1803–1863*. New Haven, CT: Yale University Press, 1959.

———. *Exploration and Empire: The Explorer and the Scientist in the Winning of the West*. New York: W. W. Norton, 1966.

———. *New Lands, New Men: America and the Second Great Age of Discovery*. New York: Viking Penguin, 1986.

Gómez, Arthur R. *A Most Singular Country: A History of Occupation in the Big Bend*. Washington, DC: National Park Service, 1990.

Griswold del Castillo, Richard. *The Treaty of Guadalupe Hidalgo: A Legacy of Conflict*. Norman: University of Oklahoma Press, 1990.

Hine, Robert V. *Bartlett's West: Drawing the Mexican Boundary*. New Haven, CT: Yale University Press, 1968.

Horgan, Paul. *Great River: The Rio Grande in North American History*. 2 vols. New York: Rinehart, 1954.

Ivey, James E. *Presidios of the Big Bend Area*. Translated by Carlos Chavez. Santa Fe, NM: Southwest Cultural Resources Center, National Park Service, 1990.

Jackson, W. Turrentine. *Wagon Roads West: A Study of Federal Road Surveys and Construction in the Trans-Mississippi West, 1846–1869*. Berkeley: University of California Press, 1952.

James, Harold L. "History of the United States-Mexican Boundary Survey, 1848–1955." In *The Border Region*, ed. D. A. Cordoba, S. A. Wengerd, and J. W. Shomaker, 40–55. 20th Annual Fall Field Conference Guidebook. Albuquerque: New Mexico Geological Society, 1969.

Jameson, W. C. *Border Bandits, Border Raids*. Helena, MT: Lone Star Books, 2017.

Kelley, Pat. *River of Lost Dreams: Navigation on the Rio Grande*. Lincoln: University of Nebraska Press, 1986.

Kelsey, Robin. "Arthur Schott: Marking the Mexican Boundary." In *Archive Style: Photographs and Illustrations for U.S. Surveys, 1850–1890*, 21–74. Berkeley: University of California Press, 2007.

Lago, Don. *The Powell Expedition: New Discoveries about John Wesley Powell's 1869 River Journey*. Reno: University of Nevada Press, 2018.

Langford, J. O. *Big Bend: A Homesteader's Story*. With Fred Gipson. Austin: University of Texas Press, 1952.

Lassiter, Berta Clark. *We Come and Go: A Handbook for the Big Bend National Park*. San Antonio: Naylor, 1949.

Latorre, Felipe A., and Dolores L. Latorre. *The Mexican Kickapoo Indians*. Austin: University of Texas Press, 1976.

Luther, Joseph. *The Odyssey of Texas Ranger James Callahan*. Charleston, SC: History Press, 2017.

MacLeod, William. *River Road Vistas: A Journey along the River Road*. Alpine: Texas Geological Press, 2008.

Madison, Virginia A., and Hallie Stillwell. *How Come It's Called That? Place Names in the Big Bend Country*. Marathon, TX: Iron Mountain Press, 1997.

Martínez, Oscar J. *Troublesome Border*. Tucson: University of Arizona Press, 1988.

Maverick, Samuel. *Samuel A. Maverick, Texan*. Edited by Mary Rowena [Rena] Maverick Green. San Antonio, TX: Privately printed, 1952.

Maxwell, Ross A. *Big Bend Country: A History of Big Bend National Park*. Big Bend, TX: Big Bend Natural History Association, 1985.

———. *The Big Bend of the Rio Grande: A Guide to the Rocks, Landscape, Geologic History, and Settlers of the Area of Big Bend National Park*. Guidebook 7. Austin: Bureau of Economic Geology, University of Texas, 1968.

Maxwell, Ross A., and John W. Dietrich. *Geology of the Big Bend Area, Texas: Field Trip Guidebook*. Midland: West Texas Geological Society, 1972.

Maxwell, Ross A., and R. H. King. *Big Bend Area, Brewster County Texas: The Fall Field Trip Guidebook*. Midland: West Texas Geological Society, 1941.

Mendoza de Lavario, Israel. *A Brief Chronicle of Presidio del Norte: Homeland of the Jumano*. Austin, TX: La Junta Press, 2012.

Möllhausen, Balduin. *Diary of a Journey from the Mississippi to the Coasts of the Pacific with a United States Government Expedition*. 2 vols. Translated by Mrs. Percy Sinnett. London: Longman, 1858.

Morgenthaler, Jefferson. *La Junta de los Ríos: The Life, Death and Resurrection of an Ancient Desert Community in the Big Bend Region of Texas*. Boerne, TX: Mockingbird Books, 2007.

———. *The River Has Never Divided Us: A Border History of La Junta de los Ríos*. Austin: University of Texas Press, 2004.

Mulroy, Kevin. *Freedom on the Border: The Seminole Maroons in Florida, the Indian Territory, Coahuila, and Texas*. Lubbock: Texas Tech University Press, 1993.

Norris, L. David, James C. Milligan, and Odie B. Faulk. *William H. Emory, Soldier-Scientist*. Tucson: University of Arizona Press, 1998.

Orozco y Berra, Manuel. *Apuntes para la historia de la geografía en México*. Mexico City: Francisco Díaz de León, 1881.

Pearson, Jon R. *Road Guide to Backcountry Dirt Roads of Big Bend National Park*. Big Bend Natural History Association, 1980.

Porter, Kenneth Wiggins. *The Black Seminoles: History of a Freedom-Seeking People*. Gainesville: University Press of Florida, 1996.

Rayner, William H. *Elementary Surveying*. New York: Van Nostrand, 1943.

Rebert, Paula. *La Gran Línea: Mapping the United States–Mexico Boundary, 1849–1857*. Austin: University of Texas Press, 2001.

———. "Unknown Works and Forgotten Engineers of the Mexican Boundary Commission." In *Mapping and Empire: Soldier-Engineers on the Southwestern Frontier*, edited by Dennis Reinhartz and Gerald D. Saxon, 156–84. Austin: University of Texas Press, 2005.

Reinhartz, Dennis, and Gerald D. Saxon, eds. *Mapping and Empire: Soldier-Engineers on the Southwestern Frontier*. Austin: University of Texas Press, 2005.

Rodgers, Andrew Denny, III. *John Torrey: A Story of North American Botany*. Princeton, NJ: Princeton University Press, 1942.

Sherburne, John P. *Through Indian Country to California: John P. Sherburne's Diary of the Whipple Expedition, 1853–1854*. Edited by Mary McDougall Gordon. Stanford, CA: Stanford University Press, 1988.

Smith, Charles I. *Lower Cretaceous Stratigraphy, Northern Coahuila, Mexico*. Report of Investigations No. 65. Austin: Bureau of Economic Geology, University of Texas, 1970.

Smith, Thomas T. *The Old Army in Texas: A Research Guide to the U.S. Army in Nineteenth-Century Texas*. Austin: Texas State Historical Association, 2000.

———. *The Old Army in the Big Bend of Texas: The Last Cavalry Frontier, 1911–1921*. Austin: Texas State Historical Association, 2018.

Smith, Thomas T., Jerry D. Thompson, Robert Wooster, and Ben E. Pingenot. *The Reminiscences of Major General Zenas R. Bliss, 1854–1876*. Austin: Texas State Historical Association, 2007.

Smithers, W. D. *Chronicles of the Big Bend: A Photographic Memoir of Life on the Border*. Austin: Texas State Historical Association, 1999.

St. John, Rachel. *Line in the Sand: A History of the Western U.S.-Mexico Border*. Princeton, NJ: Princeton University Press, 2011.

Swift, Roy L. *Three Roads to Chihuahua: The Great Wagon Roads That Opened the Southwest, 1823–1883*. Austin: Eakin Press, 1988.

Thompson, Gerald. *Edward F. Beale and the American West*. Albuquerque: University of New Mexico Press, 1983.

Turpin, Solveig A., and Herbert H. Eling Jr., eds. *Dust, Smoke, and Tracks: Two Accounts of Nineteenth-Century Mexican Military Expeditions to Northern Coahuila and Chihuahua: Colonel Emilio Langberg, 1851, and Major Blas Flores, 1880–1881*. Center for Big Bend Studies, Occasional Papers No. 11. Alpine, TX: Sul Ross University, 2009.

Tyler, Ronnie C. *The Big Bend: A History of the Last Texas Frontier*. Washington, DC: National Park Service, 1975.

Utley, Robert M. *Changing Course: The International Boundary, United States and Mexico, 1848–1963*. Tucson, AZ: Southwest Parks and Monuments Association, 1996.

Virga, Vincent, and Don Blevins. *Texas: Mapping the Lone Star State through History: Rare and Unusual Maps from the Library of Congress*. Guilford, CT: Globe Pequot, 2010.

Wallace, Edward S. *The Great Reconnaissance: Soldiers, Artists, and Scientists on the Frontier, 1848–1861*. Boston: Little Brown, 1955.

Watson, Paul. *Ice Ghosts: The Epic Hunt for the Lost Franklin Expedition*. New York: W. W. Norton, 2017. [This 1845 British expedition carried two small rubber boats.]

Webb, Walter P., *The Texas Rangers: A Century of Frontier Defense*. Austin: University of Texas Press, 2000.

Weber, William A. *King of Colorado Botany: Charles Christopher Parry, 1823–1890*. Boulder: University Press of Colorado, 1997.

Werne, Joseph R. *The Imaginary Line: A History of the United States and Mexican Boundary Survey, 1848–1857*. Fort Worth: Texas Christian University Press, 2007.

Whiting, Wm. H. C. "Journal of a Reconnaissance from San Antonio de Bexar to El Paso del Norte." In Philip St. George Cooke, William Henry Chase Whiting, and François Xavier Aubry, *Exploring Southwestern Trails, 1846–1854*, edited by Ralph P. Bieber and Averam B. Bender, 241–350. Philadelphia: Porcupine, 1974. First published 1938 by Clark.

Wilbarger, John W. *Indian Depredations in Texas*. Austin, TX: Eakin Press, 1991.

Williams, Oscar W. *O. W. Williams' Stories from the Big Bend*. Edited by S. D. Myres. Southwestern Studies Monograph No. 10., Vol. 3, no. 2. El Paso: Texas Western College Press, 1965.

———. *Pioneer Surveyor, Frontier Lawyer: The Personal Narrative of O. W. Williams, 1877–1902*. Edited by S. D. Myres. El Paso: University of Texas, 1966.

Articles

Campbell, Thomas N., and William T. Field. "Identification of Comanche Raiding Trails in Trans-Pecos Texas." *West Texas Historical Association Yearbook* 44 (1968): 128–44.

Carlisle, Jeffrey D. "Seminole Indians." *Handbook of Texas Online*. http://www.tshaonline.org/handbook/online/articles/bms19, accessed July 8, 2013. Uploaded on June 15, 2010. Published by the Texas State Historical Association.

Crimmins, Martin L., ed. "Two Thousand Miles by Boat in the Rio Grande in 1850." *West Texas Historical and Scientific Society Publications* 5 (1933): 44–52.

Cunningham, Bob, and Harry P. Hewitt. "A 'Lovely Land Full of Roses and Thorns': Emil Langberg and Mexico, 1835–1866." *Southwestern Historical Quarterly* 98, no. 3 (January 1995): 387–425.

Daugherty, Franklin W. "Las Vegas de los Ladrones and the Flynt Gang." *Journal of Big Bend Studies* 3 (January 1991): 1–28.

Faulk, Odie B. "Bartlett, John Russell," *Handbook of Texas Online*. http://www.tshaonline.org/handbook/online/articles/fba93, accessed April 2, 2019. Uploaded on June 12, 2010. Published by the Texas State Historical Association.

Flawn, Peter T., and Ross A. Maxwell. "Metamorphic Rocks in Sierra del Carmen, Coahuila, Mexico." *Bulletin: American Association of Petroleum Geologists* 42, no. 9 (September 1958): 2245–49.

Goetzmann, William H. "Science Explores the Big Bend, 1852–1853." *Password* 3, no. 2 (April 1958): 60–67 (El Paso Historical Society).

———. "The United States–Mexican Boundary Survey, 1848–1853." *Southwestern Historical Quarterly* 62, no. 2 (1958): 164–90.

Hays, John C. "Report of Col. Hays [to Peter Bell]." *Corpus Christi Star*, January 20, 1849. https://texashistory.unt.edu/ark:/67531/metapth80212/m1/1/?q=John C. Hays.

Hewitt, Harry P. "The Mexican Commission and Its Survey of the Rio Grande River Boundary, 1850–1854." *Southwestern Historical Quarterly* 94, no. 4 (April 1991): 555–80.

Hill, Robert T. "Running the Cañons of the Rio Grande." *Century Magazine*, January 1901, 371–87.

———. "Running the Canyons of the Rio Grande." *Dallas Morning News*, Aug. 5, 19, 26, and Sept. 2, 16, 23, 1934.

Hoops, Herm. "The History of Rubber Boats and How They Saved Rivers." http://www.westwatercanyon.com/herm%20hoops/History-Rubber-Boats.pdf, accessed June 6, 2017.

Kajencki, Francis C. "Charles Radziminski and the United States–Mexico Boundary Survey." *New Mexico Historical Review* 63, no. 3 (July 1988): 211–40.

Lammons, Frank Bishop. "Operation Camel: An Experiment in Animal Transportation in Texas, 1857–1860." *Southwestern Historical Quarterly* 61, no. 1 (July 1957): 20–50.

Maxwell, Ross A. "Big Bend National Park: A Land of Contrasts." *Sul Ross State Teachers College Bulletin* 28, no. 2 (June 1948): 5–24.

McCaslin, Richard B. "United States Regulars in Gray: Edward Ingraham and Company A, 1st Regular Confederate Calvary." *Southwestern Historical Quarterly* 118, no. 1 (July 2014): 24–45.

Nevill, Charles L. "The Perils of a Texas Ranger." *Austin Daily Statesman*, February 25, 1882.

Nunley, M. Christopher. "Kickapoo Indians." *Handbook of Texas Online*. http://www.tshaonline.org/handbook/online/articles/bmk09, accessed July 8, 2013. Uploaded June 15, 2010. Published by the Texas State Historical Association.

Parry, Charles C. "On Depositing the Parry Botanical Collection." *Proceedings of the Davenport Academy of Natural Sciences* 2 (1878): 279–82.

Porter, Kenneth W. "The Seminole Negro-Indian Scouts, 1870–1881." *Southwestern Historical Quarterly* 55 (January 1952): 358–77.

Preston, Charles H. "Biographical Sketch of Dr. C. C. Parry." *Proceedings of the Davenport Academy of Natural Sciences* 6 (1897): 35–45.

Rebert, Paula. "A Civilian Surveyor on the United States–Mexico Boundary: The Case of Arthur Schott." *Proceedings of the American Philosophical Society* 155, no. 4 (2011): 433–62.

———. "Views of the Borderlands: The Report on the United States and Mexican Boundary Survey, 1857–1859." *Terrae Incognitae* 37 (2005): 75–90.

Rivaya-Martínez, Joaquín, ed. and trans. "The Captivity of Macario Leal: A Tejano among the Comanches, 1847–1854." *Southwestern Historical Quarterly* 117, no. 4 (April 2014): 372–402.

Rodríguez, Oscar S. "El Mulato, Chihuahua: A Continuing Light in the Desert." Paper presented at the Twenty-Third Annual Conference of the Center for Big Bend Studies, Sul Ross University, Alpine, TX, November 12, 2016.

Skiles, J. Raymond. "Henry B. du Pont: Industrialist and Rio Grande River Runner." *Journal of Big Bend Studies* 19 (2007): 175–200.

Smith, Ralph A. "The Comanche Bridge between Oklahoma and Mexico, 1843–1844." *Chronicles of Oklahoma* 39, no. 1 (1961): 54–69.

Stockley, John. "Monclova Viejo." Paper presented at a National Park Service conference on San Antonio Missions, San Antonio, TX, 1989.

———. "Update on Monclova Viejo Based on Langberg's Diaries." Paper presented at the Third Annual Conference of the Center for Big Bend Studies, Sul Ross State University, Alpine, TX, 1996.

Swanson, Donald A. "Coacoochee (Wild Cat)." *Handbook of Texas Online*. http://www.tshaonline.org/handbook/online/articles/fcoaz, accessed June 15, 2013. Uploaded June 12, 2010. Published by the Texas State Historical Association.

Tate, Michael L. "Black Seminole Scouts." *Handbook of Texas Online*. http://www.tshaonline.org/handbook/online/articles/qlbgn, accessed on June 15, 2013. Uploaded June 12, 2010. Published by the Texas State Historical Association.

Tyler, Ronnie C. "Exploring the Rio Grande: Lt. Duff C. Green's Report of 1852." *Arizona and the West* 10, no. 1 (1968): 43–60.

Walter, Matt. "Love on the Rio Grande: The 1850 Exploration by Captain Love." *Journal of Big Bend Studies* 19 (2007): 35–45.

Werne, Joseph R. "Surveying the Rio Grande, 1850–1853." *Southwestern Historical Quarterly* 94 (April 1991): 535–44.

Willeford, Glenn P. "The Three Bells of Ojinaga." *La Vista de la Frontera* 24 (Alpine, TX: Sul Ross State University, Winter 2014): 12–13.

Wright, Paul. "More Phantom Surveys Come Home to Roost: The Search for the True 'Gano Corner.'" *Journal of Big Bend Studies* 17 (2005): 97–142.

Index

*Page numbers in italic typeface indicate illustrations.
Page numbers followed by "t" indiate tables.*

Abbott, Charles, 24–25, 27, 127–28, 136–37, 150, 161, 172, 180–81, 183, 231, 246n78, 252n178, 253n195, 255n14
Abert, John James (J. J.), 9, 30–31, 240n25
Adams Ranch House, 111–14
Aguaje del Leon, 81, 245n55
Amistad Reservoir, 55t, *158*, 189, *191*, 192
Apache(s), 51, 69, 105, 143–44, 156, 192, 207–8, 226
Apache Trail, *112–13*
Arizpe, Sonora, xv, 10
Army Corps of Topographical Engineers, 3, 4, 9, 17, 27, 30, 97, 127, 159, 240n25
army escort, 3, 6, 17, 24, 25, 32, 40, 57, 58, 71, 96, 151, 153, 155, 161, 203, 204, 207, 230
Army of the West. *See* Kearny, Stephen W.
Arroyo: Agua Verde, 168, 175–76; Altares, *84*, 89, 91–93, 136, 217; Caballo, *158*; Carreta, 188; Ceferino, *113*, 114, 117, 120, *251*; Cíbolo (El), 133, *174*, 186; El Burro, 132; El Nogal, 145, 147; el Puerto, 45; El Sauz, 64; El Zacate, 182, 186, *187*; La Cochina, *187*, 188; La Herradura, 118, 129; La Hormiga, 114; La Lajita, 147; La Parida, 188, *191*; La Piedra Parada, 119, 120, 121–22; La Presa Reventada, 117–18; La Saladita, 81, 86; Las Pompas, 175; La Tinaja del Toro, 117; La Ventura, 131; La Yegua, 124; Los Maromeros, 175; Painted Rock (*see* Lozier Canyon); San Antonio, 72, 80, 217; San Carlos, 70, 71, 78, 80; San José, 148; San Rosendo, 118, 129; Santa Ana, *130*, 135 139, 219; Tinaja Blanca, 70, 76; Ventanas, 59; Viento Negro, 186; Zacate (El), 182, 186, *187*
arroyo: definition of, 233; and location of rapids, 63

Bartlett, John Russell, 5, 17, *21*, 156, 209, 229–32, 238n7, 239n22, 240n24; and Green, 24, 42; and Iron Boats, 30–31; travels of, 6–7, 9, 10–11, 24, 150–51, 155–56; writings by, xv, 198–99, 209. *See also* Bartlett–García Conde Compromise
Bartlett–García Conde Compromise, xiv–xv, xvii, 2, 8–10, 20, 230, 239n20 239n22, 240n24
Beale, Edward F., 30

275

Big Bend National Park (BBNP), 2, *12*, 16, *34*, 81, 82, 89, 218, 227
Big Bend Ranch State Park, 16, 64, 246n67
Big Canyon, 12, *177*, 180
Bigelow, John Milton, 43, 238n7
Black Gap Rapids, 111, 121
Black Gap State Wildlife Management Area, 16, *19*, 47*t*, 115, 155, 172, *177*, 204, 227, 257n50
Black Hills, *34*, 126
Black Seminole, 143, 144, *146*, 166, 253n212, 262n4. *See also* Mascogo
Bliss, Zenas, 144
boat(s), 26–27, 40–41, 55*t*, 71, 77, 88, 98–99, 105, 123, 127, 137, 159, 161, 168, 181, 193, 234, 254–55n4; rubber, 27–29, *29*, 93, 159; wooden, 159; wreck, 15, 26, 62–63, 67, 100, 182, 186, *187*. *See also* Iron Boats Fiasco
Bofecillos Mountains, 46, 223
Bolson de Mapimi, 91
Bone Springs, 91
Boquilla Crossing, *84*, 89, 97
Boquillas, Coahuila, *106*, 226
Boquillas Canyon, *19*, 39, 47*t*, 54*t*, 104–11, 124, 153, 154, 204, 218, 226, 231, 251n169
Boquillas Crossing, 54*t*
Boquillas Finger. *See* Pico Cerda
Boquillas formation, 99, 249n128
Boquillas Hot Springs, 249n132
boundary commission, chain of command, 9
boundary commissioners. *See* Bartlett, John Russell; Campbell, Robert B.; Emory, William Hemsley; García Conde, Pedro; Salazar Ylarregui, José; Weller, John B.
boundary map(s), 3, 15, 23, *17*; accuracy of, 56, 85, 93, 99, 101, 120, 121, 202, 206–7 (*see also* individual maps); based on boat survey, 183–86; final, 82, 83, 124, 126, 127, 153, *158*, 178, 197–201; index, 17–18; intent for, 201–2; Mexican, xxiv, 2, 50–51, 52, 66–67, 83, 194, 200–201, 206, 247n100; Michler's, 205–7; No. 15, 183, 188, 190–93; No. 16, 183–84, 186, 187, *187*, 188–90, *191*, 193, 259n78; No. 17, 83, 115, 122–23, 128, *158*, 172–81, 183–84, 193, 206, 226, 252n175, 258n53; No. 18, 111, *112*, 114, 115, 119, 120–22, 176, 179; No. 19, 105, *106*, 109–11, 179; No. 20, 82–83, *84*, 85–86, 89, 93, 97, 100, *101*, 102, 105, 204, 218; No. 21, 58–66, 60, *61*, 66–67, 69, 70, 71, 73, 75, 76, 82–83, *84*, 85, 246n82, 247n100, 259n78; No. 22, 43, *44*, 50–56, *53*, 66–67, 200, 247n100; unsurveyed gap, 176, 178, 179–80, 185, 205, 206
Bourland Canyon, 115, 121
Brackettville, Texas, 68, 144, 181, 248n110, 256n21
Bullis Fold, *177*, 178
Bullis, John, 144

camels. *See* Echols, William H.
Campbell, Robert B., 157, 232
Camp Destruction, 60, 62
Cañón de la Alameda, 36, 135, 139–42
Cañón Obscuro. *See* Closed Canyon
Cañón of Bofecillos, 46
Cañón Zeferino, 114
Carmel Peak. *See* Pico Cerda
Castle Butte. *See* Cerro el Sombrero
Castle Rock, 47*t*, 60, 64, *65*
Cavasera, 148, *149*
Cerro Aguachile, 132
Cerro Agujita Negra. *See* Sentinel, The
Cerro Chino, 81, 86
Cerro de las Burras, *44*, 45–46
Cerro del Pirata, 138
Cerro el Caracol, 115, 121
Cerro el Conejo, 133
Cerro el Sombrero, 117, 119, 121, 122
Cerro la Fortuna, 131
Chandler, Marine Tyler Wickham (M. T. W.), 5, *12*, 13, 15–17 18–*19*, 20, *21*, *34*, 54–55*t*, 150, 151, 211; and Langberg's map, 33, 36, 77 88–89; and Map 20, 83, 85, 86; results of survey, 152–56; surveying

methods 36–39. *See also under* boundary map(s): No. 18, No. 19, No. 20, No. 21, No. 22, and unsurveyed gap
Cherry Springs, 97
Chihuahua, Mexico, xv, *19*, *34*, *44*, 91, 93
Chihuahua City, 7, 57, 135, 136, 148, 155
Chisos Crossing, 47*t*, 68, 88–97
Chisos Mountains, 22, 33, *34*, 68, 71, 80, *84*, 86, *87*, 89, *90*, 93–94, 100, 115, 134, 154, 164, 165, 204, 217, 218
Cibolo Creek, 52
Ciénaga del Zacate, 139
Cinco de Mayo Crossing, 189
Ciudad Acuña, Coahuila, 208
Ciudad Juárez, xiv, 4, 239n18. *See also* El Paso del Norte
Coahuila (Mexico), *19*, *34*, 91, 93, 143
Colorado Canyon, 13, 26, 45, 46, 47*t*, 49, *49*, 50, 61–63, 223
Colorado River, xiv, xvi, xix, 1, 7, 22, 28, *29*, 30–31, 57, 196, 197, 201, 213
Columbia Valley, *130*, 138, 141
Comanche, 15, 25, 51, 67–68, 91, 92, 93, 143–44, 152, 154, 203, 207, 226
Comanche Crossing, *18*, 32, *34*, 47*t*, 54*t*, 60, 64, 66, 67–73, 77, 93, 154, 231
Comanche Springs, 6, 69, *70*, 163, 164
Comanche Trail, 68, 69, *84*, 88–89, 92, 96, 102, *112*, 119, 120, 164, 217
Comanche trails, 88, 89, 91, 92, 207, 217
Comunidad Negros Mascogos, 145, 253n212
Contrabando (movie set), 60, *65*, 246n67
Contrabando Creek, 64
Cottonwood River. *See* Río Álamos
Craig, Louis S., 24, 25
Cretaceous formations, 45, 47*t*, 99, 102, 117, 129, 131, 133, 138, 142, 151, 154, 155, 164, 178, 233, 249n128, 257n37
crime, 6, 24
Cuesta de Ponze, 80, 81, 89

Dark Canyon, *60*, 64
Del Rio, Texas, *12*, 23, *3*, 192, 208, 227

Devils River, 6, 55*t*, 108, *158*, 181, 192, 193n1, 248n110, 250n155, 256n21
Disturnell, John, xiii, xiv, xvii, 7–8, 239nn17–18
Dominguez de Mendoza, Juan, 57
Dryden, Texas, *35*, *158*, 166, 262n4
du Pont, Henry B., 95
Durango, Mexico, 67–69, 91, 93

Eagle Nest. *See* Langtry, Texas
Eagle Pass, Texas, 11, *12*, 16, 23, 24, 33, *35*, 39, 129, 135, 143, 148, 150–51, 159, 181, 205, 219
Echols, William H., 41, 97
Edwards Plateau (Texas), 129
Elephant Tusk Mountain, 94
El Fortin, Coahuila, *130*, 138–39
El Indio Crossing, *187*, 189
El Mesquite Crossing, 186
El Moral, 143, 219
El Mulato, Chihuahua, 43, *44*, 51, 54*t*, 223
El Nacimiento, Coahuila, 143, 144
El Padre al Altar, 64
El Paso del Norte, as starting point, 4–5, 7–8
El Sombrero/Castle Butte, *112*–13. *See also* Cerro el Sombrero
El Vado Chisos. *See* Chisos Crossing
Emory, William Hemsley, 3–5, 9–13, *12*, 16, 20, *21*, 22–23, 25, 28, 33, 52, 54–55*t*, 57, 68, 71, 137, 150–52, 155–56, 157–58, 160, 183, 195, 200, 210–11; 1848 report by, 3, 200; and final Emory Report, 154, 197–99; and Gadsden survey, 50, 196–97; on Indian problems, 192–93; and railroad, 10. *See also* Emory Report
Emory Peak, *19*, *34*, 47*t*, 71, 75, 82, *84*, 86, *87*, 94, 244n39
Emory Report, 22, 23, 40, 154, 198–99, 200, 216, 232, 238n3; destruction of background material, 23, 82, 86, 201; final maps in 85, 166, 197, 206, 211
Encantada Pass. *See* La Encantada Pass
Encantada Valley, 134, 138

Engelmann, George, 154, 200
Ernst Valley, 107
Evans, George, *33–34*, 135–36, 139. See also Forty-Niner(s)
Ewing, Thomas, 30
expeditions, *34–35*. See also Forty-Niner(s); Hays-Highsmith Expedition; Johnston, Joseph E.; Langberg, Emilio; Whiting, William H. C.

Fernandez, Manuel, 12, 50, 223
Fillmore, Millard, 197
Finger Canyon, 115
Flores, Blas, 135
Flynt, John M., 250n155
Fort Arbuckle, 210
Fort Clark, *35*, 68, 144, 181, 208, 256n21
Fort Davis, 6, 172, 225, 227, 262n4
Fort Duncan, 11, 15, 16, 22, 23, 24, 25, 27, 32, *33*, *35*, 36, 39, 55*t*, 57, 95, 96, 126, 127, 128, 129, *130*, 135, 136–37, 143, 144, 148–52, *149*, 153, 159, 161, 180, 181–83, 190, 192 193, 205, 208, 219, 230, 231, 232, 243n38, 245n44, 246n78, 252n182, 253n195, 256n17, 18, 257n32, 258n58,
Fort Fillmore, 24, 25
Fort Gibson, 143
Fort Inge, 57, 160, 181, 245n55
Fort Leaton, *34*, 41–42, *42*, 43, *44*, 45, 52, 54*t*, 56, 97, 223, 245n55
Fort McIntosh, 156
Fort Quitman, 6
Fort Stockton, *12*, 57, 163, 164, 245n55
Fort Towson, 57
Fort Vicente, 158
Forty-Niner(s), 32, *33*, 36, 41, 80, 135–36, 138, 139, 141, 142, 143, 218, 219, 229
Fort Yuma, 196
Fraser, Captain, 28
Fredericksburg, Texas, 6, 248n110
Frémont, John C., 4–5, 27–28, 199
Fresno Creek, 60, 64
Freyhold, E., 121

Froebel, Julius, 41
Frontera, 11, 16, 17, 20, 207

Gadsden Purchase (Treaty), xv, xvii, 2, 8, 10, 50, 51, 195–96, 211, 212, 215, 232, 239n21, 244n49
Gano, John T., 100, 102, 137, 172, *173*, 225–28
García Conde, Pedro, 6–9, 230. See also Bartlett–García Conde Compromise
Gardner, George Clinton (Clint), 13, 16, 20, 25, 26, 43, 57, 156, 215,
geologic formations, 47*t*
Gerstacker Bridge, 111, *113*
Gila River, 1, 2, 4, 7, 11, 22, 30–31, 196, 239n22, 243n39
Glenn Springs, 91, 92
Graham, James D., 5, 9, 28, 31, 39, 243n39
Gray, Andrew B., 3, 5, 8, 9, 10, 229, 230, 238n7, 239n20
Green, Duff Cyrus, *21*, 24–25, 32, 40, 41, 42, 50, 57, 58, 59, 150–52, 153, 155, 161, 230–31, 245n56; and Bartlett, 24; and Indians 67, 69, 144, 145, 147; later life, 214; maps, *130*, 140–41; recommends army post, 96–97
Guadalupe Hidalgo, Treaty of, xiii, xv, xviii, 1, 2, 7, 22, 41, 195, 202, 229
Guadalupe Pass, 6
Guerrero Coahuila, 28, 35f6, 143, *149*, 151, 228

Hacienda Guadalupe, 133
Hardcastle, Edmund L. F., 3, 230
Hays, John Coffee (Jack). See Hays-Highsmith Expedition
Hays-Highsmith Expedition, 32, *33–35*, 41, 91, 92, 97, 248n109
Heath Canyon, 115
Heath Creek, 107, 110, 111
Herradura Crossing, *187*, 189. See also Arroyo La Herradura
Herrera, Francisco, 50, 223
Highsmith, Sam. See Hays-Highsmith Expedition

Index

Hill, Robert T. (R. T.), 72, 77, 94, 98, 100, 114, 115, 117, 126, 137, 249n128
hoodoos, 59, 64
Horse Canyon, *113*, 115
Horsehead Crossing of the Pecos, 6, 57, 245n55
Hot Springs (in Lower Canyons), 24, 58, *125*
Hot Springs camp, *19*, 39, 40, 119, 120, 123, 124, 127, 129, *130*, 152, 179, 231
Hot Springs Canyon, *101*, 104, 105, *106*, 111, 204. *See also* Rapids, Hot Springs
Howard, Richard A. (Dick), 91, 97, *162*, 248n109
Howard, Volney, 10
Howard's Well/Spring, *35*, 91, 251n155, 256n21
Hubert Ridge, 110
Hughes, George, 28

Iglesias, Miguel, 50, 223
Independence Creek, 163, 165, 181
Indian(s), 88, 143–44, 199, 227; attacks, 24, 57, 144, 145, 152, 156, 192, 207, 231; conflicts with, 13, 23, 81, 105, 142, 155–56, *167*, 226; encounters with, 51, 67, 192–93, 207–8, 210; relics/pictographs, 81, 104, 166; trails, 46, 68, 69, 89, 93, 97, 102, 111, 114, 117, 118, 119, 121, 129, 133, 135–36, 153, 165–66, 176, 181, *187*, 188–89, *191*, 192, 204, 205. *See also* Apache, Comanche, Kickapoo, Lipan, Seminole
Ingraham, Edward, 159–61, 215–16, 255n14, 256n20
International Boundary and Water Commission (IBWC), 93, 201, 228
Iron Boats Fiasco, xvi–xvii, 30–32
Ives, Joseph, 28, *29*

Jiménez, Francisco, 196
Johnson Ranch, 81–82, *84*, 86, 89, 92, 94, 96, 257n50
Johnston, Joseph E., 96–97, 159, 162, 164–65, 168, 170, 176, 185, *187*, 188–89, 215, 240n28, 248n109; reconnaissance map, *162*

Jones, Thomas, 195
José María Morelos, Coahuila, 132

Kearny, Stephen W., 3, 11, 22, 200, 239n19, 240n28, 246n78
Kickapoo, 143–45, 219
King Springs, 164
King's Road. *See* King's Springs
King's Springs, *34*, 163–66, 181, 190, 232

La Babia Valley, *35*, 133
La Cuesta de Malena/del Plomo, 134
La Encantada Pass, *19*, 36, 128, 135–36, 138, 141, 218, 229, 230, 231, 242n37
Lajitas, Chihuahua, 66
Lajitas, Texas, *18*, 32–33, *34*, 40, 51, 57, 59, *60*, 65, 66, 69, *70*, 71, 93, 154, 207, 223, 231
La Linda, Coahuila, *19*, *34*, 55t, *113*, 114–15, 121, 231
Langberg, Emilio, 32, 33, *34*, 36, 43, 51, 77, 80–82, 88–89, *90*, 93, 97–99, 102, 104, 108, 126, 133, 135, 136, 138, 139, 142, 143, 145, 156, 217–20, 230
Langford, J. O., 95, 249n132
Langford('s) Hot Spring(s), 94, *101*, 249n132
Langtry, Texas, *35*, 137, *158*, 188, 189
Laredo, Texas, 23, 83, 156, 157, 200, 228
La Salada (Jabalí) Springs, 218
Las Moras Spring/Crossing, 68
Las Vegas de los Ladrones, 47t, 117, 122
Leaton, Ben. *See* Fort Leaton
Leon Springs. *See* Aguaje del Leon
Lipan, 144, 166, 192, 207
Lipan Crossing, *35*, 55t, 166, *167*, 168–76, *174*, 181–88, 190, 205, 206, 208, 232, 243n38. *See also* Shafter Crossing
Llano Los Buras, 131
Lomas el Hacha, 131
Long, John (Dr.), *146*, 147–48
Los Chisos Mountains. *See* Chisos Mountains
Los Cojos, 142
Lower Madison Falls, 137

Lozier Canyon, 55*t*, *158*, *187*, 188, 190
Lujan, Natividad, 92–93

MacMahon, James, 227–28, 262n5
Maderas del Carmen Protection Area, 131
Madison Rapids, *158*, *177*, 178
Magoffin, James, 11, 240n34
Mano, 67–69
Manuel Benavides (formerly San Carlos), Chihuahua, *18*, 33, *34*, 51, 57, 67, 69, *79*, 217
Mapa de los Estados Unidos de Méjico. *See* Disturnell, John
Map of the United States of Mexico. *See* Disturnell, John
map(s), xiv–xix, xxii. *See also* boundary maps; Gano, John; Johnston, Joseph T.; Langberg, Emilio
Maravillas Creek, *113*, 121, 172, 227, 250
Mare Canyon, *174*, 175
Mariscal Canyon, *19*, 33, 39, 47*t*, *84*, 86, 93, 96, 98–104, *101*, 153, 154, 203, 204, 217
Mariscal Mine, 99, 217
Maroons. *See* Mascogo
Mascogo, 143–44, 145, *146*. *See also* Black Seminole
Maverick, Samuel, 91–93, 248n110
Maxwell, Ross, 95, 107, 227, 250n135
McClellan, John, 5–6, 20, 28, 30–31
Meade, George G. (General), 160
Mesa de Anguila, 80, 247n95
Mesa de los Fresnos, 134
Mesa San Juan, 51
Mesquite Canyon, 186
Mexican-American War, 1, 3, 4, 11, 41, 148, 160, 199, 202, 239n19
Meyers Spring(s), *35*, *158*, 166, 181, 188, 190
Michler, Nathaniel, 11–13, *21*, 23, *34*–*35*, 55*t*, 150, 152, 158, 159–61, 230, 232; and "initial point," 176–79; later life, 214–15; maps, 83, 122, *158*, 184 (*see also under* boundary map(s): No. 15, No. 16, No. 17)
Möllhausen, Balduin, 28–29

Monterrey (Mexico), *2*, 148, 155
Moran, Thomas, *74*, *75*, 115
Morris, Thompson, 150, 258n58
mortar holes, 81, 104
Mount Carmel, 94, 104, 108
Mount Carmel Cañon, 104
Mount Emory. *See* Emory Peak
Mount Picacho, *70*, *71*, *72*, 75
Mulato Village. *See* El Mulato
Mule Ear Peaks, *84*, 86, *87*, 90
Muleta Ranch. *See* El Mulato
mule train(s), 6, 11, 15, 24, 25, 33, 41, 50, 59; trails, *72*, *84*, *106*, *113*
"Murderer's Canyon," 62
Múzquiz, Coahuila, *12*, 33, *35*, 36, *130*, 135, 142, 143, 144, 145, *149*, 208, 219

Native Americans. *See* Apache, Comanche, Indians, Kickapoo, Lipan, Seminole
Nevill, Charles L., 172, 225–27, 262n4
Nuestro Padre Jesús Church, 53
Nuevo Mexico, 1, 7–9, 239n20

observatory stations, 11, 36, *187*; at Fort Duncan, Texas (Michler), 11, 23, 159, 182, 183, 196, 243n38, 258n58; at Presidio, Texas (Emory), 11, 13, 16, 36, 41, 52, 53, *53*, 54*t*,56, 85, 122, 193, 223, 230–31, 241n40, 243n38
O'Donoghue, John, 196
Oehlschlager, Theodore H., 188, 259n78
Ojinaga, 12, 53, 56, 202, 208. *See also* Presidio del Norte

Palm, Swante, 216
Palo Duro Canyon, 144
Panama, 2, 30, 196, 214
Parry, Charles Christopher, 10, 20, *21*, 22–23, 40–41, 45–46, 126, 127, 128, 140–41, 153–55, 179, 180; as doctor, 58, 124; drawings in Emory Report, 23, 105; journal, 23, 32, 40, 86, 202; later life, 212–14
Paseo de Chisos. *See* Chisos Crossing

Paso. *See* El Paso del Norte, as starting point
Paso Colorado, *174*, 175
Paso de (los) Chisos. *See* Chisos Crossing
Paso Las Pompas, 175
Pecan Creek, 147
Pecos River, *12*, 13, 15, 16, 23, 27, *44*, 57, 95, 108, 115, 124, 127, 133, 137, 151, 152, 156, 157, 159, 163–65, 168, 170, 176, 179, 181–83, *191*, 193, 195, 202, 205, 230, 232, 235
Pecos Springs, 163, 165, 166
Persimmon Gap, *19*, *34*, 91, 126
Phillips, E. A., 13, 20, 24, 119, 120, 159–60, 161, 169, 196
Pico Cerda, *19*, *34*, 94–95, 100, 102, *103*, 104, *106*, 108, 110, 124, 126, 129, 251n168, 252n181, 258n54
Pico Etéreo, *19*, *34*, 108, *109*, 110, *113*, 117, 124, 129, *130*, 131, *158*, 218, 250n136, 250n142, 251n168, 252n181, 258n54
Pico Puerto Rico. See Pico Cerda
Pico Tena. *See* Pico Etéreo
pictographs, 81, 104, 155, 188, 190, 249n132, 256n30
Piedras Negras, Coahuila, 33, *35*, 143, *149*, 150, 151, 219
Pierce, Franklin, 157, 195, 197
Pima Villages, 11, 160
point of the mountain, Parry's, 118, *130*
Polk, James K., xiii, 1, 3, 4, 197, 229, 240n28
Ponce (Ponze) Crossing, 81–82, *84*, 86, 89
Presidio, Texas. *See* Presidio del Norte
Presidio del Norte, 12, *12*, 13, 15, 16, 25, 26, *34*, 36 40, 41, *44*, 45 51, 53, *53*, 67, 78, 202, *222*, 223, 230
Presidio Monclova Viejo, Coahuila, *34*, 219, 261n6
Presidio San Carlos, Chihuahua, *18*, 78, 247n90
Presidio San Vicente, Coahuila (ruins), *19*, 33, *34*, *101*, 102, 154, *158*, 217, 230, 249n129
Providencia, Chihuahua, 80

Puerto de la Gorriona, 138
Puerto de Santa Ana, 142
Punta (de la) Sierra, *19*, 47t, *84*, 86, 89, 90, 94

Quinn, Edward, 24, 25, 147
Quitman Canyon, 69

Radziminski, Charles, 195, 215
railroad, transcontinental, route for, 8, 10, 28, 195, 196, 197, 198, 239n19, 240n28, 244n49
Rancho de Enmedio, 82, *84*
Rancho el Álamo, 134
Rancho el Fortin, 139
Rancho Nuevo, 129, 131
Rancho Santo Domingo, 133
Ranchos of Baise, *44*, 56
Rapids: Agua Verde, 168, 175, 176; Black Gap, 111, 121; Compton's, 100; Fresno, 60, 64; Hoodoos, 54t, 59, 60, *61*; Hot Springs (Lower Canyons), 24, 27, 36, 40, 58, 122, 123, *125*, 126, 127, 128, 136, 140, 152, 154, 178, 179, 231, 258; Ledgerock, 60; Lower Madison Falls, 137; Madison, *158*, *177*, 178; Maravillas, *113*, 121, 172, 227; Mariscal Entrance, 100; Matadero, 60, 69, *70*; Madera Canyon, 64; Panther, 50, 60, 63, 64; Quarter Mile, 62; Rancherias (Camp Destruction), 26, 46, 60, 61, 62, 63; Rock Slide, *70*, 73, *74*, 75–76, 77, 100, 137, 203, 226, 227, 228; Santa Elena Entrance, *72*, 83; San Francisco, 175; Sanderson, *35*, 172, *174*, 175; Silber Canyon, *177*, 178; Tight Squeeze, 100; Zacate, 182, 186, *187*
rapids, formation of, 26
Reagan Canyon, *19*, 172, *177*, 180, 204–5, 251n169
Redford, Texas, *18*, 40, 43, *44*, 45, 46, 56, 66, 223
Redford Valley, 56, 58
Ringgold Barracks, 137, 150, 151, 152, 155, 156, 159, 209, 232

Río Álamos, 148
Rio Bravo del Norte, 86
Río Conchos, *12*, *34*, *44*, 68, 223
Río Escondido, 149–50
Rio Grande City, Texas, 137, 150, 155, 159
Río Sabinas, *130*, 138, 140, 141, 142, 143, 144, 145, *146*, 147, 148, 219, 253n220
Río San Antonio, 71, 73
Rooney's Place, 99, 102, 249n123

Salazar Ylarregui, José, xv, xviii, 50–51, 223, 230
San Antonio Road, 11, 24, 42, 69, 91, 108, *174*, 181
San Carlos, Chihuahua, *12*, *18*, 32, 33, *34*, 51, 57, 59, *60*, 67, 68, 69, 71, 77, 78, *79*, 88, 89, 92, 97, 154, 225
San Carlos Creek, 54*t*, 78
San Carlos Presidio, *18*, *34*, 78, *79*, 102, 247n90
Sanderson Canyon (Rapids), 172, *174*, 175
San Elizario, Texas, 11
San Felipe Springs, 192, 208
San Fernando, Coahuila, *35*, 143, 149, 219
San Francisco Canyon, 128, *158*, 170–81, *177*, 185, 193, 202, 232, 252n175
San Francisco Creek, 122, 124, 170, 172, *173*, 180, 225, 226, 227
San Francisco ridge, 56
San Luis Potosi, Mexico, 91, 213
Santa Cruz Mountain, 45, 56
Santa Cruz, Sonora, 10
Santa Elena Canyon, *18–19*, 26–27, 33, 39, 40, 47*t*, 54*t*, *70*, 72, 73–77, *84*, 154, 225–28, 231
Santana Mesa, 50, 64
Santa Rita Copper Mines, 9, 10, 207, 229, 230, 239n20
Santa Rosa, Coahuila, *12*, *19*, *35*, *101*, *130*, 142, 145, *146*, 14–48, *149*
Santa Rosa Valley, 142
Santiago Peak, *19*, *34*, 164, 218
San Vicente, Coahuila, *101*, 102, 104

San Vicente, Texas (ghost town), 104
San Vicente Canyon, 39, 47*t*, 92, 98, 99, 100, 126, 154, 204, 217
San Vicente Crossing, *101*, 104, 217
Schott, Arthur, 10, 11,*12*, 16, 23, 55*t*, 95, 128, 156, *158*, 159, 160, 180, 181, 183, 188, 190–93, *191*, 195, 196, 197, 208, 214, 215, 230, 255n14
Schott Tower. *See* Pico Cerda
Seminole, 25, 142–47, 208, 219, 257n32. *See also* Black Seminole
Seminole Canyon, 188, *191*
Sentinel, The, *70*, 72, 73, 75
Serranía del Burro, 129
sextant. *See* surveying instruments
Shafter, William R. *See* Shafter Crossing
Shafter Crossing, 166, *167*, 227, 257, 262n4
Shot Tower. *See* Pico Cerda
Sierra Atravesada, 138
Sierra Carmel. *See* Sierra del Carmen
Sierra [de la] Encantada, 36, 134–36, 138, 139, 218. *See also* La Encantada Pass
Sierra de la Gorriona, 138
Sierra del Bravo, 129
Sierra del Carmen (Sierra [de] Carmel), *34*, 36, 94, 95, 102, *103*, 104, 110, 115, 126, *130*, 131, 133, 134, 155, 204, 218, 249n128, 257n32. *See also* Mount Carmel
Sierra de los Guajes, 138
Sierra de Muzquiz, 142
Sierra de Santa Ana Anticline, 142
Sierra Hermosa de Santa Rosa, 138
Sierra Larga, 111
Sierra Los Encinos, 71
Sierra Orégano, 138
Sierra Ponce. *See* Cuesta de Ponze
Sierra San Vicente, *101*, 102
Silber Canyon, *177*, 178
slot canyon, *49*, 49, 235
Smith, Martin L., 159, *162*, 166, 168, 183, 186, 189
Smith, Ralph, 91
Smith, W. F., 11
Soldado Crossing, 188

Solis Graben, 98, 100
Stanley, John Mix, 200, 238n3
Stillwell Bend/Creek, 55t, 111, *113*, 121
Strain, Isaac G., 31, 32n5
Straw House Trail, 107
Stremme, Christoph Conrad, 159–61, *167*, 170, *171*, 172, 216, 261n21
Stuart, Alexander H. H., 9–10, 20, 31, 192
surveying, 95; from boat, 39, 58, 66, 182–85, 190, 192, 206; instruments, 37, *37*, 38, *38*, 40, 58, 62, 77, 190, 235, 243n38; methods, 36–39, *38*, 43, 50–51, 56, 69, 71, 75, 76–77, 82–83, 88, 95, *101*, 105, 109–11, 122, 127, 168, 172, 175, 181, 182, 185, 190–94, 196, 202–7, 236, 243–44n39. *See also* triangulation station(s)

Talley Place, 96
Tapado Creek, *48*, 59, 60
Taylor, Zachary, 4–5, 148, 197, 229
Telephone Canyon, 107
Temple Canyon, *19*, *34*, *113*, 114–20, *116*, 121, 123, 154, 231
Terlingua Creek, 69, *70*, 71, 76, *84*
Terlingua Fault, 80
Texas Rangers, 77, 91, 117, 137, 172, 225–27, 250n155
theodolite. *See* surveying instruments
Thompson, Thomas, 13, 20, 24, 43, 73, 75–77, 155, 241n38, 245n56
Three Dike Hill, 46, *48*
Tinaja camp, *130*, 134, 138, 139, 141
tinaja(s), 81, 131, 234, 235, 247n96
Topographical Engineers. *See* Army Corps of Topographical Engineers
Tornillo Creek, *101*, 104
Torrey, John, 10, 20, 22, 154, 200, 212, 213, 238n3, 246n78
Tower Peak. *See* Castle Rock
traverse. *See* surveying, methods

triangulation. *See* surveying, methods
Triangulation Station Mountain, *84*, 86, *87*, 94
triangulation station(s), 43, 51, 66, 73, 83, 222–23
Trist, Nicholas, xiii–xiv, 1
Turnbull, Charles, 196

unsurveyed gap. *See under* boundary map(s): unsurveyed gap
Upper Canyons (of the Rio Grande), 51, 56, 83, 203, 207, 230
Ures, Sonora, 9, 10
US Boundary Commission Office(s), 17, 150, 159, 161, 197, 210–12, 229, 258n58

Vado de Chisos, 93. *See also* Chisos Crossing
Vado de Fleche, 88–89
Vado Ponce (Ponze). *See* Ponce Crossing
Valle el Fortin, 138–40
Valle las Norias, 133
Van Horn, Texas, 6, *12*
von Hippel, Maurice, 11–13, 20, 25–26, 50, 156, 159, 196, 201
von Humboldt, Alexander, xiii–xiv

Wagon Road (San Antonio to El Paso), 17, 57, 155, 163, 165, 245n55, 248n108
Weiss, Charles, 196
Weller, John B., 3, 4, 6, 30
Whipple, Amiel Weeks, 3, 8–10, 22, *29*, 239n20
White's Ranch. *See* Frontera
Whiting, William H. C., 41, 53, 56
Wild Cat, Chief, 142–47, 208, 219
Willow Springs, 91
Woodson Place, *90*, 91–93
Wool, John E., 148

Zaragoza, Coahuila. *See* San Fernando

www.ingramcontent.com/pod-product-compliance
Lightning Source LLC
Chambersburg PA
CBHW080238170426
43192CB00014BA/2491